Satire & The State

Satire & The State focuses on performance-based satire, most often seen in sketch comedy, from 1960 to the present, and explores how sketch comedy has shaped the way Americans view the president and themselves.

Numerous sketch comedy portrayals of presidents have seeped into the American consciousness – Chevy Chase's Gerald Ford, Dana Carvey's George H.W. Bush, and Will Ferrell's George W. Bush – all worked to shape the actual politician's public persona. The book analyzes these sketches and many others, illustrating how comedy is at the heart of the health and function of American democracy. At its best, satire aimed at the presidency can work as a populist check on executive power, becoming one of the most important weapons for everyday Americans against tyranny and political corruption. At its worst, satire can reflect and promote racism, misogyny, and homophobia in America.

Written for students of Theatre, Performance, Political Science, and Media Studies courses, as well as readers with an interest in political comedy, *Satire & The State* offers a deeper understanding of the relationship between comedy and the presidency, and the ways in which satire becomes a window into the culture, principles, and beliefs of a country.

Matt Fotis is Associate Professor of Theatre at Albright College. He is the author of *Long Form Improvisation and American Comedy: The Harold* (2014), and coauthor of *The Comedy Improv Handbook* (2015).

Satire & The State

Sketch Comedy and the Presidency

Matt Fotis

NEW YORK AND LONDON

First published 2020
by Routledge
52 Vanderbilt Avenue, New York, NY 10017

and by Routledge
2 Park Square, Milton Park, Abingdon, Oxon, OX14 4RN

Routledge is an imprint of the Taylor & Francis Group, an informa business

© 2020 Taylor & Francis

The right of Matt Fotis to be identified as author of this work has been asserted by him in accordance with sections 77 and 78 of the Copyright, Designs and Patents Act 1988.

All rights reserved. No part of this book may be reprinted or reproduced or utilised in any form or by any electronic, mechanical, or other means, now known or hereafter invented, including photocopying and recording, or in any information storage or retrieval system, without permission in writing from the publishers.

Trademark notice: Product or corporate names may be trademarks or registered trademarks, and are used only for identification and explanation without intent to infringe.

Library of Congress Cataloging-in-Publication Date
Names: Fotis, Matt, 1979- author.
Title: Satire & the state : sketch comedy and the presidency / Matt Fotis.
Other titles: Satire and the state
Description: New York : Routledge, 2020. | Includes index.
Identifiers: LCCN 2019058341 (print) | LCCN 2019058342 (ebook) |
  ISBN 9781138338111 (hardcover) | ISBN 9781138338128 (paperback) |
  ISBN 9780429441851 (ebook)
Subjects: LCSH: Presidents—United States—Humor. | Political satire, American—History and criticism. | United States—Politics and government—20th century—Humor. | United States—Politics and government—21st century—Humor. | Television comedies—United States—History. | Television and politics—United States.
Classification: LCC E176.1 .F7655 2020 (print) | LCC E176.1 (ebook) |
  DDC 792.7/60973—dc23
LC record available at https://lccn.loc.gov/2019058341
LC ebook record available at https://lccn.loc.gov/2019058342

ISBN: 978-1-138-33811-1 (hbk)
ISBN: 978-1-138-33812-8 (pbk)
ISBN: 978-0-429-44185-1 (ebk)

Typeset in Minion
by Apex CoVantage, LLC

To my First Family, thanks.

Contents

	Acknowledgments	ix
	Introduction	1
1	**From Colony to Country: A Brief Overview of American Political Satire**	23
2	**JFK**	79
3	**LBJ and Nixon**	101
4	**Ford and Carter**	122
5	**Reagan and Bush**	137
6	**The Clintons**	158
7	**Dubbya**	186
8	**Obama**	208
9	**Donald J. Trump**	231
10	**Conclusion**	262
	Index	276

Acknowledgments

As with any endeavor, there are many people responsible for this book getting done. First and foremost, thanks to Jeanette and my kids for supporting and encouraging me throughout not only this book but in life.

A special thanks to the Albright College Creative Research Experience grant that allowed me to spend two summers researching comedy. Thanks to Joey Love for his research and creative support, from preliminary research to collaborating on the *Half-Hour Hour Report*, as well as for his comedic insights, Johnny Canal, and overall Philadelphia wisdom. It is indeed too hot in the hot tub. Go Birds!

I am fortunate to have colleagues who support and champion my creative and scholarly work – there are not many theatre departments around that put political sketch comedy shows in their mainstage season. This book would not exist without Albright College encouraging me to develop courses in Comedy Studies, specifically "Satire & The State" – so thank you for championing academic inquiry and fostering interdisciplinary study. I'm also grateful to the many students who have taken those classes, for listening to me ramble about these ideas and offering interesting questions, pushing back against my assumptions, and making me dig deeper into the work. Also, thanks to that one student who got up in the middle of class to go get a WaWa hoagie.

Introduction

As long as there have been written records, there has been political satire – and probably before that, too. No doubt cave dwellers were hilarious. The ancient Egyptians and Greeks were fans of unflattering or parodic caricatures of leaders, with the Greek playwright Aristophanes bringing his political satire to the stage. From Horace to Dante to Voltaire to Jonathan Swift to Mark Twain, there is a celebrated history of Western political satire. In America, a country founded on political revolution, there is a long and varied tradition of political satire – from Ben Franklin's *Rules by Which a Great Empire May Be Reduced to a Small One* to Alec Baldwin's impersonation of Donald Trump. The American character seems particularly adapted to this type of humor. Our ingrained mistrust of government creates a questioning of authority that Canadian Lorne Michaels argues is "established in the American DNA."[1] Similarly, a fundamental characteristic of the American DNA is the constant search and fluctuation of what exactly it means to be an American. The American identity has ebbed and flowed for nearly three centuries, and the presidency has come to be a central component of that identity. George Washington was unanimously elected as the first president because everyone could agree on his American credentials. Even if the average citizen could not clearly articulate what exactly it meant to be an American, they knew Washington represented it. Over two centuries later, Donald Trump made his way to the White House with a very distinct vision of what it meant to be an American, specifically who constituted "We the people" and who did not.

The presidency has been vital to the creation of the American identity. The president is expected to speak to and for the nation. As Mary Stuckey argues in *Defining Americans: The Presidency and National Identity*, presidents have historically reflected and articulated the American character. She writes, "More than for any other participant in the national conversation, the task of articulating the collective culture, like the responsibility for managing the collective action, belongs to the president."[2] Presidents project both who we are at any one point in history, and what we aspire to be. They remind us of our values in moments of national crisis, that "the only thing we have to fear is fear itself," appeal to "the better angels of our nature," and point us toward the "New Frontier" of the future. Presidents have also used fear, warning of "American carnage," and have defined our identity by declaring who we are not, long excluding marginalized communities from the American experience. Our country's history is often presented as a singular story from a majority point of view. In reality, the American experience is multifaceted and plural. The 2016 election (and others before it) laid bare the deep divisions in America that are rooted in our collective (mis)understanding of our national identity. As the American character changed during the 20th century, presidents have worked to include more voices in the American story. The election of Barack Obama seemed like a culmination, but was brought to a screeching halt with the election of Donald Trump. While much of America's identity building comes from the president, one factor that has been central to the relationship between presidents and Americans goes the other way – satire. If presidents speak for the nation, satirists are often the ones talking back. Americans have looked to the presidency to see their values reflected and promoted. Depending on their perceived reflection of those values, satirists have made Americans laugh *with* or laugh *at* the president.

Sketch comedy has become an integral part of that national conversation. While sketch comedy hasn't fundamentally changed the presidency or the men who have occupied the office, it has shaped the way Americans view the office, the occupant, and themselves. There are numerous sketch comedy portrayals of presidents and politicians that have seeped into the American consciousness. Sometimes sketch comedy does a better job of packaging and presenting a politician than the politicians themselves, as their impression has a stronger impact than the person. Chevy Chase's Gerald Ford, Dana Carvey's George H.W. Bush, Will Ferrell's George W. Bush, and Tina Fey's Sarah Palin all worked to shape the actual politician's public persona. Darrell Hammond's Al Gore was so devastating that Gore's campaign made Gore watch *Saturday Night Live*'s debate sketch to see how poorly he was communicating with the American public – and Gore adjusted his presentation accordingly. The relationship between satire and the presidency has become fundamental to the health and function of American democracy. At its best, satire aimed at the presidency can work as a populist check on executive power, becoming one of the most important weapons for everyday Americans against tyranny and political corruption. It also can become part of our social-historical record. As comedian Godfrey Cambridge said, "A comedian is in many ways a historian. He reflects the times and the mood of the country and the world."[3] At its worst, satire can reflect and promote racism, misogyny, and homophobia. What a society laughs at speaks volumes about its values. Satiric barbs aimed at the presidency become a window into our culture, principles, and beliefs, reflecting over time what has changed in America, and what has stayed the same.

There has been a good deal written in the last two decades about the relationship between satire and politics, studying its implementation and its effects. Much of that research, however, has focused on satiric news, such as *The Daily Show*, or quantitative studies about political humor on late-night talk shows like *The Tonight Show*. These works have been essential to establishing the immediacy and influence of political satire on society. Yet, thus far, sketch comedy has taken a back seat in satiric research, especially its direct relationship with the presidency.

By focusing on sketch comedy and the presidency over its contemporary life span (1960–present), this study aims to fill the gap in satiric scholarship, as well as illuminate how sketch comedy has worked to shape and define the modern presidency. Studying this evolution can give us a unique window into American culture, illustrate the fundamental changes in American society that have occurred over the last 60 years, and potentially illuminate the future of American democracy.

Satire: A Tricky Definition

But what exactly is satire? Satire's precise definition has remained elusive. *Encyclopedia Britannica* notes in its entry for satire that "it is one of the most heavily worked literary designations and one of the most imprecise."[4] Nobody seems to be able to agree on what satire is and its effects, yet everyone seems to know what satire is and its effects. Supreme Court Justice Potter Stewart's remarks regarding obscenity seem to encapsulate society's definition of satire: "I know it when I see it."[5] While there is no one agreed-upon definition, satire is generally "a term reserved for a particular kind of humor that makes fun of human folly and vice by holding people accountable for their actions."[6] Satire is a unique form of political and social commentary that uses humor, often through irony and exaggeration, to expose hypocrisy, lies, or just plain lousy policy. As Rachel Paine Caufield argues, "by subtly exposing the audience to the critique, creating laughter, and using a combination of wit, humor, and playfulness to engage the audience, satire is *artful* political critique."[7] More than just a critique, satire either implies or overtly calls for action. It is both a tool and a weapon aimed at the powerful, to break what Stephen Koch calls "the solemn spell of pomposity, to laugh down whatever refuses to be laughed at."[8] Most scholars and critics agree that satire aims at a specific target, and, as is often the case in contemporary satire, it does so to expose "truth." As Andrew Stott notes in *Comedy: The New Critical Idiom*, "satire's appeal has traditionally rested in its ability to speak truth to power and to effect the resistance implied by George Orwell's proposition that 'every joke is a tiny revolution.'"[9] Satire, then, can be seen as a social or political critique delivered through comedic means with an overt or implied call to action. This idea of satire as a social/cultural corrective goes back centuries.

Satire's roots are in Greek comedy, but it rose to prominence in Rome. Roman satire was so crucial that satire is classified based on the two most famous Roman satirists, Horace and Juvenal. Horatian satire aims to heal through humor. It is generally gentler in its attacks and features lighthearted humor and playful critiques. Horatian satire tends to target human folly, rather than individuals and presents its targets as misguided or off course rather than inherently evil. It often uses exaggeration to point out the absurdity or ridiculousness of an idea or concept. *Gulliver's Travels*, *Dr. Strangelove*, *The Simpsons*, and *The Onion* are all examples of Horatian satire. With sketch comedy about the presidency, *The First Family* about JFK or Dana Carvey's George H.W. Bush would be examples of Horatian satire. Juvenalian satire is much sharper and aggressive than Horatian. It uses scorn, outrage, and ridicule to attack its target, which is presented not merely as wrong, but evil. Juvenalian satire often presents the world as worse than it is, relying on metaphor, irony, sarcasm, moral outrage, and the power of its pessimistic presentation of the world. While Horatian satire tends to elicit laughter, Juvenalian satire is much darker, utilizing an almost macabre sense of humor; Juvenalian satire is an indictment. Political satire that makes a strong statement like *A Modest Proposal*, or much of the sketch comedy about Richard Nixon or Donald Trump is Juvenalian satire. Dystopian satires also fall into the Juvenalian camp – works such as *Animal Farm*, *A Clockwork Orange*, or even *Catch-22*. The two can mix, such as in Will Ferrell's *You're Welcome America: A Final Night With George W. Bush*, which alternates Horatian playful critiques about Bush's malapropisms with Juvenalian attacks on his legacy in Iraq and New Orleans.

For this study, satire will be broken down into two forms: social and political. Social satire aims at things like race, religion, and cultural beliefs and practices. *Saturday Night Live*'s "The Day Beyoncé Turned Black" is a Horatian social satire about white people's reaction to Beyoncé celebrating her African American heritage in her video "Formation."[10] A sketch about Donald Trump would usually, but not always, fall under political satire. While there is undoubtedly crossover, generally speaking, anything dealing with policy or politicians is political satire, and anything satirizing cultural beliefs or attitudes is social satire. When we drill down, though, we see that not all political humor is satirical. Jokes about the president that imply resistance or offer a critique would fall under satire, while jokes that simply make fun of a president with no specific point of view or desired outcome would not. Therefore, the intent matters. Chevy Chase falling down as Gerald Ford is satiric because Chase is using the pratfall as a *commentary* on Ford, suggesting that Ford is literally falling down on the job. If, on the other hand, there was no commentary or judgment, if he just fell for an easy laugh (which some critics argue), the sketch would not be satiric. Similarly, it's also important to note that not every piece of sketch comedy is satiric. There are plenty of sketches on *Saturday Night Live* and other shows that have no satiric intent. For instance, *SNL*'s "Haunted Elevator" sketch with David S. Pumpkins is about a weird guy that's part of a Halloween ride. There are many questions about him – "Any questions? – but no inherent critique associated with him.[11]

Intent matters, but so, too, does content and delivery. According to George A. Test, satire contains four key elements: aggression, judgment, play, and laughter.[12] Satire needs to attack a target from a particular point of view, but the combination of judgment and aggression is rather common in political commentary. One can turn on the television to see scores of talking heads being judgmentally aggressive. It is the *playful* mixture of aggression and judgment that is satire's essential characteristic. As Jonathan Gray, Jeffrey Jones, and Ethan Thompson argue in *Satire TV: Politics and Comedy in the Post-Network Era*, "satire's calling card is the ability to produce social scorn or damning indictments through *playful* means and, in the process, transform the aggressive act of ridicule into the more socially acceptable act of rendering something ridiculous."[13] The combination of these four elements is what makes satire effective. As Test writes, "whether the target is vice or folly, absurdity or enemies of the state, the satirist is concerned with passing judgment."[14] In the world of sketch comedy, judgment is the sketch's satiric point. What is it that we are trying to say in this particular sketch? What are we critiquing or judging? What is the content?

In order to pass judgment, satire requires a target and an audience. Whatever the medium, sketch comedy included, satire has a similar triangular relationship to the one Sigmund Freud explores regarding tendentious jokes in *The Joke and Its Relation to the Unconscious* (1905): the person telling the joke, the object of the joke, and the person listening to the joke. In satire, that triangle becomes satirist, target, and audience. As John Gilmore argues in *Satire: The New Critical Idiom*, "satire is only effective if it is perceived by persons other than its author to be such, and responses can change depending on factors such as time and circumstances."[15] As important as intent and content are, the audience must *receive* the joke. Satire, therefore, requires a knowledgeable audience. An audience needs to "get it" to engage in the playfulness of satire. If there isn't a shared knowledge between satirist and audience, the playfulness evaporates, and a piece loses its satiric bite. In many cases, the target and the audience may be the same, or the target may be unaware of or miss the point entirely. Many conservatives approvingly watched *The Colbert Report* without realizing Stephen Colbert was satirizing right-wing opinion shows. For them, there was no satire because there was no satiric triangle – they saw no target. Time can likewise dilute satire, as a contemporary audience might understand references or circumstances that, in the future, are no longer common knowledge. A joke from 1987 about Iran-Contra might make little sense to an audience in 2020 that has no idea about the Iran-Contra affair (or make little sense to an uninformed audience in 1987). What is more pressing than dated references, however, is the growing societal divide(s) in America. As the country polarizes and the news media divides into partisan camps, the gap between satirist and audience is expanding and threatening the nature of satire. As we shall see, this has, in part, led to the development of satiric authenticity and advocacy satire that overtly asks its audience to take political action rather than relying on an implied critique.

This triangular relationship relies heavily on intent, context, and interpretation. In some cases, as with minstrelsy, the audience can receive the same message much differently and misconstrue the target, and therefore the satirical intent. A white audience may take the stupidity of a minstrel or slave character as a sign of his naiveté and inherent inferiority. A black audience may read it as an act, and therefore as a sign of resistance. Racial and ethnic humor historically has had double meanings and different readings depending on the satirist and the audience. This points to the relationship between intent and interpretation. In the above example, a black audience might immediately recognize that the target is white superiority, while a white audience might misattribute the target as black inferiority. The interpretation of the satire becomes crucial but often relies on the intent. If a white actor plays the slave character in blackface, the intent is obviously to demean. But if an African American actor plays the slave character, as was common in later minstrelsy, then the intent can be quite different.

As such, with much satire, it is critical to distinguish jokes *about* minority groups from jokes *by* minority groups. Humor used to suppress a group is fundamentally different from humor used to assert agency – intent matters. As significant as the intent is, perhaps more important is the interpretation. Herman Gray, writing about the racial satire on *In Living Color*, points to the tension that exists with racial humor's interpretation. Gray writes that this humor can be interpreted as contesting "hegemonic assumptions and representations of race in general and blacks in particular in the American social order; for others, it simply perpetuates troubling images of blacks."[16] Humor by marginalized groups often constructs the humor or satire through their marginal identity. As Lawrence Levin explains, "Marginal groups often embraced the stereotype of themselves in a manner designed not to assimilate it but to smother it. . . . To tell jokes containing the stereotype was not invariably to accept it but frequently to laugh at it, to strip it naked, to expose it to scrutiny."[17] Yet, as Gray and others argue, this embrace of self-deprecating humor or use of negative stereotypes can lead an audience to misidentify the intent or target, and therefore misinterpret the satire. Throughout American comedy, and documented throughout in the following chapters, marginalized groups have used self-deprecating types of humor to combat stereotypes and assert agency. The interpretation of the satire is critical for it to work. If audiences miss the marginalized framework, they miss the satire and oftentimes receive the opposite message. The tension and distance between the intent and interpretation can be a source of deep trauma and struggle for the satirist and marginalized communities.

Context likewise is crucial to the proper interpretation of target and intent. As such, even a dictionary can be satiric. For instance, Merriam-Webster is satirically commenting on Donald Trump's administration via its Twitter account. When Kellyanne Conway defended Press Secretary Sean Spicer's lies about the size of Trump's inaugural crowd by calling them "alternative facts," Merriam-Webster tweeted, "A fact is a piece of information presented as having objective reality."[18] They followed up two days later with "*whispers into the void* In contemporary use, fact is understood to refer to something with actual existence."[19] The dictionary tweeting the definition of a word wouldn't generally be satiric, but given the context, the satiric intent of the posts becomes evident. It also illustrates the importance of context. If someone sees the dictionary tweeting the definition of words without knowing why, then they would not interpret the tweet as satiric. More importantly, it also demonstrates the pervasiveness of satire in contemporary America – when the dictionary is satiric, you've reached a new level of absurd reality.

What About Parody?

While satire uses irony, parody mimics something – a person, genre, etc. – to point out its defects. Parody "can be understood as a polemical imitation that exposes the flaws in its 'pretext' – that which it imitates."[20] Satire and parody often work hand in hand. As Elaine May once put it, parody is "friendly satire."[21]

Parody relies on exaggeration for humor, first mimicking and then exaggerating its target. Parody frequently targets a particular person, writer, genre, or song, whereas satire tends to speak to broader issues and topics – even when it targets one person, such as the president. Parody is likewise divided into two types: parody and blank parody. Traditional parody mimics a form in a "friendly" way to point out defects, whereas blank parody tends to focus exclusively on capturing the genre itself. Weird Al's parody songs "Like a Surgeon," "Amish Paradise," and "Eat It" are good examples of blank parody, as the humor mostly resides in the similarity and subsequent exaggeration between the original song and its parody.

In sketch comedy, satire and parody frequently complement each other, such as with the 2016 *Saturday Night Live* sketch "Black Jeopardy." In the sketch, parody is used to enhance the satire. The parody in the sketch focuses on imagining a "black" version of the game show *Jeopardy*. The host is a black version of Alex Trebek, Darnell Hayes, played by Kenan Thompson, and the categories are an intentional parody featuring exaggerated "black categories," like, "Big Girls," "MM . . . I Don't Know," "They Out Here Saying," and "White People." In this sketch, a Trump supporter named Doug, played flawlessly by Tom Hanks, is the only white contestant on the show. The satire in the sketch focuses on the connections between two groups of people – African Americans and white Trump supporters – who are often at odds. Rather than focus on what divides the two groups, as would be the easy laugh, and is often the case on other "Black Jeopardy" sketches, this sketch stands out and works so well because it points out their similarities. Rather than the obvious white outsider who doesn't understand black culture, Doug answers several "black questions" correctly and seems to be fitting in quite nicely. Doug shares similar economic insecurity, finding common ground on lottery tickets instead of 401k contributions, as well as having a local fix-it guy: "You better go to that dude in my neighborhood who'll fix anything for $40." Hayes replies, "You know Cecil?!?" "Yeah, but my Cecil's name is Jimmy." They all agree that elections are rigged and decided beforehand by the elite, that you can't trust Apple with your thumbprint on an iPhone, and that Tyler Perry's movies are hilarious. It is not until the final category, "Lives That Matter," that the stark difference between contestants reemerges. We know Doug's answer the moment the topic appears, so much so that the sketch never shows his response. Instead, Hayes simply states, "Well, it was good while it lasted, Doug." The satiric point becomes apparent: race is used to divide people, pointing to the evident reality that race is a significant factor behind Trump's support. In the sketch, Doug has a great deal in common with the other contestants, yet the one thing they can't seem to agree about is politics. As Spencer Kornhaber writes in *The Atlantic*, "One implication is race isn't just an illusory divide. Another is both hopeful and a bit depressing: People casting opposing ballots in November might not realize just how much they have in common."[22] The satiric point the sketch works to demonstrate is that they *should* agree on political issues because they have so many similarities. The one obvious difference, of course, is race, and by highlighting their similarities, it illustrates how race is used to divide.[23]

As with "Black Jeopardy," the satiric element often relies on parody. The audience recognizes the "fake" part through parody (we realize *The Onion* is not an actual newspaper) so that the audience can understand the satiric element. For instance, *The Onion*'s June 19, 2018, story "Stephen Miller Furious At ProPublica For Only Releasing 7-Minute Recording of Immigrant Children Sobbing," parodies other news stories at the time about White House Senior Advisor Stephen Miller's controversial family separation policy. The *Onion* story satirizes the traditional media's biographic sketches of Miller and ProPublica's real story by representing Miller as someone who *enjoys* the sound of children crying. Rather than try to conceal the damning evidence, as an ordinary politician would, Miller wants the whole tape released.[24] This mixture of real and fake makes the satire work by highlighting the truth behind the joke – that the cruelty of Miller's policy is the very point of the policy. The ridiculousness of a joke, graphic, idea, proposal, etc. allows the satiric critique to land – for instance, being mad at only hearing seven minutes of kids crying, or selling children as food to the rich (*A Modest Proposal*), or a set of guidelines for England that will finally allow them to lose their colonies in America (*Rules By Which a Great Empire May Be Reduced to a Small One*), or simply repeating Trump's rambling ridiculousness.

On the flip side, comedy that veers too far into parody can nullify the satiric elements. In contemporary political sketch comedy, it is almost impossible to satirize a politician without also parodying him or her. An audience won't respond to a non-orange Trump with normal hair who properly pronounces the word "China." Audiences crave that entry point, without which there can be no satire. Too often, however, comedy about Trump leans too heavily on parody. When this happens, there is no critique of Trump; instead, there is only blank parody via mimicry and exaggeration. For example, in *SNL*'s 2017 "Donald Trump Trucker Rally Cold Open," the jokes tend to avoid or step around the significant issues of the week: Trump reigniting the NFL kneeling controversy, the details of the Republican tax plan, and the administration's response to Hurricane Maria in Puerto Rico. Rather than satiric critique, we get jokes about Senator Bob Corker being small, Trump mispronouncing words, and Trump guiding Mike Pence to leave various events that aren't "American" enough. The sketch is a parody of Trump. There are certainly funny moments, but most of the comedy focuses on Trump's mannerisms and personality or takes "friendly" jabs at his policies. The sketch jokes about Trump undoing Obama's policies on health care, Iran, and "ripping out all the vegetables in Michelle Obama's garden and planting McNuggets." The joke is an exaggeration (parody) of Trump's agenda to undo Obama's legacy, rather than a critique (satire) of what such an agenda means for the country.

Sketch Comedy

A comedy sketch is a self-contained 30-second to 10-minute scene based on a single premise (traditional sketch) or a satiric point (political sketch), with little character or plot development.[25] Eric Weitz, in *The Cambridge Introduction to Comedy*, describes a sketch as a single *lazzi* bit that lasts as long as the bit can sustain laughter. "The Dead Parrot" sketch from Monty Python is a good example. The premise relies on the shopkeeper selling a customer a dead parrot but refusing to acknowledge the crooked sale. John Cleese reaches for a string of euphemisms to describe the dead parrot he has been duped into buying, while the shopkeeper insists the parrot is still alive. The *lazzi* uses delay, protraction, and extension.[26] A sketch can be silly and pointless, but a political sketch has a crystal-clear point of view that trumps (no pun intended) the other dramatic elements. There are many different types of sketches, but in terms of humor, they all broadly fall into two categories: behavior or idea. A behavior sketch asks us to laugh at a character and their behavior in a given situation. Either the character or the situation is absurd. For instance, *Saturday Night Live*'s "Hot Tub Lovers" mixes both character styles in one sketch. Will Ferrell's and Rachel Dratch's outlandish "luvahs" characters are contrasted with the "normal" couple, played by Jimmy Fallon and host Winona Ryder. The comedy relies on the contrast between what each couple considers normal behavior, with Ferrell and Dratch clearly outside the bounds of normality. When Ryder's character joins the "luvahs" couple, the three are juxtaposed with Fallon, making him seem like the oddity.[27] The humor relies almost exclusively on this contrast. An idea sketch, however, is where satire more often comes into play as the humor relies on the idea or issue presented more so than a character's behavior, such as "Black Jeopardy." With sketch comedy about the president, the two types often mix. We laugh at presidents not acting presidential and their outsized personality quirks, *and* we laugh at the satiric treatment of their ideas and policies. The balance between behavior and ideas, personality and policy, has ebbed and flowed between presidents, though nearly all contemporary political sketch comedy relies on both types.

A collection of sketches is a sketch comedy revue. The form, as we know it today, developed in the 1960s at The Second City, which was building on the work of The Compass Players. According to Second City producer Bernie Sahlins, a revue is "a stage presentation that uses short scenes of varying lengths. Add music and songs and think of it as generally comical and topical by nature."[28] Traditionally, a sketch revue is a collection of scenes, songs, and blackouts that combine to explore a theme. The comedy is based on irony and satire, taking pointed jabs at social, political, and cultural norms by turning mainstream ideas about religion, race, politics, and culture on their heads. Rather than a traditional narrative, the revue's through line is its satiric point. A sketch revue might, for instance, be thematically linked by our reliance on technology, with each sketch offering a different satiric point on the way technology influences our lives. There's no main character or narrative arc; instead, the audience follows the connections between sketches as the thematic arc develops. Some characters may return throughout the revue, but generally, characters live and die with one sketch, often existing without a fully developed inner life.[29] Sketch revues are much more common on stage, as most sketch comedy on television utilizes independent sketches with no narrative or thematic relationship to the other sketches presented in a particular episode.

Performance is an integral part of sketch comedy, and more so than other types of comedy it relies on the dual presentation of the actor. Rooted in the theories of Bertolt Brecht (1898–1956), sketch comedy performance, especially satiric sketches, require the actor to present both themselves and the character they are portraying. Brecht wanted a theatre of ideas, performed in a cabaret-style setting that allowed the audience to engage intellectually with what was happening onstage rather than engage emotionally. This intellectual engagement ideally leads the audience to participate in social action/activism, an idea that later evolves into satiric advocacy where satirists, like John Oliver, explicitly ask their audience to engage in social activism. Sketch comedy's immediacy and flexibility – *SNL* does a new show each week meant to immediately comment on the news of the day – make it an ideal form for Brecht's theories. The early roots of sketch comedy, notably The Compass Players and Second City, were heavily influenced by Brecht, both politically and aesthetically. To achieve his socially conscious theatre, Brecht wanted a deliberate acting style where the actor was always aware of the triangular relationship between the actor, the audience, and the character, what Ian Wilkie calls a "reflective practitioner."[30] Rather than the actor "becoming" the character, the Brechtian relationship hinges on the actor presenting both themselves *and* the character during the performance.

We see this Brechtian style particularly in sketch comedy about the president. We read Chevy Chase's personal feelings about Gerald Ford and lay those onto the sketch to deepen the satiric take – we never forget that Chevy Chase is as much a part of the sketch as is Gerald Ford. A similar duality exists in many of the sketch comedy impressions explored in this book, most notably Will Ferrell's George W. Bush, Tina Fey's Sarah Palin, and Alec Baldwin's Donald Trump. In each instance, the audience enjoys the sketch more because they can impose the actual actor's personal opinions onto the politician they are portraying. Therefore, part of the satiric critique relies on the audience reading the actor onto the character. The audience's knowledge of his intense disdain for Trump enhances Baldwin's critique. This duality is at the heart of satiric authenticity. Crucially, the audience not knowing about the actor's personal feelings doesn't take away from the humor; instead, knowing enhances the humor. The duality also points to the commodification of sketch comedy. Part of the reason Chevy Chase played Ford as Chevy Chase is because he was building his own comedic persona – "I'm Chevy Chase. And you're not." Great "character" actors have had much less commercial success outside of the show than have the performers who have harnessed their own identity as part of their sketch comedy performance. Chase played Chase in virtually every sketch, a trend that continues through much of *SNL*'s history as the path to post-*SNL* success often relies on developing a star persona reliant on the performer's own identity. For the vast majority of the show, part of that star identity has also been reliant on a white male identity.

We see this duality throughout the history of sketch comedy, including long before Bertolt Brecht and the promise of post-*SNL* stardom. African American satirists, in particular, have always had a duality in their American identity, articulated in W.E.B. DuBois's notion of double consciousness. Expressed in DuBois's *The Souls of Black Folk* (1903), the concept stems from African Americans having to always look at themselves and their American identity through the eyes of others, namely white America. This double consciousness applies in performance as well. Bert Williams wearing blackface, for example, relies on the audience understanding that his wearing of blackface is a critique of the social construction of blackface. His dual performance of minstrel stereotypes is essential to his critique and attempted destruction of the stereotype he's portraying onstage – he is self-consciously asking the audience to view him through his own double consciousness. The satiric critique, and Williams's comedic brilliance, requires this double presentation of Williams the man and Williams the character. The negotiation between them is at the heart of his American identity.

This dual performance is likewise evident in sketch comedy shows where the comics perform as themselves during interludes or introductions to sketches. Many of television's 1950s variety shows intentionally framed the show, including its sketches and comedic bits, around the persona of the star host. In more contemporary sketch comedy, the same dynamic is at play when Dave Chappelle, Key and Peele, and Amy Schumer all perform as themselves between sketches to help frame the satiric take of the forthcoming material. We see this on *SNL* when a cast member appears as "themselves" to do a Weekend Update monologue about a particular topic or issue, as well as with the host's opening monologue and musical guest introductions. The host's real self is always present in *SNL* sketches. A great deal of the humor comes from the host either reinforcing or subverting their "normal" self. While this duality has always existed, it gains increased importance with the emergence of satiric authenticity after 9/11, where audiences began to demand that the satirist not merely present a critique, but also be "on our side" while delivering it. As such, the individual identity of a satirist, including their race and gender, can be fundamental to their effectiveness.

Furthermore, sketch comedians, like all satirists, need to be intellectually curious and adept. As James Thurber argued in 1958, "Political comedy must be grounded in serious knowledge of our nation and of the world."[31] Satirists, including sketch comedians, need to have a thorough knowledge of their targets and topics. They must be well-versed in the news of the day, be able to contextualize and ground complicated issues within history, and be tapped into the cultural zeitgeist. The sketch comedian then must take complicated issues – like immigration, health care, the Vietnam War, impeachment – and convey them to an audience in an accessible manner. Further complicating the matter, the audience holds a variety of viewpoints and presenting a sketch as "too one-sided" can alienate a large segment of the audience, blunting the satiric critique. On top of it all, it also needs to be funny. Taking a complicated issue, which is often highly charged, and making it accessible and funny is incredibly complicated. There is a fragile line between preachy and funny; angry and satiric. Former Second City Artistic Director Sheldon Patinkin argues this line is the key to satire: "If you're doing satire and comedy, you have to figure out how to do it so that the audience will laugh at what you hate, rather than just get angry at it. If you can laugh at it, you can fix it."[32] Not all satire requires laughter, but for sketch comedy, laughter is key to landing the satiric point. There has been a historical tension between laughter and anger in sketch comedy about the presidency. As times grow more turbulent, the satire becomes angrier, culminating with anger nearly completely taking over during Trump's presidency, in part, because, for many, it felt like absurdity had taken over reality.

Reality and Absurdity

In a 1985 interview with *The New York Times Book Review*, famed *Washington Post* columnist Art Buchwald summed it up: "You can't make up anything anymore. The world itself is a satire. All you're doing is recording it."[33] While presidents and leaders have been the target of satire for centuries, contemporary sketch-based satire is relatively young and has undergone a radical shift in the last 60 years. For centuries, satire has largely amplified the absurd in the real. For example, Jonathan Swift's *A Modest Proposal* amplifies the very real problem of poverty by proposing an absurd solution – eat Irish babies. Beginning with Vaughn Meader's comedy album *The First Family* (1962), many of the earliest presidential sketch and performance satirists likewise sought to illuminate the absurd within the real. Through the latter half of the 20th century, satirists mainly worked to amplify their targets, making them more extreme, more out of touch, more absurd. As G.K. Chesterton states, "the essence of satire is that it perceives some absurdity inherent in the logic of some position, and . . . draws the absurdity out and isolates it, so that all can see it."[34] The truth these satirists sought was not in the real, but the absurd amplification of the real. For example, in "Gerald Ford on Christmas Eve" he starts his fireside address early, cuts ornaments off the tree, hangs stockings upside down, and of course falls over trying to put the star on the tree.[35] From a simple trip caught on camera, Ford became "the first president to be defined by a pratfall."[36] As Ford himself notes in his autobiography, thanks to Chase's impression, anytime he "stumbled or bumped [his] head or fell in the snow, reporters zeroed in on that to the exclusion of almost everything else."[37] Similarly, *SNL*'s Phil Hartman portrays Bill Clinton voraciously eating all the McDonald's he can get his hands on. His one-on-one charm and policy knowledge are on full display, as is his uncontrollable appetite (and not just for food). Both of these examples push absurdity to reveal the satirists' points of view: Ford is falling down on the job, and Clinton's charm is both his ultimate weapon and his greatest flaw.

But what happens when the real is already absurd? Numerous events in the latter half of the 20th century saw absurdity taking over reality, beginning with Watergate and escalating through the end of the Cold War. Other events pushed absurdity further, led at times by comedians, but it was a string of real events and popular culture movements in the 1990s that pushed reality over the edge into absurd territory. The 1990s saw a series of more and more absurd "real-life" events, combined with a growing pop-culture landscape that focused on stupid or ridiculous things over anything of substance. Clarence Thomas's Supreme Court hearings in 1991 kicked off the decade's absurd public spectacles, but would pale in comparison to what was to come. Popular culture in the 1990s likewise fueled the absurdity. *The Jerry Springer Show* reveled in people acting like fools, while Howard Stern took to the airwaves to create a media empire based on crudeness and outlandishness. The most popular television shows – *Seinfeld* and *Friends* – focused on narcissistic New Yorkers dealing with outlandish scenarios or, quite literally, nothing. Back in reality, the O.J. Simpson murder trial in 1995 created a new sense of absurd reality. The trial captivated the nation, and while it reflected some very stark truths about race and the U.S. justice system (the trial came only a few short years after the Rodney King riots), it more often than not resembled the absurd antics of *The Jerry Springer Show*. O.J.'s famous gloves and Johnny Cochran's quote – "If it doesn't fit, you must acquit" – became a pop-culture phenomenon. The absurd reality of the 1990s reached the White House in 1998 with the Monica Lewinsky scandal. Much like its wall-to-wall coverage of the O.J. trial, cable news went all-in on the Lewinsky scandal, covering it around-the-clock and often sensationalizing the story rather than reporting it. As with O.J., Clinton's scandal was ever present in American life, amplified on television and a constant source of conversation. Clinton's own testimony, parsing the meaning of the word "is," added to the ridiculousness. The 2000 election and the Florida recount seemed to prove that reality had become absurd. American life was resembling *The Jerry Springer Show*. Then 9/11 turned everything on its head, jolting American life and presenting Americans with a stark new reality. The attacks were unthinkable to many Americans, and the world was suddenly much more dangerous and threatening than it had been since the end of the Cold War.

After 9/11, the truth became harder to find thanks in part to the secrecy of the Bush White House and the "patriotically correct" reporting of the media, creating a new credibility gap.[38] *The Daily Show* and *The Colbert Report* stepped into this truth vacuum. The shows rose in popularity specifically because they were speaking a truth the news media and others were not (albeit a reality leaning left). The shows called out the press for echoing not only the Bush White House, but also each other. *The Daily Show* especially gained traction as a media and "truth" watchdog. As the two shows became increasingly popular and influential, satire itself began to change. Stephen Colbert's turn as the right-wing commentator Stephen Colbert started as a traditional satiric amplification of the absurd, but throughout the show it shifted into absurdity mirroring reality. Suddenly, satire didn't need to amplify the absurd; cable news and reality TV was already doing that, so satire began pointing out the real in the absurd. Colbert's trademark "truthiness" embodied this change, satirizing the genuine (and ridiculous) notion that truth was something to be felt rather than objectively known. In sketch comedy, this shift was accompanied by a change from policy-based satire to personality-based satire, framing the president's personality as fundamental to understanding presidential policy.

The emergence of Sarah Palin in 2008 became the lynchpin for absurdity, at least in the political realm, becoming the new reality. Sarah Palin's rapid ascent during the 2008 election and Tina Fey's portrayal of her on *Saturday Night Live* fully captured satire's new role as revealing the real in the absurd. Rather than amplify the absurd in Palin's candidacy, Fey just repeated Palin's actual speeches and interviews. The "CBS Evening News: Katie Couric Interviews Sarah Palin" sketch, more fully explored in Chapter 8, is nearly identical to the actual Katie

Couric–Sarah Palin interview.[39] Palin's performance was widely seen as a disaster as she struggled to answer basic questions, like what newspapers she read. In the sketch, Fey verbatim repeats what Palin said, with a joke or two thrown in here or there. Fey's request for a lifeline in the sketch is a prime example where the real (Palin's lack of preparation to be vice president) is amongst the absurd. But the vast majority of the sketch is Fey saying nearly verbatim what Palin said. The verbatim sketch style used so effectively to satirize Palin is, in some ways, a product of reality television. The emergence of reality TV in the early 2000s amplified absurd reality to new heights. Americans watched "real" people doing "real" things in "real" situations that were highly orchestrated and constructed versions of reality. As reality TV "matured," many shows, like *Keeping Up With the Kardashians*, followed famous people living their lives who were mostly famous for being famous. That was it. This absurd television landscape not only pushed reality into new directions, but it also created a framework for verbatim comedy. Shows like *The Office* (2005–2013) used the conventions of reality TV to bring a different type of comedy to the network sitcom. Sketch comedy likewise used reality TV, both in sketches mocking it as well as in the verbatim style of sketch seen with Sarah Palin.

This verbatim sketch style has only escalated with the presidency of Donald J. Trump, who pushed all notions of normal to the wayside. Depending on one's political outlook, it is fair to say that real life has become absurd under Trump, our reality TV star president. To amplify its absurdity, rather than exaggerate reality as has historically been the practice, satirists now repeat reality nearly verbatim *via comedy shows* to remind people that what is actually happening is absurd. By repeating the real via comedy, the idea is that people will recognize the absurdity of their current reality through the delivery mechanism. If you couldn't tell that what Trump just said was absurd because he was in the Oval Office and presidents don't normally use a Sharpie to extend a hurricane's path, let us show it to you again on *SNL* so you can see just how ridiculous everything has become. Charted throughout the book and in detail for the final chapters, this verbatim style helped lead to satiric authenticity, which then led some into satiric advocacy, where satirists push for real change to our absurd world. A reality television star in his own right who became famous for mimicking reality, Trump is, in many ways, the perfect vehicle for verbatim sketch comedy. Therefore, it isn't surprising that satirists have attacked Trump in much the same way Fey attacked Sarah Palin. What is surprising is that this approach has been decidedly less effective in satirizing Trump, for numerous reasons, analyzed more fully in Chapter 9.

The Personality–Policy Spectrum

As absurdity and reality tangle, the other significant tension in sketch comedy about the president is between personality and policy. Nearly every sketch comedy presidential portrayal falls somewhere on the personality–policy spectrum. There is not quite as clear a historical shift on this spectrum as there is from absurdity to reality, with the range resetting and recalibrating for each new occupant of the White House. The very first impressions of JFK veered almost exclusively toward personality because satirizing policy was not yet wholly acceptable and because satirists genuinely liked JFK. The pendulum swung almost entirely toward policy when Lyndon Johnson took office. Nearly all of the sketch-based satire during LBJ's time in office was about Vietnam and the Johnson administration's handling of the war. Richard Nixon is the first example where personality and policy fused, as many saw Nixon's policy as a result of his personality. For satirists, Watergate happened *because* of Nixon's character. As the satiric takes of these three presidents demonstrate, satire in sketch comedy can take many forms, with the forms reflecting the satirists' intent. The critique of JFK was mainly about his Camelot persona, while with LBJ and Nixon the critiques were much more focused on the policies enacted by the two administrations. The type of sketch, therefore, reflected the intent of the satire.

Gerald Ford, the accidental accident-prone president, was the first president to have his personality satirized as a way to criticize his presidency. The satire via pratfall was less about his policies per se and more about his legitimacy and ability to be in the Oval Office. Jimmy Carter's four years saw him swing across the pendulum. Initial satire was heavily personality based but morphed into biting policy satire by 1980 as the country slid further into malaise. Reagan was perhaps our least effectively satirized president in terms of sketch comedy, though what was there tended to focus pretty exclusively on personality. George H.W. Bush would become the first president to have the entirety of his sketch persona shaped by personality. It did not matter that it wasn't necessarily reflective of Bush's actual personality. Dana Carvey's nerdy, out-of-touch Bush became the "reality" of Bush. Bill Clinton became the poster child for personality-as-policy satire. Like Nixon, many saw his personality as the cause of his policy, and in Clinton's case policy meant (for comedians at least) sex scandals. After 9/11, satire took a harder edge, and the George W. Bush satire found itself veering in all directions on the personality–policy spectrum. Eventually, it meant there needed to be more than "Bush is dumb" personality satire, but that was not always the case. Barack Obama's satiric take was a combination of JFK and Reagan. Like JFK, many satirists seemed to admire Obama and were reluctant to criticize him; like Reagan, his message of hope and optimism was challenging to mock. Like both JFK and Reagan, Obama's wit worked to neutralize many of the satiric attacks against him. Obama's race was unquestionably a factor, as a historically white liberal community of satirists found themselves unwilling and unable to take on Obama's policy.

Donald Trump represents the ultimate merger of the spectrum, a sort of über-combination of Clinton and Nixon. Like no president before him, Trump's policy *was* his personality, and his personality was, in many ways, absurd. As such, satirizing Trump's character became the best way to criticize his policies. What makes Trump so tricky to satirize effectively, paradoxically, is that his personality is so easy to ridicule. Trump's real persona is already a sketch character: the voice, the hair, the long red ties, the braggadocio, the narcissism, the lying. Satirists can focus too heavily on those distinct elements and not effectively link his personality to his policy. Because he's so easy to make fun of, he's challenging to satirize successfully. Similarly, because he was in the public eye for decades before running for office, his public persona was already fully formed. As Jody Baumgartner argues, the 2016 election demonstrated the limits of satire influencing public opinion, in no small measure due to the national prominence of Hillary Clinton and Donald Trump. She writes, "Being well-known public figures before the campaign season even began, public opinions of each were relatively immune to change as the result of watching political comedy directed at them."[40] As such, historically satire has been more influential on public perceptions when aimed at political figures when they first emerge on the national stage – like Gerald Ford and Sarah Palin – rather than aimed at already well-known politicians. Likewise, more politically active viewers are less likely to be swayed by a sketch or a politician's appearance on a talk show than less enthusiastic or knowledgeable viewers.[41]

Liberal or Conservative

While satire can be a corrective, many scholars argue that satire inherently reinforces the status quo. Satire may aim at a target, but does the satirist expect change? Is the satirist merely pointing out the vice, or, is it a dull knife pointed inward? As Wylie Sypher wrote, "The ambivalence of comedy reappears in its social meaning, for comedy is both hatred and revel, rebellion and defense, attack and escape. It is revolutionary and conservative. Socially, it is both sympathy and persecution."[42] The "Donald Trump Trucker Rally Cold Open" sketch is a prime example. We laugh at Trump, but the sketch isn't doing anything to enact change. It reinforces Trump's role as president. As Harvey Young argues, "satire normalizes Trump's presidency.... The more that he appears on SNL, the more familiar his presidency becomes. It's not that he's humanized by parody. He simply appears more recognizable as the president."[43] Anne Libera, articulating the limits of Brechtian theory, argues that satire can be too much of a balm. She explains that

> there are studies out there that suggest that people are less likely to try to affect change in a situation after being exposed to jokes about that situation. It may be that there is something in laughing at an injustice that gives us an intellectual distance rather than creating an emotional/empathic connection which could drive us to action.[44]

But as Libera points out, one of comedy's greatest strengths is creating community: "When we laugh at something together, it bonds us. We know we are not alone in our thinking. And knowing that there are others out there who agree with us is a pretty big predictor of motivation for change."[45] Is satire about the presidency working to improve the presidency? Did satire about Vietnam influence the policy of LBJ or Nixon? Does making fun of Donald Trump do anything to impact his policies or behavior? Do they work more to galvanize "the base" than to enact any tangible change? Or do these sketches simply reinforce the institutional structure of an ever-expanding and powerful position?

Satire has historically been made by and for liberals. In *Irony and Outrage,* Dannagal Goldthwaite Young demonstrates that satire has a clear liberal psychological bias. These statements are undeniably true, yet, is the *effect* of satire actually conservative in nature? As John Gilmore and others suggest, perhaps Jonathan Swift wrote *Gulliver's Travels* "not because he hoped to change human nature, but because he despaired of it."[46] Because satire ridicules nonnormative behavior, most classic and literary theory posits that satire reinforces the status quo. Amber Day argues in *Satire & Dissent* that the long-held belief among scholars that satire is conservative is

> a theory that has continued to have widespread prominence to this day, with countless thinkers arguing that satirists typically ridicule particular personalities, going after character flaws and other weaknesses, but that they rarely critique the more crucial economic and political structures of their societies. The implication is that, while satire and political humor may appear transgressive, they are "essentially conservative in thought and impact," serving to assure us that, while particular individuals are fallible, the system itself works as it should.[47]

Sketch comedy seems like a subversive art form, but has its commodification by television neutralized its revolutionary roots? In writing about the history of sketch comedy on TV, Nick Marx argues that "networks strategically create and circulate sketch comedies with identities that serve their respective financial goals. Across nearly all historical periods, social contexts, and advertising models, networks have programmed sketch shows starring comedians and targeting audiences that support the social status quo."[48] It is important to remember that sketch comedy on television, which has become the dominant medium for sketch, is a commodity. The network is trying to make a profit, not deliver cutting-edge satire. Sometimes the two goals intersect, but more often they collide, with the network almost always erring on the side of caution.

Similarly, mainstream satirists have been overwhelmingly heterosexual white men. While varying viewpoints have emerged, the history of satire comes from a traditionally privileged point of view. *Saturday Night Live*, the pinnacle of American satiric sketch comedy, is the prime example. Though President Donald Trump routinely accuses the show of being "rigged" and "liberal," it has worked more often to reinforce the status quo. The show has long presented itself from the perspective of young heterosexual white men, and has often ostracized women and minorities in the cast. This vantage point is due in part to the historic ostracizing of diverse voices. So much of comedic television is populated by white men, that when the next show comes along they hire people that they've worked with or who have experience in the industry, which tends to be white men. The next show does the same, and so on. The whiteness of the show was highlighted when there was not an African American cast member to play President Barack Obama or enough African American female cast members to have two black women in a sketch at the same time. Nick Marx argues the casting of the show, including its "progressive" original cast, worked to reinforce gender and racial stereotypes. The show's rush to produce content that appealed to network tastes (i.e., advertisers' tastes) meant that the show "ended up reinforcing – not undermining – existing social power inequalities based in race and gender."[49]

SNL is hardly alone in the privileging of whiteness. Nearly the entire history of political satire, outlined in Chapter 1, showcases the ways in which whiteness has been seen as normal, as well as the ways satire has used difference to reinforce those ideas.

These issues of diversity are still prevalent today. For instance, in the fall of 2019 *SNL* hired and then quickly fired Shane Gillis due to his history of racist humor (Gillis hardly being the only example in the recent history of *SNL* hiring a white man with a problematic history of racial humor). In the mid-1990s, John Pike, then senior vice president in charge of CBS's late-night programming, was working to bring MTV's *The State* to the network. Comprised of ten white men and one white woman, the group was hardly diverse. So, Pike suggested adding an African American performer to the group. Obviously, adding one African American cast member would not suddenly make the group diverse. The tokenism aside, the idea is a start, but Pike's alleged rationale was abhorrently racist. Pike thought having an African American in the cast would help draw in African American viewers, who Pike saw as the perfect late-night demographic because they have "no place to go in the morning – no jobs – so they can stay up as late as they like . . . [also], they can't follow hourlong drama shows – no attention span – so sketches are perfect for them."[50] Pike ultimately resigned in connection with the statement, though he denied saying it. Here is the head of a major network's late-night programming (allegedly) using minstrel stereotypes propagated for over a century by mainstream comedy to highlight political and social satire's glaring diversity problems. The situation is sickening, but also demonstrates the power of satire to influence cultural ideas and practices. It also bears repeating that *The State* had an 11-person all-white cast, with only one female member, and that was considered normal. Even if we ignore Pike's rationale, his suggestion was not to truly diversify the cast, it was to add a single African American member.

This conservative nature is not limited just to racial diversity. Satire and comedy have likewise ostracized women and female voices. Original *SNL* cast member Jane Curtin remarked on the show's attitude toward female comics, saying,

> There were a few people who out and out believed that women should not be there and believed that women were not funny. . . . You'd go to a table read, and if a woman writer had written a piece for John [Belushi], he would not read it in his full voice. He felt as though it was his duty to sabotage pieces written by women.[51]

Numerous female cast members have echoed the sentiment, including Julia Louis-Dreyfus, who is perhaps the most decorated and celebrated comedic actress of our time, who said that *SNL* "was a very sexist environment."[52] She did note that it has gotten better since her time on the show, but it points to the work *SNL* still has to do in terms of diversity and further raises questions about just how progressive the show actually is. The show's history with sexual orientation is likewise problematic, with numerous examples of homophobic sketches contrasted with only a handful of openly gay and lesbian cast members in the show's nearly 50 years. It all points to *SNL*'s positioning as an institution. As Mary Elizabeth Williams writes:

Introduction 19

If you want to make the case for "SNL" as a venue always open to making jokes at the expense of politics and power, sure, that's embedded in its DNA. But right there mixed in with that has always been a strong streak of conformity with the status quo, regardless of who gets thrown under the bus in the process. And even without the addition of Shane Gillis to its opening credits when the new season premieres next weekend, Lorne Michaels' legacy is still plenty safe from any real threat of "liberal bias."[53]

We can see this conservative nature play out within the show's diversity (or lack thereof). As the show has slowly become more diverse, there is a direct and notable impact on the show's sketch comedy portrayals. For instance, Hillary Clinton transformed from a shrill shrew to a more nuanced and sympathetic character on *Saturday Night Live* in part because the writing staff of the show transformed. It is not a coincidence that Hillary's first considerate portrayals occurred when Tina Fey became the show's first female head writer. Similarly, *Key & Peele* was able to address issues of race during the Obama presidency in much more detailed, bold, and, frankly, meaningful ways than the much whiter *SNL* ever did or could. Both cases definitively deflate the "diversity for diversity's sake" argument that inevitably appears when discussing representation in comedy. Not only were the sketch portrayals of Hillary and Obama more accurate and penetrating, but they also were plain old funnier. These examples demonstrate the importance not just of analyzing the satire, but of the satirist as well.

Does satire speak truth to power, or is it a tool to help stabilize the powerful? Some of our most successful presidents have used humor as a weapon. Lincoln, FDR, Kennedy, Reagan, and Obama all used humor throughout their presidencies to deflect criticism, mask shortcomings, further their legislative agendas, and bring the country together. Comedy about the president can certainly be a form of checks and balances, but it can also work to enhance the president's power. Comic impersonations of the president can humanize the presidency. A joke can be a reminder that the person holding the most powerful office in the land is indeed a person. By ridiculing the president's vulnerabilities or shortcomings, Americans get to see that their president is fallible. It can also work to demystify the presidency. As technology evolved, the president went from a person the average American never saw or heard speak, to someone who is almost ever present in our lives. Humor helps with that transition, both historically and currently, to link citizens to the White House. That link is essential to the creation, evolution, and maintenance of the American identity.

While satire may intend to "harm" the presidency, has it worked to reinforce the power of the office? George H.W. Bush famously fully embraced Dana Carvey's impression of him, making Bush seem like he was a part of the joke rather than the target. Humor, it seems, has come to be one of the key traits necessary for a successful presidency. Rather than being the target of satirists, has the modern presidency evolved to the point where presidents use humor to twist satiric barbs to their advantage? What happens to our perception of Bush when he impersonates Dana Carvey impersonating him? Does it take the sting out of the original and ultimately work to enhance Bush's power and popularity? What about when Donald Trump outright rejects satire about him and uses "biased" satire to assert his own authenticity? In short, what exactly is the relationship between satire and the presidency?

In the following chapters, I will first provide an overview of American satire, before examining the individual relationships between sketch comedy and the president, from JFK to Trump. While each president has a unique relationship with sketch comedy, there are larger patterns that emerge, such as the shift toward absurd reality, with each subsequent president often learning from his predecessor about how to best treat the relationship. As the country made social and cultural advances, often heavily pushed by sketch comedians, both the presidency and sketch comedy changed. Sketch comedy has shaped and reacted to the fracturing divides in American life in the wake of the social revolution of the 1960s and the "credibility gap" that emerged in the 1970s. From the conservative conformity of the 1980s to the "nothing matters" sketch comedians of the 1990s, we can see how comedy reflects and responds to the nation's highest office and the ways it influences both the presidency and the public. The changing landscape precipitated by 9/11 and exacerbated by the Bush White House resulted in a fundamental sharpening of sketch comedy that worked to expose "the truth," but that also further divides an already splintering country. The challenges of the "post-racial" mythology of Obama's presidency reflected the growing demand for diversity in comedy, all of which has been pushed to the brink by the sheer absurdity of the Trump White House. By tracing the role of sketch comedy and the presidency, we can gain a deeper understanding of how the presidency functions in America and the role of satire in shaping our national discourse and destiny.

Notes

1. Qtd. in William Horner and Heather Carver, *Saturday Night Live and the 1976 Presidential Election: A New Voice Enters Campaign Politics* (Jefferson, NC: McFarland & Co. Inc., 2018), 2.
2. Mary E. Stuckey, *Defining Americans: The Presidency and National Identity* (Lawrence: University Press of Kansas, 2004), 7.
3. Qtd. in Mel Watkins, *On the Real Side: A History of African American Comedy from Slavery to Chris Rock* (Chicago: Lawrence Hill Books, 1994), 517.
4. Robert Elliot, "Satire," *Encyclopedia Britannica*. www.britannica.com/art/satire#ref 504991.
5. Peter Lattman, "The Origins of Justice Stewart's 'I Know It When I See It,'" *The Wall Street Journal*, 27 September 2007. https://blogs.wsj.com/law/2007/09/27/the-origins-of-justice-stewarts-i-know-it-when-i-see-it/.
6. David Marc, "Foreword," in *Satire TV: Politics and Comedy in the Post-Network Era*, eds. Jonathan Gray, Jeffrey P. Jones and Ethan Thompson (New York: New York University Press, 2009), ix.
7. Rachel Paine Caufield, "The Influence of 'Infoenterpropagainment,'" in *Laughing Matters: Humor and American Politics in the Media Age* (New York: Routledge, 2008), 4.

8. Stephen Koch, "Introduction," in *American Satire: An Anthology of Writings from Colonial Times to the Present*, ed. Nicholas Bakalar (New York: Penguin Group, 1997), xiii.
9. Andrew Stott, *Comedy: The New Critical Idiom* (New York: Routledge, 2015), 160.
10. "The Day Beyoncé Turned Black," *Saturday Night Live*, 13 February 2016. www.nbc.com/saturday-night-live/video/the-day-beyonce-turned-black/2985361.
11. "Haunted Elevator (ft. David S. Pumpkins)," *Saturday Night Live*, 22 October 2016. www.nbc.com/saturday-night-live/video/haunted-elevator-ft-david-s-pumpkins/3333596.
12. George A. Test, *Satire: Spirit and Art* (Tampa: University of South Florida Press, 1991), 32.
13. Jonathan Gray, Jeffrey Jones and Ethan Thompson, "The State of Satire, The Satire of State," in *Satire TV: Politics and Comedy in the Post-Network Era*, eds. Jonathan Gray, Jeffrey Jones and Ethan Thompson (New York: New York University Press, 2009), 12–13.
14. Test, 28.
15. John Gilmore, *Satire: The New Critical Idiom* (New York: Routledge, 2018), 3.
16. Herman Gray, *Watching Race: Television and the Struggle for "Blackness"* (Minneapolis: University of Minnesota Press, 1995), 130.
17. Lawrence W. Levine, *Black Culture and Black Consciousness: Afro-American Folk Thought from Slavery to Freedom* (New York: Oxford University Press, 1977), 336.
18. Merriam-Webster. Twitter Post, 22 January 2017, 9:32am. https://twitter.com/MerriamWebster/status/823221915171061760.
19. Merriam-Webster. Twitter Post, 24 January 2017, 2:50pm. https://twitter.com/MerriamWebster/status/824026625373306884.
20. Geoffrey Baum, "Serious Comedy," *Laughing Matters*, 33.
21. Qtd. in Sam Wasson, *Improv Nation: How We Made a Great American Art* (New York: Houghton Mifflin Harcourt Publishing Company, 2017), 99.
22. Spencer Kornhaber, "*SNL's* Surprisingly Affectionate Portrayal of a Trump Supporter," *The Atlantic*, 24 October 2016. www.theatlantic.com/entertainment/archive/2016/10/black-jeopardy-snl-tom-hanks-donald-trump-supporter/505142/.
23. "Black Jeopardy," *Saturday Night Live*, 22 October 2016. www.nbc.com/saturday-night-live/video/black-jeopardy-with-tom-hanks/3333590.
24. "Stephen Miller Furious at ProPublica for Only Releasing 7-Minute Recording of Immigrant Children Sobbing," *The Onion*, 19 June 2018. https://politics.theonion.com/stephen-miller-furious-at-propublica-for-only-releasing-1826958853.
25. There is also a marked difference between a sketch and a skit. As Annoyance Theatre founder and frequent Second City director Mick Napier notes, "skits would be what cub scouts do."
26. Eric Weitz, *The Cambridge Introduction to Comedy* (Cambridge: Cambridge University Press, 2009), 108.
27. "Hot Tub Lovers," *Saturday Night Live*, 18 May 2002. www.nbc.com/saturday-night-live/video/hot-tub-lovers/3505918.
28. Bernard Sahlins, *Days and Nights at the Second City* (Chicago: Ivan R. Dee, 2001), 115.
29. On the other side, a play is a play (feel free to quote me). A play explores big ideas through the plot and character development. A play's characters live within and beyond the world of the play – the characters and story may stay with us, whereas the satiric point is what remains with us in sketch comedy. Both forms deal with big ideas; they approach them in different ways.
30. Ian Angus Wilkie, *Performing in Comedy: A Student's Guide* (London: Routledge, 2016).

31. James Thurber, "State of the Nation's Humor," *New York Times Magazine*, 7 December 1958, 26.
32. Qtd. in Mike Thomas, *The Second City Unscripted: Revolution and Revelation at the World-Famous Comedy Theater* (Evanston: Northwestern University Press, 2012), 43.
33. Qtd. in Herbert Mitgang, "Behind the Best Sellers," *The New York Times*, 4 February 1979. https://www.nytimes.com/1979/02/04/archives/behind-the-best-sellers-art-buchwald.html.
34. Qtd. in *Satire TV*, 12.
35. "Christmas Eve at the White House," *Saturday Night Live*, 20 December 1975. www.nbc.com/saturday-night-live/video/christmas-eve-at-the-white-house/2721418.
36. S. Robert Lichter, Jody C. Baumgartner, and Jonathan S. Morris, *Politics is a Joke! How TV Comedians are Remaking Political Life* (Boulder, CO: Westview Press, 2015), 45.
37. Gerald Ford, *A Time to Heal: The Autobiography of Gerald R. Ford* (New York: Harper & Row, 1979), 289.
38. Ira Glass, "599: Seriously?" *This American Life*, produced by WBEZ, NPR, 21 October 2016, audio, 63:37. www.thisamericanlife.org/599/seriously.
39. "CBS Evening News: Katie Couric Interviews Sarah Palin," *Saturday Night Live*, 27 September 2008. www.nbc.com/saturday-night-live/video/couric-palin-open/n12311.
40. Jody C. Baumgartner, "The Limits of Attitude Change: Political Humor During the 2016 Campaign," in *Political Humor in a Changing Media Landscape*, eds. Jody C. Baumgartner and Amy B. Becker (Lanham, MD: The Rowman & Littlefield Publishing Group Inc., 2018), 61.
41. Jody C. Baumgartner and S. Jonathan Morris, "The 'Daily Show' Effect: Candidate Evaluations, Efficacy, and American Youth," *American Political Research* 34, no. 3 (May 2006), 341; Matthew A. Baum, "Talking the Vote: Why Presidential Candidates Hit the Talk Show Circuit," *American Journal of Political Science* 49, no. 2 (April 2005), 213–234.
42. Qtd. in Watkins, 16.
43. Qtd. in James Warren, "Laughing at Trump," *U.S. News & World Report*, 15 March 2017. www.usnews.com/opinion/thomas-jefferson-street/articles/2017-03-15/what-to-make-of-alec-baldwins-saturday-night-live-skits-on-donald-trump.
44. Qtd. in Warren.
45. Qtd. in Warren.
46. Gilmore, 9.
47. Amber Day, *Satire & Dissent: Interventions in Contemporary Political Debate* (Bloomington, IN: Indiana University Press, 2011), 11.
48. Nick Marx, *Sketch Comedy: Identity, Reflexivity, and American Television* (Bloomington, IN: Indiana University Press, 2019), 23.
49. Marx, 31.
50. Qtd. in Marx, 117. Pike has denied the veracity of the quote.
51. Qtd. in Mary Elizabeth Williams, "Even Without Shane Gillis, 'SNL' Has Always Been a Conservative Show," *Salon.com*, 18 September 2019. www.salon.com/2019/09/18/even-without-shane-gillis-snl-has-always-been-a-conservative-show/.
52. Qtd. in Dave Itzkoff, "Julia Louis-Dreyfus on Clinton, Trump and an Election-Year 'Veep,'" *The New York Times*, 14 April 2016. www.nytimes.com/2016/04/17/arts/television/julia-louis-dreyfus-on-clinton-trump-and-anelection-year-veep.html?_r=0.
53. Williams.

CHAPTER 1

From Colony to Country: A Brief Overview of American Political Satire

Louis Rubin, Jr. writes in "The Great American Joke" that "From colonial times onward, we have spent a great deal of time and effort criticizing ourselves, pointing out our short-comings, exploring the incongruities and the contradictions within American society."[1] For Rubin, "The Great American Joke" is the contrast between the lofty ideals of the Declaration of Independence and the everyday realities of American life. Depending on the positioning of the satirist, the contrast can take many forms. For African American satirists, the difference lies between "All men are created equal" and slavery and subsequent Jim Crow laws and systemic racism. Similarly, female satirists have found themselves navigating an inherently uneven playing field, working for centuries to assert their independence and agency. Even today we see "The Great American Joke" playing out as a nation of immigrants battles over immigration, with Donald Trump winning the presidency in 2016 in no small part because of his promise to build a wall blocking immigrants from entering the country. American satire has grappled with this inherent discrepancy in its various guises for centuries, coming in four primary forms: literary, editorial cartoons, satiric news, and performance. While this study focuses on political sketch comedy related to the presidency, it is vital to position it within American political humor properly, specifically in regards to satire's role in the creation of an American identity and Americans' relationship with the presidency.

America's Comic Founding Father – Benjamin Franklin

Like many budding American institutions, from democracy to baseball, European thought and practice heavily influenced American political satire. The two most prominent influences on America's comic founding father, Benjamin Franklin (1706–1790), were Jonathan Swift (1667–1745) and Voltaire (1694–1778). The two satirists' influence is apparent in Franklin's work, most notably in his work satirizing indoctrinated thought. As such, their impact is imbedded in Franklin's expression of American identity as he simultaneously mimics and rejects their work. Early Americans struggled with adopting and adapting European thoughts and ideas as part of their emerging national identity. Simultaneously, the clearest way to assert their Americanness was by *rejecting* European thoughts and ideas.

Franklin did it better than anyone, and that is one of the reasons his work resonated so strongly with Americans.

Franklin's satire rarely attacked individuals, instead focusing on policies and ideas. He became America's most prominent satiric critic of authority, frequently unleashing his pen against the British. In his biography of Franklin, Edmund Morgan writes that Franklin often responded satirically to British policies by suggesting ridiculous proposals. For instance, in *Felons and Rattlesnakes* (1751), Franklin recommends a ludicrous trade: "the British practice of shipping convicts to the American colonies should be matched by a regular export of rattlesnakes from the colonies to Britain." As war with England loomed, Franklin advised England "that the British army be assigned to castrate all American males in order to reduce the growing and ungovernable American population."[2] Reflecting Swift's style, these ridiculous proposals severely critiqued British tyranny. In *Rules by Which a Great Empire May Be Reduced to a Small One* (1773), Franklin sarcastically offers advice to England on how to ensure losing the American colonies. His suggestions include continuing to exclude the colonies from the creation of all legislation and having them "governed by *severer* laws;" to "*suppose* them always inclined to revolt, and treat them accordingly," mainly by allowing the quartering of troops; to send incompetent governors and judges so that the colonists don't think the government is fair, just, or wise; and of course, to endlessly tax the colonies without representation.[3] Several of the grievances aired in *Rules* made their way into another document, the Deceleration of Independence, perhaps in no small measure because, in response to the Boston Tea Party, the British enacted many of Franklin's "suggestions" in the Coercive Acts of 1774.

Rules may be Franklin's most influential piece of satire, but his most famous work and the one most closely associated with the emerging American identity is *Poor Richard's Almanack*. First published in 1732 and then published annually for the next 25 years, *Poor Richard's Almanack* is not unlike other almanacs of the day. What set it apart and drove its great popularity were Franklin's sayings, aphorisms, and idioms – many of which are still part of the American lexicon.[4] Though widely known that Franklin was the author, he wrote under the pseudonym of Richard Saunders. In much the same way that viewers of *The Colbert Report* knew that Stephen Colbert was playing a part, Franklin was using Saunders as a personal vehicle. This double persona appears throughout American satire, such as Seba Smith's Jack Downing, Charles Farrar Browne's Artemus Ward, Peter Finely Dunne's Mr. Dooley, Chevy Chase's Gerald Ford, and Stephen Colbert's Stephen Colbert. The structure and content of *Poor Richard's Almanack* were not satiric, but Franklin's style defined the emerging American comedic sensibility and became an early rallying point for American identity. Franklin's plainspoken language reflects his position as a "common man," lending authenticity to his American voice. Furthermore, as Peter Robinson argues, "In Franklin's hands, humor indicated heroic defiance, mastery over the follies and flaws of both others and oneself by virtue of being able to recognize them and replace the harm they might do with ridicule or resignation as the occasion demanded."[5] Franklin was the first to assert an American voice, and he, through Poor Richard, was likewise the first to play a dual role within his satire. Franklin's "real life" dual role as satirist and Founding Father helped foment and normalize the relationship between humor and politics in American life.

The Early American Stage – The Stage Yankee to the Minstrel Show

Believe it or not, *Hamilton* was not the first play to take on American politics. The stage became a vehicle for political debate and partisan opinion as the American government tried to figure out precisely what it wanted to be. Joseph Addison's *Cato* (1713) and John Gay's *The Beggar's Opera* (1728) each became foundational to the framers of the presidency. The first play written and professionally produced by an American likewise became instrumental in formulating American's emerging identity. Royall Tyler's comedy *The Contrast* (1787) defines American identity by contrasting it against British identity. The play reflects the contrast of Americanness – we see American identity asserted not by what it is, but by what it is not. The play is written in the style of a 17th-century British Restoration comedy, and much of the comedy, ironically, comes from Tyler satirizing Americans who attempt to mimic British style, fashion, and politics. Contrasting these phony anglophiles are two truly American characters: the aptly named Colonel Manly and his honest but straightforward servant Jonathan. Manly "is the first in a long series of eighteenth and nineteenth century embodiments of idealized American manhood whose central concern, both on and off the battlefield, is their nation's moral and political health."[6] With Manly representing the more aristocratic or upper-class notions of patriotism, Jonathan allowed audiences to feel superior to him, while simultaneously sparking patriotic pride in his unbreakable moral and ethical standards. Manly's classic American patriotism inspired generations of American heroes in his mold, but it was Jonathan that became the locus of American identity. As Maura Jortner notes, Jonathan "was a perfect vehicle of nationalism, promoting and displaying an idealized relationship between the upper and the lower strata in this new national community."[7] He might be uneducated, and city types might be able to trick him, but in the end, his rural, hard-working, commonsense wisdom wins out. While there are clear parallels between Manly and George Washington, nearly every other president tried to balance these two characters – the patrician Manly and the common Jonathan – in their own personas.

Presidents balanced the two, but for "the common man" Jonathan became a rallying point for national identity. The simple, hardworking, rural stock character contains elements of Franklin's Poor Richard persona. He may lack in intellect, especially formal education, but is full of honor, gumption, and patriotism – a true common man for a country of common men.[8] One of the popular comic tools of the Yankee character, also inherent in minstrel humor, is cacography – deliberate misspelling for comic effect. In performance, this manifests itself through puns and malapropism. A clear example of "The Great American Joke," we laugh at his stupidity, while also marveling at his wisdom. As Winifred Morgan notes, for the first 65 years of the United States' existence, the answer to the question "What is an American?" "came the popular answer 'Brother Jonathan.'"[9] Morgan asserts that

Jonathan "provided a commonly accepted definition of what to expect from an ordinary American . . . [and] the idea that each American citizen had the potential to 'take charge' sparked the most overwhelmingly popular understanding of America's greatness."[10] As Francis Hodge notes, "What gave the Yankee character such a long life on the stage . . . made him so popular, not only everywhere in America but in England as well, was his status as a symbol of American democratic society."[11] His work ethic borne from rural hard work, his strong moral fiber, his mistrust of the highly educated and the elite (namely Europeans), and his ability to "take charge" came to be essential components of Americanness.

Yankee characters permeated American culture in the early 19th century and quickly found themselves influencing American ideas about the presidency. One of the more famous examples was Jack Downing, created in 1830 by journalist Seba Smith. Writing in the *Portland Daily Courier* and later in Downing's faux memoir *My Thirty Years Out of the Senate* (1859), Downing quickly went from rural Maine bumpkin who wandered into the state legislature to sell ax handles to confidant of President Andrew Jackson. The meteoric rise of the simple Downing reflected the ascent of Jackson himself, echoing the limited distance between citizen and president. Even more significantly, it illustrated the perceived promise of America – that merit would dictate a person's future, not birth or nobility (or education). The fictional relationship also helped to set up future relationships between comics and presidents, such as the similarly fictional relationship between Artemus Ward and Abraham Lincoln, as well as the very real relationship between Will Rogers and Franklin Roosevelt. As Americans moved west, the character took on frontier qualities. Johnson Jones Hooper's character Captain Simon Suggs was the most notable, a character "who became the prototype of the colorful, rascally, but witty lout that epitomized the humor and distinct vernacular dialect of the Frontier type in the mid-nineteenth century."[12] One of the distinguishing features of the Stage Yankee character, and American identity, is its malleability.

The Yankee character in its many incarnations has become a staple of American identity and American comedy, ebbing and flowing over the last two centuries to reflect the changing country – from frontiersman, to immigrant, to soldier, to blue-collar worker. Through it all, his rural hard work and mistrust of the elite remained a rallying point for national identity. In the same way that Shakespeare used fools and comics to speak truths, this seeming fool became a spokesperson for America: "The idea was that from the mouths of the ignorant a kind of wisdom might flow that was uncluttered with the deformations of learning; in the country of the common man, this ironic, often satiric voice would be the sound of the common man's wisdom."[13] It should come as no surprise then that politicians have appropriated this folksy model to increase their popular appeal for centuries. Andrew Jackson and Abraham Lincoln were among the first to embrace the rural-as-authentic trope, while we still see it in contemporary America, most notably with George W. Bush. He purposefully crafted a Yankee persona, working to distance himself from his Yale and Harvard education, instead presenting himself as a Texas rancher who'd rather clear brush than read books. Donald Trump likewise pushes the anti-intellectual strain of the Yankee type, warning his "real

American" supporters against the dangers of experts, scientists, and coastal elites. Similarly, both men used "tough" speech and presented themselves as embodiments of the rugged individualism that defined the Yankee character.

The Stage Yankee brought an American identity to the stage through comedy and satire. It wasn't until the mid-19th century, however, that the first truly American form of stage entertainment developed: the minstrel show (roughly 1830–1890). The minstrel show was hugely popular in antebellum America, with the Ethiopian Serenaders even going to the White House in 1844 for the "Especial amusement of the President of the United States."[14] Reflecting racial tension in America, most minstrel performances asked white audiences (mostly Northern white audiences) to laugh at stock characters based on negative racial stereotypes to reinforce slavery and white superiority. Frederick Douglass, who, according to Trump, is "being recognized more and more,"[15] said in *The North Star* in 1848, blackface performers were "the filthy scum of white society, who have stolen from us a complexion denied to them by nature, in which to make money, and pander to the corrupt taste of their white fellow citizens."[16] Not only did minstrel mock and demean African Americans, it did so to assert white citizenship. As Mel Watkins argues, the minstrel characters, who in many ways resembled Yankee character types, were the perfect foil for working-class whites: "What better way to fashion a common man's culture than to spotlight a comic type at which the average man could laugh, indeed, recognize some part of himself in veiled form, and at the same time feel superior?"[17] The use of verbal cacography in the back-and-forth jokes, songs, and stump speeches was a direct link to the Yankee and Frontier American characters. Only this time, the type was a tool to suppress blacks and assuage the concerns of white audiences about the brutality and morality of slavery.

It seems obvious, but it is essential to remember that "the first characteristic that is standard to minstrelsy jokes is comic material about color."[18] Blackness allowed white audiences to feel superior. As Roger Scruton writes about the superiority theory of humor, "laughter devalues its object in the subject's eyes."[19] Thanks to minstrelsy, audiences laughed *at* blackness and made it a disqualifying factor for Americanness. One of the ways minstrel did this was through exaggeration, making absurd stereotypes and then presenting them as "real." White performers would blacken their faces with burnt cork, hence the term *blackface*, and exaggerate their appearance: huge eyes, large lips, and broad noses. They would speak in an exaggerated and fictitious plantation dialect that was a significant source of humor meant to demean African Americans. Black characters either lived on Southern plantations where they were happy and secure, or in the North where they were bewildered by city life and unknowingly incapable of functioning as freemen. The inability of free blacks in the North to handle the responsibility of freedom and authority/autonomy would become a long-lasting comic trope used to suppress African Americans. While audiences laughed at the simple jokes and slapstick comedy of Northern blacks who were hopelessly out of place and the happy-go-lucky shenanigans of Southern plantation life, the sociopolitical meaning was clear: "black people belonged only on Southern plantations and had no place at all in the North."[20] As time wore on and slavery ended, the message only slightly altered in much of American comedy: blacks have no place in positions of power or authority, up to and including the presidency.

Minstrel characters were lazy, stupid, superstitious, and yet, happy as pie with their lot in life. There were many stock characters in minstrel, including the Sambo (a Stage Yankee for minstrelsy), Zip Coon, Mammy, Uncle Tom, Buck, the mulatto, the wench/jezebel, and the pickaninny. These character types became part of America's cultural and political lexicon. They also reshaped the emerging American comedic aesthetic. Tambo and Bones, who played the tambourine and bone castanets, respectively, were referred to as *endmen* (they stood on the ends of the semicircle of characters that often opened or closed a show). One of the comedic staples of the show was the comic back-and-forth with the interlocutor, who worked as a master of ceremonies and tended to speak in "proper" English. The interlocutor was in charge of the pacing of the show, and in terms of race he "represented the white presence on stage; he projected a loftier, less frantic and less ignorant image than the rest of the troupe."[21] Their back-and-forth helped establish a joke rhythm that would define American comedy: the comic–straight man dynamic. For instance:

MR. Bones: Mr. Interlocutor, sir!
Interlocutor: Yes, Mr. Bones?
MR. Bones: Mr. Interlocutor, sir. Does us black folks go to hebbin? Does we go through dem golden gates?
Interlocutor: Mr. Bones, you know the golden gates is for white folks.
MR. Bones: Well, who's gonna be dere to open dem gates for you white folks?[22]

Many of the jokes would become common within American popular culture, such as "Why did the chicken cross the road?" The answer was so obvious as to be humorous – "To get to the other side." The endmen used the joke as a way to embarrass the interlocutor.[23] The back-and-forth between the endmen and the interlocutor was a complicated comic device that worked on multiple levels. As Watkins argues:

> minstrel audiences could laugh *with* the endmen and identify with their lunacy when they ridiculed the interlocutor's pompous airs. And when the interlocutor corrected their ignorant assumptions and their butchery of the English language, the audience could laugh *at* them and feel superior to characters intended to represent simple-minded blacks, who, by this time, had become both a topic of immense concern and a source of dissension to white Americans.[24]

The jokes, therefore, worked to ease anxiety among white audience members, laughing at blacks to render them powerless.

As minstrel went on, African American performers began to act in minstrel shows. Early African American comedy stars like the virtuoso comedian Billy Kersands and the composer/songwriter James Bland achieved success playing in minstrelsy well into the early 20th century. There are a variety of reasons blacks performed in minstrel. For starters, it was one of the only avenues for black performers to work professionally. Similarly, it was a way to gain agency over their identity. As Annemarie Bean argues:

> African American minstrels were showing audiences that minstrelsy was just a show, a *performance* of color and gender rather than a presence of African American culture, even when performed by African Americans. White minstrelsy came close to defining how the minstrelized black body should sound and appear, but it did not succeed in its latent desire to contain and constrict. This attempt to define African American staged black Other was thwarted by the nuanced, rebellious, skilled, and, in the case of the African American male and female impersonators, doubly inverted performances of restaging. Ultimately, what African American minstrels created was a new form of theatre based in the skills of the performers, not in their ability to conform to stereotypes.[25]

While there was a beginning of resistance to the stereotypes, minstrelsy stereotypes pervaded the culture. Furthermore, they penetrated black humor and often boxed in African American comedians. Black comics in minstrel first faced the dilemma that nearly every African American comedian would grapple with: "the conflict between satirizing social images of blacks and contributing to white negative stereotypes of blacks in general."[26] We see the struggle over agency and identity play out over centuries, both with comics and politicians, from Bert Williams to Dick Gregory to Richard Pryor to Dave Chappelle to Barack Obama.

While we think of minstrel and slavery as part of America's past, many minstrel stereotypes permeated into American culture where they still influence us today, up to and including the White House. Ronald Reagan famously called upon minstrel stereotypes when he decried the lazy and irresponsible "welfare queens" driving Cadillacs and the "strapping young bucks" who were using food stamps for steak dinners. Reagan derided black people, presenting them as destroying America by living large on white taxpayers' dime. Reagan is hardly alone in invoking minstrelsy, as Robert Toll reminds us:

> From Aunt Jemima to Mammy in Gone with the Wind, from Uncle Remus to Uncle Ben, from Amos 'n' Andy to Good Times, the inexplicably grinning black face is a pervasive part of American culture. Only very recently have black performers been able to break out of the singing, dancing, and comedy roles that have for so long perpetuated the image of blacks as a happy, musical people who would rather play than work, rather frolic than think. Such images have inevitably affected the ways white America has viewed and treated black America. Their source was the minstrel show.[27]

The many caricatures and racist barbs thrown at Barack and Michelle Obama haunted them while they were in the White House, demonstrating how persistent these minstrel stereotypes are in American culture. Minstrelsy was an essential component of 19th-century American identity that explicitly excluded black people from Americanness. It is an obvious example of the conservative nature of satire that works to uphold the status quo, and the ugliest chapter of American comedy.

Political Cartoons – Laughing Through Pictures

As American humor developed (or devolved) on stage, satiric humor was expanding in another form – the political cartoon. Also called editorial cartoons, these images often appear alongside a news story or editorial essay about current events. They make no claims of objectivity and usually "go after public figures with vigor, subjecting them to 'exaggeration, ridicule, and sarcasm.'"[28] Unlike literary works or performances, a cartoonist must make their point in a matter of seconds. While the exact impact of political cartoons is challenging to research definitively, many have pointed to their influence on public opinion. Commenting on the work of Herblock (Herbert Block, 1909–2001) and other cartoonists' caricatures of Richard Nixon, Pulitzer Prize-winning cartoonist Patrick Oliphant remarked, "It is no stretch to claim that the political cartoon had a distinct influence on the termination of the Nixon presidency."[29] Cartoons also acted as one of the only visual representations of a president for many Americans. Before photography, film, and television made the president a well-known visible figure, Americans saw their presidents in formal portraits and or through political cartoons. Presidents likewise have understood the power of their image, which with the advent of television has only magnified. JFK arguably won the presidency because he was better able to harness his image than Nixon, while Trump has built an entire empire out of his image as a "successful" businessman.

Scholars believe the first American satirical illustration – a woodcut – was done in 1789 of George Washington riding into New York on an ass,[30] which was probably not the image the new president wanted associated with him as he began his presidency. Washington would be the first president caricatured, but certainly not the last. For example, 1801's "Mad Tom in a Rage" depicts Thomas Jefferson being spurred on by the devil to topple American democracy.[31] Technological advancements in lithography in the mid-1800s made the dissemination of illustrations in newspapers, pamphlets, periodicals, and as individual pictures more affordable. Andrew Jackson was the lucky man sitting in the White House at the time. In 1832 Jackson vetoed the rechartering of the National Bank and in 1833 ordered the removal of federal deposits from the bank. In "King Andrew The First," Jackson is depicted as a despotic monarch to criticize what was seen as executive overreach. While race was being comically (and tragically) treated onstage, much of the political satire during the Civil War (1861–1865) centered on illustrations. Northerners drew unflattering portraits of the Confederacy and Jefferson Davis, while the South caricatured Abraham Lincoln and what they considered Northern hypocrisy. Thomas Nast (1840–1902) was the North's leading cartoonist, and is widely considered the "Father of Modern Political Cartoons."[32] His 1864 cartoon

"Compromise with the South" lambasted Democrat's peace platform that sought to end the Civil War prematurely. Lincoln's Republican Party reprinted the cartoon and widely disseminated it as part of the campaign, vaulting Nast into the national spotlight and Lincoln to a second term. The cartoon was so popular Lincoln called Nast "the Union's 'best recruiting sergeant.' "[33] Ulysses S. Grant likewise attributed his 1868 election to " 'to the sword of [General Phil] Sheridan and the pencil of Nast.' "[34] Nast's reach went beyond political campaigns, with his caricatures of Uncle Sam and Santa Claus becoming American icons. He likewise created the Republican elephant and popularized the Democratic donkey.[35]

He rose to further prominence in 1871 with his months-long attacks on William "Boss" Tweed, or as Nast drew him, the Tammany Tiger. A favorite target of Nast's pencil, Tweed was the head of the very powerful and very corrupt Tammany Hall political machine in New York City. As the corruption scandal unfolded, Nast's cartoons in *Harper's Weekly* helped sway public opinion against Tweed. The cartoons were so effective that Tweed himself said of Nast's work, "Stop them damn pictures! I don't care so much what papers write about me. My constituents can't read. But damn it, they can see pictures!"[36] Tweed wasn't the only powerful man who wanted to stop the "pictures." Cartoons during the 1896 presidential race between William McKinley and William Jennings Bryan were so influential, and some thought so severe, that New York and several other states introduced legislation making it easier to sue cartoonists and newspapers for libel. The measures failed, but they speak to the power of political cartoons and again echo the fight for freedom of speech inherent in American satire. We see here, as we will see with Nixon and *The Smothers Brothers* and Donald Trump and *Saturday Night Live*, high-level efforts to quash satiric voices from criticizing the government.

The Columnist – Fanny Fern

Writing under the pseudonym Fanny Fern, Sara Willis Parton (1811–1872) wrote what many consider to be the first contemporary newspaper column. Her writing is sharp, satiric, and modern, made all the more impressive by the fact that she was a woman writing at a time when women were supposed to only write "feminine novels," not social and political commentary. Her first "Fanny Fern's Column" was published in 1852, and by 1855 the *New York Ledger* made her "the highest paid newspaper writer of her time."[37] Her columns were "ferociously funny, sharply satirical, and by nineteenth century standards extremely 'unfeminine.' "[38] Her columns explore life, relationships, business, and womanhood through a satiric lens, forcefully pushing back against male heteronormativity and asserting the rights of women. Her columns include: "Have We Any Men Among Us?" (1853), "To Gentleman: A Call to be a Husband" (1856), "Has a Mother a Right to Her Children?" (1857), "Male Criticism on Ladies' Books" (1857), "A Law More Nice Than Just" (1858), "The Coming Woman" (1859), and "A Chapter for Parents" (1863), where she calls out the gender stereotyping of parents that set boys and girls down different and destructive societal paths of expectation, with girls expected to defer to boys. We see this deference to boys especially pronounced in American comedy, where women's voices have routinely been silenced or sidelined, making Fern's contributions all the more critical.

Fern's satiric writing is some of the earliest mainstream humor written from a female perspective. It illustrates "The Great American Joke" for many female satirists – a fight for agency and equality. Reflecting the false promises of American citizenship as it pertains to women, she writes in "Independence" about the lack of freedom for women in America. She runs down a litany of ways women are not free, before asking, "Can I even be President? Bah – you know I can't. '*Free?*' Humph!"[39] For Fern and other female satirists, part of their American identity is rooted in their experiences in a country founded on the principle that "all *men* are created equal." Fern's work helps provide greater authenticity on women's struggles and points of view, as well as broadening the scope of social and political satire to include multiple voices and viewpoints. We can see Fern's influence on later satirists and comics, like Joan Rivers, Tina Fey, and Amy Schumer. Many of the struggles Fern wrote about remain in contemporary American politics. Most obviously, they endure in the media's misogynist coverage of female candidates like Hillary Clinton, Alexandria Ocasio-Cortez, and Elizabeth Warren, and the seemingly never-ending question, "Is America ready for a female president?" We also see the lack of female satiric voices play out in the satiric treatment of men and women. For instance, JFK was given a free pass for his many affairs (as were LBJ, Bill Clinton, and Donald Trump), while Hillary Clinton was pilloried as a feminazi for not wanting to bake cookies as First Lady.

The First Stand-up Comic – Charles Farrar Browne/Artemus Ward

Often referred to as the first stand-up comic, Charles Farrar Browne's (1834–1867) alter ego Artemus Ward channeled the Stage Yankee persona – a semiliterate showman who was both the butt of the joke and the source of wisdom.[40] Borrowing traits from the Stage Yankee and P.T. Barnum, Ward was both larger than life and homespun; he was rural but craved city life – a persona not unlike Bill Clinton or even Donald Trump. Browne first introduced Ward in print in 1858 and gained national notoriety through his writing in Cleveland's *The Plain Dealer*. After *The Plain Dealer*'s publisher J.W. Gray turned down Browne's offer to buy the exclusive rights to Ward for $1,200 a year, Browne took Ward to the stage. Jumping on the nation's newfound love of public lectures (and stealthily avoiding its steady mistrust of the theatre), Browne began crisscrossing the country performing as the "old showman" Artemus Ward. While on the page Ward was larger than life, onstage he was a reflection of Browne – shy, quiet, reserved, and funny. Browne made no real effort to put on the persona of Ward, much like Chevy Chase would later make no effort to sound or look like Gerald Ford.

Browne's performances as Ward captivated the nation – including its new chief executive, Abraham Lincoln. Honest Abe was "a devoted reader who found in Ward's playful jests the ideal palliative for the afflictions of the presidency."[41] Like FDR's relationship with Will Rogers, Kennedy's relationship with Mort Sahl, and Obama's with Key and Peele, Lincoln saw the inherent power of Ward's wit, using both it and his own humor during his presidency, to among other things, hold the country together. Ward and Lincoln became connected in popular culture, in part, because Browne wrote about the two on several occasions. In 1860, he published "Interview with President Lincoln" in *Vanity Fair*, in which Ward recounts a fictional tale of visiting the president-elect in Springfield, Illinois, as he is overwhelmed by people seeking political appointments. Luckily for Lincoln, Ward was there to save the president-elect and clear the room of the pariahs. Ward and Lincoln never actually met or worked together as they did in the stories; nevertheless, many Americans linked the two.

Not only was Browne perhaps the first political stand-up comic, but he was also doing it during one of the nation's most dire times. By satirizing the nation's institutions and leaders during its most arduous period, Ward, according to Peter M. Robinson:

> demonstrated to his countrymen and women that the mechanisms of democracy are necessarily forever undergoing revision, and that even in such moments of crisis (or especially during them), jokes, satire, and ridicule can render a restorative pruning effect that allows democracy to grow and adapt. Browne encouraged Americans to recognize humor as both a tonic to ease the immediate symptoms of the nation's pain and a prescription for its re-creation.[42]

Understanding the power of comedy in politics, Lincoln was a devoted reader of Ward's work, especially the 1862 collection of Ward-isms, *Artemus Ward, His Book*, which he would often read from to begin cabinet meetings. Lincoln read "High-Handed Outrage at Utica" at the September 1862 meeting that would eventually lead to the drafting of the Emancipation Proclamation. After reading the story, Lincoln reportedly said to his cabinet, "With the fearful strain that is upon me night and day, if I did not laugh I should die, and you need this medicine as much as I do."[43] Laughter, according to Lincoln, was a vital ingredient of the American spirit.

Browne, like Franklin before him, and numerous satirists after him, knew that satire was a key component of American democracy. Importantly, so too did Lincoln. Various presidents have responded to satire differently. Lincoln clearly saw it as a positive that could help hold the Union together. Lyndon Johnson likewise wrote an impassioned defense of freedom of speech during his battles with the Smothers Brothers (though he had been working behind the scenes to silence them). On the other hand, Richard Nixon kept an "enemies list" filled with comedians, and Donald Trump has repeatedly threatened to cut off the free expression of critics in the news media as well as the comedy community. Humor, as evidenced by Franklin's writings, can threaten power and the powerful, and explains why Trump, and Nixon before him, were so afraid of it. They, like satire's defenders in the White House, recognized that the public airing of grievances through comedy is distinctively American. Browne, and Lincoln, recognized that uniquely American tool, and both used it during one of America's most trying times.

The (Re)Birth of American Comedy – Mark Twain

Often cited as America's greatest humorist, Mark Twain's (1835–1910) use of vernacular language, along with his deft combination of humor and social commentary, led William Faulkner to deem him "the father of American literature." His writing was "friendly, funny, irreverent, often satirical and always eager to deflate the pretentious."[44] Twain is most well-known for his novels *The Adventures of Tom Sawyer* (1876) and *The Adventures of Huckleberry Finn* (1884/85). The latter is often cited as The Great American Novel, with Ernest Hemingway remarking in 1935 that "All modern American literature comes from one book by Mark Twain called 'Huckleberry Finn' . . . It's the best book we've had. All American writing comes from that. There was nothing before. There has been nothing as good since."[45] While the runaway slave Jim acts as the moral compass of the book, Huck is its voice. Echoing the Stage Yankee/Jonathan character, the novel is told through the voice of a country boy, Huck, who is wary of being "sivilized." Huck, like Jonathan before him, offers wisdom in the simple vernacular of hardworking America. The book is both a picture of life along the Mississippi and a scathing satire of slavery and indoctrinated thought (in this vein, it is in line with *Gulliver's Travels* and *Candide*). Like many of the great satirists, Twain's work echoed "The Great American Joke," criticizing American society for not living up to its principles.

Much like Franklin before him, Twain defined Americanness. Pulitzer Prize-winning historian Garry Wills wrote, "To understand America, read Mark Twain. . . . No matter what new craziness pops up in America, I find it described beforehand by him."[46] Twain captured the American spirit in his work, in part, because he understood the hypocrisies it contained. Historians used the title of his 1873 book *The Gilded Age* to label the late 19th-century era marked by greed, unchecked capitalism, and rampant political corruption. His satiric writings covered numerous topics, and much of his political commentary has become part of the American attitude toward politics, for instance, "Reader, suppose you were an idiot, and suppose you were a member of Congress. But I repeat myself."[47] In his 1879 essay "A Presidential Candidate," he announces a faux presidential candidacy by laying bare all of his wickedness: "I recommend myself as a safe man – a man who starts from the basis of total depravity and proposes to be fiendish to the last."[48] Donald Trump, for example, seems to have taken Twain's advice at face value, often flaunting his faults and "politically incorrect" speech. His twisted "man of the people" rhetoric is attempting to capture Twain's plainspoken prose, only without any satiric subtext.

Twain's influence and legacy are gigantic. His vernacular prose unlocked a distinctly American voice, first articulated by Franklin, and mimicked by countless satirists. Twain's writing allowed Americans to no longer look to the British for validation or erudition. He took the common man label that American's had struggled to balance against their more erudite European forefathers, and cemented it as a point of American pride. The themes of his work – social justice, hypocrisy, etc. – still resonate today, as do the simple vernacular and colloquialisms he mastered. FDR's "Fireside Chats" are a direct appeal to a plainspoken leadership style that is inherently tied to Twain. Likewise, Twain's persona can be seen in our presidents. He was vain, arrogant, and always looking for the spotlight. It was, in part, his narcissism that made him great and endeared him to Americans. While Donald Trump most obviously exemplifies these traits, nearly every president in this study shares Twain's vanity and assuredness of their own greatness.

A New Century Dawns – Mr. Dooley and Vaudeville

Americans at the turn of the 20th century were once again debating what it meant to be an American. The Second Industrial Revolution exacerbated these questions of Americanness by reshaping the economy, and through migration and immigration, reshaping the ethnic, cultural, and social makeup of American cities. Upwards of 20 million immigrants from Central, Eastern, and Southern Europe, including nearly 2 million Jews fleeing religious persecution, came flooding into America. This quick transformation intensified the question of Americanness, which became a focal point of comedy. Comedians joked about their Old World customs and beliefs, their attempts at assimilation (as well as their views of American norms), their malapropisms, and language barriers. Much like the humor in minstrel shows, these "differences" became familiar comic tropes of late 19th- and early 20th-century humor. Much like minstrelsy, the humor released anxieties about difference by showing the "other" as clownish, or inherently inferior. Many of the ethnic jokes in vaudeville acts were similar to minstrel jokes, simply changing the ethnicity of the immigrant being mocked – from German to Polish to Italian to Irish to Jewish – to reflect America's latest immigration trends. When a group had become assimilated, comics stopped mocking them and moved on to the next group. We see this villainization of immigrants starkly under Donald Trump, who, like many American politicians before him, riles up anxieties about immigrants and "the other" in order to gain power.

A good example is humorist Finley Peter Dunne (1867–1936), who created Mr. Dooley, an Irish-immigrant bartender on the South Side of Chicago who would provide political and social commentary through his Irish brogue. Again, we see the humor and wisdom of an undereducated country type (Dooley was from a small Irish town), representing wisdom. The brand had adapted for the times. Rather than a New England farmer or rugged frontiersman, the new stock character was an Irish immigrant speaking truths about society from behind the bar. Through Dooley, Dunne was able to satirize American life and political beliefs, using the fictional character's freedom to say things he couldn't say as himself, much like Stephen Colbert's fictitious Stephen Colbert. Dooley also allowed the audience to receive the message differently since it came from a fictitious Irish bartender. His position as an invented immigrant allowed audiences to feel superior rather than threatened by his critiques. Capturing the attention of President Theodore Roosevelt, who was both a fan and a frequent target of Mr. Dooley, the columns were read each week at White House cabinet meetings to gauge public opinion.[49] Though we often think of TR as the swaggering Rough Rider turned trust buster, he was also a funny man who understood the power of comedy. After Dunne satirized TR's memoir *The Rough Riders*, commenting it should have been named *Alone in Cuba*, TR reached out to Dunne and struck up a nearly two-decade-long friendship with his satiric critic. Dunne commented upon TR's death, "I never knew a man with a keener humor or one who could take a joke on himself with better grace."[50] While Dunne criticized TR, he also came to his defense. When TR invited Booker T. Washington to the White House, many Southerners vehemently objected. Dooley wrote, it is "goin' to be th' roonation iv Prisidint Tiddy's chances in th' South. Thousan's iv men who wudden't have voted f'r him undher anny circumstances has declared that undher no circumstances wud they now vote f'r him."[51] Reflecting the way many satirists defended JFK against his Cold War adversaries, or *Key & Peele*'s inherent defense of Barack Obama, Dunne understood that satire did not only need to criticize the powerful, but could also bolster them when appropriate.

Nowhere was ethnic humor more prevalent than in vaudeville. Itself heavily influenced by the minstrel show, music halls, and variety-style shows, vaudeville ushered in a new era of live performance that would influence early radio, film, and television comedy, while inadvertently leading to the creation of stand-up comedy. Vaudeville borrowed heavily from the structure of minstrel shows and similarly relied on stock characters and setup/punchline jokes. Comic duos, which resemble much of later sketch comedy, came to dominate, like Bud Abbott and Lou Costello, whose famous "Who's On First?" bit became synonymous with American comedy. It likewise privileged male humor, with female characters in vaudeville often reduced to nagging wives, floozies, or ingénues to be won. In addition to wordplay, double entendre, and slapstick, vaudeville used identity and ethnicity as a central topic for humor. The popular sketch "Cohen on the Telephone" is an excellent example of ethnic humor within vaudeville. First recorded in 1913 in England by Joe Hayman, the monologue became a staple of Jewish performers in America. In the sketch, Mr. Cohen is speaking on the telephone for the very first time. Much of the humor comes from his inability to properly use this new technology, mostly due to his thick Yiddish accent, which makes it difficult to understand what he's saying. He's calling his landlord to come fix his roof from the windstorm the night before, but grows frustrated as the landlord keeps misunderstanding him: "Are you dere? Last night de vind came unt blew donw de sutter outside mine house, and I vant you to send a car-pen-ter – a carp. . . . Oh, never mind, I'll have it fixed myself."[52] The one-sided phone call would become a staple of vaudeville and later in stand-up comedy featured in the acts of comics like Shelly Berman and Bob Newhart.

Vaudeville often asked its audience – itself a melting pot – to think (or rethink) ideas about ethnicity and Americanness. Much like with later minstrel where African Americans began performing in blackface to gain agency over their identity, as vaudeville evolved members of an ethnic group began performing ethnic humor about the group, such as Jewish comics performing "Cohen on the Telephone." This shift demonstrates the vast difference between jokes *about* a minority group as opposed to jokes *by* a minority group. Appealing to a mass audience, vaudeville's influence on generations of comedy is self-evident. Similarly, vaudeville comedy created an American identity. Leigh Woods argues in "American Vaudeville, American Empire" that vaudeville went a step further and worked to assert America's influence in the world, its "cultural imperialism." She goes on, saying, "Vaudeville signaled the growing capacity of American popular entertainments to create compelling images of both an audience and a nationhood defined in steady opposition to existing European models."[53] Vaudeville, therefore, worked once again to contrast America with Europe, this time mocking European immigrants for their non-Americanness, while also working to assert the growing influence of America on the world stage.

Williams and Walker, TOBA, and the Chitlin' Circuit

While vaudeville traded in ethnic humor, it did reflect one truth of American society: segregation. Vaudeville houses were not officially segregated throughout the country, and African American performers did appear on the various "white" circuits. When they did appear, however, there was never more than one African American act, and white comics would often resent any African American performance that was too funny. Furthermore, African American comics performing for mostly white audiences found themselves facing the dilemma of being outsiders, with the audience often expecting the performers to fulfill racist stereotypes. Bert Williams and George Walker were the most well-known African American vaudeville duo. Their bits usually focused on Walker trying to convince the "slow-witted" Williams, who was lighter skinned and wore blackface as a purposeful mask, to join him in dubious get-rich-quick schemes. The duo took on the minstrel stereotypes by playing the Sambo and Zip Coon/Dandy characters with more authenticity and layered double meaning – including Williams wearing blackface.

The duo went on to produce several iconic Broadway productions, including *In Dahomey* (1903), "the first full-length musical written and played by blacks to be performed at a major Broadway house."[54] They followed its immense success with *Abyssinia* in 1906, which featured Williams's iconic song "Nobody." The song features "an upbeat tune whose buoyant arrangement runs perpendicular to its melancholy message of isolation and disappointment, a device that's since become ubiquitous."[55] They sought to expose the artifice of blackface and minstrel stereotypes, and in the process became the most popular comic duo at the turn of the century. Upon Williams's death, W.E.B. DuBois wrote:

> When in the calm after day of thought and struggle to racial peace we look back to pay tribute to those who helped the most, we shall single out for highest praise those who made the world laugh; Bob Cole, Ernest Hogan, George Walker, and above all, Bert Williams. For this was not mere laughing; it was the smile that hovered above blood and tragedy; the light mask of happiness that hid breaking hearts and bitter souls. This is the top of bravery; the finest thing in service. May the world long honor the undying fame of Bert Williams as a great comedian, a great negro, a great man.[56]

Williams worked very carefully to present himself, both onstage and off, as a dignified American to combat the stereotypes of minstrelsy. He recognized the power of those negative stereotypes, and did what he could to undercut them. He likewise understood that his actions would be scrutinized, and if he ever messed up, it would be reflected onto all black people. His incredible grace and dignity would become a model for many minority comics and would be a burden projected onto minorities by white audiences. One need look no further than the incredibly high standards of behavior and decorum that were placed upon Barack Obama when he was president to understand the protracted battle for acceptance and equality that Williams fought.

Despite the success of Walker and Williams, African American comedians were usually excluded from the major white vaudeville theatres. The quasi-segregation, a desire to develop more authentic black comedy, and a swelling of black audiences eager for comedy, led to the founding in the 1920s of the Theatre Owners Booking Association (TOBA). Often referred to as "Tough on Black Actors" or "Tough on Black Asses," TOBA was a collection of theatres throughout the country that booked black entertainers. Though its pay and working conditions were notoriously bad, and travel in the South proved to be difficult and often dangerous, TOBA provided an outlet for black actors, musicians, dancers, and comedians. Numerous well-known bits and performers worked the TOBA circuit. Mantan Moreland, Hattie McDaniel, Stepin Fetchit, Count Basie, Boots Hope, Bessie Smith, the husband and wife comedy duo Butterbeans and Susie, and many others developed their acts on the exacting circuit. David "Pigmeat" Markham (1904–1981) likewise was a regular, and his "Here Comes de Judge" routine is perhaps the most recognizable bit from the time. Markham would play the judge, who pretty much always gave people time. In one recurring bit, Markham again announces that everyone would be doing time:

Lawyer: Your honor, that's not fair! I object!
Judge: *Object*! You object! You all the time comin' in here and objectin' me outa decisions. Why man, I got all these years in my book and somebody's gotta do 'em! Ain't gonna be me! Where's your first client ... he's guilty!
Client: Judge, please don't you remember me? I'm the man who introduced you to your wife!
Judge: Introduced me to my wife? *Life* ... you sonofagun!

According to Markham, "Negroes in the audience loved it, probably because the judge, the pompous oppressor of the Negro in so many Southern towns, was being taken down a peg by a Negro comedian."[57] The bit is one of the more readily apparent satiric examples from TOBA, with Markham clearly mocking the unjust justice system. Most black comics steered clear of overtly taking on political issues. The social climate *outside* of the theatres simply was too toxic and too dangerous for comics to directly take on the many social and political injustices of the time, with Watkins arguing that to take on these issues, particularly in the Deep South, "would have been suicidal."[58]

TOBA officially closed in 1930 when Sherman Dudley, who owned numerous TOBA theatres and is credited as the originator of TOBA, sold his theatres to a white-owned chain of movie theatres.[59] With the official circuit closed, African American performers developed what came to be known as the Chitlin' Circuit, a collection of clubs mostly in the South that featured black musicians and comedians performing for black audiences. According to Preston Lauterbach, author of *The Chitlin' Circuit and the Road to Rock 'n' Roll*, the circuit was representative of the African American experience: "The Chitlin' Circuit was African-Americans making something beautiful out of something ugly, whether it's making cuisine out of hog intestines or making world-class entertainment despite being excluded from all of the world-class venues, all of the fancy white clubs and all the first-rate white theaters."[60] Jackie "Moms" Mabley (1894–1975) was one of the circuit's biggest stars and most pointed social satirists. Her onstage persona, based in part on her grandmother, was a sharp-tongued old woman in a frumpy housedress, floppy hat, and with no teeth who lusted after younger men – "Ain't nothin' an old man can do for me but bring me a message from a young man." Playing well beyond her age, Mabley wove satiric critiques of race and gender into her performances and is one of the first stand-up comedians. Her career spanned decades, from the stages of TOBA to television. Clarice Taylor, who portrayed Mabley in her play *Moms* (1987), said of Mabley, "most of her jokes at the beginning were 'in' jokes. She talked about things black people understood. She talked about white people, and she told us things we wanted to hear about them."[61] Mabley's jokes are a direct response to the historic comic othering of black people by whites. Mabley turns the tables, joking about the "otherness" of whites as a way to assert a black identity. Mabley even included imaginary conversations between herself and the Eisenhowers, Kennedys, and Johnsons. A story in *Ebony* recounts one such breakfast conversation with Mrs. Mamie Eisenhower: "I said: 'Listen, Mame.' And she said: 'Yes, Mrs. Mabley.'" The article continues, "Her listeners crack up with laughter at the absurdity of it all."[62] The "joke" reflects the success of white America's othering of blacks. The audience laughs at the "absurd" idea that a black woman could influence the First Lady. When Michelle Obama was First Lady, she faced numerous racist attacks, being called an "ape in heels" and "Obama's baby mama," with the clear implication that she did not "look" like a First Lady. The attacks on Michelle Obama illustrate the pervasiveness of the mindset at the heart of Mabley's joke.

Will Rogers and Bob Hope

Continuing the legacy of Franklin and Twain, Will Rogers (1879–1935) was the next to claim the mantle of folksy American humorist, with *The New Republic* saying in 1927 that "Political satire in America is for the moment the monopoly of Will Rogers."[63] While his performance work made him famous, it was his political commentary that cemented his legacy. Appealing to the Stage Yankee ideal of the American character, Rogers's straightforward language, political wit, and country wisdom made him an American icon. Proving rather prescient, Theodore

Roosevelt remarked in 1918, "This man Rogers has such a keen insight into the American panorama and the American people . . . that I feel he is bound, in the course of time, to be a potent factor in the political life of the nation."[64] *New York Times* book critic John Carter wrote of Rogers, "America has never produced anybody quite like him, and there has rarely been an American humorist whose words produced less empty laughter or more sober thought."[65] Rogers defined Americanness in the early 20th century, his political observations definitively shaped the nation, and his relationship with FDR would forever redefine the relationship between satirists and presidents.

Rogers even ran for president in 1928, albeit as a joke. But it was his real relationship with the presidency that cemented the link between American comedy and the White House. As Peter M. Robinson argues, "he convinced much of America that performing political humor was more than merely good entertainment; it served a vital public service . . . [Rogers] encouraged Americans to employ humor to do the serious work of democracy, and he challenged the presidency to keep up."[66] In 1916, Rogers performed as part of *Friars Frolics*, a touring production of New York's Friars Club. When the show went to Baltimore, President Woodrow Wilson, an avid vaudeville fan, made the 50-mile drive specifically to see the show. Rogers, who had by then made it a habit to make jokes about the day's news, made several jokes at Wilson's expense. Rogers had joked about TR in 1911 when the former president was seeking to return to the White House in 1912, but his 1916 performance was the first time a comedian had made jokes about the president with the president sitting in the audience. Rogers, who remarked that it was the most nervous he ever was on stage, joked about Wilson's failed attempts to capture Pancho Villa, as well as the country's lack of military preparedness as the world was at war: "There is some talk of getting a Machine Gun if we can borrow one. The one we have now they are using to train our Army with in Plattsburgh. If we go to war we will just about have to go to the trouble of getting another gun."[67] The audience turned to Wilson to follow his lead, and when the president laughed, the audience joined in. Rogers would go on to perform four more times for Wilson as part of the *Follies*.

While Rogers joked about TR, Wilson, and his successors, including a radio impression of President Calvin Coolidge in 1928 that caused immediate controversy, it was his friendly relationship with FDR – two of the biggest celebrities of their time – that inextricably linked comedy and the presidency. Rogers introduced FDR at a political rally in September 1932 in Los Angeles, with an estimated 100,000 people in attendance. Rogers joked about FDR and politics in his signature folksy style, saying, "This is the biggest audience in the world that ever paid to see a politician. This stadium [Olympic Stadium] was dedicated to art, sports . . . and legitimate enterprises, hence there can be no politics. It was also dedicated to amusement, so politics certainly comes under that head."[68] Rogers and FDR were both masters of media, especially radio. Rogers's broadcasts paved the way for FDR, sometimes literally. Rogers often spoke directly about and sometimes even literally mere hours before FDR would take to the airwaves. According to Robinson, Rogers "primed the airwaves with humor and accustomed the nation to the easygoing conversational authority that was so critical not only to his own success onstage, in films, and over the air but also to that of the new president, who sought to interact with Americans in similarly direct ways."[69] While the two men did not always agree politically – Rogers was a staunch isolationist – they were reasonably in sync, and FDR used their relationship and Rogers overt or tacit endorsements to further his political agenda. Furthermore, their relationship broke down barriers between comedy and politics. Whereas most political humor post-1960s has sought to subvert political authority, Rogers's brand of humor and his relationship with FDR worked to reinforce and even assert the president's political power. Rogers's relationship with FDR made making fun of the president, albeit in a mild and highly good-natured manner, part of American popular culture.

America's next great comedic voice – and one of the most iconic figures in 20th-century American popular culture – was born in England. Born in 1903, Leslie Townes Hope (1903–2003), known as Bob Hope, came to America in 1907. In fact, after his 1944 White House Correspondents' Association dinner appearance, columnist Richard Wilson called Hope "another Will Rogers."[70] Like Rogers, Hope's work transcended mediums. He started in vaudeville, rose to fame on the radio, became an icon through film and television, became America's favorite goodwill comic ambassador through his many USO tours, and is one of the pioneers of stand-up comedy. For nearly a century, his political humor "walked a fine line between tolerant comedy that poked fun and biting satire that punctured, regaling audiences from all walks of life with jokes about the state of the nation's affairs and its leaders."[71] His work is marked much more so by his jokes and witticisms, such as "I love to go to Washington, if only to be near my money," but he also performed more controversial satiric material.[72]

As noted in the Library of Congress exhibit "Hope for America: Performers, Politics and Pop Culture," throughout his career:

> Bob Hope received an excessive amount of criticism when his comments seemed to cross an ever-changing line of good taste. Hope's vaudeville act was censored in Boston. On the radio, NBC received protests when Hope made jokes about electoral politics, and "faded" the audio level when he satirized the network itself. In a 1949 radio broadcast, Hope did a sketch lampooning President Harry Truman and his wife Bess that provoked many letters in protest, one of which warned, "ridicule is the surest and quickest way to weaken and destroy our respect for the highest office in our country."[73]

Hope, who regularly fought censorship, remarked in 1955, "One of our greatest freedoms is to crack jokes at our government's expense. . . . When we're afraid to be funny about our political opponents, there won't be any politics left, just dictators."[74] Again, we see the fundamental question of freedom of speech and expression tied to satirical barbs aimed at the president. Hope, like many other comedians, tied the American character to the ability to make fun of its leaders – arguing it is one of our inalienable rights. At the same time, more often than not, Hope's comedy worked to reinforce the status quo and power of the presidency. He knew and performed for 11 presidents, from FDR to Bill Clinton. His comedy fortified the dignity and respect of the office, with the majority of his jokes poking fun at the men in the office. As Hope remarked, the key to making fun of presidents is "making an insult humorous so as to only dent the presidential ego, not damage it."[75] Such a viewpoint was common for much of the 20th century, though in the age of Donald Trump, who faces vicious satiric attacks by the hour, it seems like a lifetime ago. Building on the legacy of Rogers's relationship with the White House, Hope, whose jokes might not have cut deeply, was fundamental to the 20th century's slow blurring of politics and humor. Thanks to Rogers and Hope, Americans began to expect a satiric connection between leading comedians and presidents.

Radio and Early Film

Initially featuring vaudeville performers, radio became a vast comedic outlet. The radio was not well-suited for satire, but it did house sketch comedy and comedic bits quite nicely. Much like with the development of television, radio was hungry for content, and comedy was often used to fill the void. Radio also brought the presidency closer to the average citizen. For the first time, presidents could simultaneously communicate with Americans across the country. The 1908 campaign featured recorded speeches by William Howard Taft and his challenger William Jennings Bryan, and by 1920 the practice of recording speeches and publicly releasing speech transcripts was common. In 1922, President Warren Harding became the first president to be heard on the radio, while in 1925 Calvin Coolidge became the first president to deliver a specific radio address.[76] FDR would famously master the medium with his radio addresses and "Fireside Chats," using them to speak with the American people, evoking the plainspoken vernacular language of Franklin, Twain, and Rogers. Comedians and presidents used the radio to reach a mass audience and connect Americans.

Early film was also fertile ground for comedy, but not necessarily satire. Film was better suited to the short bits and broad physicality that we today associate with sketch comedy. Laurel and Hardy, Abbott and Costello, the Marx Brothers, Charlie Chaplin, and the Three Stooges all made use of the emergent technology to showcase their comedic sensibilities to the nation. Film likewise provided an outlet for presidents to connect with Americans. Early newsreels, often shown before a film or even just on their own, were quite similar to later television news and worked to show Americans their presidents, literally. Thomas Edison filmed the inauguration of William McKinley in 1897, including the outgoing President Grover Cleveland, technically making Cleveland the first president to be filmed in office. Theodore Roosevelt was the first president to have much of his time in office captured on film, though mostly in ceremonial capacities. The photogenic TR quickly understood the power of images, often going out of his way to accommodate photographers, regularly stopping mid-ceremony to smile at the camera. In 1912, the Democratic National Committee released the first filmed campaign ad, "The Old Way and The New." Produced during the silent film era, the ad relies heavily on physical and visual comedy. "The old way" shows us fat cat plutocrats getting rich, including shoveling money from a safe into a "dough bag," while "the new way" shows us Woodrow Wilson, who will fight for the common man. The ad ends with a common man, who earlier was berated by the fat cat politician (and who is dressed not too dissimilarly from the image Will Rogers would later project), sending one dollar to Woodrow Wilson's campaign.[77]

The two new technologies, radio and film, would fundamentally change the ways presidents interacted with Americans. They likewise broadened comedy's reach, while also forcing comics to rethink their stage routines. Unable to play the same scene over and over again like they could onstage, comedians had to adapt to the new technologies. The next new technology, television, would forever change the presidency and American life.

The 1950s – Nonconforming to Conformity

The 1950s was a time of conformity, which was reflected through American's televisions sets. There were strict guidelines in virtually every form of entertainment meant to uphold decency. Senator Joseph McCarthy rose to fame through his political witch-hunt of suspected communists, while mass-marketed materialism and the suburban sprawl created a sense of "normalcy." Yet, upon closer inspection, the 1950s also saw the birth of nonconforming to conformity – on TV, on stage, and in print. As Laurence Maslon and Michael Kantor argue, the 1950s was ripe for satire: the decade "presented the American public with figures so objectionable and partisan that satire seemed to be the very least they deserved. . . . It seemed more and more permissible to tackle public figures directly and, with the passing of the revered Franklin Roosevelt, even the presidency was considered fair game."[78] On the surface, the 1950s was a time of stability and conformity. The hero of D-Day, General Dwight D. Eisenhower, sat in the Oval Office, but underneath the normality the 1950s was a time of change for America. As the suburbs flourished and the United States became a military and economic superpower, the civil rights movement was gaining momentum and the beginnings of a cultural revolution were fomenting and being fostered, in part, by comedy.

Television proved to be the perfect medium for comedy and satire: fast and visual. The new technology was hungry for content, especially comedy. Variety shows, like Ed Sullivan's *Toast of the Town* (1948–1955), which in 1955 became *The Ed Sullivan Show* (1955–1971), were popular with producers, and competitors quickly imitated the format. Soon variety shows were all the rage, mixing music, dance, and the comic sensibilities of their various stars/hosts in programs like *The Colgate Comedy Hour* (1950–1955), *The Milton Berle Show* (1948–1956), *The Jonathan Winters Show* (1956–1957), and *The Jack Benny Program* (1950–1965). Many of these early variety shows featured sketch comedy, though the sketches themselves were hardly political or satiric, and instead played on basic comic tropes that worked to reinforce the cultural status quo. Early television sketch comedy relied heavily on parody, most notably Sid Caesar's *Your Show of Shows* (1950–1954), which was more cutting-edge and subversive than its relatively conservative counterpart *The Red Skelton Show* (1951–1971), both of which were more mainstream than the decidedly offbeat but hugely influential *Ernie Kovacs Show* (1952–1962, in various forms on various networks).

The flurry of shows in the post–World War II era of early television became a turning point for American comedy. The bits and business of vaudeville and radio coalesced and adapted to the new demands of TV, and in a few short years these variety shows had transformed the style and delivery of comedy from the stage to the small screen. The traditional sitcom grew out of radio, but also the sketch comedy style of these early programs. *The Honeymooners*, for instance, began in 1951 as a short recurring sketch on the variety show *Cavalcade of Stars* and later *The Jackie Gleason Show* before becoming one of the most successful sitcoms of all time. The influence on late-night talk shows is evident, with the star-host commanding the show and bringing on guest stars and musical acts. Even the early roots of contemporary stand-up comedy are visible, with comic monologues being staples of these 1950s variety shows. Of course, sketch comedy's roots are evident as well, both in terms of structure and content. We also see the emerging tension between comics and networks. Networks (and advertisers) were more concerned with turning a profit than producing cutting-edge comedy, and from the very beginning there would be censorship battles that would become standard operating fare for sketch comedy on television. As crucial as these shows were, and as dominant as television would become, comedy was also undergoing a fundamental transformation on the theatrical stages of Chicago based on the radical notion of unscripted performance.

Improvisation was fueling a brand new performance style that borrowed from vaudeville and live television, and that would reshape American comedy. Behind Viola Spolin's theatre games based on the creative potential of play, improvisation would become, as Sam Wasson argues in *Improv Nation*, "America's farthest-reaching indigenous art form."[79] Established in Chicago, The Compass Players (1955–1958) was the first modern improvisational theatre in the world. David Shephard, who was heavily influenced by the theories of Bertolt Brecht, wanted a lively cabaret-style theatre that spoke to the concerns of the common man – and he wanted it to be as timely and topical as possible. The Compass was part of a comedic pushback against conformity culture. As Stephen Kercher notes in *Revel With a Cause: Liberal Satire in Postwar America*, "Compass Players spoke directly to the restlessness and nagging doubts of its young, educated middle-class patrons." While today much of the comedy may seem tame, it was revolutionary for its time. Kercher continues:

> To many audience members, the idea of lampooning mothers and fathers, salesman, hucksters, and professors freely onstage was liberating. The fact that Compass actors uttered obscenities and the undisguised names of national politicians confirmed that their enterprise was boldly out of step with the rest of 1950s Cold War America.[80]

Compass actor Andrew Duncan likewise talked about the connection between the performers and audience:

> To suddenly find an applied form in which to get up and start expressing the things we were thinking about and feeling at the time, with all those repressed political, social, psychological feelings . . . I mean, the freedom! . . . A lot of what we did was very negative in that we were satirizing the establishment's institutions. But a lot of it, too, was an expression of how we wanted to live, crude and pioneering as it was. And we struck a responsive chord in our audience.[81]

Improv was revolutionary. It was a natural manifestation of the freedom of speech and expression inherent in American comedy. What could be freer than improvisationally responding in the moment? While society offstage seemed to be like a scripted sitcom, improvisation allowed comics to perform without the restraints that defined American life. Contrasted with the culture of conformity of the 1950s, it is easy to see why improvisation and this new style of comedy was so popular to a younger generation. It allowed them to directly rebel against conformity and "normal" expectations. Due to a variety of factors, The Compass flamed out (a satellite Compass was opened in St. Louis, which introduced Ted Flicker and Del Close to the world). From its ashes rose perhaps the most influential American theatre of the 20th century – The Second City (1959–present). *New York Times* critic Clive Barnes summed up the company's influence in a 1969 review, stating, "The entire recent tradition of American theatrical satire can be summed up in three words: 'The Second City.'"[82] Building upon the ideas Paul Sills and others explored with The Compass, The Second City developed a system of sketch comedy derived from improvisation that satirized the social, cultural, and political issues of the day.

It isn't a coincidence that improvisational theatre in the form of The Compass Players and The Second City emerged against this backdrop of confined normality. Similarly, it isn't a coincidence that several satiric magazines emerged in the mid-1950s. The most well-known and influential of these publications was *MAD Magazine*, which came into being as we know it in 1954.[83] It took on popular culture and the growing materialism and conformity of the 1950s and worked to unmask it. As Kercher argues, "the Great American Way, as legitimated by American corporate liberalism and translated through American movies, television, comics, and advertising, was riddled with a disturbing mix of deception, sentimentality, and condescension."[84] *MAD*'s deflation of American culture was a sensation, reaching a circulation of one million by 1960. The vast majority of its readers were high school and college students. Jerry Seinfeld was one of the numerous comedians heavily influenced by *MAD*, saying, "When we grew up, poking fun of commercials or television or movies, that was not something everyone did. But *MAD Magazine* was the first place where you found that going on, and it was, like, can we *do* this? And we did."[85] Though different than traditional newspaper political cartoons, *MAD*'s visual satire likewise made it easily accessible to a broad audience. Much like contemporary satiric news, *MAD* used the trappings of modern media and advertising – using pop culture to satirize pop culture – to take down the metanarratives of the 1950s and beyond. A forerunner of *National Lampoon* and *The Onion*, *MAD* was a primary influence on many of the leading comics of the counterculture who would go on to challenge authority in more and more overt ways.

MAD, The Compass, The Second City, as well as influential satirists like Jules Feiffer and the offbeat Ernie Kovacs, were developing social satire aimed at the cultural conformity of the 1950s. These comedic outlets joined cultural forces with Beat poets, theatre of the absurd playwrights, and other counterculture figures to form a slightly less rosy picture of the 1950s. Importantly, they did it from a mainstream white-male point of view, but they did lay the groundwork for the cultural revolution of the 1960s and were, in many cases, front and center players.

Late-Night TV – Johnny Carson, the "Super Midwesterner"

The 1950s also saw the birth of late-night variety talk shows. In 1953, Steve Allen pioneered the late-night genre with *Tonight Starring Steve Allen*, which was broadcast locally in New York City. NBC picked up the show in 1954 and aired it nationally as *The Tonight Show*. Allen, "the founding father of the late-night talk show," is widely credited with creating the remarkably consistent format of late-night shows: monologue, man-on-the-street interviews, guest interviews, guest comedian, audience interaction, recurring bits, and sketches.[86] Allen left *The Tonight Show* in 1956 to host his own variety show opposite Ed Sullivan, and NBC replaced Allen in 1957 with Jack Paar, who started the tradition of molding the show into a reflection of the host – by 1959, the show was titled *The Jack Paar Show*. Paar was more contentious than Allen, and his mercurial and electric personality became the hallmark of the show. Paar had both Kennedy and Nixon on the show, marking the first time presidential hopefuls appeared on late-night TV. The appearances were not at all comedic, but they used television and comedy to help connect Americans to the presidency. Paar remained host until 1962 when he was replaced by Johnny Carson, who would host the show for the next 30 years.

Carson's Midwestern style appealed to the country and was a sharp contrast to the bold and brash style of many comedians, with Bob Newhart dubbing Carson the "Super Midwesterner." His Midwestern sensibility aligned with the Yankee type, lending him a trustworthiness that had become synonymous with "Midwestern values." Behind his trustworthiness and guarded persona, by 1965 Carson had doubled Paar's audience and was watched by 10 to 15 million viewers a night. Carson's reach and influence on American life are unfathomable in today's post-network, post-cable, online-streaming niche media market. With such a large audience, Carson had a pulpit few others could ever dream of, and his most direct message was through his nightly monologue, which George Carlin dubbed "the town square of America."[87] Carson's nightly monologue was the comedy equivalent of a presidential address from the Oval Office. Thanks to the emergence of TV, presidents found themselves speaking directly to Americans more regularly, transplanted by a box into the homes of millions of Americans.

Though not a nightly occurrence, Americans could watch the president on television during the afternoon or evening, and then tune in to Johnny Carson that night to hear his take. Carson openly joked about politics and politicians during his monologues, but was remarkably guarded about his political leanings. Nobody was ever really sure who he voted for or what party he aligned with himself. Carson hosted seven presidents on *The Tonight Show*, sometimes rehabilitating their image, like when Bill Clinton joined Johnny after his notoriously long 1998 State of the Union Address. Thanks to some self-deprecating humor and Carson's stamp of approval, Clinton escaped any lingering effects, with CNN citing it as the "fastest turnaround ever."[88] Like Bob Hope, he was rarely out in front of a politician or scandal, but he always commented on the political news of the day. His carefully guarded views were part of his savvy. With such a broad audience, Carson knew that if he became too partisan or if his jokes were too pointed, he would offend half of his audience.

What is remarkable about the history of late-night television is how apolitical it has been. David Letterman, Jay Leno, Conan O'Brien, and other hosts have generally followed Carson's lead with political humor – make a joke about politics but don't make a political statement. While Steven Colbert has brought a sharper political bite to *Late Show With Stephen Colbert*, and Jimmy Kimmel has famously jumped into political debates like health care, most late-night hosts have followed in Carson's tradition. There are undoubtedly political jokes, but often they are "mainstreamed" – jokes about the president or Congress that are already part of pop culture, rather than any stinging satiric critique. Carson reflects the satiric trend at the heart of this book – his jokes were exaggerating the real, finding little absurdities in politics. But after Jimmy Fallon's infamous hair tousling interview of Donald Trump in the lead up to the 2016 election, late-night hosts no longer could stay on the outside, throwing spitballs from the back of the class. The shift to absurdity, where Trump's seeming every step brought a new round of "did that actually happen?", caused late-night hosts to pick sides. Fallon, who had faithfully fulfilled the class clown role, suddenly found himself bombarded for being, ironically, *too* apolitical with Trump.

The Stand-up Revolution

As sketch comedy and late-night shows made inroads on television, stand-up comedy quickly developed a more personal and political style thanks to Mort Sahl (1927–), Lenny Bruce (1925–1966), and Dick Gregory (1930–2016). The three worked to transform stand-up comedy from broad jokes to social and political satire. Sahl came to be known for his political satire, with *Time* magazine dubbing him "Will Rogers with fangs."[89] He began his stand-up career in 1953 at San Francisco's hungry i, where he took the stage with a newspaper and made jokes about the news. Dressed casually in a V-neck sweater, a "perpetual grad student," Sahl was a revolutionary not only because of his politically charged material, but because he didn't tell jokes. He wrote jokes, but used the newspaper and improvisation as his tools. In an interview in 1955, he said, "What I like to do is a jazz solo in words – an improvisation on a theme. . . . The old jokes just disappeared. My material is a patchwork of old and new ad libs."[90] His jokes were off-the-cuff, and his tone was conversational, as though he was talking with the audience rather than throwing jokes at them. Fellow comic Shelly Berman described Sahl like this:

> Mort came into the nightclub era without jokes. We'd always had comedians who told jokes; good one-line strong jokes, with a setup and a slam, good punch line. And he wasn't doing that, he was making commentary on our lives, on our social life, and on our political thinking, making fun of us in some way, or showing us our silliness, and the lies we were telling.[91]

His political observations were in the moment and brought a new political bent to stand-up comedy that influenced a generation of comics, helping to pave the way for shows like *That Was the Week That Was* and *The Daily Show*. He also developed a close relationship with JFK, who later hired Sahl to write jokes for him during the 1960 campaign. The coupling points not only to JFK's savvy, but also to the growing symbiotic relationship between satire and the state.

While Sahl was satirizing the news (and helping JFK win votes), Lenny Bruce was bringing a fiercely personal form of stand-up comedy to the stage, what *Time* magazine labeled in 1959 as "sicknik." Like Sahl, Bruce didn't tell jokes. Bruce took the stage and spoke about what was on his mind, including drugs, sex, race, religion, and politics – topics that weren't talked about by comics onstage. In addition to a singular style that transformed stand-up comedy, Bruce was routinely censored and arrested for obscenity. The fact that his speech was considered "obscene" or dangerous is a testament to the power of satire. There would be no need to censor him if what he was saying did not ruffle the feathers of the powerful. His style, including his fierce advocacy for free speech, would transform stand-up, with George Carlin and Richard Pryor among the many pointing to Bruce as an influence. *Rolling Stone* summed him up, saying:

> Matching the rhythms and vernacular of jazz with feverish smarts and a filthy imagination, Bruce tumbled headlong into a series of improvisational riffs on whatever was on his mind. . . . Bruce pushed past fear and pursued his truth in the moment; it was messy, meandering, sometimes ungainly and without a perfect punchline, but his act was unlike anything that had come before it. The revolution started here. He was both the John the Baptist and the Jesus Christ of modern comedy.[92]

Bruce's comedy was much more visceral than the more intellectual Sahl. While Sahl became entwined with the political establishment, Bruce was feared by the establishment because he spoke in a more common vernacular, crude for the time to be sure, but it was the language of the common man, not unlike Franklin or Twain, taking on established institutions like the church and the government.

Meanwhile, Dick Gregory brought the civil rights struggle to the stage. He became the first black comic to crossover and find success in white clubs while still maintaining agency over his comedy and his race. His big break came in 1961 at the Playboy Club in Chicago. A 28-year-old struggling comedian, he was called in as a Sunday night replacement and almost didn't go onstage. The Playboy Club was hosting a contingent of white frozen-food-industry executives from the South, so the manager suggested postponing. Gregory insisted on performing and quickly won over the crowd – "Good evening, ladies and gentlemen. I understand there are a good many Southerners in the room tonight. I know the South very well. I spent twenty years there one night."[93] The crowd loved him. Gregory was booked for an extended run, and in February his act was reviewed by *Time* magazine. The glowing review reflected Gregory's natural, dry, and laid-back style:

> What makes Gregory refreshing, is not only that he feels secure enough to joke about the trials and triumphs of his own race, but that he can laugh, in a sort of brotherhood of humor, with white men about their own problems, can joke successfully about the NAACP as well as the PTA.

Newsweek would go on to say, "From the moment he was booked into the Playboy Club ... Jim Crow was dead in the joke world."[94] His career took off and he became a star. His comedy reflected his life – he was arrested in Selma, shot during the 1965 Watts riots, publicly protested the Vietnam War, took part in numerous hunger strikes, and even ran for president in the tumultuous 1968 election. He rarely pulled punches onstage – "A Southern liberal? That's a guy that'll lynch you from a low tree."[95] His style made the material palatable to white audiences; "he was so sweetly and serenely reasonable, so nonthreatening, so downright amiable, that you didn't realize until you were walking out of a club that he had heightened your sense of civil rights."[96] Gregory, like Bert Williams before him, brought dignity and authenticity to the stage.

While Sahl, Bruce, and Gregory weren't the only stand-ups pushing boundaries, the three men were at the forefront of the changing face of the new genre. As Gerald Nachman says in *Seriously Funny: The Rebel Comedians of the 1950s and 1960s*, Bruce, Sahl, and Gregory used their "comic tools to build a playing field much larger than comedy."[97] They transformed stand-up in a few short years from an apolitical string of rapid-fire jokes to a place where social and political satire were the main topics of conversation.

The British Satire Boom

The end of World War II shifted the balance of power in the world, with the United States and Soviet Union emerging as superpowers. The 1950s conformity and materialism in America was, in part, about adjusting to this new reality, and as we've seen, this new reality created a unique style of subversive comedy as Americans once again struggled with defining their identity. The British Empire, on the other hand, was losing influence, and by the end of the 1956–1957 Suez Crisis,[98] it was clear that Britain was no longer the world's leading power. Much like their American counterparts in the 1950s, the world promised to this generation did not exist. Like their American brethren, this in-between generation used satire to define their new worldview, with Stuart Ward arguing that resentment fueled their comedy: "While on the face of it the satire boom had the character of a good-humoured acknowledgment of new post-imperial realities, closer examination reveals an underlying resentment towards those who had promised a more grandiose role for Britain in the post-war world."[99] The result was the British Satire Boom.

On August 22, 1960, four young comedians – Dudley Moore, Alan Bennett, Jonathan Miller, and Peter Cook – changed the face of British comedy with *Beyond the Fringe*. The foursome took on the British establishment through a series of satirical sketches about the Cold War, the nuclear threat, class, religion, and was among the first to take on the government and individual politicians head-on. Peter Cook's impersonation of Prime Minister Harold Macmillan in "TV PM" was one of the first sketch comedy impressions of a leading politician.[100] While such impressions are common today, Cook's impersonation was a radical act. As Michael Palin said, "It is not easy nowadays to convey the sensational audacity, the explosively liberating effect of hearing the Prime Minister of the day impersonated."[101] Rather than merely a parody of Macmillan, Cook's impersonation focused on Macmillan's ineffectual leadership at home and abroad. As Ward argues, the impression positioned Macmillan as "an inept and inadequate world statesman – a symbol of the unrealized expectations of an entire generation."[102] The impersonation was such a sensation that Macmillan himself attended a performance. Cook saw him from the stage and improvised a series of jokes at Macmillan's expense, commenting as the PM that there's nothing he likes more than wandering into a theatre "with a stupid great grin spread all over my silly old face."[103] Macmillan didn't think that was terribly funny, but he would later defend the right of satirists to criticize the government.

The show spawned a flurry of new satirical outlets, most notably the current-events newspaper *Private Eye* (1961–present) and the BBC satiric news show *That Was the Week That Was* (*TW3*) (1962–1963). *Private Eye* worked to mix satire with investigative journalism, at once a parody and a newspaper working to uncover corruption. Much like later satiric news, *Private Eye* combined entertainment and news, and is a forerunner of *National Lampoon*, *The Onion*, and *The Daily Show*. As *Private Eye*'s circulation continued to grow, over on the BBC arguably the very first satiric news show was being broadcast. *TW3* was the brainchild of BBC Director General Sir Hugh Greene, who remarked, "I had the idea that it was a good time in history to have a programme that would do something to prick the pomposity of public figures."[104] *TW3* was hosted by David Frost, a forerunner of Jon Stewart as a comedian-journalist who is most well-known today for his series of interviews with Richard Nixon after Nixon resigned the presidency. The show opened with the theme song sung by Millicent Martin, who updated it each week to give a synopsis of the week's news, then transitioned to a topical monologue by Frost, then into sketches, songs, monologues, and debates. An early example of the entertainment–news combination, *TW3*'s writers were a mix of journalists and comedians. The show was broadcast live on Saturday evenings, and the aesthetic was purposefully rough – there was virtually no scenery or props, and cameras were often in the shots to highlight the mechanics of the show. This lack-of-style-style came to be a trademark of the show, celebrating its liveness and transparency.

Within this framework, the show took on politicians like had never been done for a mass audience. It battered "down the bulwarks of the establishment and establishing that anyone – even the Prime Minister – was fair game for satire."[105] One early sketch that drew ire from politicians was Gerald Kaufman's sketch "Silent Men of Westminster," which mocked members of parliament who sat in the House of Commons for years without ever speaking. After the sketch aired, one MP actually got up in the House of Commons to protest but was laughed down. Ironically, Kaufman himself would later become a Member of Parliament. *TW3* took on more than politicians, as they satirized societal hypocrisies at home and abroad. The minstrel style song "The Mississippi Number" satirized racism in the United States, as well as the BBC television show *The Black and White Minstrel Show* (1958–1978), a popular troupe of blackface singers singing songs of the Old South. In "Consumers' Guide Presents Its Report on Religions," Frost presented a news-style consumer report story comparing different religions: Judaism, the Roman Catholic Church, the Protestant Church, Islam, and Communism. They compared them as a typical story analyzes products by "A) What do you put into it? B) What do you get out of it? And C) What does it cost?" In "The Sinking of the Royal Barge," *TW3* satirized the way the media reported on The Royal Family, in this case covering the pretend sinking of the royal barge – "And now the Queen, smiling radiantly, is swimming for her life. Her Majesty is wearing a silk ensemble." The BBC ultimately pulled the show after its 1963 season, citing the upcoming 1964 general election and the BBC's desire to remain objective.

The show received acclaim and praise but also was derided by more conservative viewers and politicians. Tellingly, Prime Minister Macmillan defended the show against protestation from the minister in charge of broadcasting, Reginald Bevins, who vowed to "do something about this."[106] Macmillan wrote to Bevins, saying, "I hope you will not repeat not take any action about 'That was the week that was' without consulting me. It is a good thing to be laughed at. It is better than to be ignored. HM."[107] Macmillan would go on to be a favorite target of the show, frequently finding himself being "laughed at." Macmillan, as would LBJ in America with *The Smothers Brothers*, defended the show. Both men recognized an important new component of leadership: the importance of successfully navigating political satire. Macmillan and LBJ were not the first leaders to be satirized, but thanks to television's ability to reach millions of viewers, they were the first to be satirized in such a direct, negative, and public way. Their responses became almost as important as the satire itself.

Even though the British Satire Boom only technically lasted for three years, it had a long-lasting impact on comedy. There is a reasonably straight line, for instance, between *That Was the Week That Was* and *Last Week Tonight*. They took on political leaders and establishment culture directly, in novel ways, and made people laugh while doing it. Furthermore, it redefined British identity. As Stuart Ward argues, reckoning with the post-imperial world "involved a traumatic adjustment of national aspirations, and a major realignment of national assumptions." It also simultaneously demonstrated satire's conservative and progressive natures. As Ward writes:

> The comic relief provided by the satirists' relentless parodying of Britain's flagging fortunes in the post-war world provided a welcome pressure valve whereby these dramatic changes in the national self-image could be rendered less threatening. Moreover, in subjecting leading political figures and civic institutions to public ridicule, the satire boom undermined the automatic deference and respect that had traditionally occupied the core of British civic culture.[108]

The British Satire Boom, therefore, like much of presidential satire, was both a liberal and conservative movement. It worked to skewer the political and cultural establishment, but as Ward notes, it also acted as a "pressure valve" that functioned to reify the central tenets of Britain's power structure without fundamentally challenging them. Its influence on American satire would likewise funnel into the changing and fracturing nature of American identity in the late 1960s and 1970s.

Early American Sketch Comedy TV – *TW3, The Smothers Brothers, Laugh-In,* and *The Carol Burnett Show*

In the first half of the 20th century, comedy and politics seemed to work together, highlighted by the relationship between Will Rogers and Franklin Roosevelt. Comics certainly made fun of politics, but the general relationship between comedians and politicians was civil. With the rising tide of nonconforming to conformity in the 1950s, some comedians were no longer working with politicians – they were pitted against them. This growingly antagonistic relationship played out through the turbulent 1960s, in particular through satiric television shows. Comedians began pushing back against the *Leave It to Beaver* metanarrative of American life, as the inequalities of American society – in terms of race, class, and gender – began cracking through the all-is-well façade of Eisenhower's America. American identity was once again about to undergo a dramatic shift, and satire would again play a vital role. Building on the work of Second City, *MAD*, and Nichols and May, the 1960s began to use comedy to defy the establishment. The typical American family was cozily in the suburbs, and satirists sought to reach them through their television sets.

In May 1963, America took its turn at satiric news with WNEW-TV in New York, creating a syndicated pilot called *What's Going On Here?: A Shrewd and Somewhat Rude Look at the News*. The pilot was critically acclaimed, with the *New York Times* saying the show was "a breakthrough in the use of sauce and sass as instruments of comment on the passing scene."[109] Even President Kennedy seemed to be a fan, with *Time* magazine reporting that Kennedy "laughed and stayed with the show to the end."[110] Despite its initial success, plans for further syndication stalled. Ed Sullivan briefly resuscitated the show, but after a sketch comparing a rambling commentator giving an update on the events in Southeast Asia was juxtaposed with President Kennedy likewise fumbling over an explanation, Sullivan and CBS decided to cancel the remaining two segments. Absurdity and reality were a bit too close for comfort for network executives, thus ending *What's Going On Here?* and its brief entry into satiric news.

Once again, the inherently conservative nature of satire won out, as the network was fine with light jokes but did not want anything severely criticizing the president. The same notion played out with the American version of *TW3*. NBC bought the rights to *TW3*, and in the show's pitch Leland Hayward, Marshall Jamison, and head writer Robert Emmett sought to pitch the show's satire as fresh, but not inflammatory. In their proposal, they said the audience would be "invited to join a group of varied performers who, with impudence and humor, will turn the week upside down and take it to pieces, investigating, commenting and laughing at the foibles of American life." The pitch continued by highlighting the central role of political and social satire within the American identity, saying, "For it is true that our countrymen have always had the healthy capacity to laugh at themselves."[111] The pilot episode aired on November 11, 1963, with Henry Fonda in the anchor role, and included Henry Morgan, Gene Hackman, and Mike Nichols and Elaine May amongst its performers. The pilot was a critical darling, and watching the show became a sign of one being in the cultural vanguard. Viewers were likewise effusive in their praise, with one woman writing, "American[s] are adult enough (I hope) to appreciate a topical satire on politicians, businessmen and clergymen. . . . After ten years of [sitcoms'] death-grip on TV humor, it's about time someone did do an adult, timely show of satire."[112] The viewer's assertion reflected the new satiric mood under Kennedy, but that all quickly changed.

Just as *TW3* began in America, satire faced a crossroads with the assassination of President Kennedy on November 22, 1963. Many felt that satirizing politicians was now inappropriate, including satirists themselves. The Second City removed all political content, with Sheldon Patinkin saying, "After the assassination, we could not get audiences. People wanted to laugh, but I don't think anyone knew what to laugh at, or if they could."[113] The JFK satire boom was over in an instant. *TW3* in Britain produced a nonsatiric tribute to President Kennedy, which NBC reaired to great critical acclaim. In part due to the hugely positive response to the BBC tribute, NBC announced in December that they would air the American *TW3* on Friday nights. Corporate sponsorship proved difficult, and many politicians argued airing the show was a mistake. Nevertheless, in one of the few instances of networks taking a risk on satire NBC pushed forward with the show.

Aired live on Friday nights from New York, the show featured news stories, sketches, songs, and editorial commentary. Anchored by Elliot Reid and David Frost, the show targeted culture and politics. In part an after-effect of JFK's assassination, and in part because the satirists tended to agree with LBJ's social policies, the show was generally friendly to Great Society liberalism. As Kercher notes, "On domestic political issues, particularly America's civil rights crisis, *TW3* performed sketches and delivered punch lines with astringent irony. Reminiscent of liberal cartoonists' work, multiple *TW3* jokes and sketches took aim at the racial intolerance of Southern Senators, the John Birch Society, the KKK, and other conservative organizations."[114] During the 1964 election season, *TW3* regularly satirized the Republican presidential contenders Barry Goldwater and Nelson Rockefeller. Frost remarked about Goldwater that he was "a great eighteenth-century American," and the GOP is "on the way back. And who knows, one day it may even go forward."[115] *TW3* did take on liberal politicians as well, including President Lyndon Johnson. While Hayward and others worried that audiences would be wary of criticizing the president given the circumstance he assumed office, *TW3* routinely attacked Johnson on a wide array of issues mostly related to foreign policy or his rough Texan persona. The show, much like its British predecessor, burned out, in part due to network pressure. Its relatively short run, however, does not impede its influence. The first show of its kind in America, *TW3* would influence comedy and satiric news for generations. Building on *TW3*'s success, a string of satiric sketch comedy shows emerged in the late 1960s that pushed political and social satire further than it had ever gone before.

The most overtly political of those shows was *The Smothers Brothers Comedy Hour* (1967–1969). More fully explored in Chapter 3, the show was helmed by Tom and Dick Smothers. The antiauthoritarian show featured sharp satire, parody, and a host of musical guests, including the folk-singing brothers themselves. The show had a strong liberal political bent that was somewhat masked by the Brothers' folksy presentation. Their liberalism, however, didn't stop them from taking on President Johnson, both metaphorically and literally. As the show's Vietnam criticism ramped up, Johnson worked behind the scenes to stifle parts of the show, though when he left office he wrote a famous letter defending the show's right to satirize the president. During its brief run, *Comedy Hour* and CBS executives, pushed by both LBJ and then Nixon, routinely clashed over the content of the show, leading to censorship, lawsuits, and the show's cancellation. The show was much more critical than *TW3* of American foreign and domestic policy, namely the Vietnam War, and didn't pull punches regarding their feelings about LBJ or Nixon. As David Bianculli argues in *Dangerously Funny: The Uncensored Story of The Smothers Brothers Comedy Hour*, Tom and Dick were the right folks at the right time as the tumultuous events of the late 1960s unfolded around them, and they reacted to them:

> They were the first members of their generation with a prime-time pulpit, and they used it. Each season, the average age of their writing staff got younger, and the satiric edge of the material being televised – or censored – got sharper. Yet in an era when most families still watched television together, in the same room on the same TV set, the greatest and most impressive achievement of *The Smothers Brothers Comedy Hour* was that it spoke to and attracted young viewers without alienating older ones. With its humor, guest list, and high caliber entertainment, it bridged the generation gap at a time when that gap was becoming a Grand Canyon–like chasm.[116]

The Smothers Brothers tapped into the moment, and their comedy, as well as their censorship battles, reflected the rising cultural tensions of the late 1960s.

Influenced by both *TW3* and *The Smothers Brothers*, producer George Schlatter saw the potential of a satiric current-events sketch comedy show. He came up with *Rowan & Martin's Laugh-In* (1968–1973), which satirized current events, but mainly steered clear of the types of political topics that got the Smothers Brothers into trouble. The show was titled as a take on the sit-ins and be-ins of the civil rights movement and hippie culture. Rather than promote the show's progressive nature, the name was a pun poking fun at the movements without picking a side. The show harkened to the variety shows of the 1950s and the traditions of vaudeville more so than to the social commentary of *The Smothers Brothers*. Ironically, the show that tried its best to skirt major political issues came to be synonymous with Richard Nixon. His appearance and utterance of "Sock it to me!" during the 1968 campaign were arguably as important as anything Nixon did on the campaign trail (discussed more fully in Chapter 3). As Maslon and Kantor argue, "it lasted three seconds – tops – but it may have ushered in five and a half years of the most controversial presidency in American history."[117] Whether or not his appearance was the lynchpin of his election is debatable, but it did work wonders to lessen Nixon's sour personality. Hosted by Dan Rowan and Dick Martin, a comedy team with roots back to 1950s Las Vegas, *Laugh-In* was like a hip cocktail party full of funny and beautiful people. The sketches were fast, really fast, and the speed allowed them to touch on taboo subjects and quickly move on, though by and large, the jokes weren't biting satire. Instead, *Laugh-In* was filled with one-liners, slapstick, zingers, sexual innuendo, and gags, and was more a montage of funny bits than a sketch show with a beginning, middle, and end. While *The Smothers Brothers* satirized politics and pop culture through fully developed sketches, monologues, and songs, *Laugh-In*'s humor was reminiscent of the gags and back-and-forth of vaudeville and burlesque, updated for the 1960s. The goal was a laugh rather than a satiric critique.

The Carol Burnett Show (1967–1978), anchored by Carol Burnett, found its success through parody. Featuring a shockingly stable cast for a show that ran for 11 seasons – Vicki Lawrence, Harvey Korman, Lyle Waggoner, and later Tim Conway and Dick Van Dyke (for half of the final season) – the humor depended much more on parodic takes on movies and television than on political satire. Parodies such as "As the Stomach Turns," a recurring soap-opera parody; Rhoda Dimple, Burnett's take on Shirley Temple; as well as a series of mock-commercials were the backbone of the series. Film parodies likewise were a signature of the show, with their 1976 parody of *Gone With the Wind* – "Went with the Wind!" –featuring Burnett's Scarlett O'Hara fashioning a gown from curtains, and descending the stairs with the curtain rod still in place. In addition to its parodies, *The Carol Burnett Show* was known for the actors' mugging. The cast routinely broke during sketches, capturing the spontaneity of the moment, and then milking it for as long as humanly possible. The tight-knit ensemble, their apparent joy in performing, and their genuine love of one another made the show highly relatable and enjoyable for audiences, but not exactly a satiric juggernaut.

While *TW3* and *The Smothers Brothers* took politics head-on, *Laugh-In* and *The Carol Burnett Show* mostly sidestepped politics. *Laugh-In* certainly captured its era in terms of style, and there was inevitable anarchy to its speed, but *The Carol Burnett Show* was almost shockingly apolitical. For a show that featured a female as the lead comic – and one that ran for 11 seasons overlapping the 1970s women's movement, Vietnam, Watergate, and more – the show mostly skirted politics. Perhaps that's why it lasted so long and *TW3* and *The Smothers Brothers Comedy Hour* flamed out so quickly. It did present a female perspective on pop culture and domestic issues, but it lacked the teeth of the other sketch comedy shows of the time. More closely aligned with the silliness and playfulness of *Your Show of Shows*, *The Carol Burnett Show* reflected more mainstream American comedy of the 1970s – big, broad, and playful.

The Flip Wilson Show

Another show that surprisingly steered clear of overt political statements was *The Flip Wilson Show* (1970–1974). One of the highest-rated shows of the time, it was the first late-night variety show to be hosted by an African American. Wilson got his big break via Redd Foxx, who during an interview on *The Tonight Show* said that Wilson was the funniest comedian working. Wilson was subsequently booked on the show in 1965, leading to a spate television appearances, a special in 1969, and then his own show. On his show, Wilson did a satiric news segment with George Carlin and created several iconic sketch comedy characters, including Sonny the White House Janitor; Reverend Leroy; and his most famous character, Geraldine Jones. Sonny the White House Janitor was a classic "fool" character. He knew more about running the country than the president. Reverend Leroy was a fast-talking con man who was the pastor of the "Church of What's Happening Now." In one sketch, he's going to Las Vegas to observe and "slow down" the sin there. Reverend Leroy was one of the first mainstream "black preacher" comic types, but it was Geraldine that was Wilson's signature character. Sassy, sexual, flirty, and self-absorbed, Geraldine was a regular on the show, often interviewing guests on the show such as Muhammad Ali, and in a later Kennedy Center appearance in 1983, Ronald Reagan. Wilson said of the character, "Geraldine is an attitude. I can go into any conversation now as Geraldine and ad-lib right along, because Geraldine doesn't have to bite her tongue. Flip Wilson might hold back on saying something but Geraldine will jump down your throat."[118] Once again, we see the duality of performance. The audience knows Wilson is Geraldine, allowing them to layer his persona onto the character. Similarly, as Wilson notes, the character allowed him to say things he couldn't say as himself.

Geraldine was a comedy phenomenon, spawning three catch phrases that have become part of American culture: "When you're hot, you're hot; when you're not, you're not," "The Devil made me do it," and "What you see is what you get!"[119] Any social commentary or satire was implicit in the show, rather than overtly part of the comedy. His avoidance of social commentary brought him both admirers and detractors, and despite the relatively short run of his show its influence runs deep. Wilson's nonpolitical approach allowed conservatives to label him as proof that African Americans had achieved equality. If there were systemic problems, then surely Wilson would have addressed them. Since he didn't, it was proof to conservatives that no such problems existed. Much as many pointed to Obama's election as the end of racism in America, conservatives saw Wilson's success as proof that the lack of success for other African Americans was not a systemic problem, but a personal one inherent to African Americans – an idea planted into the American consciousness and continually reinforced through the demeaning comic portrayals of blacks from the minstrel show through radio, film, and television.

National Lampoon

If Carol Burnett was mainstream humor in the 1970s, *National Lampoon* (1970–1998) was the black sheep. Comedy in the 1970s was ironic, anarchic, and anti-establishment. It was less politically overt than its 1960s predecessors, as evidenced by the shift in sketch comedy from the Smothers Brothers to Carol Burnett, yet it in some ways had a more revolutionary tone. While comedy in the 1960s pushed back against the establishment, comedy in the 1970s created a counteruniverse. Stand-up comedians, inspired by Lenny Bruce and led by George Carlin and Richard Pryor, were breaking the mold and performing more personal and more culturally charged material. Meanwhile, Steve Martin and Andy Kaufmann were performing ironic-style stand-up that critiqued pop culture rather than politicians.

National Lampoon became the ironic and anarchic voice of a new generation. Rather than satirizing individual politicians, *National Lampoon* took on the entirety of popular culture – it was at its core social satire. The magazine featured satirical essays and humor, illustrations, and fake advertisements. Printed monthly and usually organized around a particular theme for each issue, the magazine was immensely popular. The *National Lampoon* brand expanded into radio, theatre, and film, forming the bedrock for what would become *Saturday Night Live* and creating iconic American films such as *Animal House*, *Caddyshack*, and the Chevy Chase *National Lampoon Vacation* film series. Their early 1970s issues reshaped comedy and its role in creating and critiquing popular culture. Their 1974 book, *National Lampoon 1964 High School Yearbook*, was a sensation. The book was illustrative of the *Lampoon*'s parodic/satiric style. They would copy the original publication's style almost to the letter, but would slightly alter minute things – a prime example of pulling the absurd out of the real. For example, a *Playboy* parody featured the signature foldout, but the model's tan lines were reversed, so her body was pale, but her breasts were heavily tanned. With the *Yearbook*, "this method – a nearly flawless graphic rendering, perverted – reached a kind of consummation."[120] The *Yearbook* captured suburban American life in the 1960s by recreating a fictional yearbook in a fictional high school in Dacron, Ohio. As Andrew Ferguson argues, "the yearbook parody is a pitiless critique of life in these United States – every bit as forlorn as *Winesburg, Ohio* or *Spoon River Anthology*. But it is even more insidious because you can't stop laughing."[121] Appealing to a generation who had graduated high school in the 1960s, the book spoke to all the trappings and tribulations of suburban American life, only with an ironic and anarchic 1970s spin.

National Lampoon also took on political satire but did it through popular culture. The magazine famously parodied advertisements, commenting on the way they influenced and shaped American culture. In its *National Lampoon Encyclopedia of Humor* (1973), they printed a now-famous parody Volkswagen ad that satirized Ted Kennedy's famous 1969 Chappaquiddick accident. Kennedy, who was drunk at the time, drove his car off a bridge and into a shallow body of water. He fled the scene, and his passenger, Mary Jo Kopechne, died in the semisubmerged vehicle. Kennedy failed to report the accident for ten hours, and the resulting scandal ended his presidential aspirations, though, tellingly, not his political career. The *Lampoon* piece also parodied an actual VW Beetle ad bragging that the vehicle's underside is so well-built that it would float on water. The *Lampoon* ad shows the same "floating" VW, with the caption, "If Ted Kennedy drove a Volkswagen, he'd be President today." It is one of the most well-known pieces of satire in existence. Volkswagen didn't find it funny – calling it a "tasteless publication of [a] tragic mishap" – and sued for $30 million.[122] In the settlement, *National Lampoon* recalled the issue and published an apology: "Even if Ted Kennedy had driven a Volkswagen he wouldn't be president today." Yet again, the tension between free speech and censorship played out through satire.

The *Lampoon* brand also found its way into sketch comedy through *The National Lampoon Radio Hour* (1973-1974) and *Lemmings* (1973), both more fully explored in Chapter 3. In 1975, the three founders, Doug Kenney, Henry Beard, and Robert Hoffman, took a buyout that many mark as the beginning of the end for the magazine. Though it remained in print for another two decades and spawned a variety of film and other spinoffs, it's most prominent influence came from its earliest publications. The *Lampoon*'s style of outsider comedy exists across genres, most notably in stand-up comedy with comics like George Carlin, Richard Pryor, Andy Kaufman, and Steve Martin. Likewise, in 1975, much of its staff and talent pursued other opportunities, namely a new sketch variety show called *Saturday Night Live*.

Saturday Night Live

Saturday Night Live premiered on October 11, 1975, as a comedy variety show. It became an instant hit with younger viewers, taking on popular culture in much the same vein as *National Lampoon*. *SNL*'s popularity with younger viewers illustrates the relationship between comedy and American identity. *SNL*'s baby boomers sought to assert a more confrontational and assertive style of comedy than the mass-appeal 1950s variety shows of their parents. Comedy became one of the key internal markers for boomers to distinguish themselves from their parents. Similarly, the 1990s' Gen-X shows – *The State, Mr. Show, The Ben Stiller Show* – rebelled against *SNL*'s boomerism by embracing a "nobody cares" ironic detachment, that was then contrasted with the latest generational shift to comedy that cares *very deeply* about social issues. This generational identity marking through comedy bled into the show, unintentionally helping *SNL* become the nation's leading voice in political satire thanks to the confrontational nature of Chevy Chase's stumbling Gerald Ford. The show's political commentary and impressions have pervaded popular culture, completely altering the relationship between sketch comedy and the presidency. Americans began looking to *SNL* for insight on the president and the week's news. *SNL* brought the presidency to the masses more effectively and more intimately than any other piece of satire in American history, forever changing the way Americans related to and visualized the presidency. The relationship between the show and each individual president, which will be detailed in the following chapters, profoundly altered American politics and culture. The impact of *SNL* has been widely debated, as has the show's intent. As noted in the Introduction, many view *SNL* as an inherently conservative institution that might poke fun at the president, but never truly threatens the system of power. At the same time, conservatives, especially Donald Trump, have labeled the show as an inherently liberal institution, pushing a biased liberal agenda, with Trump going so far as to link *SNL* with all other negative news coverage of him as "fake news." Whether it is seen as liberal or conservative, the show is undoubtedly at the center of contemporary American political satire, wielding a power that no other satiric outlet has ever attained.

The Richard Pryor Show

The most celebrated comic of his time, and perhaps even today, Richard Pryor was a revolutionary stand-up comic. He didn't really tell jokes, he told stories and played characters, and brought his life and upbringing to the stage in a raw and unique way that allowed him to make an audience laugh as he dissected American life. Before Pryor became the Richard Pryor of comic lore, he began his career as Richie Pryor, a straight-laced comic working in a style very similar to Bill Cosby. When working in Las Vegas in 1967 for yet another mostly white crowd, Pryor famously had an epiphany, walked offstage, took what was essentially a sabbatical in San Francisco, and completely changed his act to focus on his own experiences being black in America. For African Americans, "The Great American Joke" has always been the contrast between American ideals and the African American experience. As Watkins writes:

> [B]lacks' humor is most often not predicated on fabricated scenarios intended merely to entertain or *symbolically* expose absurdity; instead, since black life in America is rife with examples of such absurdity, much black humor derives from a candid, unflinching view of everyday life. To some extent, mainstream America's social reality *is* African American's humor, a fact that no doubt prompted Dick Gregory's sardonic claim that "the white man is our greatest

clown." The irony of receiving flagrantly inequitable treatment in a society that boasts of its democratic heritage has been a main source of black humor from slavery.[123]

Building on the success and style of Dick Gregory, Pryor shifted his focus to encapsulate this "joke," working to reveal authentic black humor in a public setting like no comic before him. His commentary on the justice system from his 1975 album *Is It Something I Said?* is an excellent example: "You go down there lookin' for justice, and that's what you find – Just Us." Most importantly, he made these experiences universal. They weren't just comments on black life, they were commentary on American life. Pryor became the synthesis of centuries of African American comedy, bringing together its many threads into one dynamic, and downright hilarious, package.

While he's most known as a stand-up and film star, the short-lived *The Richard Pryor Show* proved enormously influential, and became yet another touchpoint in the battle between censorship and free speech. The very first episode was supposed to open with Pryor standing naked, with his genitals removed like a Ken doll. Ironically, network censors cut the sketch about network censorship. Pryor was furious, ultimately cutting the show from the original ten episodes to four. *The Washington Post* wrote a scathing take about network censorship, saying,

> When a network says it wants Richard Pryor, it apparently means it wants Richard Pryor's good and exploitable name without also accepting the special combustible qualities that made him valued and popular in the first place. So if NBC should buy the movie "Jaws" for TV, expect to see everything but the shark.[124]

Each sketch was scrutinized, and Pryor famously battled with the network over creative control, even making a sketch out of it. "Censored Audio" features Pryor delivering a scathing monologue about NBC's censorship, but his audio is cut out and replaced by an NBC announcer. As Pryor fumes onscreen, we hear the announcer tell us that "By the way, I don't mind the fact that NBC never aired the opening of my first show. I know they were just thinking of me. They always put me first. And that's why for me, they'll always be number one."[125] The show ultimately only lasted those four episodes, but its mark on comedy was long-lasting. Its mixture of comic and dramatic scenes, its frank discussion of race, and its unapologetic style all can be seen in future shows like *In Living Color*, *Chappelle's Show*, and *Key & Peele*.

Pryor became the next comic to capture the American voice. Ben Franklin created "an American voice," and we can see how important emulating and adapting that voice was for satirists. While capturing the American voice was crucial to forming an identity, in satiric performance, it became more important to relay what Americans did *not* sound like. This vocal othering began with contrasting against a British accent in *The Contrast*, then emerged in force with the plantation dialect of minstrel characters, a voice that would haunt African Americans for over a century. The various ethnic dialects used in vaudeville likewise presented Americanness against the foreign accents of the immigrants coming to America at the turn of the century. Most significantly, in the late 20th century, we began to see the reclamation of these ostracized voices in the work of comics like Richard Pryor, who channeled a linguistic style that was once used to "other" blacks and made it foundational to his American identity.

Eddie Murphy

Saturday Night Live would not be on the air today if not for one man: Eddie Murphy. When Lorne Michaels left the show in 1980 over a contract dispute, the majority of the original writers and cast left. Viewers left, too. It was good fortune for Ronald Reagan, as the show hit one of its lowest points during his first term, so there was not much *SNL* satire aimed at him. There is little doubt that had a young, cocky, and hilarious Eddie Murphy not joined the cast the show would have ended like so many other sketch comedy shows after a good but short run. Quite simply, Murphy was a star. According to Dick Ebersol, who took over as producer after a half season of Jean Doumanian, "Eddie is the single most important performer in the history of the show. He literally saved the show."[126] He was also the first cast member to satirize race regularly. Original cast member Garrett Morris, the only African American in the original cast, was hardly utilized during his time on the show. Murphy was not going to let that happen to him. His recurring characters in sketches like "Mr. Robinson's Neighborhood," "Gumby," "Stevie Wonder," "James Brown's Hot Tub," "Velvet Jones," and "Professor Shabazz K. Martin" made Murphy must-see comedy. In 1984's "White Like Me," Murphy puts on "white" makeup to explore the concept of two Americas, one for whites and one for black people. He discovers that white people are living a secret life, filled with cocktail parties on public transportation and free money from banks. At the end of the sketch, Murphy directly addresses the camera, echoing "The Great American Joke," saying, "So what did I learn from all of this? Well, I learned that we still have a very long way to go in this country before all men are truly equal. But I'll tell you something, I've got a lot of friends, and we've got a lot of makeup."[127] Murphy would turn his *SNL* persona into Hollywood stardom, becoming the first African American mega-movie star. Murphy had a string of blockbuster comedies, including *48 Hours*, *Trading Places*, and *Beverly Hills Cop*. In *Trading Places*, he returned to the two Americas premise of "White Like Me." The movie's entire premise asks if an uneducated black man can succeed if given the same opportunities as a white man. Spoiler alert: he can. Murphy simultaneously transcended race and completely embodied his race. Dick Gregory had made white audiences laugh, Richard Pryor made African American experiences universal, and Eddie Murphy, in his own words, was "the first black actor to take charge in a white world on-screen. That's why I became as popular as I became. People had never seen that before."[128] He was a superstar, and he did it by playing a self-assured, arrogant, cocky, funny, and unapologetic black man.

Sketch TV Strikes Back – *In Living Color, MADtv,* and *Chappelle's Show*

Since its inception, *Saturday Night Live* has dominated sketch comedy on television. Many shows have emerged to either challenge *SNL* or present a different perspective. Second City's *SCTV* was the first to appear, debuting the year after *SNL* hit the airwaves. Featuring the cast of Second City Toronto, *SCTV* didn't do political satire and never aimed to take on *SNL*, instead focusing on the small details, silliness, and idiosyncrasies that make life hysterical. While other sketch shows have found success, such as *Fridays* (1980–1982), which briefly challenged *SNL* (explored more fully in Chapter 5), in the early 1990s a new generation of sketch comedians began to challenge the traditional stalwart by carving out their own niche in the new post-network television landscape. *The Kids in the Hall* (1989–1995), *The Ben Stiller Show* (1989–1990, 1992–1993), *The State* (1993–1995), *The Dana Carvey Show* (1996), *Mr. Show* (1995–1998), and *The Upright Citizens Brigade* (1998–2000) each created distinct worlds apart from the sketch comedy giant and were hugely influential within the comedy world, but none found a mass popular audience.

Like most mainstream comedy, *Saturday Night Live* has been an overwhelmingly white show presenting a white-male point of view through a white cast with a white writing staff. In 1990, Keenen Ivory Wayans brought a new type of sketch show to television with *In Living Color* (1990–1994). The show unapologetically presented a different point of view, featuring a mostly African American cast and humor rooted in the black experience in America. It became an instant success, winning the Primetime Emmy for Outstanding Variety, Music or Comedy Series in 1990, just months after its premiere. Its special broadcast opposite the Super Bowl halftime show garnered record ratings and prompted the NFL to start booking A-list musicians for future Super Bowl halftime shows. As David Peisner states in *Homey Don't Play That!: The Story of In Living Color and the Black Comedy Revolution*:

> There had been black sketch shows before *In Living Color*, including the short-lived but influential *Richard Pryor Show* more than a decade earlier. That this was the first one that found an audience said as much about that audience as it did about the show. The culture was changing. For more than fifty years, black life on screens big and small had looked even more demeaning than it did in the real world. Stereotypes were indulged. The Civil Rights Movement came and went without too many substantive changes in front of or behind the camera. There had been important breakthroughs – Bill Cosby, Flip Wilson, Redd Foxx, Richard Pryor – but the march of progress was exceedingly, agonizingly slow. Until suddenly it wasn't. . . . *In Living Color* – a black show created by a black man that seemed to effortlessly cross over to a mainstream audience ready and waiting for it – was in many ways at the center of it all. As Keenen put it, "We became this bridge in America between white suburban kids and urban kids."[129]

Recurring sketches such as "Homey D. Clown," "The Homeboy Shopping Network," "East Hollywood Squares," and many others put black culture front and center in a way no other comedy show would or could. The show's success reflected a changing American identity, especially in terms of how Americans viewed race. The show obviously did not eradicate racism or lead to racial harmony, but it spoke to the evolution of American identity, in part by finally giving a mainstream voice to African American satire.

The show's success was short-lived. Wayans and Fox Network executives clashed over censorship and syndication, ultimately leading Wayans to stop appearing in sketches in 1992. His brother Damon, a breakout star, left the show after the third season, while his other brother, Marlon, departed as well. By the fourth season, the entire Wayans family had left the show, though Keenen retained his executive producer title. The show itself began to rely on more crude humor in the fourth and fifth seasons, with less of the character-driven culturally satirical content that had made the show so cutting edge.

When *In Living Color* went off the air, Fox replaced it with *MADtv* (1995–2009). Ostensibly named after *MAD Magazine*, the sketch show bore little resemblance to the magazine – the rights to *MAD* were purchased from EC Comics after its founder William Gaines died (Gaines reportedly despised television). *MADtv* branded itself an edgier, brasher, bolder, more diverse, and younger *Saturday Night Live*. Celebrating its 20th season in 1995, *SNL* was once again being pronounced dead – *New York Magazine* ran a lengthy article detailing *SNL*'s fall from grace titled "Comedy Isn't Funny: *Saturday Night Live* at Twenty – How the Show That Transformed TV Became a Grim Joke."[130] While *MADtv* never quite succeeded in toppling *SNL*, it pushed the giant while simultaneously providing a new outlet for sketch comedy and launching the careers of numerous young comedians, including Patton Oswalt, Keegan-Michael Key, and Jordan Peele.

While the show didn't mimic the magazine, it did push the envelope in the same way. *MADtv* was bold and broad, filled with pop-culture parodies and often going for big jokes or physical humor. *MADtv* had a more diverse cast than *SNL*, though they were hardly diverse, and a more varied audience. While *SNL* continued to play as and to a white suburban audience, *MADtv* was speaking to a different audience while also capturing the crossover of young white suburban viewers. The show delved into politics but was more popular for its broader character sketches. Keegan-Michael Key explained that one of his favorite sketches was a political debate sketch where halfway through the Democrat and Republican begin speaking in unison to tell everyone how very different they are. What viewers responded to more often was his Coach Hines sketches:

> I was a walking cartoon – a sight gag. I had super-high shorts up my ass, my fuckin' whistle, and a stupid soup-strainer mustache, and that's what they were tuning in for. I adored playing that character, even if none of the Coach Hines scenes are my favorite. There was really well-executed political satire on that show, but I feel like that was not what they were going for, necessarily.[131]

At its heart, *MADtv* had the same challenges as *SNL* – it was a network show broadcast for a mass audience. *SNL* was better at political satire, so *MADtv* tried to become the home for broad and brash character-based sketch comedy. While *Mr. Show* on HBO could take more creative risks due to its status as a cable show (and one that was bounced around between terrible timeslots), *MADtv* was playing to a much broader audience and therefore tended, like *SNL*, to create accessible and broad comedy. As Key notes, *MADtv* faced the same commodification issues that all television sketch comedy faces: "Comedic/artistic consideration versus commercial consideration."[132] *MADtv* never managed to conquer *SNL*, but it did push *SNL* to reinvigorate itself and provided a long-running alternative form of broad and brash sketch comedy.

Chappelle's Show (2003–2006) became the first non-network sketch comedy show to gain massive popular and critical success. Broadcast on Comedy Central and starring Dave Chappelle, the show made its name through its commentary on race and the cultural climate in post-9/11 George W. Bush America. The show had its share of recurring characters like Tron Carter, Tyrone Biggums, and Charlie Murphy's "True Hollywood Stories," along with popular catchphrases – "I'm Rick James, bitch!" – but its sketches on race were its hallmark. Sketches like "Black White Supremacist," "The Niggar Family," "I Know Black People," "Racial Draft," "Wayne Brady's Show," and "Black Bush" (more fully explored in Chapter 7) both played upon and inverted racial stereotypes and taboos while presenting an America where racism is still inherently ingrained and inherently illogical. These layered sketches brought about the show's popularity, but also became part of its downfall.

Chappelle began to have misgivings about the show's racial humor, unsure if people were laughing at the stereotypes themselves instead of their satiric treatment. During its third season, Chappelle left the show amid a personal identity crisis. Chappelle was filming the "Stereotype Pixies" sketch, in which four men – Black, Asian, White, and Hispanic, respectively – are put into situations with racially stereotyped behavior. The black man must decide between chicken and fish on an airplane flight. A pixie dressed stereotypically and often absurdly racist – with a matching racist dialect – appears to each man encouraging him to make the racially appropriate choice, in this case, to pick chicken. During the taping of the sketch, in which Chappelle's pixie appears in blackface, "one spectator, a white man, laughed particularly loud and long." According to *Time*, "His laughter struck Chappelle as wrong, and he wondered if the new season of his show had gone from sending up stereotypes to merely reinforcing them." According to Chappelle, "When he laughed, it made me uncomfortable."[133] Chappelle left the show, leaving the third season in hiatus. Ultimately Comedy Central aired the already filmed sketches as the "Lost Episodes" without Chappelle as host. Chappelle's crisis points to a long-held tension in American identity in terms of race, one that has often been exacerbated and exploited by comedy: Americans have long laughed *at* the "other," so Chappelle's uncertainty about what exactly the audience member was laughing at has roots that run back centuries.

Sitcom Satire – *The Simpsons* and *South Park*

While TV is a great medium for satire, the sitcom has proved more elusive. Shows like *M*A*S*H* (1972–1983), *All in the Family* (1971–1979), and *Sanford and Son* (1972–1977) all had elements of social satire, but by and large sitcoms have steered clear of any overt political satire. The televised satire that has found mainstream success has come via animated shows. Two of the longest-running satirical sitcoms, *The Simpsons* (1989–) and *South Park* (1997–), both use animated worlds to critique the real world. *The Simpsons* is the longest-running sitcom of any kind and follows the trials and tribulations of Homer and his family in the fictional town of Springfield. Originally a recurring short sketch on *The Tracey Ullman Show* (1987–1990), *The Simpsons* has become a cultural and critical phenomenon. Centered on the modern Everyman Homer Simpson, a less racist, more stupid, but entirely loveable Archie Bunker, *The Simpsons* uses pop culture to critique politics, religion, culture, and, of course, pop culture.

Most of the political satire on *The Simpsons* is aimed at the system, taking shots at the left and right along the way. Lisa Simpson, the middle child, hopelessly striving for a more just world, rarely finds success in her progressive pursuits. More often than not, she is ignored by the town until it is (almost) too late. Her inability to find sustainable success is a critique of both sides – it critiques conservatives for not doing more to do things like protect the environment, and critiques the left for its inability to connect with "everyday" voters, while it critiques a system where doing the right thing is often at odds with getting ahead. In "Mr. Lisa Goes to Washington," Lisa is crushed to find out that her congressman and the entire American political system is not the idyllic democracy she learned about in school. It is, instead, corrupted by money and power. Springfield's public employees and elected officials are equally corrupt and incompetent. Mayor Quimby and Chief Wiggum are inept, crooked, and seemingly entrenched in the system. *The Simpsons* present a world where the only way to get ahead is to play the system and bend the rules. Yet, *The Simpsons* also offers us a world where doing the right thing is still a worthy pursuit. Sometimes Lisa does win, or she at least convinces her father that doing the right thing is possible. It presents a world with a corrupt system, but it ultimately challenges us to do better.

The Simpsons presents a political system that is corrupted but perhaps salvageable, while *South Park* goes a step further and offers an inherently irredeemable system. Set in South Park, Colorado, the show follows its four young protagonists, Stan, Kyle, Kenny, and Cartman, as they crudely navigate their way through both mundane and truly bizarre scenarios. The show is the most prominent satiric voice criticizing liberals, becoming a rallying point for mocking political correctness. The show's criticism of liberalness gone amok has created a generation of what Andrew Sullivan dubbed "South Park Republicans: irreverent young people driven rightward by the priggishness of the other side more than by any doctrinal commitment."[134] Cocreator Matt Stone summed it up himself in 2005 when he said: "I hate conservatives, but I really fucking hate liberals."[135] The show's satire mirrors libertarian ideology – individual freedom at all costs while keeping government out of pretty much everything. Some have argued that *South Park* unintentionally created the alt-right,

> which can resemble an extended *South Park* episode for people who have forgotten that it is meant to be a joke. There is the same anti-elitism, the same

appeal to educated young men who resent being trampled in thought and speech. But none of the same lightheartedness and humanity, none of the same rigorous equidistance between the absurdities of right and left.[136]

While it's a bit extreme to pin the alt-right on *South Park*, there is a pretty straight line between libertarians and *South Park*.

While *South Park* aims at liberals, the show also became one of Trump's earliest critics, before controversially backing off of satirizing him altogether. In the show's 19th season, Trey Parker and Matt Stone warned about the dangers of laughing at Trump when he was still a long-shot candidate. In "Where My Country Gone?" the show warns about the risks of not taking a joke candidate seriously. In the *South Park* universe, Canada has elected its version of Trump with disastrous results. A Canadian refugee warns that "It was a joke! We just let the joke go on for too long. He kept gaining momentum, and by the time we were all ready to say, 'Okay, let's get serious now, who should really be president?' he was already being sworn into office."[137] Yet by 2017, Parker and Stone had decided to stop satirizing Trump because "satire has become reality."[138] Yet the show also has preached for 20 years that caring about anything is uncool. As *The Onion AV Club* said, the show's philosophy has pretty much been, "Everything and everyone are full of shit – *hey, relax, guy*."[139] This philosophy endeared the show to its viewers and led it to become a loud libertarian satiric voice, but also makes it challenging to give prescient warnings about caring about the dangers of a looming national political threat. The season 20 premiere episode in September 2016, just a month before the election, posited the choice as one between a Giant Douche and a Turd Sandwich, perfectly capturing the show's long-standing ideology of there being no difference between political parties, and therefore no point in picking a side. When caring about anything is what you satirize, the message about caring about something can be hollow. The two messages of the shows – the system is corrupt but fixable or the system sucks so who cares – represent a two-decade fracturing begun in the 1970s of American's attitudes toward the government. The growing cynicism of *South Park* would be exacerbated by satiric news and conservative media (and later Donald Trump), creating both liberals and conservatives wary of trusting the government or news media.

The Satiric News Rebirth – *The Onion* and *Politically Incorrect*

While most contemporary satiric news exists on television, one of the most prominent satiric news outlets is the satiric newspaper *The Onion*. It parodies a traditional newspaper with an authorial voice mimicking the Associated Press. Its style is a direct reflection of the shift from reality to absurdity, with each subsequent issue having to exaggerate reality less and less as reality itself becomes the absurdity. Not every news story is satiric ("Struggling Used Bookstore Has Tried Everything But Organizing Books by Genre and Author"), but it has come to be a reliable source of political satire. The same August 9, 2018, issue had the story "Pentagon Officials Listen in Silence as Mike Pence Details Plans for Angel-Guided Defense Weapons System." Vice President Pence has used religion to justify any number of policy proposals, from denying evolution to belief in gay conversion therapy to justifying discrimination against gay people. Coupled with President Reagan's very real (and very absurd) "Star Wars" missile defense plan in the 1980s, it is not much of an exaggeration to think Pence would actually push for a religious-style "Star Wars" plan.

When most people think of satiric news, they think of The Daily Show. But as we've seen, The Daily Show wasn't the first satiric news show to enter the infotainment sector; it wasn't even the first to take on the rising tide of cable news. In 1993, Bill Maher launched Politically Incorrect With Bill Maher, somewhat ironically on the cable station Comedy Central. Formatted as a mix of a late-night talk show, debate, and comedy show, Maher took on the news of the day featuring guests across the political and entertainment spectrum, such as Jerry Seinfeld and Ann Coulter. The show moved from Comedy Central to ABC in 1997, where it ran until its cancellation in 2002. Maher found himself in hot water, not for the first or last time, after he commented that the 9/11 hijackers were not cowards, in response to President Bush and Congress calling the hijackings "heinous and cowardly attacks." Maher countered, saying, "We have been the cowards, lobbing cruise missiles from 2,000 miles away. That's cowardly. . . . Staying in the airplane when it hits the building, say what you want about it, it's not cowardly."[140] The show was canceled at the end of the season, according to ABC because of low ratings, but most suspect it was due to Maher's comments. He would take the show to HBO with Real Time With Bill Maher, which as of this writing, is still on the air, and still angering folks on both sides of the aisle. Aside from angering everyone, the show, and the satiric news genre in general, became largely responsible for the American public's conflation of comedy and politics. Shows like Politically Incorrect and The Daily Show, as well as SNL, made the merger seem obvious, reflecting the long tradition of humor and politics and cementing it as part of American democracy.

The Satiric News Boom – *The Daily Show* Universe

When Politically Incorrect left Comedy Central, the network wanted another satiric news show to take its place – The Daily Show. The original incarnation, hosted by former ESPN SportsCenter anchor Craig Kilborn, premiered in 1996 and was more of a spoof of Entertainment Tonight than network news. In 1999, Jon Stewart took over as host and transformed the tenor of the show. Focusing more on politics, The Daily Show rose in prominence during the hotly contested 2000 election, and by 2004 had become a leading voice not just in comedy, but in the "real" news business. A 2004 report found that in the 18- to 35-year-old demographic, "more people got their news from The Daily Show than any national news broadcasts."[141] A 2006 study, "No Joke: A Comparison of Substance in The Daily Show with Jon Stewart and Broadcast Network Television Coverage of the 2004 Presidential Election Campaign," found that there was virtually no substantive difference in the

2004 election coverage between *The Daily Show* and network news broadcasts.[142] The show was the perfect vehicle for the times, with *The New York Times* saying:

> *The Daily Show* resonates not only because it is wickedly funny but also because its keen sense of the absurd is perfectly attuned to an era in which cognitive dissonance has become a national epidemic. Indeed, Mr. Stewart's frequent exclamation "Are you insane?!" seems a fitting refrain for a post-M*A*S*H, post-"Catch-22" reality, where the surreal and outrageous have become commonplace – an era kicked off by the wacko 2000 election standoff in Florida, rocked by the terrorist attacks of Sept. 11 and haunted by the fallout of a costly war waged on the premise of weapons of mass destruction that did not exist.[143]

The Daily Show certainly was well positioned to document the country's move toward absurd reality. As noted by *The New York Times*, the early 21st century has been marked by unreal moments, from the 2000 election debacle to the 9/11 terrorist attacks to the Bush White House lying the country into war, to the very persona of Donald Trump. *The Daily Show* has been a steady force trying to pull the real out from the absurd.

Politicians took note of *The Daily Show*'s influence, routinely making campaign stops on the show. Barack Obama was on the show, as were Hillary Clinton, Bill Clinton, Tony Blair, Al Gore, Joe Biden, Jimmy Carter, and Michelle Obama, with many of the candidates seeking the 2020 Democratic nomination making an appearance. The show has been less friendly for Republican politicians, who often find themselves the butt of the joke. Notable Republican presidential contenders have been guests on the show though, like Ben Carson, Lindsey Graham, Rand Paul, Newt Gingrich, and Chris Christie. While their appearances are geared at making them seem more moderate, by 2020 it has become almost an essential stop for Democratic politicians to prove their progressive chops – a clear illustration of the importance of satiric authenticity. Furthermore, the interviews reflect the liminal status of the show as both comedy show and news report. Stewart and Trevor Noah make jokes with their guests, but they also ask difficult questions and discuss serious issues. *The Daily Show* has made candidate appearances on late-night comedy both normal and required.

The most notable *Daily Show* spinoff, Stephen Colbert's *The Colbert Report*, in many ways became the face of satire during George W. Bush's second term. A satire of *Fox News*'s cult of personality news shows, most notably Bill O'Reilly's *The O'Reilly Factor*, it was hosted by Stephen Colbert's conservative alter-ego Stephen Colbert. Modeled as a *Fox News* show, with obvious winks that it's not real, *The Colbert Report* mimics the style of those shows. A great example is during a segment called "The Wørd." The screen is split in half during the segment. On the left side, Colbert discusses the topics being addressed, but on the right side of the screen a list of bullet points analyzes the argument. Unlike the similar format on O'Reilly's "Talking Points," for Colbert the bullet points actually undercut Colbert the commentator's message. Essentially, Colbert follows the logic of conservative arguments to their extreme, but still logical ends, so that Colbert can show what he perceives to be the absurdity of their arguments. Unlike Jon Stewart on *The Daily Show*, who takes an outsider's perspective on the news, Colbert embodies the people that Stewart and others mock. On *Charlie Rose*, Colbert described the difference saying,

> Jon deconstructs the news and he's ironic and detached. I falsely construct the news and am ironically *attached*. . . . Jon may point out the hypocrisy of a particular thing happening in a news story. . . . I illustrate the hypocrisy as a character. That's Jon being Jon. And that's me not being me. That's me being the Stephen Colbert guy.[144]

Colbert is consciously playing a part.

Performing in character at the 2006 White House Correspondent's dinner, Colbert delivered what has become one of the most iconic pieces of political satire in the 21st century. Standing mere feet from President Bush, he gave a speech that was on the surface defending the president but was a line-by-line deconstruction of the president's policies. Everyone in the audience knew that Colbert wasn't defending Bush. Neva Chonin said in the *San Francisco Chronicle* that Bush was listening to Colbert "eviscerate his administration on live television. I wasn't just watching a comic's routine; I was witnessing courage incarnate . . . [we need] a few more Colberts."[145] The power of comedy evident in Colbert's speech is an example of "holding a politician's feet to the fire," only it is the political satirists doing the work instead of journalists. This has placed satiric news in an awkward and somewhat ironic place. Sophia McClennen and Remy Maisel argue in *Is Satire Saving Our Nation*:

> Even though satire has always been a form of comedy that asks the audience to be critical, today it is often the source of serious news, and regularly it is the only source audiences consult due to frustration with and distrust of the mainstream news media. In the past, satire mocked news sources the public had already consumed. Today, satire is often the *only* source of news the public consumes.[146]

A part of the shift toward absurd reality is reflected in this shift in Americans' news sources. Watching a "fake" news show and getting an arguably better news report than the actual news is pretty darn absurd. In addition to *The Colbert Report*, there have been several other *Daily Show* spin-offs, most notably *Full Frontal With Samantha Bee* and *Last Week Tonight With John Oliver*. Both shows have come to embody the satiric authenticity and satiric advocacy that has marked much of the satire during Trump's presidency. Both Bee and Oliver implore their audiences to not only laugh at Trump, but to resist actively.

Sketch TV 21st-Century Style – *Key & Peele* and *Inside Amy Schumer*

The election of Barack Obama in 2008 famously led to many declaring America a post-racial society (while the election of Donald Trump in 2016 showed the complete fallacy of that statement).[147] During Obama's presidency, sketch comedy continued to satirize the increasingly complicated politics of race, and nobody did it better than *Key & Peele* (2012–2015). More fully explored in Chapter 8, the show features former *MADtv* cast members Keegan-Michael Key and Jordan Peele. *Key & Peele*, like *In Living Color* and *Chappelle's Show* before it, made race a defining topic. Yet, unlike its predecessors, the duo presented a more nuanced world of race, particularly of black men. Their most well-known sketch, "Luther," exemplifies the bifurcated world many black men inhabit, including President Barack Obama. In the sketches, Peele plays a level-headed and cool President Obama, while Key embodies his anger translator Luther, who angrily yells what the president is really thinking and feeling. The sketch is a literal manifestation of the dual-performance mode described in the Introduction, with both characters representing Obama. The duo's success in comedically satirizing race and culture made their show a comedy phenomenon.

Inside Amy Schumer (2013–2016), also aired on Comedy Central, used cultural attitudes about gender as the main topic of its humor. Based around Schumer's stand-up comedy, which is equal parts crude, crass, and sexual, the show presented a female perspective mostly lacking in mainstream sketch comedy. For instance, the sketch "You Would Bang Her?" features an all-male focus group discussing Schumer's show. As the focus group participants are asked questions about the content of the show, the respondents only focus on her looks, ultimately devolving into a discussion of if they would "bang her."[148] The sketch deftly illustrated the different standards and expectations placed upon female comedians, ones that ignore their satiric voices and instead reduce women to sexual objects. The show often mixed political humor and gender. It took on rape culture in "Football Town Nights" and "A Very Realistic Military Game," satirizing the culture that enables and supports violence against women. Social control of women's bodies is likewise at the heart of "Birth Control." A parody of birth control and drug commercials in general, it satirizes both the inherent misogyny related to birth control as well as its incredibly stringent regulation compared to the lax regulations regarding guns. In the sketch, which is reminiscent of Fanny Fern's "Male Criticism on Ladies' Books," Schumer must ask all of the males in her life if she should get birth control, before finally getting a one-month supply with no refills. A young boy then approaches the pharmacist, asking for a gun. The pharmacist nonchalantly slides the boy a gun across the counter before declaring, "Remember, that's your right."[149] Schumer's show took on an inherently misogynist culture, pointing out the often-absurd lengths required of women to conform to the illogical expectations placed upon them.

The sketch comedy landscape at the beginning of the 21st century is ever-present. There's hipster comedy on *Portlandia* (2011–2018); surreal comedy on *The Eric Andre Show* (2012–), *Comedy Bang! Bang!* (2012–2016), and *I Think You Should Leave* (2019–); the goofy premise and pop-culture parody of *Human Giant* (2007–2008) and *The Kroll Show* (2013–2015); and the all-access comedy platform of *Funny or Die* (2007–). Sketch has likewise become slightly more diverse, with shows like *Alternatino With Arturo Castro* (2019) and *A Black Lady Sketch Show* (2019), as well as the Canadian all-female show *Baroness von Sketch Show* (2016–)

and the highly diverse all-male show *Tallboyz* (2019). On stage, numerous groups across North America are showcasing a variety of comedic voices, like the Native American group The 1491s, the all-Asian American group Model Majority, and the long-running GayCo sketch group in Chicago. While some comedy has taken direct aim at politics, others have either tangentially commented or avoided it altogether.

Sketch comedy, in particular, became a means to navigate, debate, and postulate what it means to be an American. It also, particularly in the latter half of the 20th century, became a town hall for what we want and expected in a president. Those answers often varied greatly depending on the president, but just as importantly, on the identity of the satirist. African American satirists, for example, had to push back against mainstream white satirists' derogatory and demeaning caricatures to establish and defend their own American identity, first fighting stereotypes and later working to reclaim agency over their own identity. Women have similarly struggled for agency over their identity and place in American society, continually fighting against negative stereotypes and for a seat at the comedy table. Satire has reflected these and other anxieties about our differences. It has been used to exacerbate those differences, but also to assimilate those differences. Those differences have ebbed and flowed over nearly three centuries, and have manifested in the various incarnations of American identity. Who Americans are has been a question that has always been central to our history. We often look to the presidency as a sign of what it means to be an American. We look to the Oval Office to reflect what traits we value at any one particular time – honesty, hard work, common sense, a moral sense of duty and honor, and an indefatigable American spirit (whatever that means). And in our genuinely unique American way, one of the keys we have used to navigate the relationship between American identity and the presidency is humor. When Americans like the reflection, satire tends to be more light-hearted and celebratory. When we don't, the satire takes on a more Juvenalian tenor and reflects the tensions in society that are often exacerbated by the person in the White House. The first president in this study, JFK, epitomizes the former, while the last president, Donald Trump, represents the latter.

Notes

1. Louis D. Rubin, Jr., "The Great American Joke," in *The Comic Imagination in American Literature* (New Brunswick, NJ: Rutgers University Press, 1973), 3–15.
2. Edmund Morgan, *Benjamin Franklin* (New Haven: Yale University Press, 2002), 35.
3. Benjamin Franklin, "Rules by Which a Great Empire May Be Reduced to a Small One," 11 September 1773, in *American Satire: An Anthology of Writings from Colonial Times to the Present*, ed. Nicholas Bakalar (New York: Meridian, 1997), 53–61.
4. "No pains without gains" (1745); "Haste makes waste" (1753); "Wish not so much to live long as to live well" (1738); "Lost time is never found again" (1747); "Well done is better than well said" (1737); "Early to bed, early to rise, make a man healthy, wealthy, and wise" (1735). Franklin did not originate many of the quotes/sayings attributed to him, but he did put them into his particular American style, and the quotes have primarily come to be associated with him.

5. Peter M. Robinson, *The Dance of the Comedians: The People, the President, and the Performance of Political Standup Comedy in America* (Amherst: University of Massachusetts Press, 2010), 21–22.
6. Gary Richardson, "Plays and Playwrights: 1800–1865," in *The Cambridge History of American Theatre, Volume I*, eds. Don Wilmeth and Christopher Bigsby (Cambridge: Cambridge University Press, 1998), 276.
7. Maura L. Jortner, *Playing 'America' on Nineteenth-Century Stages: Or, Jonathan in England and Jonathan at Home* (Ph.D. diss., University of Pittsburgh, 2005), 28.
8. Men is specifically used here as early American identity was synonymous with male identity.
9. Winifred Morgan, *An American Icon: Brother Jonathan and American Identity* (Cranbury, NJ: Associated University Press, 1988), 11.
10. Morgan, *An American Icon*, 11–12.
11. Francis Hodge, *Yankee Theatre: The Image of America on Stage, 1825–1850* (Austin: University of Texas Press, 1964), 4.
12. Mel Watkins, *On the Real Side: A History of African American Comedy from Slavery to Chris Rock* (Chicago: Lawrence Hill Books, 1994), 61.
13. Stephen Koch, "Introduction," in *American Satire: An Anthology of Writings from Colonial Times to the Present*, ed. Nicholas Baker (New York: Meridian, 1997), xvii.
14. Watkins, 88.
15. Dan Merica, "Trump: Frederick Douglass 'Is Being Recognized More and More,'" *CNN*, 2 February 2017. www.cnn.com/2017/02/02/politics/donald-trump-frederick-douglass/index.html.
16. Qtd. in Eric Lott, "'The Seeming Counterfeit': Racial Politics and Early Blackface Minstrelsy," *American Quarterly* 43, no. 2 (June 1991), 223.
17. Watkins, 62.
18. Annemarie Bean, "Black Minstrelsy and Double Inversion, Circa 1890," in *African American Performance and Theater History: A Critical Reader*, eds. Harry Elam, Jr. and David Krasner (Oxford: Oxford University Press, 2001), 172.
19. Qtd. in John Morreall, *The Philosophy of Laughter and Humor* (Albany: State University of New York Press, 1987), 168.
20. Robert Toll, "Behind the Blackface," *American Heritage* 29, no. 3 (April–May 1978). www.americanheritage.com/content/behind-blackface.
21. Watkins, 90.
22. Qtd. in Watkins, 90.
23. Robert Toll, *On with the Show: The First Century of Show Business in America* (New York: Oxford University Press, 1976), 95.
24. Watkins, 91–92.
25. Bean, 187–188.
26. Watkins, 114.
27. Toll, "Behind the Blackface."
28. Josh Compton, "More Than Laughing? Survey of Political Humor Effects Research," in *Laughing Matters: Humor and American Politics in the Media Age*, eds. Jody Baumgartner and Jonathan Morris (New York: Routledge, 2008), 40.
29. Patrick Oliphant, "Why Political Cartoons Are Losing Their Influence," *Nieman Report*, 2004. http://niemanreports.org/articles/why-political-cartoons-are-losing-their-influence/
30. It should come as no surprise that none other than Benjamin Franklin composed the first published political cartoon in an American newspaper. The "Join, or Die" cartoon

was drawn for the Albany Conference (1754), where the colonies convened to discuss defense strategies regarding the French and Indian War.
31. Some scholars argue that the "Tom" depicted is not Jefferson but rather Thomas Paine, who was writing scathing newspaper editorials about the United States moving toward a monarchy.
32. Fiona Deans Halloran, *Thomas Nast: The Father of Modern Political Cartoons* (Chapel Hill: The University of North Carolina Press, 2012).
33. Qtd. in Dan Gilgoff, "Political Cartoonists Impact Presidential Races," *US News & World Report*, 28 February 2008. www.usnews.com/news/articles/2008/02/28/political-cartoonists-impact-presidential-races.
34. "Thomas Nast Biography," Billy Ireland Cartoon Library & Museum, The Ohio State University. https://cartoons.osu.edu/digital_albums/thomasnast/bio.htm#top.
35. The donkey first appeared in 1828. Republican critics of Andrew Jackson called him a "jackass," and used the donkey as an anti-Jackson image. Jackson, however, loved the image and used the donkey on his campaign posters. Nast employed the elephant in an 1874 *Harper's Weekly* cartoon titled "The Third Term Panic." Fearing a third term by Ulysses Grant, the cartoon depicts a donkey in a lion's skin scaring away the other zoo animals – the only one undeterred is an elephant with the words "the Republican vote" on its hide.
36. Qtd. in Alleen Pace Nilsen and Don L.F. Nilsen, "Political Cartoons: Zeitgeists and the Creation and Recycling of Satirical Symbols," in *Laughing Matters: Humor and American Politics in the Media Age*, eds. Jody Baumgartner and Jonathan Morris (New York: Routledge, 2008), 67.

Nilsen and Nilsen go on to say that Tweed offered Nast half a million dollars to "study art in Europe. Ironically, Nast chose to stay in the United States, while Tweed fled to Europe only to be arrested and brought back for trial when a Spanish official recognized him from one of Nast's drawings" (67).
37. Joyce Warren, ed., *Ruth Hall and Other Writings by Fanny Fern* (New Brunswick, NJ: Rutgers, The State University, 1986), xviii.
38. Nicholas Bakalar, ed., "Fanny Fern," in *American Satire: An Anthology of Writings from Colonial Times to the Present* (New York: Meridian, 1997), 162.
39. Qtd. in Lauren Berlant, "The Female Woman: Fanny Fern and the Form of Sentiment," *American Literary History* 3, no. 3 (Autumn, 1991), 443.
40. Browne reportedly added the "e" to his last name to give it a more British flair, and in his mind, lend his name esteem and credibility.
41. Robinson, *The Dance of the Comedians*, 11.
42. Robinson, *The Dance of the Comedians*, 20.
43. Qtd. in Brad Scriber, "Artemus With A U," *American: American University Magazine*, March 2015. www.american.edu/magazine/article/artemus-ward.cfm.
44. "Mark Twain Biography," Biography.com, A&E Television Networks, 27 April 2017. www.biography.com/people/mark-twain-9512564.
45. Qtd. in David Ulin, "Celebrating the Genius of 'Huckleberry Finn,'" *The Los Angeles Times*, 14 November 2010. http://articles.latimes.com/2010/nov/14/entertainment/la-ca-mark-twain-20101114.
46. Garry Wills, "Our Best Political Novel," *The New York Times*, 6 June 1976. https://archive.nytimes.com/www.nytimes.com/books/97/06/01/reviews/wills-twain.html.
47. Walter Moss, "Mark Twain's Progressive and Prophetic Political Humor," *History News Network*, 13 August 2012. https://historynewsnetwork.org/article/147643.
48. Mark Twain, "A Presidential Candidate," *The 50 Funniest American Writers* (*According to Andy Borowitz)*, The Library of America, 2011, 5.

49. Charles Fanning, *Finley Peter Dunne & Mr. Dooley: The Chicago Years* (Lexington: The University Press of Kentucky, 1978), 199.
50. Qtd. in Michael Medved, "Lessons of Mount Rushmore Presidents Could Help Donald Trump Redeem His Presidency," *USA Today*, 27 August 2018. www.usatoday.com/story/opinion/2018/08/27/donald-trump-scandal-conviction-manafort-plea-cohen-advice-rushmore-column/997775002/.
51. Qtd. in Elmer Ellis, *Mr. Dooley's America: A Life of Finley Peter Dunne* (Hamden, CT: Archon Books, 1969), 160.
52. Joe Hayman, "Cohen on the Telephone," Columbia Records, 1913. www.youtube.com/watch?v=7cUWk942JPE&feature=youtu.be.
53. Leigh Woods, "American Vaudeville, American Empire," in *Performing America: Cultural Nationalism in American Theater*, eds. Jeffrey Mason and J. Ellen Gainor (Ann Arbor: University of Michigan Press, 1999), 74.
54. Gerald Bordman, *Musical Theatre: A Chronicle* (New York: Oxford University Press, 1978), 190.
55. Jesse David Fox, "The 100 Jokes That Shaped Modern Comedy," *Vulture*, 2015. www.vulture.com/2016/01/100-jokes-shaped-modern-comedy-c-v-r.html?mid=fb-share-vulture.
56. Qtd. in David Suisman, "Bert Williams and George Walker—Victor Releases (1901)," Library of Congress, 2003, http://www.loc.gov/static/programs/national-recording-preservation-board/documents/WilliamsAndWalker1901Recordings.pdf.
57. Qtd. in Watkins, 370–371.
58. Watkins, 381.
59. Preston Lauterbach, *The Chitlin' Circuit and the Road to Rock 'n' Roll* (New York: W.W. Norton and Co., 2011), 302–304.
60. Qtd. in Tanya Ballard Brown, "The Origin (And Hot Stank) Of The 'Chitlin' Circuit," *NPR*, 16 February 2014. www.npr.org/sections/codeswitch/2014/02/16/275313723/the-origin-and-hot-stank-of-the-chitlin-circuit.
61. Qtd. in Leslie Bennetts, "The Pain Behind the Laughter of Moms Mabley," *The New York Times*, 9 August 1987. www.nytimes.com/1987/08/09/theater/theater-the-pain-behind-the-laughter-of-moms-mabley.html?search-input-2=moms+mabley.
62. "Behind the Laughter of Jackie (Moms) Mabley," *Ebony* 17, no. 10 (August 1962), 89–90.
63. Gilbert Seldes, "Satire, Death of . . .," *The New Republic*, 5 January 1927. https://newrepublic.com/article/78757/satire-death-will-rogers.
64. Qtd. in Greg Mitchell, "Will Rogers: Tribute to a Political Hero at the 75th Anniversary of His Death," *Huffington Post*, 16 August 2010. www.huffingtonpost.com/greg-mitchell/tragic-day-for-america-wh_b_683284.html.
65. Qtd. in Mitchell.
66. Robinson, *The Dance of the Comedians*, 57.
67. Qtd. in A. Scott Berg, *Wilson* (New York: G.P. Putnam & Sons, 2013).
68. Qtd. in Robinson, *The Dance of the Comedians*, 83.
69. Robinson, *The Dance of the Comedians*, 91.
70. "Hope for America: Performers, Politics and Pop Culture," *Library of Congress Exhibition*, 11 June 2010. www.loc.gov/exhibits/hope-for-america/from-my-house-to-the-white-house.html.
71. "Hope for America."
72. Sheryl Cannady, "Library Opens New Exhibition Honoring Bob Hope and Political Satire," *Library of Congress*, 27 May 2010. www.loc.gov/item/prn-10-130/.

73. "Hope for America," www.loc.gov/exhibits/hope-for-america/hope-and-satire.html.
74. "Hope for America."
75. Qtd. in "Hope for America," www.loc.gov/exhibits/hope-for-america/hope-and-the-presidents.html.
76. "Warren G. Harding Becomes the First President to be Heard on the Radio," *History.com*, 28 July 2009. www.history.com/this-day-in-history/harding-becomes-first-president-to-be-heard-on-the-radio.
77. "1912 – First Presidential Campaign Film," *C-SPAN*, 17 August 2015. www.youtube.com/watch?v=uq-6d77iVE0.
78. Laurence Maslon and Michael Kantor, *Make 'Em Laugh: The Funny Business of America* (New York: Hachette Book Group, 2008), 65.
79. Sam Wasson, *Improv Nation: How We Made a Great American Art* (New York: Houghton Mifflin Harcourt Publishing Company, 2017), xi.
80. Stephen Kercher, *Revel with a Cause: Liberal Satire in Postwar America* (Chicago: University of Chicago Press, 2006), 127.
81. Qtd. in Kercher, 127.
82. Clive Barnes, "Revue in New Version of Eastside Playhouse," *New York Times*, 16 October 1969.
83. It had been in print for two years but was rebranded after the 1954 Senate investigation into juvenile delinquency. EC Comic was under fire for their horror comics, which caused publisher William Gaines to cancel them. The only comic left in his publishing house was *MAD*, which was a spoof of other comic books and didn't conform to the industry's voluntary Comics Code Authority. Virtually out of options, Gaines opted out of the Code, and *MAD Magazine* as we know it was born.
84. Qtd. in Kercher, 108.
85. Qtd. in Maslon and Kantor, 64.
86. Richard Severo, "Steve Allen, Comedian Who Pioneered Late-Night TV Talks Shows, Is Dead at 78," *The New York Times*, 1 November 2000. www.nytimes.com/2000/11/01/arts/steve-allen-comedian-who-pioneered-late-night-tv-talk-shows-is-dead-at-78.html.
87. Qtd. in Maslon and Kantor, 94.
88. Judy Woodruff, "Johnny Carson's Political Legacy," *CNN*, 27 January 2005. www.cnn.com/2005/ALLPOLITICS/01/27/johnny.carson/.
89. "Comedians: Will Rogers with Fangs," *Time Magazine*, 25 July 1960.
90. Qtd. in James Curtis, *Last Man Standing: Mort Sahl and the Birth of Modern Comedy* (Jackson: University Press of Mississippi, 2017), 22–23.
91. Qtd. in Maslon and Kantor, 333.
92. Matthew Love, "50 Best Stand-Up Comics of All Time," *Rolling Stone*, 14 February 2017. www.rollingstone.com/culture/culture-lists/50-best-stand-up-comics-of-all-time-126359/lenny-bruce-105883/.
93. Qtd. in Dennis McLellan, "Dick Gregory, Groundbreaking Comedian and Activist Who Ran for Chicago Mayor, Dies at 84," *Chicago Tribune*, 19 August 2017. www.chicagotribune.com/news/obituaries/ct-dick-gregory-dead-20170819-story.html.
94. Qtd. in McClellan.
95. Tom Porter, "Dick Gregory: Here's All You Need to Know About the Pioneering Comedian and Civil Rights Activist Who Died, Aged 84," *Newsweek*, 20 August 2017. www.newsweek.com/dick-gregory-heres-what-you-need-know-about-pioneering-comedian-and-civil-652431.
96. Gerald Nachman, *Seriously Funny: The Rebel Comedians of the 1950s and 1960s* (New York: Pantheon Books, 2003), 481.

97. Nachman, 481.
98. Egyptian President Gama Abdel Nasser nationalized the Suez Canal in 1956, which led to an invasion by Israel, France, and Britain (which previously controlled the canal). The United States and the Soviet Union, on opposite sides, both urged an end to the conflict. Prime Minister Anthony Eden secretly colluded with France and Israel on the invasion and was accused of misleading the House of Commons. His more substantial blunder was not recognizing that the United States was the stronger power, and when President Dwight Eisenhower failed to support the invasion, it was clear to all that Britain was no longer an equal partner with the United States. As Keith Layborn noted in *Fifty Key Figures in Twentieth Century British Politics*, Eden's "obituary writers recognized that he was the last British Prime Minister to believe that Britain was still one of the great powers. Suez exposed that belief as an illusion" (102).
99. Stuart Ward, "No Nation Could be Broker': The Satire Boom and the Demise of Britain's World Role," *British Culture and the End of Empire*, ed. Stuart Ward (Manchester: Manchester University Press, 2001), 92.
100. An audio version of the sketch can be heard at this link. www.youtube.com/watch?v=ywiPY_aUfoI.
101. Qtd. in Ward, 99.
102. Qtd. in Ward, 99.
103. Qtd. in Andy Parsons, "Andy Parsons on Peter Cook: The Pure Filth that Inspired My Career," *The Guardian*, 6 May 2015. www.theguardian.com/stage/2015/may/06/andy-parsons-on-peter-cook-the-pure-filth-that-inspired-my-career. Season 2, Episode 10 of *The Crown* recreates Macmillan's visit to the show.
104. Andrew Crisell, *An Introductory History of British Broadcasting*, 2nd Edition (London: Routledge, 2002), 124.
105. "BBC Marks TW3 Anniversary," *BBC*, 26 November 2002. http://news.bbc.co.uk/2/hi/entertainment/2516511.stm.
106. "BBC Marks TW3 Anniversary."
107. Harold Macmillan, "Television Satire," *The British National Archives*, 12 October 1962. www.nationalarchives.gov.uk/education/resources/sixties-britain/television-satire/.
108. Qtd. in Ward, 108.
109. Jack Gould, "British-Style Satire," *New York Times*, 13 May 1963, 59.
110. "Something's Going on Here," *Time*, 24 May 1963, 72.
111. Qtd. in Kercher, 364.
112. Qtd. in Kercher, 368.
113. Qtd. in Wasson, 95.
114. Qtd. in Kercher, 373.
115. Qtd. in Kercher, 376.
116. David Bianculli, *Dangerously Funny: The Uncensored Story of The Smothers Brothers Comedy Hour* (New York: Touchstone, 2009), xv.
117. Maslon and Kantor, 97.
118. Qtd. in Louie Robinson, "The Evolution of Geraldine," *Ebony*, December 1970, 182.
119. Mel Watkins, "Flip Wilson, Outrageous Comic and TV Host, Dies at 64," *The New York Times*, 27 November 1998. www.nytimes.com/1998/11/27/arts/flip-wilson-outrageous-comic-and-tv-host-dies-at-64.html.
120. Andrew Ferguson, "Class of '64 Reunion," *Slate.com*, 2 January 2004. www.slate.com/articles/arts/culturebox/2004/01/class_of_64_reunion.html.
121. Ferguson.

122. "Volkswagen Settles Suit Against National Lampoon," *New York Times*, 30 October 1973. www.nytimes.com/1973/10/30/archives/volkswagen-settles-suit-against-national-lampoon.html.
123. Watkins, "Flip Wilson," 475.
124. "A Pryor Restraint," *The Washington Post*, 14 September 1977. www.washingtonpost.com/archive/lifestyle/1977/09/14/a-pryor-restraint/b90f2673-29c1-4cc0-bcf7-48690916cfef/.
125. "Censored Audio," *The Richard Pryor Show*, 27 September 1977. www.youtube.com/watch?v=2ahpgVVIfzE.
126. David Peisner, *Homey Don't Play That! The Story of In Living Color and the Black Comedy Revolution* (New York: Atria/37 INK, 2018), 54.
127. "White Like Me," *Saturday Night Live*, 15 December 1984. www.nbc.com/saturday-night-live/video/white-like-me/n9308.
128. Qtd. in Peisner, 56–57.
129. Peisner, 3.
130. Chris Smith, "Comedy Isn't Funny: *Saturday Night Live* at Twenty – How the Show That Transformed TV Became a Grim Joke," *New York Magazine*, 13 March 1995.
131. Qtd. in Tim Greiving, "An Oral History of *MADtv*, the Sketch Show That Never Quite Changed Comedy," *Vulture*, 18 May 2016. www.vulture.com/2016/05/oral-history-madtv.html.
132. Qtd. in Greiving.
133. Christopher John Farley, "Dave Speaks," *Time*, 14 May 2005. http://content.time.com/time/magazine/article/0,9171,1061512-6,00.html.
134. Janan Ganesh, "Did South Park Accidentally Invent the Alt-Right?" *Financial Times*, 5 May 2017. www.ft.com/content/c69fa756-30be-11e7-9555-23ef563ecf9a.
135. Qtd. in Sean O'Neal, "*South Park* Raised a Generation of Trolls," *The Onion AV Club*, 25 July 2017. https://tv.avclub.com/south-park-raised-a-generation-of-trolls-1798264498.
136. Ganesh.
137. Qtd. in Megan Garber, "*South Park's* Creators Have Given Up on Satirizing Donald Trump," *The Atlantic*, 3 February 2017. www.theatlantic.com/entertainment/archive/2017/02/south-parks-creators-are-giving-up-on-satirizing-trump/515616/.
138. Qtd. in Garber.
139. O'Neal.
140. Qtd. in Josh Gerstein, "Terror Attacks Spark Cowardly Debate," *ABC News*, 26 September 2001. https://abcnews.go.com/Politics/story?id=121312&page=1.
141. Maslon and Kantor, 127.
142. "It's No Joke: IU Study Finds The Daily Show with Jon Stewart to be as Substantive as Network News," Indiana University News, 4 October 2006. http://newsinfo.iu.edu/news-archive/4159.html.
143. Michiko Kakutani, "Is Jon Stewart the Most Trusted Man in America?" *The New York Times*, 15 August 2008. www.nytimes.com/2008/08/17/arts/television/17kaku.html.
144. Qtd. in Charlie Rose, "A Conversation with Comedian Stephen Colbert," *Charlie Rose*. www.charlierose.com/view/interview/93, 8 December 2006.
145. Neva Chonin, "Truthiness to Power," *San Francisco Chronicle*, 7 May 2006.
146. Sophia McClennen and Remy Maisel, *Is Satire Saving Our Nation: Mockery and American Politics* (New York: Palgrave Macmillan, 2014), 7.

147. Nikole Hannah-Jones, "The End of the Postracial Myth," *The New York Times Magazine*, 15 November 2016. www.nytimes.com/interactive/2016/11/20/magazine/donald-trumps-america-iowa-race.html.
148. "You Would Bang Her?" *Inside Amy Schumer, Comedy Central*, 1 April 2014. www.cc.com/episodes/689scb/inside-amy-schumer-you-would-bang-her – season-2-ep-201.
149. "Birth Control," *Inside Amy Schumer, Comedy Central*, 21 April 2015. www.cc.com/video-clips/whzt7k/inside-amy-schumer-birth-control.

CHAPTER 2

JFK

There was an undercurrent in American comedy during the 1950s, the decade Arthur Schlesinger, Jr. called "the most humorless period in American history," of nonconforming to conformity.[1] As noted in the previous chapter, the countercultural explosion of the 1960s owed a debt to the work of *MAD Magazine*, Jules Feiffer, Mort Sahl, and The Compass Players. The emergence of The Second City in 1959 created a politically charged world of sketch comedy that took on the "consensus culture" of the 1950s by humorously exploring "misunderstanding, alienation, and pain."[2] In 1960, after one of the closest elections in American history, the young and debonair John F. Kennedy represented a cultural shift for the United States. Kennedy celebrated the change, saying in his inaugural address, "Let the word go forth from this time and place, to friend and foe alike, that the torch has been passed to a new generation of Americans."[3] Kennedy's election similarly ignited a satiric explosion. Historian Stephen Kercher wrote that

> After Kennedy was elected president, smart, irreverent political commentary, long absent from the American scene, appeared poised to make a remarkable comeback. With the young, witty, urbane John Kennedy in the White House, satiric expression, long a resource for cultural dissent, became for many American liberals a source of affirmation and a sign of better days to come.[4]

America was changing, and political humor was entering a new decade with "vigah."

Sketch comedians ridiculed many of the presidents explored in this book. Kennedy, on the other hand, was often celebrated. He was young, cool, and handsome. Rather than challenge him, comedians often tried to be associated with him – nearly everyone wanted to be a part of Camelot. Kennedy reignited political satire, but he also proved a difficult target for young liberal satirists. The Second City's Avery Schreiber spoke about the difference of having Kennedy in office:

> With Eisenhower we had had a perfect target . . . we were young, he was old . . . Kennedy was a different story. He was very close to an age we could communicate with. The only way you could make fun of the man was on

subjects of his accent, his wealth, and his social activities. It wasn't easy. We sided with what the man wanted to do.[5]

During JFK's famous birthday celebration at Madison Square Garden in 1962, where Marilyn Monroe sang him "Happy Birthday," *Variety* remarked that "the present administration is enamored of, and in turn admired by, large segments of entertainment."[6] We see here one of the earliest examples of what happens when satirists like the American vision of the person in the White House. Satirists largely agreed with and supported Kennedy, so much of the satire about him worked to celebrate his vision rather than criticize it. By and large, satirists liked the Kennedy mystique.

That is not to imply that Kennedy was without faults. He suffered major political defeats, including the disastrous Bay of Pigs invasion, and made little legislative progress. He likewise had his share of personal flaws. Yet, satirists, and the press, overlooked many of Kennedy's flaws, including his well-known sexual proclivities. Alison Dagnes argues in *Sex Scandals in American Politics* that those personal affairs were not considered newsworthy. Kennedy was hardly the first president to have what we would now consider a scandalous sex life. Still, it is important to note many of his personality flaws were deemed off-limits to both the press and satirists. Bill Clinton, and to a lesser extent Donald Trump, would later be ridiculed for their sexual misconduct, though even three decades later many of the jokes about Clinton celebrated his sexual proclivities. It is significant, therefore, to emphasize the notion that the satirist, or journalist, matters. Kennedy was mostly covered by and satirized by men, who felt that the sexual proclivities of the president weren't newsworthy or worth satirizing. Therefore, we can certainly make a connection between the relatively light treatment of Kennedy by satirists, specifically in terms of his sexual activity, and the overwhelmingly white male demographics of those satirizing him. We can also see here an example of the conservative nature of satire, with satirists essentially protecting Kennedy because they thought they were protecting the office.

Outside of social norms that concealed bad presidential behavior, Kennedy also had lighter treatment because Kennedy was funny. He did not always use humor, and certainly steered clear of jokes when dealing with serious issues, but Kennedy knew that comedy could be an asset. As a senator and early presidential candidate, Kennedy used his wit to display his charm and diffuse potential pitfalls. Speaking at the 1958 Gridiron Club dinner, Kennedy reportedly brought down the house with his speech, including a now-famous joke about his father, Joseph Kennedy. Pretending to read a fictional telegram from his father, Kennedy said, "Dear Jack, don't buy a single vote more than is necessary. I'll be damned if I'm going to pay for a landslide."[7] By making the joke about his father buying votes and using it against himself, Kennedy took some of the bite out of the barb – "my father's money and influence is not something to worry about; it's just a joke." If Kennedy is making the joke, it makes it more difficult for a satirist to criticize him for it because it no longer appears to be a revelatory truth. Instead, it is merely a satirist repeating the president. We will later see satirists simply repeating a president to point out the words' inherent absurdity, such as Trump out of the blue trying to buy Greenland. There was no absurd amplification with Kennedy because what he was saying was real – his father's money *was* an important part of JFK's campaign – he was trying to lessen its impact.

This type of self-deprecatory humor is often wielded by politicians and can go a long way toward inoculating them against the actual criticism being leveled. Kennedy was particularly adept at this type of humor, maintaining his Camelot social status by poking fun at his Camelot social status. As argued in "The Political Ethology of Debate Humor and Audience Laughter," "this type of humor establishes a more equal relationship of identification with the speaker, by highlighting, in a socially preemptive manner, the candidate's personal flaws." Kennedy acknowledged the influence of his father's money so that the press and satirists wouldn't "discover" it. It made him seem more authentic and honest. Moreover, "individuals making the self-deprecatory comments present themselves as having so much social status that they can afford to, in essence, make themselves more equal with their audience by sacrificing prestige."[8] In Kennedy's case, the sacrifice of cachet actually worked to enhance his prestige and likeability. One thing JFK had to spare was mystique, so by joking about himself he actually enhanced his mystique. Rather than display weakness, JFK's self-deprecating humor was a sign of his confidence. It was also an important signal to satirists that it was, if not encouraged, acceptable to make jokes about him.

Kennedy was so in tune with the power of comedy that during the 1960 presidential campaign Kennedy hired stand-up comedian Mort Sahl to write jokes. Sahl, the preeminent stand-up at the time and an ardent Adlai Stevenson supporter, helped Kennedy use humor to broaden his appeal and ease concerns about Kennedy's youth, lack of experience, and Catholicism. Kennedy used one Sahl joke in response to criticism that if elected Kennedy would dig a tunnel to Rome (implying the Pope would be the one running the country), responding "I'm against public works progress of any kind."[9] Sahl eventually went back to making jokes *about* Kennedy rather than *for* him, but even then, the vast majority of Kennedy comedy was flattering. William White wrote in *Harper's* that the "Humor Quotient may be the most important index to watch in the first Presidential campaign of a new and – hopefully – funnier decade."[10] Satirists were more than happy to play along with Kennedy. Much of the satire during his time in office worked to reinforce a positive image of Kennedy while taking on his Cold War adversaries.

The Second City and the Premise

Kennedy awoke liberalism in comedy, bringing about a renewed interest in social and political satire. Robert Hatch wrote in the *Nation* that there was "a new spirit of mischief" that had arisen shortly after "moving day at the White House."[11] Writing about Second City, one critic said in 1962, "For years many of us have complained that our revues are lacking in biting political satire . . . here ye, here ye, here it is – the political revue in all its mordant glory."[12] The election of Kennedy signaled to many the return of political satire. Kliph Nesteroff said that "Comedy about JFK was to the early 1960s what Monica Lewinsky jokes and Bill Clinton impressions were to the 1990s. It was everywhere."[13] The *type* of comedy between the two presidents, however, was quite different. Jokes about JFK were relatively fawning, while Clinton humor painted him as more nefarious, though ultimately much of the humor about Clinton still worked to buoy him. JFK humor was even different than his contemporaries. While Peter Cook was lambasting Prime Minister Harold Macmillan in Britain as part of *Beyond the Fringe*, American sketch comics took a different tack. Rather than attack Kennedy, many of them championed Kennedy. Rather than target the president, they targeted Kennedy's opponents. Kennedy impressions were widespread to be sure, but much of the satire was focused not on Kennedy himself, but his conservative antagonists in the United States – Nixon and Barry Goldwater – and his adversaries overseas, Nikita Khrushchev and Fidel Castro.

The Second City was at the forefront of the sketch comedy boom. As noted in the previous chapter, Second City was born out of the ashes of Chicago's Compass Players. Arguably the most influential American theatre of the 20th century, The Second City opened on December 16, 1959, on North Wells Street in Chicago in what had been a Chinese laundry, with *Excelsior and Other Outcries*. Building upon the Brechtian ideas and social satire Paul Sills and others explored with The Compass, The Second City developed a system of sketch comedy derived from improvisation that satirized the social, cultural, and political issues of the day. Original members like Roger Bowen, Howard Alk, and Andrew Duncan "believed that they might use the stage to alert audiences to political issues marginalized by America's cold war consensus."[14] Barbara Harris told *The Village Voice* that Second City did things that "you couldn't put into a play . . . [like] people starving in Vietnam [and] the Bomb. . . . You can only do it at Second City."[15] Much of Second City's earliest work was more critical of the social conditions of the 1950s and 1960s than it was of Kennedy, treating him more as a savior than a villain. Behind this new type of socially relevant and subversive comedy, Second City was immediately successful, so much so that they had to quickly move to a larger space on Wells Street to accommodate the growing crowds.

The theatre was designed to evoke a 1920s-style cabaret theatre, with patrons free to eat and drink, and the ornate architecture on display ironically. The cast would perform in suits and formal dresses, itself a satiric mask about the conformity culture, with a set of only a few bentwood chairs and a handful of props. The Second City embraced the pace and tone of The Compass's improvised acts but relied on scripted sketch comedy. Nevertheless, the target of their satire remained similar to their predecessors – popular culture, relationships, sex, religion, and the cultural/generational clashes that would come to define the 1960s. The Second City worked to deconstruct the "normalcy" of the 1950s, focusing much of their attention on domestic bliss – or lack thereof. Second City scenes presented the darker side of sitcom suburban life. In "Just Rehearsing Dear," a man in his basement explains to an imaginary judge why he killed his wife. When his wife calls out from offstage, "George, what are you doing down there in the basement?" he replies, "Just rehearsing, dear."[16] In "Museum Piece" in 1961, a beatnik and a middle-class woman meet at the Art Institute, where the beatnik tries to get the woman to liberate her senses to get in touch with the art. She has a breakthrough of sorts, but when the beatnik attempts to make his move (mostly to stay at her apartment), the two remain alienated and apart. Many early Second City sketches focused on alienation and a failure to fit in. "Vend-a-Buddy" featured Alan Arkin feeding coins into a robot that speaks "platitudinous words of hollow comfort," in hopes that the robot will sympathize with his plight. It does not. This social satire resonated with a new generation that felt isolated by the 1950s consensus-culture of normality. These sketches reflect satire's principal role at this point in history. The president was not their primary focus. Instead, they saw conformity culture as the greatest threat to American identity, and they saw Kennedy as part of their crusade to end it.

In New York City, Ted Flicker, who worked with the St. Louis branch of The Compass Players, opened a new theatre with a similar aesthetic to Second City: the Premise. Flicker pitched the Premise as "fresh as the day's newspaper . . . a theatre whose actors are able to improvise and comment every night on the events of the day."[17] Like its Chicago competitor, the Premise satirized conformity and placed itself on the outside looking in. A 1962 review of the Premise stated, "As with a lot of modern American humour, psychiatric disorder is the basis of much of the show's best material."[18] Similar to Second City and Jules Feiffer, the Premise became a home for a new breed of young urban neurotics. In the sketch "The Chess Story," Joan Darling plays a young woman playing chess with a male stranger in Washington Square. As the game unfolds, Darling dissects every move psychologically, eventually breaking: "Compromise is the basis of a healthy relationship! This is not going to be like all the others, with give, give, give on my side and take, take, take on the other."[19] The Premise would get more overtly political, but like Second City, much of the material was social satire reflecting the changing identity of America. The mental toll of the 1950s was a considerably more frequent topic of humor than Kennedy's policies. In fact, JFK was seen as a remedy to the 1950s more so than a problem for the 1960s. Both Second City and the Premise became home to hip, subversive sketch comedy, and both would latch onto the Kennedy administration for laughs.

The most well-known recurring sketch involving Kennedy at Second City was the "Kennedy–Khrushchev Press Conference," in which Kennedy and Khrushchev answer audience questions. The sketch was included in numerous revues, becoming a critical and fan favorite. Initially, Roger Bowen played Kennedy with Alan Arkin as Khrushchev, who would answer in Russian gibberish. Severn Darden served as Khrushchev's interpreter, thereby doing a lot of the heavy lifting for the improvised bits. This recurring sketch routinely made Khrushchev the center of the jokes. One such exchange was captured in 1962 by *Time* magazine:

Question: Would Mr. Kennedy comment on the slogan "Better Red than Dead"?

Kennedy: (hemming and hawing) These are obviously both extreme positions. I have tried to keep my Government on the solid middle road between them. That is to say – half dead and half Red.

Question:	What will Mr. Khrushchev say at the next disarmament conference?
Khrushchev:	We in the Soviet Union believe that total disarmament is necessary for peace. We are always for peace. Anybody who stands in the way of peace will be destroyed.[20]

Kennedy is certainly mocked a bit in the exchange, but the punchline is aimed at Khrushchev. In 1961's *Seacoast of Bohemia*, another Kennedy–Khrushchev press conference celebrated Camelot, when Khrushchev remarked that if his wife "were young, thin, and rich, she, too, could be like Jacqueline Kennedy."[21] One evening during a Kennedy–Khrushchev press conference, Groucho Marx was in the audience. Andrew Duncan was playing Kennedy and Arkin was Khrushchev with Darden serving as his interpreter. Arkin's Khrushchev was wearing a peaked cab driver's hat. When the group turned to the audience for questions, Marx asked a series of more and more detailed questions about the hat, with the audience and performers laughing harder and harder as the questions became more and more specific. The simple joke illustrates the satiric tradition of exaggerating the absurd in the real. By drilling down on the hat, Marx was pointing out the absurdity of the situation. The very real tensions between Kennedy and Khrushchev were ever-present, with the threat of nuclear war looming over every interaction. Against that backdrop, a joke about a hat releases the tension by making something so trivial as a hat vitally important.[22]

In addition to the press conference sketches, Second City drew on Cold War mania. Second City's *To the Water Tower* (1963) featured several Kennedy Cold War sketches, including a Kennedy–Khrushchev press conference and the sketch "How To Sell a Fallout Shelter." In the latter, a bomb shelter salesman trains potential employees: "Here's your chance, fellows, to get into orbit with a 100-megaton opportunity. Fallout shelters – how does that grab you?" Offering customers a double-your-money-back guarantee if the shelters don't work, he adds, "There's only one thing that could possibly screw us up. . . . World peace."[23] Arthur Gelb's review of the 1963 New York performance said the sketch would "double you up with laughter."[24] As with the Marx joke, the humor here also is meant to diffuse Cold War tension rather than mock the president. As such, the Premise likewise targeted Khrushchev. In one sketch in their Washington, D.C. branch, where folks like Lyndon Johnson and Hubert Humphrey were spotted in the audience, Khrushchev is asked to respond to a report that a Soviet foreign minister had died in a car accident: "Thanks, but it's tomorrow morning."[25] Both groups likewise took aim at the escalating Cold War tensions between the United States and Soviet Union, including Vietnam. The Premise often performed a 1961 sketch involving an American and a Soviet official trying to persuade a Laotian farmer why their aid is preferable to the other's. The two officials begin fighting with one another, unintentionally killing the farmer.[26] The dangers of the Cold War for both companies are presented as a result of Soviet aggression, with Americans, helmed by Kennedy, standing as the bearers of freedom. The above sketch demonstrates America's complicity, but the overarching narrative was the danger of the Soviet Union.

The Premise and Second City were not shy about their affection for Kennedy, and both groups worked to ingratiate themselves. The Premise opened a Washington, D.C. branch purposefully to attract the attention of the Kennedy administration. Performing at the Shoreham Hotel, the Premise quickly became a hotspot: "Washington officialdom has been heading for [the Premise] with increasing enthusiasm to listen gleefully to the demolition of its most earnest endeavors."[27] The Kennedys, likewise, were fans of the various satiric takes on their lives, or at least they were in public. Second City actress Barbara Harris remarked, "The Kennedy's loved us. They were always following us around."[28] This symbiotic relationship undoubtedly affected the young satirists, who felt a kinship with the Kennedys. It undoubtedly made them less likely to criticize JFK and more likely to defend him.

Both Second City and the Premise got their chance to defend Kennedy during a pair of trips to London in the early 1960s. In a 1962 performance at London's Establishment Club, Second City found themselves defending their president:

> They were forced to respond to the left-leaning audience's angry and hostile requests for scenes involving the Cuban Missile Crisis. Del Close, a Stevenson stalwart like Sahl who on the Second City stage in Chicago repeatedly took shots at the Kennedy administration's aggressive anticommunist, anti-Castro foreign policy, took charge of the situation and instructed his colleagues to defend President Kennedy from criticism. In addition to pulling a scene critical of American foreign policy, Close engaged the combative London audience with tart reminders of British failures in the Suez. "I would like to point out," Close likewise told the audience, "that you are also members of NATO and that we are in this together."[29]

It is impossible to imagine a similar scenario involving Nixon or Trump, and likewise illustrates satire defending the status quo.

Conversely, when the Premise went to London, they called on Kennedy to defend them. Performing improvised material was technically illegal in England at the time, because all content needed approval before a performance by the Lord Chamberlain. Not having set scripts proved to be a challenge. Additionally, impressions of heads of state were frowned upon (even today, it is illegal in Britain to show televised footage of Parliament for comedic purposes). To get around the Lord Chamberlain, Flicker recorded hours of improvisation and compiled a transcript over a thousand pages long. He figured nobody would read that much. When they got to London, the group inserted five sketches about the Kennedys and one sketch about a racist governor who dies and goes to heaven only to find that God is black. Word spread quickly, and the Lord Chamberlain demanded a final play text sent for approval before he would allow the performances to continue. Flicker then sent a cable to the White House asking for permission to make fun of the Kennedys. The First Lady's press secretary responded quickly: "No objection Premise continue scenes." Unconvinced by the First Lady, the Lord Chamberlain threatened to send Her Majesty's troops to the theatre to shut down the Premise. It did not get that far, as the Lord Chamberlain and Flicker worked out an arrangement that the group could continue to improvise as long as they did not advertise. The Premise did both. It seemed that even if the Lord Chamberlain had issues, the public did not. Not only did the public embrace the show, so, too, did Prime Minister Harold Macmillan, who went to see the Premise and reportedly enjoyed the show. One night after the show, an audience member allegedly approached Flicker and told him:

> If you make fun of Prime Minister Macmillan . . . and Prime Minister Macmillan comes to see you and enjoys it or does not leave the theater in a rage: or if you are able to get your president to wire you permission to make fun of him, you can't really be striking any telling blows, can you?[30]

He had a point and again we see the conservative nature of satire working more to bolster the status quo.

Reports vary about how Flicker handled the situation at the moment, some say he brushed it aside, while in a later interview Flicker pointed to the moment as an epiphany about the limits of satire, saying, "We're doing something wrong; that man [Macmillan] should be running from the theatre in horror, going to the Lord Chamberlain to close us down."[31] Feeling that the Premise was not a productive outlet for political satire, Flicker closed the Premise and later opened The Living Premise, a company dedicated to providing an African American perspective on the growing racial tensions in America. The Living Premise was an integrated cast that featured Godfrey Cambridge and Diana Sands, both of whom had been part of the successful Broadway play *Purlie Victorious*, which satirized race relations but proved to be unpopular with white audiences (Cambridge had also been in Jean Genet's *The Blacks*, while Sands was in Lorraine Hansberry's *A Raisin in the Sun*). Opening on June 13, 1963, The Living Premise had a similar performance aesthetic to Second City and the Premise, but its content focused on race. In "The Emasculation of Militant Negro Organizations by White Northern Liberals," three black militants plot to kidnap Jackie Kennedy at a department store, while in "The Negro Sexual Myth," a white woman is pursuing a black man, demanding that he not "treat me like a white woman – let yourself go."[32] Conservative audiences were not big fans, but what ultimately brought the company down was the tensions between the cast. The white cast members grew to resent the black members and did not honestly believe the hardships they portrayed onstage. Joan Darling, a holdover from the original Premise, was "stunned" when Cambridge, Sands, and Al Freeman "suggested that the Kennedy administration was not doing all that it could to support the civil rights cause."[33] The cultural clash explored by The Living Premise foreshadowed satire during Lyndon Johnson's administration that was more focused on cultural and political issues than on the man in the White House. It also demonstrates the importance of diverse perspectives, as well as the historic difficulty in asserting marginalized viewpoints.

In light of the MacMillan affair, the Premise's rebranding, and the growing commercial success at Second City, where corporate executives often sat in the audience ready to laugh at themselves, had satire been co-opted? Was the London audience member correct? If the targets were enjoying the satire, could it be effective? Had Kennedy used the Premise and Second City to enhance his image and to further his agenda? Or did Kennedy's stamp of approval – literally in the Premise–Lord Chamberlain case – signal that satirists no longer had to fear going after the government? With Joseph McCarthy and the Red Scare still in everyone's collective short-term memory, and Eisenhower not one to tell or take a joke, was Kennedy playing along to restore a healthy dialogue between comedy and government? Many thought Kennedy was partly responsible for the satiric boom that traveled from Britain to America in the early 1960s. Russell Baker wrote in the *New York Times* that "one of the Kennedy Administration's brighter achievements in 1962 has been its restoration of the sound of laughter."[34] On the other hand, perhaps the satire was ineffective because, as some have argued, satire itself is ineffective.

Alan Arkin said in an interview that Second City had no particular affinity for Kennedy and did not think that their work was making much of an impact beyond giving an audience a chance to blow off some steam. Arkin pointed to a Tony Holland satiric monologue about satire's enormous impact on the world, saying,

> Here's a letter from Mrs. Jerome Whatsis from West Jesus, North Dakota. She says, "Dear Sir: I don't know what I would do without satire. When my husband is home sick in bed and my children are screaming for food and there's no money, I thank God there's such a thing as satire." . . . Well, this is only one of the influences of satire. We all know how much satire did to stop the rise of Hitler in Germany in 1931.[35]

Yet perhaps "blowing off steam" was precisely what Americans needed at the time. Nuclear war was a very real threat, and the man responsible for negotiating that threat was Jack Kennedy. By lightly satirizing him, often by building him up, satirists were not necessarily ineffective. Not all satire about the president need be negative to be effective. Kennedy not only represented an end to 1950s normalcy, but he also held the promise of 1960s liberalism. Tearing him down did not serve the purposes of the era's satirists – they wanted Kennedy to succeed. Satirists liked the America JFK reflected and projected, therefore they worked to mostly support his vision. The threats to America, in their eyes, were not in the White House, they were Khrushchev and Castro. Barry Goldwater's conservative vision for America was more worrying than Joe Kennedy's money or Jack Kennedy's womanizing. For satirists, celebrating Kennedy was the best way for them to realize the American they wanted to see.

The First Family

The Kennedy administration and the Cold War were favorite topics of sketch comedians onstage, but the most far-reaching Kennedy satire was Vaughn Meader's comedy album *The First Family* (1962). A relatively unknown piano-playing comic, Meader went from obscurity to comedy royalty to comedic outcast almost overnight. The Maine native had been working in New York City clubs for a short time, one of any number of comics trying to make a living. His shtick was not even Kennedy when he started – initially, he made up comic songs. Fortunately for Meader, he had three things going for him: (1) Kennedy had just been elected president, (2) he looked like Kennedy, and (3) with a slight tweak, his natural Maine accent sounded more like Kennedy than Kennedy sounded like Kennedy. In fact, most future Kennedy impressions sound more like an impression of Meader than of Kennedy. As with most presidential impersonations, Meader's centered on one singular element around which the rest of the character revolved. In Kennedy's case, it had to be his voice. Anthony Atamanuik, a comic known for his Donald Trump impression, says that a good impression isn't about the look as much as it is about the presence. Speaking about Meader's Kennedy, he said, "the presence of the person is what you feel, like there's a will that presents Kennedy in that moment."[36] Meader threw in his JFK impersonation while doing his act, and as the audience responded, he began incorporating more and more Kennedy until being Kennedy became Meader's complete (comic) identity.

On July 3, 1962, Meader appeared on CBS's *Celebrity Talent Scouts*, an early version of later talent-seeking competitions like *Star Search* and *American Idol*. He did some straight material that didn't garner much laughter (much like his traditional act), then Meader stepped behind a podium and became Jack Kennedy. The audience is audibly stunned at first. Comedians did not typically make fun of the president, but more importantly, Meader looked and sounded *so much* like JFK. Almost simultaneously, the audience falls hook, line, and sinker for the impression. Unlike earlier impressions on the radio where there was no visual cue, viewers could see that Meader wasn't Kennedy. Though he looked very much like JFK, he unquestionably was not, and therefore Meader was able to avoid any confusion or public outcry about trying to trick people into thinking he was JFK. It sounds obvious to us today, but because the audience could *literally* see him they were able to enjoy the parodic impression.

Part of the reason comics didn't impersonate presidents was because many thought it demeaned the office and was in bad taste. Tellingly, after his *Talent Scouts* appearance, Meader wrote a letter to Kennedy:

Dear Mr. President,

I respectfully call your attention to the Talent Scout Show which we taped last night for viewing on CBS Television Tuesday night, July 3, 10:00 PM. I impersonated you but I did it with great affection and respect. Hope it meets with your approval.

Respectfully,
Vaughn Meader[37]

Others worried that a vocal impression would fool people into believing the president was speaking when he was not, which could not only cause confusion but could be an enormous national security risk.

When Will Rogers impersonated President Calvin Coolidge on the radio in 1928, it was so novel that many thought it was real. Rogers had to issue an apology, saying,

> My Dear Mr. and Mrs. President, I find that due to my lack of good taste, or utter stupidity, that I have wounded the feelings of two people who I most admire.... If you can see it in your heart, you and that dear wife of yours to forgive me, I will certainly see that it, or nothing approaching it, will ever happen again.[38]

He did it again, and six years later Rogers again found himself writing an apology to the president after an impersonation, this time writing FDR: "When you are wrong you are just all wrong." To which FDR replied, "I must have guessed wrong too, because I liked it."[39] In 1937, the *New York Times* reported that NBC and CBS had banned presidential impressions except during "news dramatizations," and even then, there were strict regulations. Larry Nixon defended WMCA's decision to pull Arthur Boran's FDR impression during the Press Photographers Association dance by saying the radio was "no place to mimic the voice of the President of the United States."[40] Many questioned if it was proper to make fun of the president. There was also fear, both during FDR's time and in 1962, that a vocal impression might cause a panic if people thought the president was saying the jokes. If radio was "no place" for satirizing the president, TV was the perfect place. Because the audience could literally see Meader, television gave him the leeway to make fun of Kennedy. The newness and freshness made Meader's impression take off – quite literally no one had ever *seen* anything like it.

Almost immediately, Meader's career skyrocketed. He began doing mock press conferences as Kennedy, usually with a plant or two in the audience to ask some questions, but mostly working improvisationally. The press conference was the perfect setup to satirize Kennedy. Because JFK was so adept on TV, audiences were very familiar with Kennedy's speech and mannerisms, more so than any previous audience with any prior president. We take the president appearing on television as par for the course now, but in 1962 Kennedy was the first president to appear on TV regularly. Kennedy was also the first president to appear on a late-night talk show, appearing on June 16, 1960, on *Tonight Starring Jack Paar* during his campaign against Richard Nixon. The appearance was hardly Bill Clinton wearing sunglasses and playing "Heartbreak Hotel" on the saxophone on *The Arsenio Hall Show* three decades later, but it did demonstrate Kennedy's ease in front of the camera. He largely avoided comedy, speaking about the dangers of communism before taking questions from the audience – about the dangers of communism. Nixon himself would also have an equally serious appearance on Paar's show, before returning in 1963 to, shockingly, play the piano. The 1960 appearance of both men was met with more scorn than celebration. Ed Koterba wrote in the *Reading Eagle* that Nixon's appearance was "revolting."[41] Writing about both men and the disturbing new trend, the *New York Times*'s James Reston said with scorn:

> From now on, it will be important to analyze not only who has the best speech writers but who has the best gag-writers. . . . The historians and the

philosophers of the country would like to question them both on serious matters, but the comedians have priority. Just who gains from all this and why these two deadly serious and tense young men want to prove that they are funny and relaxed is not quite clear. It is a precedent, all right, and anyone who wonders why is obviously a stuffed shirt.[42]

The two appearances did set a precedent, though it would take another few decades to fully come to fruition. Coupled with the immense influence of the televised debates and Kennedy's media savvy, it was becoming clear that TV was the new power-medium in politics.

It is not an accident that Second City's and Meader's most popular Kennedy sketches were mock press conferences – Kennedy's media-savvy was part of his appeal. Kennedy himself was so good during press conferences that it was only natural that comic impressions of him at a press conference would be too (and would feed the idea that the real Kennedy was good at them). Therefore, the audience was able to be in on the joke in a way that no previous audience really could. Kennedy being quick on his feet turned out to be a boon to comics versed in improvisation. The quicker-witted Meader and The Second City were perfectly set up for the moment. The symbiotic relationship between the president and his impersonators worked to further the careers of both Meader and Kennedy; the more Meader (and Second City actors) seemed like Kennedy, the more the audience laughed. The more the audience laughed, the more they liked the real Kennedy. Jerry Stiller commented that Meader's

> press-conference routine was one of the greatest inventions I can remember. . . . You'd say, My God, how'd he learn to do that? It was like someone morphing into another human being, without it being an impersonation. There were no tricks or funny mannerisms or anything. It was all done with his brain.[43]

Meader's quick wit in the press conferences matched Kennedy's wit, giving Meader's impression a sense of authenticity that other JFK impressions lacked. In one such press conference, he was asked about Barry Goldwater running for president in '64 as Kennedy's Republican challenger, to which Meader's Kennedy responded: "I think Senator Goldwater is a fine man and would make a fine candidate in '64. 1864."[44] Meader was hardly the only comic doing a Kennedy impression, but his took off like no other.

Meanwhile, comedy writers George Foster and Earle Doud and disc jockey Bob Booker had begun to write a radio script about JFK and his family. They just needed a leading man. Doud, joined by comic Chuck McCann, went on a scouting mission to see Meader's act after Booker and Doud had seen Meader on *Celebrity Talent Scouts*. McCann remarked that Meader "was kind of a country hick from Maine, just another barrelhouse piano player, but his voice was very New England. . . . He barely imitated Kennedy, because he *was* that voice."[45] They hired Meader and paired him with Naomi Brossart, who breathlessly voiced Jackie. Jim

Lehner, Bradley Bolke, Chuck McCann, Bob McFadden, and Norma MacMillan voiced the other characters on the album. With their Kennedy in tow, the group set about making their album, a series of short sketches parodying life in the Kennedy White House.

The problem was, no label wanted it because they feared no radio station would broadcast it. Impersonating the president was not done. ABC-Paramount Records president and former Eisenhower press secretary James Hagarty said the idea of *The First Family* was "degrading to the presidency [and] every Communist country in the world would love this record."[46] All the major labels turned them down until tiny Cadence Records gave them the green light. They recorded the album on October 22, 1962, the very same night as Kennedy's Cuban Missile Crisis speech. Recorded in front of a live studio audience, the team immediately knew they were on to something. The blistering laughter almost becomes another character. Initially, Cadence Records President Archie Bleyer was furious with the laughter, exclaiming, "We can never release this! There's too much laughter! They're laughing over the lines! We're going to have to do it again."[47] So they did it again the next week, and the audience was silent, so they released the original recording instead.

The First Family turned out to be a massive hit, becoming the fastest-selling record of all time, not just the fastest-selling comedy record, the fastest-selling record period. It sold over 7.5 million copies and won the 1963 Grammy for Album of the Year. *Billboard* said, "There has never been an album that has broken so many records, or set so many new ones."[48] Music stores in New York had to extend their hours to accommodate demand, while eight new pressing plants were hired to keep up with the printing demands. *The First Family* wasn't the first comedy album – Lenny Bruce, Shelly Berman, Jonathan Winters, Bob Newhart, and Nichols and May had all released successful albums. It wasn't even the first comic presidential impression on the radio, as Dean Murphy, Will Rogers, and others had impersonated FDR in the 1930s. Yet somehow, *The First Family*, a sketch comedy album by an unknown comedian featuring unknown voice talent released on a small independent label, surpassed them all. Meader suddenly found himself making regular appearances on shows like *The Ed Sullivan Show*. *The First Family* proved that making jokes about the president was a lucrative business – a business that would continue to grow exponentially over the next half-century. A string of imitation albums quickly followed, most of which hoped to ride on *The First Family*'s coattails or confuse shoppers into buying the wrong record, like *The Family at the White House*. Further albums tried to take on other first families, like *The Other Family* about Nikita Khrushchev, or *The Last Family* about Fidel Castro. An imagined black president was at the center of *Funniest Dream on Record* – there was even a *Sing-Along with JFK*.

Kennedy's Cuban Missile Crisis speech has obviously received more historical attention, but October 22, 1962, marks the seminal moment in contemporary sketch comedy satire about the presidency. In the blink of an eye, the album opened the floodgates to presidential impersonation. Suddenly, something that "was just not done," was being done all the time. As the following chapters unfold, we will see the evolution from "just not done" to "everybody's doing it" to "no need to satirize Trump he's parodying himself." While satire about the presidency is everywhere in contemporary America, including coming out of the mouth (or Twitter feed of the president), it was virtually nowhere in 1962. The turning point that set it all in motion was *The First Family*. The record's success, and future satirical depictions of the presidency, also hinged on Kennedy's reaction to the heretofore never before seen record.

The Kennedy administration, like most Americans, first heard the album on the radio. Intentionally designed to have short sketches that fit between commercial breaks, *The First Family* enjoyed success thanks to generous radio airplay. According to Nicholas Cull, presidential advisor Arthur Schlesinger, Jr. was driving to work and thought he was listening to a routine Kennedy press conference. A reporter asked, "Now that you are in office, what do you think the chances are of a Jewish president?" In Kennedy's signature voice, Schlesinger thought he heard the president say, "Well I think they're pretty good. Let me say, I don't see why a person of the Jewish faith can't be president of the United States. I know that as a Catholic I could never vote for him, but other than that. . . ." Schlesinger almost drove off the road. When he got to the White House, he sounded the alarms, warning of a possible Orson Welles *War of the Worlds*–type panic.[49] Others say Schlesinger's response was more measured, but he did write a memo for the president that would impact all future presidents. Schlesinger wrote, "This raises the question of what in hell a president of the United States ought to do about mimicry."[50] The *Los Angeles Times* likewise reported that "Many people started to write the White House, asking what in the world the President was doing talking that way right on the air for all to hear."[51] One story in the *New York Times* recounted an exchange Attorney General Robert Kennedy, Jack's brother, had while trying to make a phone call: "'Yes, yes, I tell you I AM the Attorney General.' After a pause, the Attorney General said, 'Very Well,' and hung up. 'That guy thinks I'm Vaughn Meader,' he said. 'He's going to call me back just to make sure.'"[52]

Kennedy's administration set about contacting the FCC to try and ban broadcasts of the album, or at the very least, to preface any of the sketches with a disclaimer. None of that came to fruition because Americans loved the record. Publicly, Kennedy used the impersonation to help boost his popularity. Privately, many close to him said he disliked it, and he did pressure the FCC to stop the parody. While he didn't like it, the record was a hit, and he saw the opportunity it provided to enhance his image. As Peter Robinson writes,

> Prior to his apparently gracious news conference response, Kennedy met with aide Kenneth P. O'Donnell and assistant press secretary Malcolm M. Kilduff. They agreed 'that nothing could be done about this particular record. However, . . . it might be useful to get some trade magazine to blast this sort of thing.[53]

Kennedy wanted to make sure his team controlled this newfound territory. He wanted to appear like a good sport, but he also wanted the impact of the record blunted. In short, he wanted to use the record rather than let it use him. He knew that his image could be enhanced by publicly playing along. As Leo Braudy writes,

> Kennedy combined the desire to be seen and the desire to be desired with an impalatable distance, an abstract immediacy. A child of his era, the first president to have grown up entirely with the movies and the twentieth century, he was steeped in the awareness that being seen on the screen can heighten desire even as the solitude of the image also distances it into something timelessly appealing.[54]

In other words, he knew how to manipulate the media to his advantage, and he wasn't going to let *The First Family* pass him by without capitalizing on its popularity.

Kennedy reportedly bought 100 copies of the record to give out as Christmas gifts. At a December 1962 press conference, Kennedy was asked about the explosion of satire aimed at the White House, including *The First Family*, and "whether they produced annoyment or enjoyment." Kennedy laughed, "Annoyment? No. Yes, I have read them and listened to them, and actually, I listened to Meader's record, but I thought it sounded more like Teddy than it did me."[55] He reportedly played the record before a cabinet meeting, and later opened dinner with the Democratic National Committee by saying, "Vaughn Meader was busy tonight, so I came myself."[56] Kennedy's embrace of humor may have created the wave of Kennedy-related humor. Thomas Lask argued in the *New York Times* that Kennedy's wit encouraged comedians to satirize the president because he was "sharp and witty enough to appreciate what they were doing and big enough to laugh at it himself."[57] Whether he liked the album was immaterial, Kennedy was making the most of it.

Listening to the record today, it sounds like a love letter to Kennedy, the promise of his administration, and the excitement the young Kennedy family brought to the White House. The liner notes sound almost preposterously naïve today:

> This album is for fun! Things are being suggested and said here about some of the great people of our time, and perhaps the very fact that they are able to laugh with us and enjoy this album is in part what makes them the great people they are. No one has more respect for the high offices and the people suggested here than those of us who had a hand in putting this together. This album can be played loudly at any time, night or day, in front of anyone, anywhere people have a right to laugh. We hope that someday soon everyone, everywhere, will have that right to laugh.[58]

As innocent as it sounds, the notes are a direct appeal to American values of freedom and liberty. The album is a symbol of America's greatness, of Kennedy's superiority to Khrushchev. In America, ordinary citizens can make fun of the president without fear of retribution. In the Soviet Union, an album like *The First Family* would have gotten Meader killed or imprisoned. The album, therefore, is a direct appeal to the inherent democratic ideals at the heart of Americanness – the very ideals that were at stake in the Cold War. Laughing with the Kennedys was a slap in the face not to JFK, but to the Soviet Union. Kennedy himself recognized the importance of publicly supporting the album and the right to criticize him. Perhaps a bit hyperbolic, but the album did signify, as satire has throughout America's history, the freedom of speech so central to our concept of what it means to be an American. So much of the JFK satire celebrates not just JFK, but the American values satirizing him represented. Part of winning the Cold War was asserting and protecting the constitutional right to laugh at Kennedy.

When evaluating the satiric bite, it's important to remember that the album was one of the first of its kind, created in a world that wasn't yet as cynical or suspicious of its presidents. As noted, the album itself was a revolution, the first of its kind, and one that was inherently celebrating America's values. Audiences weren't accustomed to presidents being the target of satirical impressions, heck, they weren't even used to hearing presidents speak. Before FDR's "Fireside Chats," Americans rarely heard or saw their president, therefore much of the presidential satire focused either on their policy or on a caricature of their persona – political cartoons of King Andrew Jackson in full royal regalia, Abraham Lincoln with the ears of an ape or comically long legs, and Theodore Roosevelt's impossibly wide grin. Even the venerable Will Rogers received harsh backlash when he went on the radio and pretended to be Calvin Coolidge doing an ad for Dodge – the January 6, 1928, *New York Times* headline read "Criticize Will Rogers for Joke on Coolidge; Many Protest His Use of President's Name in Radio Hook-Up for the Dodge Car." Mort Sahl had begun to criticize and joke about the president in the late 1950s, but even then he was doing it onstage in nightclubs for a limited audience.

In that light, it is not surprising that the album steers clear of political scandals – from JFK's womanizing to the Bay of Pigs. Instead, the jokes center on how *not* normal the Kennedy's are by putting the Kennedy's in typical situations at the White House. Jack was a sitcom dad; Jackie, his whispering wife; Caroline, the precocious little girl; and John John, the babbling baby boy. One such "normal" sketch features Kennedy appropriating bathtub toys, giving nine PT boats apiece for Caroline and John, but warning that "The rubbah swan is mine!" The final sketch of the album, "Bedtime Story," comes close to satirizing policy. Jack tells Caroline her favorite bedtime story, in the process summing up the Camelot-Kennedy connection:

JFK: There was this tall man with a lot of hair. He was a prince and a great warrior. And the people of his country picked him to be their leader because he could protect them and lead them on to the new frontiers.
Caroline: Tell me about when he had the trouble.
JFK: Well Caroline, first he had trouble with the steel duke. And then all the money lords gave him trouble, then all the other lords wanted to take his job away. But when he talked everyone believed him and he remained as their leader. One day the evil prince with the black beard from the island in the south and the terrible fat bear from the cold

	north came and they tried to hurt the prince. But the prince was too smart and he chased them away. So the handsome prince and all the people of his country lived happily ever after.
Caroline:	Ohh, I was scared. But hooray for the prince and thank you daddy. Good night.
JFK:	Goodnight Caroline, goodnight.
	(We hear footsteps and the bedroom door open and then close.)
Caroline:	These sessions do him so much good.

In "Economy Lunch," Kennedy is hosting a lunch for world leaders. From the seating chart, where Kennedy tries to avoid having enemies sit next to one another, to Khrushchev smacking his shoe on the table, the sketch is another example of comedy defending Kennedy and delivering punchlines about his adversaries. Chinese President Chiang Kai-shek orders a club sandwich, and Kennedy asks, "Would you like it with a little mayo?" "Please! Not to mention that name!" Egyptian President Abdel Nasser orders a pastrami sandwich, "I can never get it at home." Khrushchev forgoes ordering a sandwich, "You don't have to order special for me, I'll have a bite of everybody else's." In "Relatively Speaking," the close ties of the Kennedy family and Kennedy administration gets satirized.

Jackie:	Family, family, family. Jack, there's just too much family. Can't we ever get away alone?
JFK:	Jackie, I promise we'll get away tomorrow. No more, uhhh, family for a while. I promise. Now, uhh, turn off the light. Good night, Jackie.
Jackie:	Goodnight, Jack.
JFK:	Goodnight, Bobby. Goodnight, Ethel.
Bobby and Ethel:	Goodnight, Jack. Goodnight, Teddy.
Teddy:	Goodnight, Eunice. Goodnight Peter . . .

Layered within the Kennedy political satire is an interesting critique of Kennedy's relationship with the media – an early example of pop culture comedy about pop culture. The album opens with a traditional broadcasting pitchman announcing:

> Ladies and Gentleman, I'm speaking to you from a typical American home in Hyannis Port, Massachusetts. Since January of 1960, this family of smiling and happy people have undergone a change. You might say they've been engaged in a new and different type of experiment. Sir, as head of this average family, what was this new experience undergone by you and the members of your household?

Meader's Kennedy replies, "Well, after ah, two years of brushing with ah, Crest toothpaste, our group had twenty-one percent fewer cavities with Crest." The sketch "After Dinner Conversations," frames the Kennedy family dinner conversation as a JFK press conference.

Jackie: (in a breathless whisper) Yes, I should like to ask a question –
JFK: Would you stand, please?
Jackie: Yes, I should like to ask a question –
JFK: Would you please identify yourself.
Jackie: I'm your wife. I should like to ask the following question: (she starts speaking in French) –
JFK: No, speak English, Jackie!
Jackie: I noticed that you didn't touch your salad, either at dinner tonight or dinner last night. Would you tell us why, please?
JFK: Well, let me say this about that. Number one, in my opinion, the fault does not lie as much with the salad as it does with the dressing being used on the salad. Now let me say that I have nothing against the dairy industry; however I would prefer it if in the future we stuck to coleslaw. Next question. Yes, the baby in the back row, Baby John.
John: (Incoherent baby talk)
JFK: I believe I answered that question at dinner last night. Now if you remember, here is what I said at that time: (incoherent baby talk).

"The Tour" parodies Jackie Kennedy's famous televised White House tour from February 1962, "A Tour of the White House With Mrs. John F. Kennedy." The sketch follows Jackie as she takes a reporter through the White House. She points out the various paintings as "This one. And that great big one over there. . . . And finally this one over here," while the dust on a piece of furniture in the President Grant Drawing Room, the White House lawn, and carpenters working on a project were "gifts." A later sketch satirizes sitcom-style marriages, with Jack and Jackie having this sitcom-esque exchange:

Jackie: Isn't it nice being here alone on a Saturday night, just the two of us for a change?
JFK: That's what you said last Saturday and the Saturday before that and the Saturday before that. Don't you want to see a movie?
Jackie: Fine. There's a wonderful abstract Swedish picture playing.
JFK: I knew you'd say that. I know where there's a good Italian moving playing, seeing as how you like foreign films.
Jackie: Wonderful, which one?
JFK: Hercules.

The album naturally featured Meader's famous press conference sketches. In one of the album's most memorable exchanges, Meader's Kennedy responds to a question about when the United States will send a man to the moon with, "Whenever Senator Goldwater wants to go."

Meader enjoyed the limelight and success the album brought, but was leery of becoming too closely associated with Kennedy. He only agreed to do a second *First Family* album after he was hit with a million-dollar lawsuit. In November 1963, Meader recorded a new non-Kennedy album, *Have Some Nuts!!!*, with MGM/Verve as part of a two-record deal. He didn't do any Kennedy material, instead doing a variety of characters all named Vaughn Meader – a man buying a grave for his turtle, a salesman, an advertising client, an interview with a dog behavior expert, and other sketch comedy types. But it didn't matter. On November 22, 1963, John F. Kennedy was assassinated. The golden age of satire he had ushered in was gone, and Vaughn Meader's career was over. Legend has it that Meader hopped into a taxi at the Milwaukee airport, when the cab driver asked him, "Did you hear about Kennedy in Dallas?" Meader, who heard thousands of Kennedy joke-pitches since the release of the album, thought this was another pitch. "No, how does it go?" Meader replied. Lenny Bruce took the stage that night, reportedly the only comedian to perform in New York, and accounts vary, but said something between, "Poor Vaughn Meader" and "Boy, Vaughn Meader is fucked."

In a weird testament to the effectiveness of Meader's impression, Meader became a symbol of Kennedy's tragic death. His appearances all but vanished, save for a painfully awkward appearance on *The Ed Sullivan Show* in early 1964. Nobody wanted to see Meader because he was so closely associated with Kennedy. *The First Family* was pulled from stores, Meader's television appearances were almost all canceled, nobody wanted to book him in clubs, and his appearance at the 1964 Grammys was canceled. He had to fight with Verve Records to get *Have Some Nuts!!!* released, which was predictably a flop. One club owner reportedly responded to a pitch to book Meader, saying, "I need this act like I need a hole in the head."[59] The nation so closely associated Meader with Kennedy that they projected their grief onto him. Another story claims that a construction worker who saw Meader on the street put down his jackhammer, took Meader's hand, and with tears streaming down his face, expressed his sympathies. Meader himself realized that his career was probably over, proclaiming that he, too, died on November 22, 1963, calling himself in 1979 "A living reminder of tragedy." Audiences pitied him, and that was his death sentence: "There's one thing a comedian does not need, and that's pity.... Anger and hatred beat pity. You can't make a crowd laugh when they're feeling sorry for you."[60] Kennedy satire had built the man up, and in turn, built up American's sense of their own greatness and potential. *The First Family* and other Kennedy satire simultaneously humanized and mythologized the man. Americans were laughing *with* Kennedy and *at* his adversaries. The satiric mood around Kennedy was mostly triumphant, so when he was killed it was a devastating blow to the psyche of the country.

Kennedy's assassination was a turning point in American life, and that extended to comedy. Alexander Woo summed up Meader's relationship to Kennedy, saying, "In the end, the story of Vaughn Meader is in many ways the perfect distillation of what John F. Kennedy meant to the country. Kennedy's ascension inspired an unexceptional nightclub performer to reach exceptional heights, and Kennedy's demise erased it all just as quickly."[61] It also marked a turning point in media – television was now king. Americans turned to Walter Cronkite and television news, with its ability to more immediately report on unfolding events than newspapers. Over the 1960s, sketch comedy would migrate to television, culminating in 1975 with *Saturday Night Live*. It wasn't only the medium that was changing – comedy changed as well, taking a turn to more cynical and pointed satire. In the immediate aftermath of Kennedy's assassination, many comedy theatres closed, with Lenny Bruce's appearance being the exception, not the rule. *TW3* released an entirely straight episode that celebrated Kennedy's life. When Second City reopened, the audience and performers alike were unsure how to handle the situation, knowing that everything had changed but not yet knowing what that change meant. Del Close took the stage and told the audience, "Let's make a deal: we won't stand around wondering why you're here if you don't sit back wondering why we're here."[62] The show went about as normal as possible until Close asked for an audience suggestion after intermission. Someone shouted out, "The Kennedy assassination," to which Close replied, "Just what the fuck was it you wanted to see, sir?" It was Second City's first "fuck."[63]

Notes

1. Qtd. in Sam Wasson, *Improv Nation: How We Made A Great American Art* (New York: Houghton Mifflin Harcourt Publishing Company, 2017), 59.
2. Stephen Kercher, *Revel with a Cause: Liberal Satire in Postwar America* (Chicago: University of Chicago Press, 2006), 165.
3. John F. Kennedy, "Inaugural Address," *National Parks Service*, 20 January 1961. www.nps.gov/jofi/learn/education/upload/inaugural-address.pdf.
4. Kercher, 194.
5. Qtd. in Jeffrey Sweet, *Something Wonderful Right Away: An Oral History of The Second City & The Compass Players* (New York: Limelight Edition, 1978), 299.
6. Robert Landry, "JFK – Show Biz in Love," *Variety*, 23 May 1962.
7. Qtd. in Theodore Sorensen, *Kennedy: The Classic Biography* (New York: Harper Perennial Modern Classics, Reissue Edition, 2013), 119.
8. Patrick A. Stewart, Reagan G. Dye and Austin D. Eubanks, "The Political Ethology of Debate Humor and Audience Laughter: Understanding Donald Trump, Hillary Clinton, and Their Audiences," in *Political Humor in a Changing Media Landscape*, eds. Jody C. Baumgartner and Amy B. Becker (Lanham, MD: The Rowman & Littlefield Publishing Group Inc., 2018), 122.
9. Qtd. in Kercher, 212.
10. William Smith White, "Humor in Politics," *Harper's*, February 1960, 97–102.
11. Robert Hatch, "Theatre," *Nation* 193, 14 October 1961, 254.
12. "Second City Reunion," *Cue 31*, 27 January 1962, 11.
13. Kliph Nesteroff, *The Comedians: Drunks, Thieves, Scoundrels and the History of American Comedy* (New York: Grove Press, 2015), 198.
14. Kercher, 248.
15. Qtd. in Michael Smith, "Nymphet with Sex – and Something More," *Village Voice*, 31 May 1962, 8.

16. Qtd. in Lee Gallup Feldman, *A Critical Analysis of Improvisational Theatre in the United States from 1955–1968* (Ph.D. diss., University of Denver, 1969), 140.
17. Qtd. in Kercher, 248.
18. Bamber Gascoigne, "American Quartet," *Spectator* 209, 3 August 1962, 159.
19. "The Chess Story," on the LP *Off Broadway: The Premise* (Vanguard, 1961).
20. Qtd. in "Political Humor, 1962," *Time* 79, no. 6, 6 February 1962, 72.
21. Qtd. in Dan Dietz, *Off Broadway Musicals, 1910–2007: Casts, Credits, Songs, Critical Reception and Performance Data of More Than 1,800 Shows* (Jefferson, NC: McFarland & Company Inc., 2010), 395.
22. Alan Arkin, *An Improvised Life: A Memoir* (Philadelphia: Da Capo Press, 2011), 53–55.
23. Qtd. in "Political Humor, 1962," 72.
24. Qtd. in Dietz, 460.
25. "Political Humor, 1962," 72.
26. Feldman, 123.
27. Arthur Gelb, "Political Satire Invades Capital," *New York Times*, 30 January 1962, 22.
28. Qtd. in Kercher, 236.
29. Kercher, 236.
30. Qtd. in Wasson, 84.
31. Qtd. in Ketcher, 262.
32. Qtd. in Leonard Harris, "Races Mix in 'Premise,'" *New York World-Telegram*, 14 June 1963.
33. Kercher, 267.
34. Russell Baker, "Observer," *New York Times*, 13 December 1962, 6.
35. Qtd. in Sweet, 224.
36. Qtd. in Mo Rocca, "Mobituaries: The Other Kennedy," CBS News, 20 January 2019. www.cbsnews.com/news/mobituaries-the-other-kennedy-vaughn-meader-mo-rocca/.
37. Qtd. in Peter M. Robinson, *The Dance of the Comedians: The People, the President, and the Performance of Political Standup Comedy in America* (Amherst: University of Massachusetts Press, 2010), 137.
38. Qtd. in William Wan, "The Surprisingly Dark, Twisted History of Presidential Impersonators in America," *The Washington Post*, 27 June 2016. www.washingtonpost.com/news/post-nation/wp/2016/06/27/the-surprisingly-dark-twisted-history-of-presidential-impersonators-in-america/?utm_term=.72d8e7b7d7d4.
39. Qtd. in Wan.
40. Qtd. in Jacob Smith, *Spoken Word: Postwar American Phonograph Cultures* (Berkeley: University of California Press, 2011), 125.
41. Ed Koterba, "Assignment Washington," *Reading Eagle*, 27 August 1960, 4.
42. Qtd. in Travis M. Andrews, "From Kennedy to Trump, the Much-Deplored History of Presidential Candidates on Late-Night TV," *The Washington Post*, 22 September 2016. www.washingtonpost.com/news/morning-mix/wp/2016/09/22/from-jfk-to-nixon-to-trump-presidential-candidates-and-their-goofiness-on-late-night-tv/.
43. Qtd. in Tim Carvell, "Exactly 40 Years Ago, for a Brief Shining Moment, Vaughn Meader Was the Second Most Famous Man in America," *Entertainment Weekly*, 28 March 2003.
44. "Vaughn Meader as JFK," YouTube, 29 December 2010. www.youtube.com/watch?v=35aO9GdOAZ0.
45. Qtd. in Nesteroff, 197.

46. Jennifer Boylan, "He Played Kennedy. Then he Became Himself," *New York Times*, 21 November 2017. www.nytimes.com/2017/11/21/opinion/vaughn-meader-kennedy.html.
47. Qtd. in Nesteroff, 197.
48. Qtd. in Jeff Jacoby, "When the Joke was on JFK," *Boston Globe*, 20 November 2013. www.bostonglobe.com/opinion/2013/11/20/when-joke-was-jfk-was-gentle-even-affectionate/5qocrzr9B6g3ot9DmzgecM/story.html.
49. Nicholas J. Cull, "No Laughing Matter: Vaughn Meader, the Kennedy Administration, and Presidential Impersonations on Radio," *Historical Journal of Film, Radio and Television* 17, no. 3 (1997), 384–385.
50. Qtd. in Mo Rocca, *Mobituaries: Great Lives Worth Reliving* (New York: Simon & Schuster, 2019), 255.
51. Merriman Smith, "Spoofing Kennedys on Air Causes Stir," *Los Angeles Times*, 2 December 1962, 13.
52. "Random Notes from All Over: 'This IS the Attorney General,'" *New York Times*, 24 June 1963, 14.
53. Robinson, 135.
54. Leo Braudy, *The Frenzy of Renown* (New York: Random House, 1986), 568.
55. "Clip from President John F. Kennedy's 46th News Conference – December 12, 1962," *YouTube*, 11 December 2012. www.youtube.com/watch?v=oC8ViHIuwuM.
56. "Vaughn Meader, Satirist of Kennedy Family, Dies," *Washington Post*, 1 November 2004. www.washingtonpost.com/wp-dyn/articles/A14717-2004Oct31.html.
57. Thomas Lask, "Now They Kid the Politicos," *New York Times*, 2 April 1967, 122.
58. "Liner Notes," *The First Family*, 1962.
59. Qtd. in Carvell.
60. Qtd. in Carvell.
61. Alexander Woo, "Dead Comedian of the Week: Vaughn Meader, Assassination Victim," *Deadspin*, 11 August 2011. https://deadspin.com/5829643/dead-comedian-of-the-week-vaughn-meader-assassins-victim.
62. Qtd. in Wasson, 93.
63. Qtd. in Wasson, 93.

CHAPTER 3

LBJ and Nixon

Lyndon Baines Johnson and Richard Nixon had two of the most tumultuous presidencies in U.S. history. Coming on the heels of the JFK assassination, amid the civil rights movement, and consumed by the Vietnam War, Johnson and Nixon oversaw a deeply divided nation that was beginning to lose trust in its government – mostly *because* of Johnson and Nixon. Satire, as well, was in a strange place in 1964. When JFK was in office, our Cold War enemies were apparent and the satiric targets were obvious, but suddenly nothing was clear. The whirlwind after JFK's assassination just created more confusion. The Second City's Sheldon Patinkin summed up the country's comedic mood when he said, "people wanted to laugh, but I don't think anyone knew what to laugh at, or if they could."[1]

As LBJ took the oath of office, America was entering an unprecedented period of change and social upheaval. LBJ was an outsider in the Kennedy White House and relatively unknown to the nation when he assumed the presidency. His time in office was an enigma, at times loved and hated by virtually everyone on both sides of the aisle; he was the perfect metaphor for a country in the middle of an uncertain time. His personal behavior was crude, rude, and obnoxious, yet he was one of the most skilled politicians to ever hold the office. He was the architect of the Great Society and much of the contemporary social safety net, like Social Security and Medicare. Yet he is also inextricably tied to the escalation of the war in Vietnam. He forged ahead and passed the 1964 Civil Rights Act and 1965 Voting Rights Act when no one thought it possible, but the most lasting image of him is protesters chanting, "Hey, Hey, LBJ, how many kids did you kill today?" He was liberal to some and conservative to others – seemingly able to let down anyone and everyone. LBJ's paradoxes funneled into satire, where most of the humor focused on Vietnam and the Johnson administration rather than on the president himself. When LBJ left office an even more polarizing figure took his place: the one and only Richard Milhous Nixon. If LBJ was able to sidestep personal satiric attacks, Nixon was perhaps the all-time favorite target for satirists. From his famous appearance on *Rowan & Martin's Laugh-In* to his resignation from the presidency, few presidents can claim a more turbulent time in office than Nixon.

In the space of a few years, the country, and satire, had changed dramatically. Gone were the lighthearted jabs lovingly tossed at Kennedy (and the great optimism he represented), replaced by razor-sharp barbs meant to inflict damage, which in the wake of Watergate, gave way to ironic detachment. In a few short years, Americans went from being unsure if a comic could make fun of the president to searing humor aimed at wounding the presidency. Humor about Kennedy, exemplified by The First Family and its cultural craze, sought to bring Americans closer to the presidency. Meader's and other comic impressions and The Second City's "press conferences" worked in many ways to enhance the prestige and power of the office – Kennedy was not only the subject of the humor, but he was often the star. Comics and audiences alike thought they were laughing *with* the Kennedys. After Kennedy's assassination and with the escalation in Vietnam and the growing "credibility gap," humor under LBJ and Nixon began to subvert the presidency. Satirists worked to belittle the men occupying the office. Satirists no longer playfully poked fun at the president. Instead, their satire pointed out hypocrisies and what they felt were often misleading and harmful policies. Satirists were no longer helping to build up the public persona of the president. Instead, they were pulling presidents down precisely because they felt the actions of the men in the Oval Office were pulling down the presidency. They were enhancing the power of both the comedians mocking them, and more importantly, the audience laughing *at* the president. It also marks the beginnings of satire's shift to pointing out the absurd in the real. According to playwright and director George Abbot, LBJ was himself absurd: "Humor is exaggeration and President Johnson is his own exaggeration."[2]

There was another stark difference between Kennedy and Johnson/Nixon: their use of mediatized humor. John Kennedy was a master of media, often using humor to deflect potential pitfalls or enhance his image. Some even credit Kennedy's media mastery for his win over Nixon. Kennedy had a quick wit and seemed to delight in holding press conferences and other media engagements. Whether he found "annoyment or enjoyment" in the satire directed at him didn't matter – he exploited the opportunities they presented. Johnson's humor was more akin to your uncle, who tells tired puns and dirty jokes at Thanksgiving. Nixon probably did not tell a single joke in his entire life. Johnson was undoubtedly the superior politician to Kennedy – nobody could get a bill through Congress like Johnson. Yet he never seemed to connect politics to culture or use humor as a political weapon the way Kennedy could. LBJ never fully grasped that the presidency was a different animal than the Senate and didn't understand that humor from the Oval Office was a legislative tool. As Peter Robinson writes,

> Whereas Kennedy worked news conferences like an entertainer in the midst of cold war tensions, Franklin Roosevelt confronted deep adversity by displaying a buoyant jocularity to journalists and the public, and Abraham Lincoln countered criticism with an instinctive and self-effacing use of humor during the Civil War, Johnson could bring no such talent to bear to help alleviate the horrific crisis caused by the war in Vietnam.[3]

Johnson also wasn't great at taking a joke, often responding vindictively rather than with a smile. Nixon would make Johnson look like a great sport, keeping a long and detailed "enemies list" filled with satirists who made fun of him.

The Committee

By the mid-1960s, the most overt political sketch comedy wasn't happening at Second City or with the Premise: it was happening in San Francisco at The Committee. Alan Myerson was growing tired of Second City. He felt the company was catering to corporate interests and going too easy on the Kennedy administration. Myerson had been hired by Second City in 1961 to direct the new wave of performers, but found the material lacking because there was "no real solid political stance in the theatrical culture there."[4] Second City was likewise growing weary of Myerson, who reportedly picketed the theatre during the Cuban Missile Crisis. Myerson and Latifah Taormina, his wife, picked up and moved west to San Francisco, home of Mort Sahl and the growing counterculture movement. The Committee, named after the House Un-American Activities Committee, set to work, with Myerson hiring former Compass, Second City, and Premise actors. Funded by a wide array of San Francisco elites and Berkeley professors, The Committee performed for an audience made up of "hangers out, college kids, old beatniks and liberal dentists."[5] Their performance aesthetic was a mix of Second City and the Premise. They did both sketches and improvised work (including pioneering work on what would become the long-form improv structure the Harold), but with a notably more political bite, and eventually, a robust drug-use through-line. Myerson specifically came to San Francisco to be more political than the "people" scenes of Second City; The Committee's "main mission was to afflict the comfortable."[6] He wanted to do sketches like "Sportscasters," which featured two broadcasters doing a play-by-play call of a battle in the Mekong Delta.[7] By 1964, The Committee was on Broadway in New York and a sensation in San Francisco. According to Kercher, "What won the admiration of student radicals and exurbanites alike were the Committee's satiric commentaries on the absurdity of the cold war, racism, and the hypocrisy of white, middle-class liberals."[8] The sketch "Failure 101" drew laughs and ire from the left, and was precisely the kind of satire Myerson wanted to be doing at Second City. In the sketch, a student taking an oral examination cites Adlai Stevenson as the perfect example of failure, calling him a "true Renaissance Man of failure," failing in a wide array of pursuits.[9] "The Party" satirized enlightened liberals who like to tell black people at parties that they, too, like Ella Fitzgerald (before ignoring them for the rest of the night) as a way to make themselves feel like true racial heroes. The Committee likewise pushed sexual freedom; in "Summer Vacation" two young women home from college discuss their first year away from home, including their sexual experiences. The Committee also became a leading satiric voice against the Vietnam War, protesting the war on stage and in the streets, one of the earliest examples of satiric advocacy.

"Hey, Hey, LBJ" – Mr. President-of-All-the-People

There was plenty of political and social satire in the late 1960s, but even at The Committee there was not a lot of satire directly involving LBJ in the form of impersonations. Comics in every genre took on the Johnson administration, usually focusing on Vietnam. Comedy albums were trying to capture the success of *The*

First Family – LBJ Menagerie, LBJ in the Catskills, Here Comes the Bird, and *Meet the Great Society* – but none of the impressions stuck to LBJ. Second City and other sketch comedy often portrayed the wheeling-and-dealing-Texan version of Johnson. One Second City sketch in 1964 sums up the persona in the following exchange:

LBJ: Goldwater's charges about my conflicts of interest are getting embarrassing.
Aide: What do you plan to do, sir?
LBJ: Well, first I'll put the White House in Lady Bird's name.[10]

Much of the humor about LBJ focused on his Texan visage. He was personally such a change from JFK that there was a lot of satire contrasting the two, from Camelot to Texas, with Johnson's wheeling-and-dealing front and center. Still, little of the satire during his time in office was aimed at his personality, nearly all of it focused on his administration's policies.

On television, *TW3* took the first mass media shots at Johnson, satirizing his president-for-everyone approach. David Frost said of LBJ's 1964 campaign: "President Johnson has remolded the Democratic Party into the fresh, invigorated, cautious, conservative, liberal, radical force it is today."[11] Similarly, the January 10, 1964, American premiere opened with *TW3*'s signature song satirizing the week's events with Audrey Meadows singing, "Everybody likes LBJ . . . General Motors, General Taylor, Norman Thomas, Norman Mailer. . . . People for segregation . . . people for miscegenation like Lyndon."[12] Another sketch poked fun at the high rhetoric of Johnson and his down-in-the-mud political operation, marrying the criticism of his "for-everyone" rhetoric and his wheeling-and-dealing persona:

LBJ: I see a land where love reigns. I see great farms and giant cities. I see men at work, children at play, women at peace.
Voters: O, what else do you see, Mr. President-of-all-the-People?
LBJ: I see an end of divisions and controversies. I see small men growing large and closed minds opening wide.
Voters: O, is there nothing more that you see, Mr. President-of-all-the-People?
LBJ: I see a mandate for happiness. I see the determined faces of millions – fat and skinny, tall and short, bold and shy – crying as one, "Onward to the Great Society!"
Voters: And how will all these things come about, Mr. President-of-all-the-People?
LBJ: I shall wheel and deal.[13]

Johnson's political life was an embodiment of "The Great American Joke." His vision for a Great Society was idyllic, but his methods were reminiscent of political strong-arming. This juxtaposition became a source of contrast between Kennedy and Johnson. JFK's rhetoric was grandiloquent and he politically remained above the fray, whereas LBJ seemed to love the fight. In May of 1964, LBJ ordered the lights at the White House to be turned out at night as a display of the nation economizing. *TW3* countered with "Pennies for the President," which equated the dimming of the lights with the dimming of presidential intellect from Kennedy to Johnson.

While there was satire directly aimed at LBJ, such as "Pennies for the President," most of it revolved around LBJ's policies, paradoxes, and of course, Vietnam. A February 1964 sketch satirized LBJ's Cold War foreign policy. In the sketch, a State Department employee agrees that U.S. foreign policy is "fraught with contradictions and hypocrisy.... We sell wheat [to the Soviet Union] so we can build more missiles." When asked what happens when the Soviets can't pay for the wheat, he replies, "Then, of course, we'll know they can't be trusted and it will prove we were right in selling them the wheat [and building the missiles]."[14] In a Second City sketch, an American sergeant is teaching a Vietnamese peasant how to use an M1 rifle that has been "kindly" provided by the United States. The peasant begins to use the bayonet to tend the soil, and the sergeant berates the peasant and tells him the bayonet is meant to "stick IN PEOPLE." He demonstrates on a Vietcong dummy, which enrages the peasant, who stabs the sergeant before returning to his chores.[15] The Vietnam satire and cultural criticism would quickly sharpen. Barbara Garson's satiric play *MacBird!* (1967) put Johnson into the plot of *Macbeth*, humorously speculating that he plotted Kennedy's assassination to gain power, egged on by the duplicitous Lady MacBird.[16] Originally a short sketch, Garson expanded the sketch into a full-length play that was a controversial sensation. Garson laughed off the suggestion that she was seriously implying Johnson engineered Kennedy's murder, saying, "I never took that seriously. I used to say to people, if he did, it's the least of his crimes.... It was not what the play was about. The plot was a given."[17] The play's cynical view of liberal politics and Johnson himself was a clear reflection of Johnson's reputation by 1967.

As Johnson's administration moved forward and the war in Vietnam escalated, the satire coalesced around the country's growing anti-Vietnam sentiment. Johnson's 1968 State of the Union Address proved to be a tipping point for The Committee. As Johnson simultaneously called for peace and an escalation of the war in Vietnam, while also pledging to defend the United States from the domestic threat of drug use, member Howard Hesseman had to be restrained from breaking the TV he was watching. The Committee's director, Alan Myerson, who heard Hesseman's story, immediately announced that the group would improvise what had happened that night on stage. The group initially resisted, but Myerson threatened to leave the group. Hesseman, Garry Goodrow, and Mimi Farina reenacted watching Johnson's address. Peter Bonerz played Johnson, pantomiming the speech while wearing a cowboy hat as Jim Cranna read portions of Johnson's speech over the loudspeaker. When Hesseman went to turn off the TV, Bonerz's Johnson kept pantomiming, so Cranna kept speaking, eventually repeating the phrase, "You can't turn me off. I'm you. You can't turn me off. I'm you." Hesseman turned to the audience to recount what had happened the night before, underscored by Cranna's mantra. Hesseman called to the audience: "It's fun to hate." Eventually, the audience joined in, "It's fun to hate." The chanting escalated until Hesseman cried out, "Let's kill this fucker!" The hatred spread through the theatre. Hesseman then stopped the audience, as the LBJ "You can't turn me off. I'm you." slogan continued to repeat. Hesseman then said, "Okay, that didn't work. We can't kill him. Let's see if we can love him to death." The performers and the audience then began trying to love one another – kissing and hugging as the boundary between stage and audience disappeared. Then suddenly – blackout. In the darkness, Farina spoke a single word: "Vietnam."[18] The sketch encapsulated the counterculture's many often-conflicting feelings about Vietnam and LBJ. It also illustrates much of the satire about LBJ – Vietnam overshadowed the president. Johnson is obviously connected, but the major target of the sketch, and many others, was the war and the political system that supported it. LBJ was part of that system, an important part to be sure, but the war was bigger than Johnson. The sketch likewise showcased the very intense feelings of the era's satirists. Members of The Committee were heavily involved in social activism – comedy was only one of their outlets.

The Smothers Brothers

One show that regularly took on LBJ (and featured several Committee members on its writing staff) was *The Smothers Brothers Comedy Hour*. The Brothers are most well-known today for their epic censorship battles, which often involved their critiques of the Johnson administration. Most of the show's satire and its countercultural appeal was tied up with music – both the Brothers' folk songs and those of their guests. Johnson and CBS were upset with the Brothers' treatment of the Vietnam War, especially upset at calling the war a folly. After one 1967 sketch ribbed the president and his top-secret barbeque sauce, Johnson called CBS Chairman William Paley in the middle of the night to complain. Paley reportedly asked the Brothers to ease up, and in return, he'd allow the Brothers to have Pete Seeger on the show. Seeger, a folk singer, had been blacklisted and hadn't appeared on television in 17 years. Seeger appeared the following week on September 10, 1967, to sing "Waist Deep in the Big Muddy," a thinly veiled attack on Johnson and the Vietnam War. CBS refused to air the song because Seeger refused to cut the final verse of the song, which said, "Waist deep in the Big Muddy, and the big fool says to push on." Tom complained to both CBS and the press, and a year later Seeger appeared again and was allowed to sing the entire song. Predictably, CBS was inundated with complaints.

The Smothers Brothers summed up the attitude of many toward Johnson's presidency in a cold open in its second season. Dick commented on Johnson recently asking people to refrain from traveling overseas and spending money abroad and asks his brother what LBJ should do to make people want to stay in the United States, to which Tom replies, "Well, he could quit."[19] And then he did, though not because of the Smothers Brothers. The relationship between Johnson and the Brothers dramatically shifted when Johnson announced on March 31, 1968, that he would not be running for re-election. Tom reportedly wrote a letter to Johnson, not necessarily an apology for the way the show treated LBJ, but to say that he respected Johnson even though they disagreed on various matters. Johnson wrote back to the Brothers, who would read the letter on what would be the last episode of their show:

> To be genuinely funny at a time when the world is in crisis is a task that would tax the talents of a genius; to be consistently fair when standards of fair play are constantly questioned demands the wisdom of a saint. It is part of the price of leadership of this great and free nation to be the target of clever satirists. You have given the gift of laughter to our people. May we never grow so somber or self-important that we fail to appreciate the humor in our lives.[20]

LBJ's letter, written only days after Nixon was elected, is a testament to the role of satire in American life. Here we have the President of the United States, who has been ridiculed by satirists across the country for years, defending the right of satirists to criticize him by invoking the central tenets of American identity – free speech and expression. It is almost like an affirmation of *The First Family*'s liner notes, a response from the president. He further articulates that right by stating that part of the president's job is to allow satirists to target the office. The letter not only defended the central role of satire within the state, but it also became a weapon used against future presidents who criticized satirists. There is some irony, of course, because while in office LBJ worked behind the scenes to censor the Brothers, but his public statement became a de facto endorsement from the office. When Trump began to criticize *SNL* for criticizing him, it appeared, thanks in part to LBJ's letter, that Trump was going against the foundational principles of the office. In fact, LBJ's letter became a widely circulated meme in 2017 to push back against Trump's attacks on the show.

With Johnson out of the race, the show ran its own candidate in 1968. Cast member Pat Paulsen announced his tongue-in-cheek candidacy for president on the show, running under the Straight Talking American Government Party (STAG). Paulsen rose to popularity on the show through his fake editorials, including one in support of network censorship. His mock campaign biography eerily mirrors Trump's presidential campaign strategy, saying that Paulsen ran his campaign "using outright lies, double talk and unfounded attacks on his challengers. Who thought that this style would be the method of campaigns in the future?"[21] In one sketch on *Comedy Hour*, Paulsen's face was presented in a split-screen so that the left and right sides of his face were moving and speaking differently. Delivering his answers in his characteristic deadpan, the satirical point of political doublespeak was obvious. Though his candidacy was a joke, he talked about current issues and sought to point out flaws within the system. When asked about the draft, he said, "A good many people feel that our present draft laws are unjust. These people are called soldiers."[22] He attacked his opponents, Richard Nixon, Hubert Humphrey, and George Wallace in campaign speeches, and responded to criticism with his trademark, "Picky, picky, picky." Robert Kennedy played along with the joke, doing an interview with Tom Smothers and speaking with Paulsen himself in which he admitted Paulsen's "candidacy makes me very nervous," though I "think he's peaked too early."[23]

Even with Johnson no longer pressuring CBS executives, the heat stayed on the Brothers – Nixon would only intensify it after he took office in 1969. At first, CBS executives would cut out objectionable words or phrases from sketches on the master tape. Eventually, they began cutting entire segments. The edits angered the Brothers, especially because Tom had contractual control over the scripts. Other artists often came to the Brothers' defense. In 1968, George Harrison appeared on the show to offer his support:

Tommy: (To George.) You have something important?
George: Something very important to say on American television.
Tommy: You know, a lot of times we don't have an opportunity to say anything important BECAUSE it's American television. (Laughter.) Every time you try to say something important they uhh . . . (makes gesture of pushing a censor button).
Dick: (Makes gesture of cutting across his throat.)
George: Well, whether you can say it or not, keep TRYING to say it![24]

The Brothers were representing the long strain of American satirists who had to fight censorship, and their battles were more public than many of the earlier similar censorship battles of other comedians.

While the Brothers continued to push the envelope, CBS executives tightened the clamps. CBS began demanding that the Brothers deliver final tapes ten days before air so that they could be edited. CBS affiliates likewise began cutting content at their discretion. At the beginning of their third and final season, the Brothers wanted to open with Harry Belafonte singing "Don't Stop the Carnival" against a video of violence during the 1968 Democratic National Convention. CBS cut the entire segment. To shake salt in the wound, CBS replaced it "with a five-minute campaign ad from Republican presidential nominee Richard M. Nixon."[25] David Steinberg's sermons were also routinely censored, including speeches playing on the trend of late-night television sermonettes. Steinberg regularly performed improvised sermons while he was with Second City, and the Brothers wanted him to do them for their show as well. His first encounter with the censors was during the October 27, 1968, episode, and centered on a sermon about Moses and the burning bush:

Steinberg: Moses was wandering in the wilderness, when he saw a bush that was burning, yet it would not consume itself. A voice came out of the heavens. "Moses, take off your shoes from off of your feet," God said in His redundant way. "For the land that you are standing upon is holy land." Well, Moses took his shoes off, approached the burning bush, and burnt his feet. God went, "Aha! Third one today!"

The above aired, but there was a second part to the joke that was cut by CBS:

Steinberg: We're not sure what he said, but there are many New Testament scholars who, to this day, believe it was the first mention of Christ in the Bible.[26]

By cutting a reference to Moses taking the Lord's name in vain, CBS echoed the censorship of Lenny Bruce, who likewise took on the church and found himself in hot water. The censorship also fundamentally alters the joke by changing the punchline and literally removing the social satire about religion in contemporary America. For the Smothers Brothers, it was this type of censorship that was unacceptable.

The March 9, 1969, show proved to be a pivotal point in the censorship battle. CBS showed a rerun rather than the new episode, claiming that the latest episode did not arrive in time for review. In that episode, Joan Baez delivered a monologue about her then-husband David Harris, who was headed to jail after refusing military service. The episode eventually did air three weeks later, with Baez's monologue edited so that she stated that her husband was in prison, but the reason he was there was cut. Tom Smothers was furious and began putting obscenities in scripts to spite the network. Tensions were high, but CBS renewed the show for the 1969–1970 season. With Nixon now in the White House and pushing for greater governmental control over broadcasting, the writing was on the wall. As Bianculli argues, "Undeniably, CBS wanted Tom and Dick Smothers off the air because of the ideas they were espousing on their show, but eventually removed them by claiming the Brothers had violated the terms of their contract by not delivering a copy of that week's show in time."[27] The cancellation led to the Smothers Brothers filing a breach of contract lawsuit – *Tom Smothers et al. v. Columbia Broadcasting System, Inc.* The courts ruled in favor of the Smothers Brothers, but they would never get back their show or reach the same type of platform again. The Smothers Brothers were another in a long line of sketch comedians to face pressure, and ultimately censorship, for their political comedy. While they eventually won their lawsuit, their platform was gone. Yet their spirit and their court victory can be seen in the outspoken comic voices that followed. Along with Lenny Bruce, George Carlin, and Richard Pryor, no comedian did more to champion free speech on stage than the Smothers Brothers. Their influence is felt every time a comedian takes a swipe at a politician.

With Johnson's not running for reelection, the 1968 election became even more volatile, all of which came to a head at the 1968 Democratic Convention in Chicago. Against a backdrop of civil unrest and a few blocks from the epicenter of the historic riots, The Second City mounted their latest revue, *A Plague on Both Your Houses*. Myerson was hardly alone in criticizing The Second City, with many feeling that the theatre had lost its edge. *A Plague on Both Your Houses* would prove to be anything but safe. The revue's opening sketch featured a Chicago cop beating a young man he believes is a demonstrator. When the man says, "Wait, I'm a reporter!" the officer stops beating the man, takes out a gun, and shoots him. The title song for the revue likewise played on the charged climate of the city. J.J. Barry remembers the audience getting up, "tears in their eyes, and the arms went up in peace symbols. It was like a revival, man!"[28] The show revitalized Second City's political reputation, but despite Barry's memory, it polarized its audience. Ira Miller, who often played LBJ at Second City, remarked on the show's staunch anti-Vietnam stance. While the show took a firm stand, it wasn't necessarily great sketch comedy. Patinkin said *A Plague on*

Both Your Houses "was too angry. It wasn't funny enough."[29] Patinkin's theory that satire can't be too angry helps illustrate the historical shift of satire. At the time, audiences were growing weary of anger-based satire, such as the sketches at The Committee. Yet, in contemporary sketch comedy, anger-based satire is a requirement of satiric authenticity. Audiences in Trump's America *demand* the satirist be angry as proof of their satiric authenticity – you can't just mock Trump, you need to despise him. Laughter in many ways acts as a release of anger for those disaffected by Trump's presidency. How long it will last remains to be seen.

At the time in 1968, though, Patinkin was right – the show was too angry, and audiences agreed as the show didn't do well financially. Second City brought in a new cast, who called their next show *The Next Generation*. Harold Ramis was a part of the new cast, who eschewed Second City's traditional business attire for bell-bottoms and long hair. They weren't exactly popular either, with some reviewers calling for a return of the old guard. Still, they represented the new wave of satire taking hold – firmly rooted in counter culture, drugs, and a sense of disillusionment. As an example of the changing tide, in 1969 Abbie Hoffman was on trial for conspiracy and intent to riot during the 1968 Democratic Convention. Being Abbie Hoffman, he spent his days in court. Then at night, he regularly showed up at Second City, jumping onstage to play in a sketch about his trial, playing the judge, and finding The Second City players guilty every night. It was a weird time.[30]

Richard Nixon

Richard Nixon, like LBJ, wasn't particularly adept as a comedian, but he did understand comedy's power better than LBJ – his appearance on *Laugh-In* proves as much. That's not to say Nixon had a rosy relationship with comedy. He was targeted in just about every medium in just about every way. And he hated it. Nixon's thin skin made Johnson look like he didn't have a care in the world. Not only did Nixon abhor satirists mocking him, he held firm to the idea that the presidency was above mockery. *Tonight Show* host Jack Parr wrote about listening to *The First Family* with Nixon: "Most of us laughed, and here is what may surprise you: Mr. Nixon walked over and lifted the playback head off the recording and said, 'That man is the President of our country. Neither he nor his family should be the butt of such jokes.'"[31] Nixon's comments reflect one of the major criticisms historically lobbed at satirists – they are damaging the institutions they claim to be protecting. Obviously, Nixon is perhaps not the greatest spokesperson for protecting the integrity of the office of president, but it is important to note that he not only despised jokes aimed at him, but he saw the entire enterprise of satire as inherently bad for the country. Satirists, on the other hand, thought Nixon was inherently bad for the country. Nixon satire went well beyond a gentle comedy album, and like Bill Clinton, Nixon would remain the target of satirists long after he left the White House. He had been a target of satirists long before he made it to the White House. In fact, from 1952 to 1972, Richard Nixon appeared as a candidate for the executive branch (president or vice-president) five times, all but 1964, so he was an ever-present figure for nearly two decades *before* he became president. Herblock, the famed political cartoonist who won a Pulitzer Prize for his Watergate cartoons, had been caricaturing Nixon since 1948.

After losing in 1960 to Kennedy and then losing the 1962 race for California governor, many thought Nixon's political career was over – including Nixon himself, who bitterly said to the media, "You won't have Richard Nixon to kick around anymore." But Nixon was tenacious and mounted one of the greatest political comebacks of all time, emerging victorious from the hotly contested 1968 election. The country was deeply divided, Vietnam was on everyone's mind, and the country had experienced a shocking string of assassinations. Nixon himself was a highly polarizing figure, often exacerbating divisions. He had been on the national stage for nearly two decades, first serving as Eisenhower's vice president. His campaign revolved around racially coded policies like "law and order" and "states' rights." With Alabama segregationist George Wallace running as a third-party candidate, Nixon knew he couldn't win the Deep South. Instead, he executed a coded campaign aimed at the "silent majority" – conservative white voters, who, after the 1964 Civil Rights Act and 1965 Voting Rights Act, were no longer solidly Democratic. He provided a more restrained option than Wallace for people who weren't happy about the social movements of the 1960s. These folks who did not protest the Vietnam War or civil rights, and who generally remained quiet in public about their politics, propelled Nixon to victory. The strategy worked, but it further divided the country.

In terms of his presidency, most people remember Nixon as the only president to ever resign from office. But Nixon had several notable achievements as president. One of the great ironies of Watergate is that Nixon won the 1972 election in a landslide – he didn't need to break into Democratic headquarters to steal information. As part of his 1968 campaign, Nixon promised "peace with honor" in regards to Vietnam, announcing a secret plan to withdraw U.S. forces known as Vietnamization. The strategy took a long time to unfold and did not work out as Nixon planned, but he did sign a peace agreement with North Vietnam in January of 1973. He was more successful in other areas of foreign policy, notably with his 1972 trips to the Soviet Union and China, working to open diplomatic channels with the two powerful communist nations. His summit with Soviet leader Leonid Brezhnev led to a treaty to limit the production of nuclear weapons. On the home front, Nixon established the Environmental Protection Agency, ended the draft, and was in office when Neil Armstrong stepped on the moon. But most people remember Watergate. The 1972 break-in at the offices of the Democratic National Committee was eventually tied to Nixon. The president had installed tape recorders in the Oval Office so that he could have a record of his time in office. Despite initially protesting innocence and ignorance, the tapes proved that Nixon had not only known about the break-in but had been working behind the scenes to obstruct the investigation. On August 8, 1974, in a nationally televised address, Nixon announced he would resign the presidency effective the next day.

Laugh-In – Five Seconds That Changed the World

Rightly or wrongly, many attribute Nixon's narrow loss to Kennedy to his visual appearance during the 1960 televised debate. Whereas Kennedy seemed cool and collected, Nixon was sweaty, pale, and uncomfortable. Nixon had many faults, but being stupid wasn't one of them. Nixon quickly learned the power of media; he made a 1963 *Tonight Show* appearance and wowed the audience by playing an original composition on the piano – he even made a joke. In 1968, he used a television appearance to help catapult him to the presidency. The relationship between the presidency and mass media was still evolving, especially when it came to television. For many, "the august institution of the presidency was seen as too dignified to be subjected to anything more than the most mild and bipartisan ribbing, especially on that low-brow medium known as television."[32] *Laugh-In* was a countercultural institution. With its hippie design aesthetic and rapid-fire jokes, it was everything Nixon was not – young and hip. The show was not as overtly political as *The Smothers Brothers*, though Tommy Smothers made an appearance to say, "Let's all get behind President Johnson and push."[33] The political nature of the show was simply in its aesthetic. They didn't need to make political jokes – the culture clash was on full display in the "Summer of Love" joke wall. At the same time, it was also inherently conservative. Rowan and Martin were old Vegas performers; they weren't interested in cutting political satire. The duo found themselves on the Watergate tapes, but instead of something scandalous, it was a phone call in 1973 where Nixon thanks the duo for a bit they did for Nixon's 60th birthday. The show's creative team was also politically spread across the spectrum. Whereas liberal satirists make most contemporary satiric shows, *Laugh-In* had numerous Nixon supporters on staff.

One such Nixon supporter was writer Paul Keyes, who convinced Nixon to make a cameo on the show. It was the standard operating procedure for *Laugh-In* to feature celebrity cameos dropping in for a quick one-liner. Keyes suggested Nixon could say another of the show's catchphrases, "You bet your sweet bippy," but Nixon was having none of it, reportedly telling advisers, "he didn't know what 'bippy' meant, and didn't want to find out."[34] Nixon instead agreed to say, "Sock it to me." According to producer George Schlatter, the taping was anything but easy:

> Nixon defined square. He was the original cube, but he'd do anything Paul said because he adored him. So, he says, "Sock it to me?" I say, "If you could just kind of smile and say it." He says, "OK, comedy is new to me." Six takes later, I took the tape underneath my arm, ran back to NBC like a bullet, and put it in the next show. . . . Sometimes people say I helped get Nixon elected. I've had to live with that.[35]

Nixon's September 16, 1968, appearance wasn't the ultimate tipping point in the 1968 election, but it did work to soften Nixon's image and appeal to younger voters. The five-second clip is notably awkward, and Nixon is not a natural comedian, but it put him on the highest-rated television show in 1968 less than two months before the election. Contrasted with his sweaty and angry 1960 television appearance, being composed and not embarrassing himself was a huge win. Nixon also aired a campaign commercial during the episode, showing that he'd learned a lot about the medium since 1960.

The appearance is all the more shocking when you take into account Nixon's inherent distrust of the media, which he blamed for his 1960 defeat. Nixon hadn't appeared on *Meet the Press* or *Face the Nation* in years, and his advisers strongly advised against his *Laugh-In* appearance due to its apparent liberal bent. Many, including Nixon, were also worried that his lack of comic timing would make him the butt of the joke. Yet there he was on a comedy show just weeks before the election. His team took steps to make sure he would not be the butt of the joke, appearing in a suit in front of a plain brown backdrop instead of *Laugh-In*'s colorful set. There would be no water thrown in his face, no trap door, or any of the other shenanigans that usually went with saying, "Sock it to me." Nixon was not going to let a TV appearance cost him another election – he completely controlled the presentation and his image. While Nixon gambled on a sketch comedy appearance, his challengers refused to appear. Hubert Humphrey's campaign manager thought appearing on the show would make Humphrey look beneath the office. Nixon's appearance was the first time a presidential candidate had appeared on a sketch comedy show, and it would lead to the FCC implementing an equal time rule for candidates appearing on television. We take our politicians appearing on comedy shows as a requirement for running for office, but at the time it was a considerable political risk for Nixon – one that paid off handsomely.

David Frye and the Nixon Impression

By the time Nixon assumed the presidency, the country was no longer afraid to mock the president. The years between *The First Family* and Nixon's election saw massive cultural and social upheaval. Comedians being kind to the president was no longer a requirement – ask LBJ. Nixon was attacked by comedians of all stripes – including long after his death. The longest-lasting of these was the Nixon impression. To this day, comedians still impersonate Richard Nixon. The Nixon voice – "I am not a crook!" – is still an iconic part of American culture. David Frye was the leading Nixon impressionist to emerge in the 1960s and 1970s. The man who would become famous for impersonating Nixon cut his presidential teeth on LBJ (and did impersonations of many cultural and political figures of the time, including Bobby Kennedy, Hubert Humphrey,[36] William F. Buckley, Jr., and Jack Nicholson). Frye, a short man who bore little resemblance to the tall and imposing Johnson, nevertheless channeled Johnson's tough Texan persona. Usually wearing a pair of wire glasses, he'd

> squint, raise his eyebrows as high as they'd go, tuck in his chin, and contort his mouth into a reptilian grin. In so doing, he looked uncannily like an unflattering caricature of Johnson. . . . Frye's LBJ revealed himself as a fearsome predator as he drawled out lines like, "Believe me, I tried to be a good king."[37]

Frye's LBJ was tame compared to his ruthless depiction of Nixon.

Frye would come to be closely associated with Nixon, and much like Vaughn Meader, most contemporary Nixon impersonations are actually impersonations of Frye. While Frye's physical appearance was all wrong for LBJ, his droopy, sad, and somewhat desperate mannerisms were a perfect match for Nixon's persona. Like most good impressions, Frye's Nixon was about an attitude rather than impeccable mimicry. In an interview with *Esquire* in 1971, Frye said,

> I do Nixon not by copying his real actions but by feeling his attitude, which is that he cannot believe that he really is president.... He's trying to convince himself when he says, "I am the president!" And then moving eyes and tongue merely to symbolize the way his mind is working.[38]

Frye made numerous television appearances with his Nixon impression, and released a series of comedy albums centered on Nixon, including *I Am the President* (1969), *Richard Nixon Superstar* (1971), and *Richard Nixon: A Fantasy* (1973).[39] What marked Frye's Nixon as unique – and in stark contrast to Meader's Kennedy – was the nastiness at the heart of the impression. While Meader's Kennedy was imbued with love, Frye's Nixon was mean. William Wan described *Richard Nixon: A Fantasy* akin to witnessing "in real time a brutal and total evisceration of the Oval Office in the court of public opinion."[40] Frye's Nixon was the polar opposite of Meader's Kennedy, as evidenced by Frye's paranoid and insecure Nixon stating, "The only way I'm going to leave the White House is to be dragged screaming and kicking ... because my fellow Americans, I love America, and you always hurt the one you really love."[41] According to Mark Deming, "Frye wasn't afraid to twist the knife when doing material on the president.... *I Am the President* is a sharper and more aggressive piece of political satire than what most mainstream comics were willing to serve up at the time."[42] Yet, both men were satirizing the president in a way they felt helped the country. Meader built JFK up to help promote his vision and win the Cold War, while Frye tore Nixon down because Frye saw Nixon as the country's most pressing threat. In both instances, we see a clear illustration of how satire reflects the American identity projected from the White House.

Not surprisingly, Nixon was not a fan of Nixon impersonations. As noted, he kept a detailed enemies list, which included numerous comedians. He also wasn't very adept at recognizing a joke. Rich Little, another famous Nixon impressionist from the 1970s, spoke about doing his Nixon impression in front of Nixon:

> The first time I did Richard Nixon in front of him he didn't know who I was doing, which was kind of embarrassing. I did Nixon at a garden party in San Clemente back in the 60s and everybody gathered around and I was doing my Nixon right in front of him and he turned to his wife Pat and said, "Why is this young man speaking in this strange voice?" ... He had zero sense of humor.[43]

Nixon impressions may be the longest-lasting form of satire aimed at the president, but it was hardly the only type.

Watergate

A turning point for the country as well as political satire, Watergate unleashed a wave of comedy. Nixon–Watergate comedy was nearly inescapable. *Time* said in June 1973, "Though the Watergate revelations grow grimmer each week, nightclub audiences these days must be getting the impression that the debacle is the world's funniest subject. Comics across the country are milking Watergate for every plausible or implausible laugh that it is worth."[44] Dozens of comedy albums were released, editorial cartoons were filled with Watergate jokes, and stand-ups – including Johnny Carson on *The Tonight Show* – cracked jokes about the scandal. The jokes were everywhere, but they didn't always play well. While some comics and audiences couldn't get enough, others actively avoided Watergate material. A Watergate fatigue settled on the country, and some comics and audiences didn't want to address the scandal that was ever-present in American life. Furthermore, Watergate comedy marked the beginning of a slow transition in political sketch comedy where instead of finding the absurd in the real, comics began presenting the real as absurd. Watergate was so audacious (and in its own way farcical) it hardly needed comedic amplifying. Anthony Holland commented on the new climate, saying,

> I was glad I left Second City during the Kennedy administration. When Kennedy was assassinated, I could no longer have done political satire. But then, political satire no longer has the kind of meaning it once held for me. You hardly need Second City to interpret Watergate. The news is so grotesque you don't need to interpret it satirically. Just pick up the paper and read it.[45]

A September 8, 1973, *New York Times* article "Watergate Comics Find the Joke is on Them," likewise found that many comics were either sick of Watergate or steered clear of it in their acts because audiences were tired of Watergate. While some comics found Watergate off-putting, many more found it to be a necessity to address. For example, Frye's *Richard Nixon: A Fantasy* featured Nixon addressing the nation:

> Today I have regretfully been forced to accept the resignation of 1,541 of the finest public servants it has ever been my privilege to know. As the man in charge, I must accept full responsibility, but not the blame. Let me explain the difference. People who are to blame lose their jobs: people who are responsible do not.[46]

For Frye, Nixon staying in office was unacceptable and Watergate was the ultimate proof.

In terms of sketch comedy, National Lampoon and the Second City exemplified the split approach to Watergate. Originally released as a single in 1973 and expanded into a full comedy album in 1974 on Blue Thumb Records, National Lampoon's *The Missing White House Tapes* continued the tradition of political comedy albums. The album's two sides differ significantly, with the first side featuring a compilation of doctored clips of the actual Richard Nixon confessing his guilt in Watergate (the original single featured Nixon confessing to Watergate). The B side featured a series of sketches featuring John Belushi, Chevy Chase, and many others, some of which appeared in *Lemmings* shows, the magazine itself, and previous *Lampoon Radio Hour* broadcasts. The sketches all loosely are connected by the "Impeachment Day Parade" ceremonies, with the coverage anchored by Chevy Chase and Rhonda Coullet. "Pennsylvania Avenue" features Big Dick and Shredder Monster in a *Sesame Street* parody that discusses the difference between nine tapes and seven tapes – a satiric take on the two missing White House tapes. Listeners learn the difference between lying and misspeaking. In "Senate Hearing," a reporter twists the famous question asked of Nixon, saying, "What did the President know and when did he stop knowing it?" The most famous sketch on the album is "Mission Impeachable." A parody of *Mission: Impossible*, the sketch opens with Chevy Chase narrating the traditional MI mission task:

> Good morning, Mr. Hunt. Several high-ranking members of the Democratic Party are attempting to seize control of the government of the United States by legitimate means. They plan to use a free press, open discussion of the issues, and the universal franchise in an all-out effort to win the presidency. Should they succeed, all our efforts to repeal The Bill of Rights, pack the Supreme Court with right-wing morons, intimidate the media, suppress dissent, halt social progress, promote big-business, and crush the Congress will be destroyed. Your mission E, should you choose to accept it, is to stop these men, once and for all, by ensuring that the weakest of them, Senator George McGovern, wins the nomination, and then sabotaging his campaign by any possible means. You will have at your disposal, electronic bugging equipment, burglary tools, wigs, voice alteration devices, a camera disguised as a tobacco pouch, forged documents, a safe house, five-hundred loyal but clumsy humans, and two-million-dollars in one-hundred dollar bills. As always, if any member of your CIA force is caught or killed, the President will disavow any knowledge of your activities. This administration will self-destruct in sixteen months. Good luck, Howie.[47]

Reflective of much Watergate satire, the sketch demonstrates the beginnings of the shift away from absurd amplification. While there are some obvious jokes and opinions, most of the "mission" is simply a description of the 1972 election and its aftermath as told via *Mission: Impossible*. Unlike with later verbatim repetitions with Sarah Palin and Donald Trump, the sketch here does amplify the absurdity. It does not, however, need to invent the absurdity – very little is needed to exaggerate the situation or make it more absurd. Yet, we are not quite to the point of printing a verbatim Trump speech about Black History Month in *McSweeney's*.[48]

After the "Mission Impeachable" sketch, the "Impeachment Day Parade" ends with the anchors wrapping up the proceedings:

Wallace (Chase): Well, that's about it for America's day of shame. The president has been officially impeached, and the eternal microphone has been switched on as the CIA brass band plays Wiretaps. But, Barbara, this is not only an historic

	moment, it's also a personal one. What has impeachment meant to the little people? The ordinary, simple people? You, for example, Barbara.
Barbara (Coullet):	Well, Wallace, I just don't think the American people should in any way be ashamed of this tragic occurrence. Although a bunch of bleeding-heart do-gooders have used constitutional force to do away with our beloved president, this country is still founded on the age-old traditional values of bribery, violence, and assassination. And just because there are a few good apples in the barrel, doesn't mean that the vast majority aren't rotten through and through.
Wallace:	Okay, good thinking, Barbara.[49]

The very last track is of Gerald Ford. Though Chase would come to be associated with Ford through his *Saturday Night Live* impression, he is not the voice of Ford here; John Belushi plays Ford, though it is the same bumbling and incompetent Ford persona.

In Chicago, Second City tackled Watergate in its August 1973 mainstage revue – *Phase 46, or, Watergate Tomorrow, Comedy Tonight*. More accurately, unlike *National Lampoon*, Second City avoided Watergate. Despite the title, the revue was not about Watergate. Directed by Del Close, the decision to exclude Watergate was intentional. In an August 3, 1973, interview with the *Chicago Tribune*, Close said, "We're not doing any Watergate shtick because we're tired of it – and our company is no longer a bunch of angry actors."[50] Reflecting the aforementioned Watergate fatigue, Second City opted to avoid the topic altogether. The *Chicago Sun-Times* review noted the omission, but went on to say that "I had gone prepared to enjoy myself and the mission was accomplished."[51] Second City seems to have taken Patinkin's warning about angry satire to heart. The company that cut its teeth by satirizing the establishment was now avoiding one of the biggest political scandals in the country's history. The push and pull for comics about Watergate would resurface a few decades later with Donald Trump's presidency. *South Park* and other comics eventually swore off comedy about Trump, noting that there was simply nothing more to be said. Yet comedy about Nixon was hardly over with Watergate; in fact, it seemed to pick up as he left office.

Watergate marked a shift for political satire. Watergate itself seemed to be a satiric comedy bit. There was no need to amplify the reality of the situation because the truth was so surreal. Not only did it start the turn toward the absurd in the real, Watergate became a pop-culture brand – every political scandal since has had the word "gate" added onto it. As Russell Peterson argues in *Strange Bedfellows: How Late-Night Comedy Turns Democracy Into a Joke*:

> Mass-marketed irreverence is such a fixture of our contemporary landscape that it is difficult to believe it was not always so common. But it took a change in public attitudes, the construction of a comedy-media infrastructure, an event like Watergate to definitively prove that topical comedy could be big, and – if handled in the proper way – not at all risky business. One could

imagine the ghost of Artemus Ward, lounging in his I AM NOT A CROOK T-shirt, digging into a bowl of impeach-mint ice cream, watching Carson's monologue, and chuckling approvingly.[52]

America's fascination with Nixon has permeated popular culture, comedy, movies, plays, Halloween costumes, and more. Decades after his presidency, Nixon remains a fixture – it seems that we still do have Dick Nixon to kick around.

Like Bill Clinton a generation later, Nixon remained a favorite target. Gerald Ford was *SNL*'s first target – explored in the next chapter – but Nixon didn't escape The Not Ready for Primetime Players' wrath. Like nearly all Nixon impressions, Dan Aykroyd's Nixon was merciless. Ken Tucker argued that "Aykroyd seemed to slip into Nixon's skin, where it was sweaty and the urge to hunch and beetle his brow was reflexive. The president may have been pardoned, but Aykroyd was unforgiving."[53] The most well-known Nixon sketch is "Nixon's Final Days" (1976). Written by Al Franken and Tom Davis and originally workshopped at The Brave New Workshop in Minneapolis, the sketch is a take-off on Bob Woodward and Carl Bernstein's book *The Final Days*. In the sketch, Aykroyd's Nixon is wandering the halls of the White House late at night. Nixon approaches a portrait of Abraham Lincoln. According to Franken, "Danny had the gift of bringing a three-dimensional humanity to his characters, and you almost feel sorry for Nixon when Danny says to Lincoln's portrait: 'Abe, you were lucky. They shot you!'"[54] Nixon has brief interactions with his daughter and son-in-law, as well as Henry Kissinger – to whom Nixon asks, "Don't you want to pray, you Christ-killer?" Eventually, Nixon is alone again, and returns to Lincoln's portrait. Nixon continues, "Why, Abe? Why me?" Lincoln's portrait snaps back, "Because you're such a dip." Aykroyd commented on the sketch when Davis died in 2012, saying,

> Tom was very, very oriented towards human feelings and very sensitive. . . . So, when they wrote the Nixon piece, which was lifted right off the pages of history, it's a little sentimental, it's a little sad. When Nixon goes to his knees you almost feel sorry for him, because he's at the bottom.[55]

You almost feel bad for Nixon, but you ultimately don't. Aykroyd's Nixon returned multiple times over the next few years, but even after Aykroyd left *SNL* the Nixon impersonations continued. From 1982 to 2009, Tony Rosato, Joe Piscopo, John Turturro, and Darrell Hammond all portrayed the former president on the show.

From November 1963 to August 1974, America underwent a fundamental change – and presidential humor reflects that transformation. In the span of a decade, the loving heart of Meader's *The First Family* was a relic from a different country. Comics were no longer afraid to ridicule and attack the president. LBJ and Vietnam began turning the tide toward angry satire, while Nixon and Watergate turned satire cynical. Watergate satire helped illuminate the scandal, and was for some a respite, for others a reminder of America's failure. However audiences interpreted it, satire about Watergate bred cynicism. After Vietnam, civil rights, a series of assassinations, and a country starkly divided, Americans and satirists no longer trusted their government. The two sides were pitted against one another – satire and the state had become satire versus the state. With *Saturday Night Live* establishing itself as a leader in political satire, the next occupant of the White House was going to have to deal with a different satiric world than his predecessors.

Notes

1. Qtd. in Sam Wasson, *Improv Nation: How We Made A Great American Art* (New York: Houghton Mifflin Harcourt Publishing Company, 2017), 95.
2. Qtd. in "American Humor: Hardly a Laughing Matter," *Time*, 4 March 1966, 46–47.
3. Peter M. Robinson, *The Dance of the Comedians: The People, the President, and the Performance of Political Standup Comedy in America* (Amherst: University of Massachusetts Press, 2010), 164.
4. Qtd. in Stephen Kercher, *Revel with a Cause: Liberal Satire in Postwar America* (Chicago: University of Chicago Press, 2006), 250.
5. Art Peterson, "North Beach History: How 1960s Troupe 'The Committee' Influenced American Comedy," *Hoodline*, 27 June 2016. https://hoodline.com/2016/06/north-beach-history-how-1960s-troupe-the-committee-influenced-american-comedy.
6. Peterson.
7. Their 1973 album *Wide Wide World of War* likewise satirically turned the war into a sporting battle.
8. Kercher, 253.
9. Kercher, 254.
10. Qtd. in Gerald Gardner, *Campaign Comedy: Political Humor from Clinton to Kennedy* (Detroit: Wayne State University Press, 1994), 238.
11. Qtd. in Gardner, 235.
12. Qtd. in Kercher, 376.
13. Qtd. in Gardner, 237.
14. Qtd. in Kercher, 377.
15. Qtd. in Kercher, 377.
16. Garson later said the only person she felt she treated unfairly was Lady Bird Johnson. In 2008, the sketch comedy group The Whitest Kids U Know did a sketch likewise saying LBJ engineered the Kennedy assassination.
17. Qtd. in Jane Horwitz, "She Hopes 'MacBird' Flies in a New Era," *The Washington Post*, 5 September 2006. www.washingtonpost.com/wp-dyn/content/article/2006/09/04/AR2006090400993.html.
18. Wasson, 124–126.
19. Qtd. in David Bianculli, *Dangerously Funny: The Uncensored Story of The Smothers Brothers Comedy Hour* (New York: Touchstone, 2009), 161.
20. Qtd. in Bianculli, 317.
21. William Grimes, "Pat Paulsen, 69, a Parodist of Presidential Doubletalk," *New York Times*, 26 April 1997. www.nytimes.com/1997/04/26/us/pat-paulsen-69-a-parodist-of-presidential-doubletalk.html.

22. Qtd. in Suzanne Raga, "Comedian Pat Paulsen's Sincerely Insincere Presidential Campaigns," *Mental Floss*, 1 March 2016. http://mentalfloss.com/article/70735/comedian-pat-paulsens-sincerely-insincere-presidential-campaigns.
23. "Pat Paulsen and RFK." www.youtube.com/watch?time_continue=9&v=ktg4fomzeR0.
24. *The Smothers Brothers Comedy Hour*, 17 November 1968.
25. Bianculli, xvi.
26. Bianculli, 230.
27. Bianculli, xvii.
28. Qtd. in Jeffrey Sweet, *Something Wonderful Right Away: An Oral History of The Second City & The Compass Players* (New York: Limelight Edition, 1978), 359.
29. Qtd. in Mike Thomas, *The Second City Unscripted: Revolution and Revelation at the World Famous Comedy Theater* (Evanston, IL: Northwestern University Press, 2009), 43.
30. Chris Jones, "Second City and the Democratic Convention: When Abbie Hoffman Improvised About Himself," *Chicago Tribune*, 31 August 2018. www.chicagotribune.com/entertainment/theater/ct-ae-1968-convention-culture-jones-0902-story.html.
31. Jack Parr, *P.S. Jack Parr* (New York: Doubleday, 1983), 134.
32. Ryan Lintelman, "In 1968, When Nixon Said 'Sock It To Me' on *Laugh-In*, TV Was Never Quite the Same Again," *Smithsonian Magazine*, 19 January 2018. www.smithsonianmag.com/smithsonian-institution/1968-when-nixon-said-sock-it-me-laugh-tv-was-never-quite-same-again-180967869/.
33. Qtd. in Laurence Maslon and Michael Kantor, *Make 'Em Laugh: The Funny Business of America* (New York: Hachette Book Group, 2008), 98.
34. Lintelman.
35. Qtd. in Marc Freeman, "'Laugh-In' at 50: How the Comedy Helped Elect Nixon and Set the Stage for 'SNL,'" *Hollywood Reporter*, 22 January 2018. www.hollywoodreporter.com/live-feed/laugh-at-50-how-comedy-helped-elect-nixon-set-stage-snl-1074575.
36. Hubert Humphrey reportedly said of Frye's impression of him: "I think Frye is terrific. We had a wonderful time playing his record. I don't think I talk that way, but I guess a man can't judge these things himself. My friends and family tell me that he sounds exactly like me. Political satire is healthy. David Frye is extremely talented at it." Richie Unterberger, "Liner Notes for David Frye's I Am the President/Radio Free Nixon," www.richieunterberger.com/frye.html.
37. Joe Blevins, "I am the President: The Rise and Fall of David Frye," *Vulture*, 8 December 2015. www.vulture.com/2015/12/i-am-the-president-the-rise-and-fall-of-david-frye.html.
38. Qtd. in Kevin Dolak, "Satirist and Impressionist David Frye Dead at 77," *ABC News*, 30 January 2011. https://abcnews.go.com/Entertainment/david-frye-famous-richard-nixon-impressionist-dies-77/story?id=12797928.
39. Frye released two later albums featuring his Nixon impression – *Frye is Nixon* (1996) and *Clinton: An Oral History* (1998).
40. William Wan, "The Surprisingly Dark, Twisted History of Presidential Impersonators in America," *The Washington Post*, 27 June 2016. www.washingtonpost.com/news/post-nation/wp/2016/06/27/the-surprisingly-dark-twisted-history-of-presidential-impersonators-in-america/?utm_term=.72d8e7b7d7d4.
41. Qtd. in Wan.
42. Mark Deming, "I Am the President – AllMusic Review," *AllMusic.com*. www.allmusic.com/album/i-am-the-president-mw0000977333.
43. Qtd. in Nicki Gostin, "Rich Little: 'Back in the 70s Everyone (in Hollywood) Was Republican!'" *Fox News*, 5 January 2017. www.foxnews.com/entertainment/rich-little-back-in-the-70s-everyone-in-hollywood-was-republican.

44. "Show Business: Watergate Wit," *Time*, 25 June 1973.
45. Qtd. in Sweet, 270.
46. Qtd. in Roy Reid, "Watergate Comics Find the Joke Is on Them," *The New York Times*, 8 September 1973, 12.
47. National Lampoon, *Missing White House Tapes*, Blue Thumb Records, 1974. www.youtube.com/watch?v=lxfZt4vbg4I.
48. Donald J. Trump, "My Very Good Black History Month Tribute to Some of the Most Tremendous Black People," *McSweeney's*, 1 February 2017. www.mcsweeneys.net/articles/my-very-good-black-history-month-tribute-to-some-of-the-most-tremendous-black-people.
49. National Lampoon.
50. Qtd. in Kim Howard Johnson, *The Funniest One in the Room: The Lives and Legends of Del Close* (Chicago: Chicago Review Press, 2008), 177.
51. Qtd. in Johnson, 176.
52. Russell Peterson, *Strange Bedfellows: How Late-Night Comedy Turns Democracy Into A Joke* (New Brunswick, NJ: Rutgers University Press, 2008), 35.
53. Ken Tucker, "The History of 'SNL's' Presidential Impersonators," *Entertainment Weekly*, 27 August 2004. https://ew.com/article/2004/08/27/history-snls-presidential-impersonators/.
54. Al Franken, "Al Franken: My 10 Favorite 'Saturday Night Live' Political Sketches," *The Washington Post*, 22 October 2016. www.washingtonpost.com/lifestyle/al-franken-my-10-favorite-saturday-night-live-political-sketches/2016/10/17/56e9d5be-8739-11e6-92c2-14b64f3d453f_story.html?utm_term=.560a7419d454.
55. Rolling Stone, "50 Greatest 'Saturday Night Live' Sketches of All Time," *Rolling Stone*, 3 February 2014. www.rollingstone.com/tv/tv-lists/50-greatest-saturday-night-live-sketches-of-all-time-12735/50-supreme-court-spot-check-221122/.

CHAPTER 4

Ford and Carter

Vaughn Meader was the first comedian to impersonate a president on TV, and Richard Nixon was the first presidential candidate to appear on a sketch comedy television show, but Gerald Ford was the first president to have his image shaped by televised sketch comedy. Assuming the presidency after Nixon's resignation, Ford later pardoned Nixon in a controversial move that would politically define his presidency. His public image, however, was characterized by a new television show that debuted in the fall of 1975 – *Saturday Night Live*. Ford and Jimmy Carter became the first presidents to navigate the emerging comedic power of *SNL*. Ford and *SNL*'s battle to shape Ford's public persona "set up a precedent for '*SNL*' as a place that would help define our opinion of national leaders almost as much as their own words and deeds could."[1] *SNL*'s role in the 1976 election helped cement it as the leading voice in national political satire, and William Horner and Heather Carver argue in *Saturday Night Live and the 1976 Presidential Election* that *SNL* influenced the 1976 election more so than any other election. Ford's opponent in 1976, the slick-talking, holier-than-thou Georgia peanut farmer Jimmy Carter got his own *SNL* treatment, becoming the first president to have his persona shift from hero to failure.

Chevy and Gerry – The Accidental Accident-Prone President

Gerald Ford was perhaps our most athletic president – he played college football at the University of Michigan, winning back-to-back national championships in 1932–1933 – so it is ironic that his lasting sketch comedy legacy is Chevy Chase falling. Unfortunately for Ford, several public stumbles were caught on camera, most notably a tumble down the stairs of *Air Force One*. Chevy Chase latched onto this moment, with a helping hand from the media, to create the persona of Ford as a stumbling fool – the accidental accident-prone president. The press and Chase fed one another, with any stumble by either man turning into news. Ford wrote in his memoir *A Time to Heal: The Autobiography of Gerald R. Ford* that "The news coverage was harmful, but even more damaging was the fact that Johnny Carson and Chevy Chase used my 'missteps' for their jokes. Their antics – and I'll admit I laughed at them myself – helped create the public perception of me as a stumbler. And that wasn't funny."[2] Chase and Ford battled over Ford's image, with Chase presenting Ford as a man who accidentally became president and was quite literally falling down on the job. Ford was unaware of the cultural power that *SNL* would wield. To be fair, how would Ford, or anyone, have known that a sketch comedy show airing at midnight on Saturdays would fundamentally change the presidency.

Chase's Ford is one of the most iconic political impersonations in *SNL*'s history. Indeed, the novelty and singularity of *Saturday Night Live* played a part in the influence it had on Ford's public persona. It helped *SNL* that Ford unexpectedly came onto the national political landscape as a relative unknown. Ford served in the U.S. House of Representatives from 1949 to 1973, representing Michigan, but was hardly a national figure. When Vice President Spiro Agnew resigned in 1973, Republican Congressional leaders backed Ford and pressured Nixon to make him the new vice president. Nixon nominated Ford, and Congress confirmed him in December of 1973. By August 1974, Nixon would resign, and Ford would find himself president of the United States, becoming the first person to become president without having been elected to either post in the executive branch. In September 1974, Ford pardoned Nixon, a highly controversial move that many saw as part of a corrupt pact between the two men – Ford would pardon Nixon if Nixon would name Ford vice president. No such agreement existed, but the damage to Ford's popularity was immediate and immense. When *SNL* debuted in October of 1975, Ford was unpopular and still searching for his presidency's identity in the wake of pardoning Nixon. Chevy Chase and The Not Ready for Prime-Time Players were more than willing to help step into the void and shape Ford's legacy.

What makes Chase's Ford all the more striking, and in stark contrast to Fey's Palin and pretty much every other political impression on the show, is that Chase's portrayal of Ford was a (non)impression. As Lorne Michaels said, Chase "made absolutely no attempt to look like Ford. . . . I loved that because it was so much in the spirit of the show. He just said he was Ford, and he was. He was playing an attitude."[3] Chase wore no character makeup, didn't change his hair, didn't attempt to sound like Ford, to walk like Ford, or adopt any of Ford's mannerisms. In "Ford on the Phone," the sketch starts with subtitles that say "This is not a good impression of Gerald Ford."[4] He was Chevy Chase and, instead of mimicking Ford, latched onto the idea that Ford was an affable oaf who literally stumbled into the presidency. In speaking of Dan Aykroyd's similar (non)impressions of Nixon and Jimmy Carter (though Aykroyd attempted some mimicry), Jeffrey P. Jones argues that "perhaps the inability to impersonate with accuracy gave the performances special power or leeway for political commentary."[5] Aykroyd's Carter is much more of a mimetic performance, explored below, but Chase made zero effort to mimic Ford. By not locking himself into a literal impersonation, Chase was able to lay his commentary onto Ford freely. Chase also was building the Chevy Chase brand. He didn't want to become known as the guy who plays Ford, he wanted to be a star.

Setting aside Chase's personal branding for a moment, the non(impression) allows the Brechtian technique of presenting both the actor and the character to come through more fully. Unlike Vaughn Meader, who audiences delighted in projecting as JFK, audiences never forgot that they were watching Chevy Chase. This duality allows the performer, as Jones notes, to create "humorous situations that the audience *reads onto* the politician."[6] Rather than an impression that gets laughs for its accuracy and attention to personal mannerisms, the (non)impression works to get laughs through satirizing policy and personality. Chase's Ford didn't just fall for the easy laugh – though, as Chase said in 1976, "Ford is so inept that the quickest laugh is the cheapest laugh, and the cheapest laugh is the physical joke." He fell because Chase felt Ford was metaphorically falling down on the job.[7] The pratfall was an embodiment of Ford trying to rise to the occasion of the post-Watergate presidency and falling flat on his face. It was quite clear that Chase did not think Ford was up for the job. Audiences knew that, so the Brechtian dual presentation of Chase and the character Ford deepens the satire. Chase's Ford wasn't just a pratfall for a pratfall's sake. Because the audience was simultaneously receiving Chase's personal beliefs of Ford and projecting them onto the actual Ford, the pratfall takes on a deeper, more layered meaning. This Brechtian dual presentation is essential to understanding Chase's satiric take on Ford.

So why haven't we seen any other (non)impressions? Partly this is due to Chase's star status. The impression was as much about him as it was about Ford. Chase didn't think Ford should be president, but more importantly, he did think Chevy Chase should be a star. Chase played Ford to enhance his persona as much as he did to define Ford's persona. Similarly, the novelty of a sketch comedy show's biggest star mocking the president made it must-see-TV. The novelty of Chase not even trying to imitate Ford was so unique that it was in itself worth tuning in to see – it was a clear symbol for the show's comedic aesthetic. Quite simply, the situation was so perfect that it is unlikely ever to be replicated again. Ford was unknown and the circumstances in which he became president were utterly bizarre, giving *SNL* a relatively blank slate and the freedom to sort of do whatever they wanted. *SNL* was unknown as well, so it had virtually no expectations to fulfill; they could portray Ford however they wanted without worrying about preconceived audience expectations. Add in that the hot new show's brightest young star was the one playing the president, and a comedy cocktail was created that will be difficult to ever duplicate. We expect *SNL* to impersonate the president now. We also expect a heightened reality with those impressions – the *SNL* president is supposed to be a comic version of the real president. As such, we now expect an impression that looks like the president. But in 1975, there were no expectations of how a sketch comedy show should impersonate the president because there had never been a sketch comedy show that regularly impersonated the president.

Chase first appeared as Ford in *SNL*'s fourth episode on November 8, 1975, during the show's cold open. As the first "Weekend Update" anchor, Chase had already been making jokes at Ford's expense from behind the news desk, but it wasn't until episode four that Chase's iconic (non)impression debuted. Dressed in a tuxedo but in no other way representative of President Ford, Chase steps to the podium. The subtitles/chyron read, "This is not the President of the United States. . . . But he thinks he is." When combined with the fact that Ford wasn't elected president, along with Chase's distinct political opinion of Ford – "He had never been elected, period, so I never felt that he deserved to be there to begin with" – the subtitle/chyron takes on a double meaning and signaled to everyone that *SNL* was not going to be kind to Ford.[8] This point of view defines *SNL*'s satiric point. The subtitles are, in their own way, the most biting satire lobbed at Ford: he shouldn't be president and he is too dumb to realize it. Everything flows from this premise. Chase begins his speech but misreads his cards, switching between third and first person, before announcing that a mystery person running for the 1976 Republican nomination will probably win (Ronald Reagan). Throughout the speech, Chase verbally and physically stumbles, falling several times and banging his head on the podium – each time popping up with "No problem! No problem!" Chase ultimately falls entirely to the ground before springing up and delivering the show's signature line, "Live from New York, it's *Saturday Night!*" The sketch led to a series of sketches with Chase as Ford, each one featuring new and elaborate ways of falling. The sketches became an early highlight of the show and helped bolster its place at the cutting edge of political satire. Between tumbles, Chase's Ford continued to commit obvious blunders, starting his Christmas address early ("Christmas Eve at the White House"), misreading his written speech ("Introducing President Ford"), and using a glass as a phone ("Ford on the Phone"). As 1976 and the Republican presidential primary rolled around, it was clear that Ford had a Chevy Chase problem.

April 17, 1976 – The First Presidential Appearance on *SNL*

George Washington shaped our expectations for presidential behavior, and Ford set the equally important benchmark for how a president should respond to *Saturday Night Live* – to laugh. Ford was stung in private but put on a good face in public. From Ford to Obama, each president generally laughed off their *SNL* impressions, some joining in and others keeping their distance. Donald Trump instead famously clashed with Alec Baldwin and *SNL*, but, by and large, presidents have followed Ford's lead. Not all presidents have been quite as generous as Ford, probably because they learned a lesson from Ford's willingness to play along. Comedy writer turned top Ford aide Robert Orben summed up Ford's comic sensibility, saying Ford "was someone who was not afraid to have fun at his own expense."[9] A kindly man, Ford also thought laughing at himself was good politics. The country was still reeling from Nixon and Watergate, and Ford thought that laughter could help heal the nation. Writing in his book *Humor and the Presidency*, Ford said: "the media and general public still resented any hint of 'imperial' trappings in connection with the presidency or the White House."[10] A country still dealing with the fallout from Watergate could use a laugh and a president who, unlike Nixon, didn't take himself too seriously. Lorne Michaels found Ford's willingness to laugh refreshing, noting that "You couldn't imagine Nixon signaling that this was O.K … [Ford was telling us] we could all move on from this"[11] – the "this" Michaels is referring to being Watergate. Ford didn't anticipate the tenor of

SNL, failing to grasp its new generational style of confrontational humor. Watergate did not end cynical satire, it pushed it into a new realm.

In speaking about the administration's attitude toward *SNL*, Nessen remarked, "It was just after Watergate, the Vietnam War was still going on, inflation was a problem. There was a general feeling in the White House that we didn't want to spend a lot of time on this."[12] But they did. So much so that Nessen himself ended up hosting the show. It wasn't just Ford being a good sport. His team thought being a part of the comedy could help lessen the comedy's impact, leading to what *SNL* writer Michael Douglas called "a battle of co-optation."[13] This "battle" has been raging for nearly half a century. The history of *SNL* and the presidency has been a negotiation between which entity defines the president. *SNL* wants to define the president's persona on their terms, and of course the president wants to establish their own persona. Some presidents have tried to use *SNL* to help them appear more in touch or "cooler" than they are, like George H.W. Bush, while others opted to ignore it, like Bill Clinton. Donald Trump has famously fought *SNL*, yet he is still fighting "a battle of co-optation." Trump challenges the show in part to help define himself as someone willing to take on the "rigged media" and coastal elites. He also fights them because he is a thin-skinned narcissist. Ford was the first to fight this battle, though he didn't quite realize that it was a fight, and brought the proverbial knife to a gunfight.

Amid a heated Republican primary, Ford's press secretary Ron Nessen hosted *Saturday Night Live* to help combat Chevy Chase's devastating Ford (non)impression, marking the first time a politician appeared on *SNL*. According to Nessen, he first encountered the show in January 1976, and watched as Chase's Ford and Buck Henry as Nessen plotted their next steps in the sketch "Operation Stumblebum." Nessen saw firsthand the power of Chase's dimwitted Ford. In the sketch, Chase asks Henry's Nessen about Nessen's job security. Replying that the decision is up to the president, Chase responds, "Well, I guess we'll find out sooner or later then, won't we?" The sketch also featured a solution to Ford's stumbles – everyone around him should repeat the blunder to make it appear natural. When Chase tries to light the bottom of his pipe, Henry's Nessen does the same. Nessen was unhappy with the way the press had been portraying Ford, yet found *SNL*'s portrayal humorous. As Doug Hill and Jeff Weingrad note, "Nessen had spent a significant amount of time and energy trying to overcome that image [of a bumbler]. Yet here was Chevy Chase taking Ford's buffoonery almost as far as it could go in the opposite direction," a portrayal Nessen embraced.[14] Nessen asked for a copy of the tape to be sent to the White House so he could watch the sketch again. Nessen immediately saw the power *SNL* possessed, and he thought Ford's best strategy was to play along. They thought if Ford appeared to be on the satirists' side rather than the satirists' target, he could negate the impact of Chase's impression. They were wrong.

During the New Hampshire primary, Al Franken, then an *SNL* writer, suggested to Nessen that he host the show. Accounts vary about whether Franken was serious, but Nessen took him seriously. In March 1976, Ford and Nessen tested the wisdom of appearing on *SNL* by inviting Chase to perform at the Radio and

Television Correspondents' Association dinner. Chase made his usual jokes about Ford and took a few stumbles, but the real star of the evening was the president himself. When Ford got up to speak, he purposefully pulled the tablecloth off his table, pretended to trip and dropped his script, and then stepped to the podium to offer his take on Chase's signature "Weekend Update" line, "Good evening. I'm Gerald Ford, and you're not." The appearance was a hit, with Ford's ability to laugh at himself the star of the evening. The seemingly budding good-natured relationship between the White House and *SNL* convinced Nessen that hosting would go a long way to solving Ford's image problem, writing that "Encouraged by Ford's enthusiastic spoofing of his klutz image, I resolved my lingering doubts and confirmed that I would appear as guest host on 'Saturday Night.'"[15] The decision backfired.

SNL epitomized the anarchic humor of the 1970s. Gone were the days where a comedian and president could have a friendly and mutually beneficial relationship like the one shared by Will Rogers and Franklin Roosevelt. In a post-Watergate world, the state was not to be trusted. The comedian's job was to point out the defects of the establishment and revel in the anarchy. Ford and Nessen's miscalculation about hosting *SNL* lies in their misunderstanding of the changing comedic landscape. The satirists had changed, and so, too, had the audience – especially the young and liberal audience tuned in every Saturday night. Nessen thought he could use *SNL* and didn't realize that he was the one being used. *SNL* wasn't *Your Show of Shows*; Chevy Chase wasn't Vaughan Meader. Too much had happened. *The Smothers Brothers* and *National Lampoon* signaled the changing tide, but it wasn't until *Saturday Night Live* – the April 17, 1976, episode in particular – that the antagonistic relationship between comedy and the state came into full view. While *SNL* would more fully embrace Jimmy Carter (and later Barack Obama), there would be no such embrace of Ford. The show's credibility with young viewers, its position as the voice of a new generation, and their very authenticity as a comedic institution holding truth-to-power depended on them pushing back on Ford, not embracing him. With the benefit of hindsight and nearly 50 years of *SNL* history, it is easy to see that Nessen's appearance was not going to help Ford, but it is still hard to imagine that Ford and Nessen thought *SNL* would let the White House control the narrative. Writer Rosie Shuster summed up show's attitude for the episode: "The President's watching. Let's make him cringe and squirm."[16] Michaels insisted that it wasn't the show's intention to "take the President and shove his press secretary up his ass," but as Franken notes, "It just kind of worked out that way."[17] That the White House didn't anticipate the show's attitude is difficult to understand.

The episode opened with the real Gerald Ford in a taped segment from the Oval Office delivering the show's signature line, "Live from New York, it's *Saturday Night!*" He would also appear on "Weekend Update" in another brief taped clip repeating his "I'm Gerald Ford, and you're not" line from the Correspondents dinner. The taped cold open was a historic moment, marking the first time a sitting president appeared on *SNL*. More importantly, it also gave the episode – and all the highly controversial subsequent sketches – the appearance of having Ford's blessing. Nessen himself then took the stage to deliver his opening monologue, which featured him joking about working for the president and managing Ford's stumbles: "What the president really said was . . ." and "What the president really bumped into was . . .". By having Ford and then Nessen appear at the very top of the show, it served to act as the duo giving their blessing to an episode that ultimately sought to humiliate them. As such, it illustrated the show's very point: Ford is in over his head, so much so that he doesn't even realize that this show is going to eviscerate him.

Accounts vary about Nessen's involvement in creating/writing/approving the sketches, but most agree that Nessen (and by proxy Ford) remained relatively hands-off, not wanting to appear as if they were censoring the material. Nessen didn't even arrive until Thursday (it is customary for the host to be there on Monday), so the show had already gathered momentum and a voice without its host present. The appearance was a lose-lose situation in terms of content. Nessen and Ford couldn't appear to censor the content because that would defeat the purpose of the appearance; at the same time, by not taking an active role in creating/editing the content the duo put themselves at the mercy of an anarchic group of young comedians who didn't think Ford should be president. Putting themselves in the situation in the first place showed a severe misunderstanding of *SNL* and a significant error in judgment. The press and others were shocked that Nessen didn't do more to control the show's narrative. Johanna Steinmetz of the *Chicago Tribune* was on set during rehearsals and wrote:

> Nessen vetoed none of his material on the show and appeared to enjoy other sketches in which he did not participate. . . . The most controversial sketch in which Nessen appeared was one in which he played himself to Chase's hilarious rendering of an uncoordinated, obtuse President Ford. . . . During the dress rehearsal of that sketch, an Emmy Award winning writer on the show's staff was heard to remark to a colleague: "What we are watching may be the most amazing piece of TV ever done." Replied the second writer: "It's almost like heresy on Nessen's part, isn't it?"[18]

This Chase–Nessen sketch was the only Ford sketch of the night, aside from "Weekend Update" jokes, but managed to hit virtually every Ford stereotype. Yet it wasn't necessarily the sketches directly taking on Ford that caused Ford problems – it was everything else.

The rest of the episode proved more problematic than Nessen's implicit stamp of approval on Chase's Ford. The other sketches pushed the limits of good taste and were an obvious challenge. Dan Aykroyd's now-famous "Bass-O-Matic" infomercial, where he puts a bass into a blender and Laraine Newman seemingly drinks the blended fish, was the *least* offensive sketch of the night. Attempting to push the limits of good taste – "let's make [Ford] cringe and squirm" – the rest of the episode was equal parts raunchy and outrageous. "Flucker's Jam" spoofed Smucker's jam, with flavors such as Nose Hair, Painful Rectal Itch, Dog Vomit, Monkey Pus, and Mangled Baby Ducks jams. Nessen did a recurring bit of press secretaries throughout history, such as Catherine the Great's press secretary announcing her tragic death (legend has it she died having sex with a horse) – Nessen announced she died "in the saddle" and would forever be known as "Catherine the Mashed." John Belushi did a sketch about a new army recruiting tactic, where Belushi smoked pot and offered the army as "a joint venture that works." Ford's son Jack had earlier admitted to smoking pot, and Ford's wife Betty had revealed in a *60 Minutes* interview that her children had probably tried marijuana. "Weekend Update" was Ford centric and included Gilda Radner's Emily Litella editorializing on presidential erections. Later sketches included a carbonated douche called "Autumn Fizz" – "the douche with the effervescence of uncola"; an interview with Nessen about politicians' sexual behavior; the home movie (the digital short of the time) featuring four men singing and peeing in urinals; and "Supreme Court Spot Check," which featured the nine Supreme Court Justices monitoring a couple having sex to make sure they aren't breaking any laws due to a recent court ruling about specific sexual acts – one Justice remarked, "I'm a little nervous about where that mouth is heading." The non-Ford sketches basked in their offense and their "can you believe we're getting away with this?" sensibility.

Nessen's appearance almost immediately backfired, as the press and many in the Ford administration questioned Nessen's judgment. Rather than showing Ford was in on the joke, the episode not only continued to mock Ford, but it showed how out of touch the administration was – the kids were making fun of their parents, and the parents were willingly and blindly playing along. Jerald terHorst, who briefly served as Ford's first press secretary, lambasted Nessen and the administration in the *Chicago Tribune* about the seeming lack of awareness surrounding Nessen's appearance: "It should have started with the question: 'Why?' What good, for the government, for Ford, for the country, would be served by Nessen's participating in such a show? That question wasn't asked, or it certainly would have had to be answered in the negative."[19] Nessen's appearance provided a blueprint for how *not* to handle *SNL*. Rather than solve Ford's image problem, Nessen's presence exacerbated Ford's image as a president in over his head – and just in time for the 1976 election.

Dan and Jimmy – Candidate Carter

The 1976 presidential election would be the first in the *Saturday Night Live* era. As Chase's Ford demonstrated, *SNL* had already become a national player in political sketch comedy. The Democratic frontrunner and eventual nominee (spoiler: he became president) was the peanut farmer turned Georgia governor Jimmy Carter. *SNL* had proven itself adept at satirizing a sitting president, but Carter presented a new challenge. Like Ford, Carter was relatively unknown nationally, so *SNL* would likewise have an outsized role in shaping Carter's public image. Since Chase made it so clear that he did not think Ford should be president, did that mean *SNL* would "endorse" Carter? Would their satiric treatment take it easy? Would the show speak truth to power, or would they become a partisan pawn? The answer to that question, in part, rested with Dan Aykroyd's impression.

In contrast to Chase, Dan Aykroyd attempted a more traditional impersonation with Jimmy Carter, though nowhere near today's 100% mimicry standard. Aykroyd didn't physically resemble Carter, and by today's standards, his character looks almost nothing like Carter, but Aykroyd did dye his hair gray, adopt a Southern drawl, and craft a Carter-esque smile. In an odd turn, Aykroyd kept his mustache, which Carter did not have, really never referring to it or using it in any way – it was just sort of there. Whereas Chase was Chevy Chase when playing Ford, Aykroyd approached Carter as a traditional acting role. In describing his approach, Aykroyd said,

> It wasn't that I said oh, "I want to do Jimmy Carter." It was an assignment from Lorne Michaels . . . so I took a look at Carter, the cardigan sweater, the smile, the eye contact, the sandy hair, and in the Peter Sellers mode of impersonations and impressions took all of those attributes and put them all together, watched hours of video tape and performed the impression based upon basically that premise. Of an assignment and then having to take on the physical attributes and come forth with an impression, so it was really just a function of me being one of the hired actors on the show.[20]

As Carter went from candidate to president, his portrayal on the show shifted, and he began receiving harsher treatment. Initially, Carter was presented as a clear alternative to Ford. That's not to say that Carter got off scot-free, but Ford clearly received harsher treatment. Chase's Ford was too stupid to be president – Aykroyd's Carter was almost too smart to be president. Chase's Ford was stumbling and bumbling – Aykroyd's Carter was smooth and slippery. Chase's Ford was humble and simple – Aykroyd's Carter was arrogant and holier-than-thou.

The Debates and the Faux Debates

The 1976 presidential debates were the first such debates since the famous (or infamous) 1960 debates between Kennedy and Nixon. Johnson saw no need to debate Barry Goldwater in 1964, and Nixon learned his debate lessons and steered clear in both 1968 and 1972. An FCC ruling in 1975 eliminating the equal time clause helped clear the way for the 1976 debate (essentially Ford and Carter wouldn't have to share time with any third-party candidates). Both candidates were eager to show the country that they were more than the bumbling-stumbler and the shifty-Southern-smiler. The *SNL* faux debates between Chase's Ford and Aykroyd's Carter also marked another first for the show in what has become one of its signature political sketches.

In what now seems like an incredibly odd decision, the first *SNL* debate occurred *before* the real first debate. There are several assumptions one can make about what will happen at a debate, but by going first, *SNL* lost the ability to react to the debate and reframe the candidates' performance. The post-debate spin, of which *SNL* is a part, has become almost more important than the actual debates themselves. By going before the debate, the show lost the opportunity to satirically spin the debate. Instead, they tried to define the parameters of the debate, which proved to be less effective. One lost comedic moment was the audio gaffe during the actual first debate. For nearly half-an-hour, the audio feed cut out, and Ford and Carter awkwardly stood on the stage behind their podiums silently waiting for the problem to be fixed. To sweeten the comedic pot, the audio cut out on a question about the government's control over intelligence agencies, leading the networks to assure viewers that the CIA did not cut the audio feed – talk about absurd reality. *SNL*'s debate missed the audio outage, but hit on many of the issues of the debate. Chase's Ford was clumsy and dim; Aykroyd's Carter was smiling and avoiding direct answers. At the end of the debate, Chase's Ford pours water and falls over the podium. Chase's fall during the evening's rehearsal was so severe that after the show he had to be hospitalized and missed the next show. Aside from Chase's injury, the debate sketch is mostly forgettable.

The second faux debate was *SNL*'s first post-debate debate. Both debates became focused on real gaffes by the candidates. During the actual debate, Ford committed one of the greatest debate blunders in history when he remarked that "there is no Soviet domination of Eastern Europe and there never will be under a Ford administration." The blunder was so evident that the moderator offered Ford a chance to clarify or retract his statement, which he shockingly did not. As the whole world knew, the Soviet Union in the 1970s exacted nearly complete control over Eastern Europe, for the president to say otherwise was shocking. Ford later corrected himself, but the damage was done. On Carter's end, his gaffe came in an interview with *Playboy*, where he stated, "I've looked on a lot of women with lust. I've committed adultery in my heart many times."[21] The two men and their various gaffes set the stage for *SNL*. By going after the debate this time, *SNL* had the opportunity to ridicule the candidates' performance. Going first neutered *SNL*'s greatest strength – its flexibility to be topical.

During the *SNL* debate, both candidates addressed their latest blunders. Chase's Ford responded to a question about his last visit to Poland by saying, "Last year I visited the capital of Poland, and let me just say from the outset that Milwaukee is a beautiful city."[22] Carter responded to a question about his *Playboy* interview, saying,

> I don't think there's such a thing as being too honest, Ms. Montgomery, and just to prove it, I'm going to answer honestly how I feel right now. I want to say that you're a very attractive woman, and your hair looks kind of silky and kind of soft, and at this moment in my heart, I'm wearing a leather mask and breathing in your ear.[23]

Ford's rebuttal is to announce that he's only lusted after two women in his life, "my lovely wife, Betty, and my lovely mother, Mom." The *SNL* debate didn't tip the scales but is a clear example of absurd amplification. They exaggerated reality to reflect the "truth." It also revealed the show's preference for Carter. *SNL*'s treatment of the Carter *Playboy* interview is telling. The "Debate '76" sketch turns the Carter blunder into a new joke at *Ford*'s expense. The episode continued the Carter favoritism, with "Weekend Update" jokes again targeting Ford, joking about him bragging that he committed celibacy. The final *SNL* debate was staged as a mock beauty pageant. The candidates wore old-timey bathing suits and showed off their talents. Ford's talent was voting, but while trying to vote he has trouble getting into the voting booth and falls. Carter's talent was dentistry, and he successfully performs oral surgery. The satiric debates helped frame *SNL*'s takes on the candidates – Ford was too stupid, and Carter was slippery but smart.

"Weekend Update" and the Unreleased Campaign Ads

The October 30, 1976, episode featured one of the most overt political statements in *SNL*'s history. The last episode aired before the election, "Weekend Update" released two "lost" campaign ads they claimed to have discovered. The Ford campaign ad targeting Carter features Carter working on his farm, before cutting to scantily clad women. Aykroyd's voiceover announces that Americans need a president who "lusts your lusts." The ad is an over-the-top parody of Carter's *Playboy* interview. It's funny, but not exactly biting political satire. Carter's campaign ad targeting Ford, however, takes an entirely different tone. While the ad targeting Carter was populated by actors, the ad targeting Ford was actual footage of Ford's speech pardoning Nixon. As Ford speaks, more real footage of Ford and Nixon together is shown, before returning to Ford in the Oval Office signing Nixon's pardon. Don Pardo's voice over announces "Four More Years," as the video cuts to footage of Nixon waving his famous "V for Victory" sign.

The two ads were in stark contrast. If it wasn't clear before (and it was), it was clear after the ads aired that *SNL* wanted Carter to win the election. In *Saturday Night: A Backstage History of Saturday Night Live*, Hill and Weingrad argue that Michaels loved the ads: "Lorne is proudest of the time *Saturday Night* replayed, three days before the 1976 election between Ford and Jimmy Carter, the speech in which Ford announced his pardon of Richard Nixon."[24] *SNL* would be accused of bias many times over the next four decades, and Michaels and the cast routinely refute those claims. As Hill and Weingrad note:

> *Saturday Night*'s principal goal, as it has been for satirists throughout history, was to reveal the underlying absurdity of the political game, whoever was in power – playing, as Lorne put it, "the loyal opposition." *Saturday Night* took its opposition further than other television shows. Theirs wasn't the all-in-good-fun, deep-down-we're-all-patriots humor of Bob Hope, or the more corrosive but still liberal style of Johnny Carson. *Saturday Night* wore its contempt for the political status quo on its sleeve.[25]

It's difficult to take at face value that *SNL* wasn't biased against Ford. One can argue that their bias shouldn't matter since political satire inherently takes a side, but to claim there was no bias, especially after the "Weekend Update" ads, is absurd. We have seen numerous examples of satire's conservative nature, but *SNL*'s treatment of Ford is an explicit example of satire's liberal nature. The two ads are quite simply not fair. One can argue that it isn't *SNL*'s job to be fair, but it is absurd to argue that there was no bias in the show's treatment of Ford.

Carter the President

After the election, *SNL* had two new challenges – Chevy Chase left the show, and there was a new president in the White House. Nearly every sketch comedy program was based around a star, or at the very least, like with *The Colgate Comedy Hour*, a rotating cast of stars. Chase was the undisputed star of *SNL*. When he left, the show faced a crossroads – replace him with a new star, say, John Belushi, or stay true to its ensemble roots? The show chose the latter, which became central to the show's evolution. The other challenge was the new occupant of the White House. How would they deal with President Carter? Would the show continue to champion Carter, or would they lambast him now that he was in charge? The Carter presidency presented more firsts for *SNL* and political sketch comedy. Carter would be the first person to go from candidate to president in the *SNL* era, and he'd also be the first president to have his persona change as his presidency evolved. Three sketches illustrate *SNL*'s shifting portrayal of Carter the president: "Ask President Carter" (1977), "Jimmy Carter on Inflation Cold Open" (1978), and "The Amazing Colossal President" (1979). Unlike Ford, the Carter administration pled ignorance when it came to Carter's portrayal on *SNL*. They claimed not to watch the show, and they steered clear of pulling a Nessen. Due to *SNL*'s presence in the early years, it's hard to believe that they completely ignored the show, especially early on when Aykroyd's Carter was relatively flattering.

"Ask President Carter," aired during Carter's first year in office, played on the image that Carter was, in the words of Franken, who cowrote the sketch, "supremely competent in every way."[26] In the sketch, Aykroyd's mustachioed Carter is doing a call-in radio show with Bill Murray's Walter Cronkite. While Carter's micromanaging was seen by many as his ultimate undoing, at first, it was presented comedically as his strength compared to the dim-witted Ford. In the sketch, Carter is taking unscreened phone calls on wide-ranging topics. The first caller is a postal worker in Kansas, who asks President Carter about a jam in the post office's sorting machine. Carter, who knows everything, responds, "Vice President Mondale and I myself were just talking about the Marvex 3000 this morning." Carter then goes into great detail to help the caller clear the jam and reset the machine. Carter later deals with a caller who is on an acid trip. Cronkite tries to end the call, but Carter steps in: "Just a minute Walter, this guy's in trouble. I think I better try to talk him down." Carter gets a description of the pills before identifying them as "Orange Sunshine." Carter begins to talk the caller down and gives him tips on overcoming the trip before a final reassurance: "Just remember you're a living organism on this planet, and you're very safe. You've just taken a heavy drug. Relax, stay inside, and listen to some music, okay? Do you have any Allman Brothers?" He ends the phone call by saying, "You know I'm against drug use myself, but I'm not going to lay that on you right now. Just mellow out the best you can."[27] The sketch presents Carter in a highly flattering light. He's cool, calm, relatable, and able to solve any problem. Carter speechwriter Hedrick Hertzberg was likewise impressed, "It wasn't just that the segment was so admiring of his competence and the depth and breadth of his knowledge. . . . It was also that the segment made Carter out to be knowledgeable about and tolerant of and maybe even experienced with psychedelic drugs."[28] Not only did the sketch highlight Carter's intellectual dexterity, it made the Christian Carter seem hip and cool.

As Carter's term unfolded, the real Carter proved to be less nimble, knowledgeable, and effective than Aykroyd's initial impression. As inflation and gas prices continued to rise, Carter's image as the expert of everything fell apart. In "Jimmy Carter on Inflation Cold Open" (1978), Aykroyd's Carter, sans mustache, addresses the nation with a "plant-side chat" to discuss how things grow, even if we don't want them to, like inflation. Carter's know-it-all persona is on display again, but rather than talking down someone high on acid, Carter tries to deflect from the growing economic crisis in America. Carter goes on to explain the concept of inflation before discussing how the best way to combat inflation is through high unemployment, so "people won't have jobs or money to spend. This is a program my administration has actively pursued." Carter finally asks that all Americans sacrifice to help the country and "take 8% of your money and burn it." Carter calls in his daughter Amy to be the first to sacrifice. They take a dollar out of her peanut piggy bank to burn – setting the dollar on fire and putting it in an ashtray that reads "The Buck Burns Here."[29] While the sketch stays true to the original slick-talking and highly intelligent Carter, those traits became distinctively negative attributes. Carter again tries to talk and intellectualize his way through what felt like an unfixable problem.

In 1979, America's economic crisis was worsening, and Carter was seen by many as an ineffective president. To make matters worse, in March of 1979 the Three Mile Island nuclear reactor melted down, adding to America's growing energy crisis and the growing sentiment that the Carter administration was itself melting down. The following Saturday, *SNL* aired "The Amazing Colossal President," in which Bill Murray spills a Pepsi on the control board of the Two Mile nuclear reactor, triggering a meltdown (the sketch is often referred to as "The Pepsi Syndrome"). After several minutes, Aykroyd's Carter enters. As the guide explains where they are, Carter replies, "Of course, I'm familiar with nuclear facilities. You know, I'm a nuclear engineer." As they try to explain what happened, Carter interrupts them, "Sounds to me a lot like a Pepsi Syndrome. Were there any soft drinks in the control room?" To which the workers' reply, "Okay. You've got me. You're too smart for me, Mr. President." As his wife Rosalyn, played by Laraine Newman, begs to leave, Carter insists on checking on the core reactor: "I think I know how to handle myself around a nuclear facility." Carter emerges moments later, glowing. The sketch cuts to two days later, and Carter's health is still unknown. Eventually, we learn that Carter has grown to 90 feet tall. Carter appears to address the media and his wife, assuring them that he's okay: "First, let me say that this experience has not changed my commitment to nuclear power, nor do I believe that my enormous size will in any way limit my abilities to perform my duties in my office." He does inform everyone that he's fallen in love with the female maintenance worker who was also in the reactor and grown to an immense size.[30] Once again, Aykroyd's signature Carter trait – he knows it all . . . even when his know-it-all persona causes him to grow 90 feet tall from a nuclear disaster – is on display. He only enters the reactor's core because he thinks he'll know what to do to fix it, and much like his micromanaging was negatively impacting the economy, Carter's know-it-all meddling leads to him suffering nuclear fallout. Importantly, Carter's core trait does not change through the three sketches. It is the effect of his know-it-all persona that changes.

The 1970s was a tumultuous decade in America, and the country's leadership didn't seem up to the task. From Watergate and Nixon's resignation to Ford's stumbles to Carter's micromanaging, America seemed stuck. Sketch comedy reflected the country's malaise, presenting a Ford falling down on the job and a Carter too full of himself to realize he was doing the same. These public personas were in no small way shaped by their sketch comedy impressions. The emergence of *Saturday Night Live* in 1975 forever changed the relationship between sketch comedy and the presidency. As Ford and Carter navigated these uncharted waters, it had become clear that a president's *SNL* impression was now something to manage actively. At the same time, it is easy to take *SNL*'s political influence for granted. We must remember that the show never set out to be solely political satire. Its emergence as a part of the national political conversation is in no small part due to the success of Chase and Aykroyd. As James Andrew Miller, author of *Live From New York: The Complete, Uncensored History of Saturday Night Live*, said, "If Chevy hadn't been as good with Ford, and Danny hadn't been as good with Carter, I don't think *SNL* would have rocketed off in terms of political satire and impersonations the way it did."[31] It's not a stretch to say that Chase and Aykroyd changed the political landscape by making fun of the president every Saturday night.

Notes

1. Alan Sepinwall, "The 'Saturday Night Live' Story Told Through Its Sketches," *UProxx.com*, 12 February 2015. https://uproxx.com/sepinwall/saturday-night-live-at-40-the-snl-story-told-through-its-sketches/.
2. Gerald Ford, *A Time to Heal: The Autobiography of Gerald R. Ford* (New York: Harper & Row, 1979), 289.
3. Diane Holloway, "Presidents Become Boobs, Bumblers on 'SNL,'" *Washington Times*, 24 February 2001, D4.
4. "Ford on the Phone," *Saturday Night Live*, 25 November 1975. www.nbc.com/saturday-night-live/video/ford-on-the-phone/n8613.
5. Jeffrey P. Jones, "With All Due Respect: Satirizing Presidents from Saturday Night Live to Lil' Bush," in *Satire TV: Politics and Comedy in the Post-Network Era* (New York: New York University Press, 2009), 41.
6. Jones, 41.
7. Qtd. in "The Ridicule Problem," *Time*, 5 January 1976.
8. "Chevy Chase Turned Star Athlete into a Klutz," *Toronto Sun*, 28 December 2006, 7.
9. Qtd. in Mark Leibovich, "Chevy Chase as the Klutz in Chief, and a President Who Was in on the Joke," *The New York Times*, 29 December 2006. www.nytimes.com/2006/12/29/washington/29chevy.html.
10. Qtd. in Leibovich.
11. Qtd. in Leibovich.

12. Qtd. in Steve Hendrix, "'SNL' Has Skewered Every President Since Ford, and All of Them Reacted the Same Way – Until Now," *Chicago Tribune*, 14 October 2018. www.chicagotribune.com/entertainment/tv/ct-ent-snl-presidents-20181014-story.html.
13. Kathryn Cramer Brownell, "The *Saturday Night Live* Episode That Changed American Politics," *Time*, 15 April 2016. http://time.com/4292027/gerald-ford-saturday-night-live/.
14. Doug Hill and Jeff Weingrad, *Saturday Night: A Backstage History of Saturday Night Live* (New York: Vintage, 1986), 179–180.
15. Ron Nessen, *It Sure Looks Different From the Inside* (Chicago: Playboy Press, 1978), 173–174.
16. Hill and Weingrad, 184.
17. Qtd. in Al Franken, *Rush Limbaugh is a Big Fat Idiot* (New York: Random House, 1996), 40.
18. Qtd. in William Horner and Heather Carver, *Saturday Night Live and the 1976 Presidential Election: A New Voice Enters Campaign Politics* (Jefferson, NC: McFarland & Co. Inc., 2018), 66.
19. Jerald terHorst, "Nessen's Saturday Nightmare," *Chicago Tribune*, 23 April 1976.
20. Qtd. in Horner and Carver, 97–98.
21. Qtd. in Robert Scheer, "The Playboy Interview: Jimmy Carter," *Playboy* 23, no. 11 (November 1976), 63–86.
22. "Debate '76," *Saturday Night Live*, 16 October 1976. www.nbc.com/saturday-night-live/video/debate-76/3004161.
23. "Debate '76."
24. Hill and Weingrad, 183.
25. Hill and Weingrad, 183.
26. Al Franken, "Al Franken: My 10 Favorite 'Saturday Night Live' Political Sketches," *The Washington Post*, 22 October 2016. www.washingtonpost.com/lifestyle/al-franken-my-10-favorite-saturday-night-live-political-sketches/2016/10/17/56e9d5be-8739-11e6-92c2-14b64f3d453f_story.html?utm_term=.560a7419d454.
27. "Ask President Carter," *Saturday Night Live*, 12 March 1977. www.youtube.com/watch?v=-68iTvhWNB0.
28. Qtd. in Hendrix.
29. "Jimmy Carter on Inflation Cold Open," *Saturday Night Live*, 15 April 1978. www.nbc.com/saturday-night-live/video/jimmy-carter-on-inflation-cold-open/3007609.
30. "SNL Transcripts: The Pepsi Syndrome," *Saturday Night Live Transcripts*, 7 April 1979. https://snltranscripts.jt.org/78/78ppepsi.phtml.
31. Qtd. in Josef Adalian, "How Each Era of *SNL* Has Ridiculed American Presidents," *Vulture*, 2 June 2017. www.vulture.com/2017/06/snl-how-each-era-has-ridiculed-american-presidents.html.

CHAPTER 5

Reagan and Bush

In the 1960s and 1970s, the country was bouncing between outrage, cynicism, fear, and malaise. The movements of the 1960s splintered the country, the failures of the Vietnam War were fresh, Watergate still cast a shadow over the White House, economic "stagflation" had taken hold of the country, and, in 1979, 52 Americans were taken hostage in Iran after the U.S. Embassy in Tehran was seized. Jimmy Carter ordered a rescue mission in April 1980, but it was a failure, resulting in the deaths of eight American service members. As the 1980 election approached, the country desperately needed a surge of optimism. Enter Ronald Reagan. A former radio sportscaster and film actor, Reagan seamlessly stepped into the role of an optimistic president. Like FDR and Kennedy before him, Reagan knew how to work the media, with natural humor playing a central role in his public persona and policy salesmanship. While Reagan knew how to use humor to sell his image and largely avoided the target of satirists, his vice president and successor, George H.W. Bush, became the target of one of the most iconic presidential impressions of all time.

The 1980s are viewed by many as one of America's greatest decades – a time of renewed optimism, excessive wealth, and American military power. For conservatives, Reagan was the embodiment of their philosophy of smaller government-bigger military. While Reagan may have emulated FDR and Kennedy in front of a microphone, he rejected their political philosophy. In his 1981 inaugural address, speaking while the Iranian hostages were being released, Reagan uttered what would become a rallying cry for the Republican Party: "Government is not the solution to our problem, government is the problem."[1] Unlike FDR, Reagan's solution to America's problems was not to introduce new government programs. Reagan's idea was to unleash the American spirit of optimism and inventiveness, to awaken nostalgia for an America that probably never existed by *cutting* government programs. He slashed taxes on the wealthy, rolled back government regulations, and poured money into the military to outspend and defeat the Soviet Union. The American economy rebounded, money flowed, the Berlin Wall came down (on George H.W. Bush's watch), and America regained its forward momentum.

At the same time, and primarily because of Reagan's policies, the 1980s became a time where societal inequality sharpened. The divide between the haves and have-nots exacerbated. With massive tax cuts for the wealthy and increased military spending, Reagan's government cut heavily on social programs and education spending. Reagan's administration ignored the growing HIV/AIDS epidemic, undoubtedly worsening the crisis and costing lives. In 1981, Reagan fired over 11,000 federal air traffic control workers who were on strike, weakening the power of organized labor and fundamentally redefining American labor relations. Reagan's second term was under a cloud from the Iran-Contra affair, a secret arms deal that sent arms to Iranian terrorists holding seven Americans hostage in Lebanon despite a U.S. trade embargo with Iran. Fighting a war with Iraq, Iran bought roughly $30 million of weapons from the United States, who then covertly funneled nearly $18 million via the CIA to secretly support the Contras (who were funded primarily with drug money) fighting against the communist Sandinistas in Nicaragua. Reagan denied negotiating with Iran or the terrorists, though he later retracted the statement and maintained that he did not know money from the arms deal funneled to the Contras. The Reagan-appointed Tower Commission found that Reagan's lack of oversight allowed those working under him, including Oliver North, to send the money to the Contras. Fourteen people were charged in the affair, though not Reagan, and his legacy largely ignores the entire ordeal. Through it all, love him or hate him, Reagan maintained his optimism and easy humor.

Timing Is Everything – The Teflon-Coated Presidency

Reagan was a natural in front of the camera, using his charm, optimism, and good humor as a political tool. Even his opponents could agree that Reagan was funny, and he used that humor in a myriad of ways. Reagan was always quick with a one-liner, even after an assassination attempt. After being shot by John Hinkley, Jr. in 1981, Reagan reportedly said to his doctors, "I hope you're all Republicans."[2] He used humor to deflect from criticism of his agenda, such as when he said, "Sometimes our right-hand does not know what our far-right hand is doing." Reagan had a special place for jokes about the Soviet Union (often repeating Russian jokes about life in the Soviet Union). Reagan joked about America's Cold War rival to deflect tension, raise American spirit, embarrass Soviet leaders, and push his administration's staunch anticommunist policies. He told them virtually every time he met with Soviet leader Mikhail Gorbachev, and they always satirized some aspect of Soviet life. One such joke involves the long wait times Soviets had to endure for products that were readily available to Americans. The premise of the joke is that it takes ten years to buy a car in the Soviet Union. A person pays, then in ten years, they can pick up their vehicle. Reagan said:

> He laid down his money, and then the fella that was in charge said to him, "Okay, come back in ten years and get your car." And he said, "Morning or afternoon?" And the fella behind the counter said, "Ten years from now, what difference does it make?" "Well, the plumber's coming in the morning."

Like FDR and JFK before him, Reagan was not only funny, but he knew how to harness humor to enhance his presidency. Reagan used humor to embarrass the Soviets, allowing Americans to laugh at our Cold War adversary and relish the freedoms of America. Even if times were tough for Americans, Reagan continually positioned the Soviet Union as the butt of the joke, letting Americans feel superior to their adversary and to neutralize their threat – the Soviets aren't going to beat us, they can't even buy a car.

As Peter Robinson argues in *Dance of the Comedians*, "As with [Charles] Browne's transformation into Artemus Ward and [Samuel] Clemens's into Mark Twain, Ronald Reagan redefined himself through performance and good humor as he negotiated the modern American frontiers between old truths and new opportunities and between authenticity and illusion."[3] Reagan the actor was fully aware that part of the job of the modern presidency was playing the role of the president. The president had not only to be a politician; the president had to radiate celebrity. With his background in performance, Reagan understood that perception was reality. Being perceived as a strong leader was every bit as important, if not more so, than actually being a strong leader. Reagan knew that part of defeating the Soviet Union was the perception that America was winning. Joking about the difficulties of Soviet life was part of this larger strategy. His carefree demeanor set the tone for Americans and was proof that America was superior to the Soviet Union.

Since Vaughn Meader's JFK, another growing part of the job of the modern presidency involved dealing with presidential impersonation. Reagan impressions were everywhere, from big names like Johnny Carson to impressionists like Jim Morris and Rich Little to up-and-coming standup comics like Jamie Foxx. Reagan impersonations, much like the familiar caricatures of Nixon, continued to be performed long after the president left office. Yet nothing seemed to stick to the Gipper. *Newsweek* wrote in 1984, "That immunity from all the usual laws of politics – the Teflon Factor – is the ultimate mystery of Ronald Reagan's success."[4] The phrase was coined by Democratic Congresswoman Pat Schroeder in 1983, when she said, "Mr. Speaker, after carefully watching Ronald Reagan, he is attempting a great breakthrough in political technology – he has been perfecting the Teflon-coated presidency. He sees to it that nothing sticks to him."[5] Invoking the commonly used nonstick coating, the Teflon moniker was meant as an insult and often tossed at him by his critics, but like most Reagan satire, it worked more to enhance his image.[6] Reagan turned the criticism into a positive, it was proof of his leadership and America's unbreakable spirit. Reagan radiated American optimism, and nothing could contain it.

The Reagan administration seemed like it would be fertile ground for satire. Reagan himself was likewise ripe for ribbing. The cowboy-turned-actor-turned-president and his overly sunny demeanor were low-hanging fruit. Not to mention, the 1980s were also a time of great international upheaval. The Cold War was reaching its climax, and the Iran-Contra affair threatened to take down Reagan's presidency. Despite what seems like a great satiric mixture, there was little effective satire of Reagan. There were lots of funny bits and jokes about Reagan, such as Johnny Carson's May 7, 1982, "Who's on First" *Tonight Show* spoof of Reagan and chief of staff James Baker preparing for a meeting with Chinese Premier Hu, Yasser Arafat, and Secretary of the Interior James Watt. While a smart take on the classic Abbott and Costello bit, it doesn't exactly satirize Reagan. It is a prime example of much Reagan humor: funny, but not effective satire (and a pretty good stand-in for much of Carson's political humor). Even *Saturday Night Live* mostly fell flat with Reagan. *SNL* had shaped the presidency of Gerald Ford and effectively satirized Jimmy Carter, but the show seemed incapable of landing any lasting satiric punches on Reagan.

Throughout nearly all forms and genres, Reagan remained an elusive target. There were jokes at his expense, but he avoided any defining impressions or satiric takes. Part of this is due to his media-savvy and optimistic nature – he was funny and effortless and happy. He laughed at himself and was always ready with a humorous retort. Unlike Johnson or Nixon, humor didn't bother Reagan. Jules Feiffer attributed part of Reagan's Teflon coating to the natural transition of America turning into a movie; another step in satire's development from pointing out the absurd in the real to the real in the ridiculous:

> If you live in a society which is nothing more or less than a movie version of itself, where a movie star plays president, though we know it's not really happening; where he gets shot, but walks into the hospital wisecracking, because it's not really happening; where he survives an assassin's bullet, which we know doesn't happen in America – assassins don't miss in real-life America, only in the movie version; where the would-be assassin also thinks he's in the movies and is shooting the president to impress a teenage prostitute who is only a movie teenage prostitute, but in real life (if such exists) is a Yale undergraduate; where the secretary of state says he is in command and breaks down on camera, much like "Seven Days in May"; and where the lesson learned out of this experience by the First Lady of the land is not that we should control guns – no, that we should control movies.[7]

If Kennedy was America's first TV president, the result of advertising and the consumer culture of the 1950s brought to life, then Reagan was America's first movie president, the result of heroic metanarratives that were true in fiction, but not in real life. Trump's presidency would later turn America into a reality TV show with himself as host. Reagan understood that there was no real difference between movie reality and real life. It didn't matter if the heroic metanarratives weren't *really* true, if they *seemed* like they were true, then they were true. Reagan's presidency was at times indistinguishable from a movie about the presidency. Reagan played the role of president to the point that the reality and performance were often fused – and that was, as Feiffer argues, part of Reagan's appeal.

Great timing is a key for success in both comedy and the presidency – and in Reagan's case, the combination of the two. Reagan assumed office as both *SNL* and Second City were amid massive turnover and internal tumult. Second City celebrated 25 years in 1984, but to many, the theatre was a tourist trap rather than a place for cutting-edge political satire. In 1985, Andrew Alexander bought the company from Bernie Sahlins, and there was an often-rocky transition. The Chicago company was entering a period of complacency and change. The Toronto branch of Second City was much more successful during this period, including the production of the television show *SCTV*. The Toronto branch was inherently less political than the Chicago branch, and for obvious reasons, less interested in satirizing American politics. As innovative and funny as *SCTV* was – and it was a landmark in television sketch comedy – it was almost wholly apolitical. Second City would remain a force in political satire, but more so as a training ground for satirists. Television had become too dominant, *SNL* too entrenched. As former *SNL* writer Douglas McGrath put it, *SNL* is "the Empire State Building of satire, the one that you find first on the crowded skyline."[8] Even if Second City had been in its satiric heyday, it's hard to imagine it having a significant national impact on perceptions of Reagan – that should have been *SNL*'s job, but like Second City, *SNL* was at its lowest point.

In May 1980, the end of the *SNL*'s fifth season, Lorne Michaels requested a one-year hiatus to pursue other projects and suggested that writers Al Franken, Tom Davis, and Jim Downey temporarily take his place. Unfortunately, NBC Executive Fred Silverman wasn't a fan of Franken, who satirized Silverman on "Weekend Update's" "A Limo for A Lame-O," which criticized Silverman's excessive use of limousines paid for by NBC. Among a myriad of other factors, including Silverman blaming Michaels for approving the sketch, NBC was unable to reach a new deal with Michaels, who subsequently left the show. A majority of the cast and writing staff went as well. Michaels was replaced by Jean Doumanian, who, after a year of bad reviews – and one Charles Rocket "fuck" on live TV – was replaced by Dick Ebersol, who ran the show until Michaels returned. According to cast member Tim Kazurinsky, Ebersol wanted to avoid political and controversial content: "I had just come out of Second City, and he tells me, 'I don't want to do political things. I don't want to do controversial things. Who do you do impressions of? Can you do Mickey Rooney?'"[9] Ebersol wanted to satirize pop culture, not the president of the United States. Writer Barry Blaustein commented on the atmosphere under Ebersol, saying:

> Reagan's election set the tone . . . and there was palpably a move toward conservatism at the network. We tried ideas for sketches that the network would shoot down. The censors would say, "You can't do that." We'd point out they did something similar with Aykroyd three years earlier, and the censor would say, "Yeah, but that was then, this is now. Things are different." There was to be no mention of the Iran hostage crisis. Ironically, when the crisis was over, we did a whole show with every hostage sketch we could think of.[10]

It wasn't just network executives who were turning more conservative. Network executives had always been conservative, they had always wanted to avoid major political statements, evidenced by the many censorship battles already discussed. Ebersol's edict was reflective of the nation's mood. The country had become more conservative, at least temporarily, and wanted a break from the stinging political satire and cultural upheaval of the previous two decades. Angry satire was dead; after all, it was a new morning in America.

Nevertheless, for satirists who wanted *SNL* to continue its tradition of satirizing the president, the new edict was blasphemous. Brad Hall echoed Blaustein, representing the frustration of many of the writers and cast, saying,

> There was a lot of news going on, Reagan era. There was stuff we could've been parodying. I don't think Ebersol wanted that. And I don't think NBC did. Someone's taste did not run toward satire. And so the very thing that originally made the show popular was really resisted. We had people that could do good impressions of all the right people. You look back, it's kind of bizarre, the election in 1984, there's almost no political humor during an entire political election. Nothing. And for me, doing the news, it was really frustrating ... they were much more keen on doing "President Reagan had his hand stuck to his head today" and show a picture.[11]

Gone were the irreverent and radical days of the original cast, replaced with a more conservative edict and a broader comedic palate. We again see the tension between sketch comedy and television. The comedians want to be edgy, but the networks want to make money. When the two conflict, the network almost always wins out. This relationship is a key factor in the argument that satire is inherently conservative.

If not for the arrival of Eddie Murphy during the sixth season, *SNL* might not have lasted what many view as the least successful period for the show. With little political satire, Murphy was essentially the only reason to tune in. When Murphy left in 1984, Ebersol hired the already established Billy Crystal and Martin Short, leading to one of the best seasons of the show. In addition to bringing in already-established stars, Ebersol wanted to rebrand the show in other ways, including cutting the "live" aspect of the show. Luckily that didn't happen, and Michaels returned in 1986. Following Ebersol's lead, Michaels hired established actors to replenish the cast, including Joan Cusack and Robert Downey Jr. The show struggled, and NBC President Brandon Tartikoff was set to cancel the show. Ironically, it was Tartikoff who fought to keep the show on the air in the early 1980s when other executives wanted to cut it, citing the importance of a live sketch comedy show. Tartikoff relented and gave the show a 13-episode renewal instead of the usual 22-episode renewal. Michaels fired the cast and returned to *SNL*'s roots by hiring unknown up-and-coming comedians, including Phil Hartman and Dana Carvey – who would go on to play Reagan and George H.W. Bush, respectively.

During *SNL*'s tumult, ABC debuted its *SNL* rip-off, *Fridays*. About the only difference between the shows was that *Fridays* was based in Los Angeles and aired on Friday nights – everything else was a straight copy of the original. One significant difference was the cohesion of the cast. Whereas the original *SNL* cast had worked together at Second City or with *National Lampoon*, most of the *Fridays* cast was coming together for the first time. Many of them would go on to comedy greatness, including Larry David, Larry Charles, Elaine Pope, Mark Blankfield, and Michael Richards. Critics were unkind to the show initially, seeing it as a lesser version of its older sibling. Yet the show began to gain traction, in part because of its pitfalls. As Dennis Perrin writes,

> Whereas *SNL* displayed a certain control, reflective of Lorne's demeanor, *Fridays* pelted the audience with whatever they could grab. Sometimes the sketches seemed formless, rushed, half-digested. Death, drugs, celebrity, religion, and political corruption were the main topics. Recurring characters like a gay monster mime or a little boy torturing his toy soldiers were barely coherent. If *SNL* was classic rock, then *Fridays* was decidedly punk.[12]

When Michaels left *SNL*, *Fridays* began to gain traction. Critics reversed their initial disdain, especially compared with the flatness of Doumanian's *SNL*. Dick Ebersol even flew out to Los Angeles to try and recruit the cast to leave *Fridays* and join *SNL*. None of them did. They saw themselves as the new satiric revolutionaries, *SNL* the wavering establishment. The show tackled topics that *SNL* wouldn't, venturing into "Salvadoran refugee camps. Torture centers. Iron Curtain undergrounds. PLO bunkers. . . . The audacity of it was amazing."[13] When Reagan was shot by John Hinckley, *Fridays* responded with a series of personal monologues – some completely serious – from the cast members about their memories from other assassinations in the country's recent past. Just when it seemed like *Fridays* was going to take over *SNL*, ABC pushed the show to a later timeslot to make room for *Nightline*, which was covering the Iran hostage crisis. Its ratings fell, and it was canceled in March 1982.

Reagan had the good fortune of being in office during *SNL*'s downturn and before *Fridays* could become a national phenomenon. That said, Reagan sketches appeared somewhat regularly on both shows, though *SNL*'s early efforts lacked the same bite and impact of the Ford and Carter sketches. The impotence is due in part to the network edicts, but also the fact that so many different actors portrayed Reagan on the show. Reagan was first impersonated by Chevy Chase in 1976, before Harry Shearer, Charles Rocket, Joe Piscopo, Randy Quaid, Robin Williams, and finally Phil Hartman, who seemed to best capture Reagan, all played the Gipper. Hartman didn't begin doing Reagan until 1986, by which time public perceptions of Reagan were firmly entrenched. Whereas relatively few people nationally knew much about Gerald Ford when Chevy Chase began shaping Ford's image on *SNL*, by 1986, Reagan was in his second term and had been in the public spotlight one way or another for nearly his entire adult life. With a public persona fully entrenched, *SNL* could not possibly have the same impact on Reagan as it did on his predecessors. The most successful Reagan *SNL* sketch worked because it flipped Reagan's public persona on its head.

Often cited as one of *SNL*'s all-time best political sketches, 1986's "President Reagan, Mastermind," posits that Reagan's cheerful ignorance is just a sham to hide his true Machiavellian intentions. Beneath the façade is a ruthless and highly intelligent leader with the brainpower and stamina to outthink and outwork everyone and anyone. Aired during the Iran-Contra affair, many were painting Reagan as a forgetful and aloof old man who was out of the loop and exploited by his nefarious underlings. Reagan famously responded to questions during his 1990 deposition over Iran-Contra with "I don't recall," or "I can't remember," and often couldn't remember key players in the saga. While many saw this as a ploy, others suspected that Reagan had early onset Alzheimer's disease (he was diagnosed with the disease in 1994). Questions about his mental health also arose during his time in office. During the first presidential debate in 1984, Reagan often looked flustered or confused, losing his train of thought during speeches. His performance in the debate began to raise questions about Reagan's health and ability to remain sharp for another four years. Reagan's age suddenly became a critical issue in the election. The consummate performer, Reagan turned that troubling performance into one of the most memorable debate moments in history. Asked during the second and final debate whether age should be an issue in the campaign, Reagan, who was 73 and at the time the oldest president in American history, responded, "I will not make age an issue of this campaign. I am not going to exploit, for political purposes, my opponent's youth and inexperience."[14] The moment was so good, even his opponent, Walter Mondale, couldn't help but laugh. It also all but sewed up Reagan's reelection, which he would win in a historic 49-state landslide. Patrick Stewart argues that Reagan's humor inoculated him "from future age-related concerns by highlighting his cleverness and ability to connect with the audience."[15] A joke neutralized his biggest liability and pushed him to victory.

But Reagan's mental state was no laughing matter. Though it was, and still is, a subject that's generated a lot of debate. Reagan's children speculated over his mental health. Ron Reagan's book *My Father at 100* suggested that his father may have shown signs of Alzheimer's in his first term, though Ron is quick to point out that no one knew or suspected, and had his father been diagnosed, he would have surely resigned. Ron's half-brother Michael vehemently challenged his brother's claim. Former White House correspondent Lesley Stahl wrote in her 2000 memoir, *Reporting Live*, that "Reagan didn't seem to know who I was. He gave me a distant look with those milky eyes and shook my hand weakly. Oh, my, he's gonzo, I thought. I have to go out on the lawn tonight and tell my countrymen that the president of the United States is a doddering space cadet."[16] Eventually, Reagan came around, so Stahl decided not to report to her fellow countrymen, though later admitted in interviews that she now believes the administration was working to cover up his condition.

Reagan's physicians denied any presence of the disease while in office. Nevertheless, many aides and reporters have debated the issue and shared stories similar to Stahl's of Reagan checking out and in. The one thing that is relatively consistent across accounts is that when the cameras were rolling (or clicking), Reagan would spring to life. In "President Reagan, Mastermind," the script is flipped. When the cameras are present, Reagan is old and frail, and it's when they turn off that Reagan springs to life. Hartman portrays Reagan as an actor, playing the part of a cheerful and confused grandfather in order to carry out his various plots. Rather than the Reagan who reportedly would fall asleep during meetings, Hartman's Reagan is equally adept with Swedish interest rates as he is speaking Arabic – it's his younger underlings who can't keep up. While the real Reagan relished photo-ops, like with the top Girl Scout cookie salesperson, Hartman's Reagan sees them as a waste of his time – "This is the part of the job I hate." Rather than the out-of-the-loop grandpa, Hartman's Reagan was the Nixonian Machiavellian mastermind of the Iran-Contra affair. His only hurdle to success was the fact that his staff wasn't able to keep up with him. After detailing the plan, CIA Director William Casey (Jon Lovitz) interrupts:

Casey: Mr. President, you're going so fast. There's still a lot about the Iran-Contra affair I don't understand.

Reagan: And you don't *need* to understand! *I'm* the President! Only *I* need to understand! Is that clear?[17]

The premise of the sketch is smart, but what makes it truly great is Hartman's performance. He swiftly and seamlessly shifts between smiling grandfather and cunning politician. He flies through complicated jargon and military tactics with ease before effortlessly slipping back into the gentle, soft-spoken grandfather. Hartman eschews the dual-performance style. He is an actor playing a part; his own persona disappears into the character. It made Hartman one of the show's most versatile and all-time great performers, but it also made his Reagan less satirically biting. The timing was more important than Hartman's performance in terms of its satiric bite, but it is worth noting that there was no association between Hartman's personal politics and Reagan. As good as the sketch is, it ultimately didn't do much to change public perceptions of Reagan because it came so late in Reagan's tenure.

Fridays took shots at Reagan before he even took office, though due to its limited run and relatively low visibility it didn't dent Reagan's persona. John Roarke's Reagan was childlike – still believing in Santa and blissfully unaware of the world around him. Roarke happily wobbles across the stage with a combination of tense rigidity and unintentional aimlessness; his head uncontrollably bobbing the whole time. *Fridays* aired nearly a dozen Reagan sketches during its three-season run. One of the most unique was a parody of *Altered States* – "Altered Statesman." In the sketch, Reagan uses a sensory deprivation tank and psychedelic mushrooms to hallucinate a solution to America's woes. Echoing Reagan's campaign slogan "Let's Make America Great Again," Roarke's Reagan believes the answer to America's future lies by rekindling its past. Harkening to an imagined halcyon past is a long-standing American political trope. It evokes "simple times" that never existed, but makes people nostalgic for American values of freedom and liberty. Nostalgia is often invoked in times of change or unease about the future. Reagan's nostalgic pitches worked to link the past to the future, reminding Americans that we were great before and can be great again. As Neel Burton writes,

> Our everyday is humdrum, often even absurd. Nostalgia can lend us much-needed context, perspective, and direction, reminding and reassuring us that our life (and that of others) is not as banal as it may seem, that it is rooted in

a narrative, and that there have been – and will once again be – meaningful moments and experiences.[18]

Given the malaise of the 1970s, from Watergate to stagflation, it is not surprising that Reagan used nostalgia to bolster American's outlook for the future.

In the sketch, Reagan tells Melanie Chartoff's Nancy Reagan, "I'm always trying to get back to the past. The days when America was strong, and great. I think I've found a way. The key lies in that tank."[19] Rather than discovering what can make America great again from the past, Reagan transforms into a Richard Nixon–ape hybrid who terrorizes the night. When Reagan returns home and gets in bed, he begins channeling LBJ, JFK, Jimmy Carter, and Richard Nixon. If anything, the sketch is harsher toward Nixon than Reagan, proving that Nixon remained a favorite satiric target nearly a decade after leaving the Oval Office. "That Darn Reagan" imagined Reagan as the star of a 1950s-style family sitcom featuring Reagan balancing the day-to-day affairs of the presidency, like hosting dinner with the Russian ambassador, with his home life. Reagan appears as a typical sitcom dad in over his head who cares more about watching his favorite television shows than Soviet missiles.[20] The sketch has one of the clearest satiric takes on Reagan, satirizing how he was playing the part of president to evoke nostalgic tropes of America's greatness while ignoring the real-world stakes of the Cold War.

Fridays also launched one of the most ambitious presidential sketches of alltime with "The Ronny Horror Picture Show," a 20-minute parody/homage of *The Rocky Horror Picture Show*. Much like the film, on a dark and stormy night, a young liberal couple, Brad and Janet, go to an eerie mansion to seek help after their car breaks down on their way to an antinuke rally. Like the film, the Transylvanians want to seduce the young couple – to be conservatives. The sketch aired only a month after the 1980 election and reflected what many liberals felt to be the final blow to the liberal spirit of the 1960s, soon to be replaced by a new era of 1980s conservatism. Complete with song and choreographed dance, the sketch is remarkable for its ambition. Songs like "Let's Fight the Big One," a parody of the film's classic "Time Warp" song, make sharp satiric critiques of Reagan's impending conservative agenda. But it is Roarke's turn as Reagan/Frank-N-Furter that seals the sketch's punch. Parodying Tim Curry's famous "Sweet Transvestite" song/performance, the song "Arch Conservative" at first seems like an easy joke by putting Reagan in a garter, but the song moves beyond parody:

> **RONNIE:** How do you do?
> I see you've met . . .
> My faithful – Vice President
> I'm sure he would deny
> But I know he'd like to be
> The White House – resident
> Don't be put off

	By what you've heard
	I'm not a power-mad glutton
	You should just feel relieved
	That the world is safe
	Don't forget who pushes – the button.
	(Ronnie takes off the cape – revealing lingerie underneath.)
RONNIE:	I'm just an arch-conservative,
	Anti-intellectual – chief executive
	From Cal-i-for-ni-a, ah ha ha
	Let me tell you the score
	I think liberals are a bore
	All they do is sit and complain
	I'm a man of action
	I've aligned with any faction
	How do you think I won – the campaign?
	I'm just an arch-conservative
	Anti-intellectual – chief executive
	From Cal-i-for-ni-a, ah ha ha
	So try it our way.
ALL:	Way!
RONNIE:	It's not as bad as they say
ALL:	Say!
RONNIE:	Well, I think our party may just suit you
	I've been, um, making a man.
ALL:	Ooooh!
RONNIE:	A Re-pub-li-can
ALL:	Ahhh!
RONNIE:	My hopes for America's future
	I'm just an arch-conservative
	Anti-intellectual – chief executive
	From Cal-i-for-ni-a, ah ha ha![21]

Reagan goes on to decry the failure of liberalism and pines for a return to optimism. At which point Larry David, as Richard Nixon, breaks through the wall riding a motorcycle, launching into "Holey Moley." Reagan then unveils his creation for the future of conservatism and America – which turns out to be a radical Black Panther who vows to take down Reagan. The liberal hope shines through at the end as the cast takes on Reagan through "Let's Fight the System." The great liberal hope of the song seems naïvely idealistic in retrospect, Nevertheless, the sketch is one of the best satires on Reagan (even though he wasn't technically president yet), in an era that lacked biting satire. The sketch uses the countercultural cache of *Rocky Horror* to assert that there will be resistance to Reagan's conservative agenda. It positions Reagan out of his element to take him down a peg, to demonstrate that his conservatism is a performance.

There were other satiric takes on Reagan, but again, nothing entirely stuck. *Doonesbury* cartoonist Gary Trudeau and composer Elizabeth Swados wrote a satiric musical revue of Reagan – *Rap Master Ronnie* (1984) – that sought to satirize Reagan before the 1984 election. Later turned into a television movie, the revue features Reagan going to the inner city to film a campaign ad to encourage African Americans to vote for him. Despite the title, only the opening number is a rap, in which Reagan touts his record on civil rights: "I have an open mind on civil rights/My youngest son grew up in tights." This type of humor, bland and ridiculing the other, is typical of the revue. The other songs fall into traditional 1980s pop and focus more on the inhabitants of Reagan's America rather than the president himself – the Moral Majority, yuppies, Soviet relations, civil rights, welfare, and the war on drugs. The revue encapsulates Reagan satire – funny bits but nothing that cuts too deeply. As the *UPI* review states, "Trudeau has dragged President Reagan into a dark alley off-Broadway to give him a good going over, but not to worry. There's no real harm done to Reagan's image or reputation in the satirical musical revue."[22] And that was the point. Trudeau himself said that he didn't like satire that is "unrelenting in its hipness and scorched-earth mentality, something we hope we've overcome in this revue."[23] It reflects the backlash to the anger and bitterness of 1960s and 1970s satire. It was an attempt to go back to the lighter fare of *The First Family*. But it was a different world now, leading the revue's jokes to seem flat. The stage show received mixed reviews, with the *New York Times* mostly lauding the show, but still pointing to the already tired tropes of Reagan comedy.[24] The later 1988 television adaptation was seen as completely tired and worn out. The *Los Angeles Times* called it "incredibly, incessantly unfunny," complaining that most of the jokes were of the "same old 'Well . . . I can't remember my own name' routine."[25]

The British television show *Spitting Image* likewise satirized Reagan, this time in their signature marionette puppet style. Several American spin-offs of the show were produced for NBC, including 1986's *Spitting Image: Down and Out in the White House*. David Frost introduced the episode, though rather than follow the sketch comedy structure of the British show, the American version was a single storyline that followed a conspiracy to replace Reagan with a double for the upcoming election. The show was critically acclaimed but did not do well in the ratings. Nevertheless, several other *Spitting Image* spin-offs followed, including 1987's *Ronnie & Nancy Show*, in which Nancy Reagan is holding an anniversary party while Reagan's aides try to prevent a nuclear attack that Reagan accidentally ordered, and the mock-documentary *Bumbledown: The Life and Times of Ronald Reagan* in 1988. Once again, the main point of these shows was that Reagan was old, confused, and stupid. With so many of the same Reagan jokes circulating, outside of Hartman's portrayal in "President Reagan, Mastermind," it is not hard to see why there was so little that satirically stuck to Reagan. Americans did not want sharp satire. They wanted lighter fare so that they could put the tumult of Vietnam and Watergate behind them – as much as anything, that was Reagan's promise. Americans, by and large, wanted a new morning for America, not a stinging satiric critique of its president. His successor wouldn't be so lucky.

"Nah-Gonna-Doet" – George H.W. Bush

George H.W. Bush's term forever redefined the relationship between comedy and the presidency. Bush's presidency sits as a holding period between two distinct periods, and between two distinct and charismatic presidents. Bush's presidency existed from the beginning in the shadow of Reagan and ended up in the shadow of Dana Carvey, whose *SNL* Bush developed a more personal relationship with the American people than the real Bush. Many Americans only remember the tics, continuous hand gestures, and catchphrases made famous by Dana Carvey – "Nah-Gonna-Doet," "Wouldn't be prudent," "That's bad – bad!" – and forget that Bush was in the White House when the Cold War ended, oversaw the controversial North American Free Trade Agreement (NAFTA), initiated Operation Desert Storm, and was at the helm during the 1990–1991 economic recession. His long career in government and his time in the Oval Office became footnotes to Carvey's impression. While Carvey usurped Bush's persona, Bush, in turn, worked very hard over several years to make himself a part of the joke rather than the butt of the joke, forever changing the relationship between satirist and target.

Dana Carvey was obviously not the only comedian to impersonate Bush. A variety of comedians impersonated Bush across mediums. One of the first popular impersonations was done by Jim Morris, who impersonated Bush at the 1989 White House Correspondents Dinner. The performance is a good impersonation of Bush, but what's more important is how Bush reacted to the mockery. Bush demonstrated his ability to take a joke and become a part of the fun like no other president. Morris recalled that Bush "was very generous that way and self-effacing with his own humor. . . . I felt like he was an old friend. He made you feel very comfortable. He wanted to know about your personal life."[26] Morris's routine is tame compared to what Stephen Colbert would later do to George W. Bush in 2006 at the same event. Morris's jokes are closer to the light-hearted jabs of Vaughn Meader, which allowed Bush to laugh along because there was no serious critique of Bush's policies. Jim Carrey played Bush on *In Living Color*, though there were not many sketches directly about or featuring the president on the show. All George H.W. Bush satire takes a back seat to Carvey's *SNL* sketches.

On the surface, Bush doesn't seem like an obvious target. Aside from holding the highest office in the land, there wasn't a lot to make fun of with Bush. The biggest laughs in the 1988 *SNL* presidential debates came from Jon Lovitz's impersonation of the Democratic nominee Michael Dukakis, who responded to Carvey's Bush longwinded answer about a time machine with the now famous, "I can't believe I'm losing to this guy."[27] At the time, it didn't seem like Bush was going to become an iconic *SNL* president. Carvey himself commented that when he was assigned Bush by Michaels, "There's nothing to do."[28] Bush was a little nerdy, sure, but he didn't have a signature accent like Kennedy, Carter, or Clinton; he didn't have any significant scandals like Nixon, Reagan, Clinton, or Trump; he didn't have a unique physical quirk to exaggerate as Chase did with Ford. He was already nationally known after serving for eight years as vice president. Bush was a straight-laced career government employee. At a 1992 White House event, Carvey-as-Bush explained his impression: "Start out with Mister Rogers – 'It's a beautiful day in the neighborhood' – then you add a little John Wayne . . . [together] you've got George Herbert Walker Bush."[29] Carvey's impression, which relied on catchphrases and hand gestures, went beyond the mockery of Chase's Ford into deeper territory. Carvey satirized Bush's nerdy personality as a means to critique Bush's policy. It was lighthearted, but as Bush's term wore on the criticism escalated. According to Carvey,

> So in the beginning of George Bush's tenure, he was so damn popular, I think he saw some of those sketches where the angle was how happy he was. It wasn't until the last eighteen months, where we had the recession and the no-new-taxes thing, where some of the stuff was heavier hitting.[30]

Like Carter, Bush would see his portrayal shift during his presidency.

One of the first Carvey-Bush sketches was the cold open on April 22, 1989, roughly 100 days into Bush's term. As noted, the humor primarily comes from Bush's sunny disposition and eagerness for approval.

> A week from tomorrow will mark the end of the first hundred days of my administration. Thank you. Thank you. . . . I could rest on the laurels of my compromise budget package, or bask in the glow of my childcare tax credit proposal. But that's not enough. Sure I've kept my campaign promises. Willie Horton is still in jail. Pledge of Allegiance being recited. Thousand points of light, still operating. Coming in from all those areas, the way that light just comes all in there, sure. Couple of things have gotten kind of nasty out there. Acid rain, it's a problem. The "frivilization" of the drug trade. It's bad – it's bad! That oil spill up there, up in that whole area. That oil spill up in that whole thing up there. Oil spill, too soon to comment. All the facts aren't in on it. Can't make that judgment, wouldn't be prudent at this time. But Bar and I, happy. Dan Quayle, gaining acceptance. The women's issue, taken care of. People say the economy has problems. Try telling that to that guy out there in Oregon who's working on that thing doing it going round and round with that whole area out there. And that guy's doing a dandy job, good for him. I'm not backing off one iota. Me, I'm good. Relaxed. Voice low, confidence factor way up.[31]

So much of the humor relies on Carvey's performance. He mines laughter from hand gestures and facial expressions, using vocal tonality to punctuate a joke – even using Bush's fake laughter to generate real laughter. Carvey's performance reestablishes the dual-performance mode, but rather than reading Carvey's politics onto the performance, it is Carvey's joy and skill that illuminate the portrayal. He seemed to be having such a good time playing Bush and audiences fed off of his energy.

Only a year later, in May 1990, Carvey's Bush was playing defense. The humor still relied on Bush's faux optimism in the face of bad news, but there is much more satire involving Bush's policies, specifically a new tax increase.

> In the past when I've spoken to you from this office here the news has always been good – not bad! – good! Berlin Wall, collapse of Communism, that

Noriega thing over there – good, good, good. It's no wonder I'm up around that 80% approval area. But now tonight the news I have to bring to ya' it's not good, in fact it's kind of bad. Maybe after ya' hear it my approval rating will slip down to 75% (laughs). Little joke there for ya'. During my campaign for president, certain things were said, things like "Read my lips – no new taxes." Now when I said it, I meant it. I meant all three words. I meant "no," I meant "new," I meant "taxes." Meant 'em all. But situations change. Spring becomes summer. Sunny days become cloudy up there. Sincere growth projections prove overly optimistic. Expenditures have continued to grow – up here (hand gesture). Right there, there's those expenditures up in that area. Revenues remain flat, right down here (hand gesture). See this gap here, that's what I want to talk about. This budget deficit. The most frightening thing I've ever seen in my life, right here. Doesn't go away. You can move it (hand gesture). Still the same size, flip it, turn it, throw it up, do anything you want – don't think I haven't tried: still there! You can move it in and out, results are always the same. We got that debt thing happening. We need cash. Lots of cash. Sort of boggles my mind, but don't fear, gotta plan. Gotta good plan. Gonna tell you right now, not avoiding it, gonna come at you with it, ready to tell you. Let the telling begin. Gonna come out with it. Here it comes. Gonna tell ya', not afraid. Read my lips. I'm gonna . . . I'm gonna . . . rai- . . . I'm gonna . . . raise . . . raise . . . I'm gonna . . . raise . . . ta-ta-ta . . . gonna raise . . . ta-ta-ta-ta-tax-taxes (in a whisper). There I said it, loud and clear. Now you might ask me, who is the money gonna come from? Could tax the poor, haven't got the money, wouldn't work. The rich, tax 'em all you want. They're slippery suckers. They'll incorporate meal deductions, they'll laugh at ya'. Don't want to be laughed at by a tax lawyer down there doing that laughter thing he does. That leaves us with the beautiful middle class. Dependable. Always there. Family people. Don't know about keeping receipts. Don't have a lot of paper laying around. Solid people, don't think we don't love ya', little tax payers (laughs). Now of course, the Democrats will urge a big tax increase – 8–10–12% – nah-gonna-doet. I'm talking 3–4% tops, no more than 5. That's it. So read my lips: no huge new taxes.[32]

While all the vocal inflections and hand gestures are still getting laughs, the content is much more critical of Bush and his policies.

Carvey's Bush was a leader who wasn't in total command, a man whom everyone respected but didn't necessarily trust to get the job done right. His nervous laughter is exposing the frailties of a not-quite-confident leader, a man too worried about his approval rating. A patrician who is never able to connect with the average American directly. David Sims argues that "Carvey skewered Bush with the little details, making him an eye-roll-worthy '80s dad who claimed to have all the answers to the country's problems but largely obsessed over what was or wasn't 'prudent.'"[33] The December 15, 1990, cold open is an excellent example of Carvey using Bush's politician-speak and hand gestures to satirize Bush's policy through personality:

But as commander-in-chief, I am ever cognizant of my authority to launch a full-scale orgy of death there in the desert sands. Probably won't, but then again, I might. And if we do go to war, I can assure you – it will not be another Vietnam. Because we learned well the simple lesson of Vietnam: "Stay out of Vietnam." They'll beat you bad, b-a-a-d. They're bad! But this time is different, because the world is behind us. Critics say, why is the U.S. doing all the work? Not true. Seventy-eight countries are contributing to Operation Desert Shield. Not all are sending troops – sure. But giving what they are able. From Belgium, nylon helmet covers. From New Zealand, socks, ranging from sizes six through twelve. Six is small. Twelve, that's big. Me, I'm a ten and a half. Could wear a ten. Wouldn't be prudent. From the Congo, Ray-Ban sunglasses – two pair. From Yugoslavia, men's swimming trunks. From Mexico, salsa. And the list goes on. You see, world behind us, not like Vietnam.[34]

Quite simply, Carvey turned Bush into a goofy nerd who would awkwardly laugh at his own jokes to cover his insecurities, a career politician who was slightly out of touch and wasn't as adept at playing the part of the president as Reagan. Carvey's Bush was a harmless aging man at the helm of a country that was passing him by.

Part of what made Carvey's impression so effective was its frequency. Reagan sketches were relatively rare, but Bush sketches were on nearly once a month. Moreover, most of Carvey's appearances were in the cold open as a monologue, rather than as a traditional scenic sketch. It was usually just Carvey's Bush giving a direct address from the oval office without any other trappings or other scenic devices that would cue the audience that this was meant to be silly. Carvey's Bush was the president sitting at his desk and addressing the nation, which made him seem more like the real Bush. Americans saw Dana Carvey's Bush on their televisions almost as much as the real Bush. Carvey's Bush was certainly more entertaining to watch, and as such, many Americans found Carvey's Bush more authentic. Bush wasn't very warm and, unlike Reagan, wasn't a natural in front of the camera – he wasn't must-see TV. Carvey's Bush, on the other hand, was riveting. His hand gestures alone were worth tuning in to watch. In part, that's probably why Bush himself liked the impression so much – it made him captivating. As William Hughes argues,

> There's an energy and vitality to Carvey-Bush that's weirdly flattering in its way, the dynamism of a master comedian who's found a character he can really sink his teeth into. Sometimes prissy, bordering on incoherent – as when sinking into his "Nah Gonna Doet" catchphrase – Carvey nevertheless made the man riveting to watch, something a politician has probably got to enjoy, even if it's just by proxy.[35]

Like Chase's Ford, Carvey's Bush is almost more about Carvey than Bush. Unlike Chase, it is because of Carvey's comedic skills rather than his political bent. Bush became a recurring sketch comedy character for Carvey, not unlike The Church Lady or Hans from Hans and Franz. It just so happened that this recurring character happened to be president of the United States.

By contemporary standards, Carvey's satiric take on Bush is relatively soft. There is nothing mean or menacing about Carvey's Bush. Instead, he's an out-of-touch career politician who doesn't quite have his finger on the pulse of the nation. He's a soft-spoken geek trying to talk tough – telling Saddam Hussein, "I'm going to talk tough now, Mr. Hussein. Watch me talk tough."[36] Carvey's Bush is aware that he isn't a great president – always worried about his approval rating going down – "that's bad . . . bad!" Carvey's Bush is unnatural on camera, aware that he isn't in-touch – he knows he doesn't "get it," but tries anyway. It is one of the kindest negative satiric takes on a president. Carvey takes shots at Bush and presents him as someone not up to the challenges of the office, yet he never demeans or belittles Bush. The satire is very light, and most of the comedy comes from Carvey's excellent performance. Carvey joyously plays Bush, imbuing him with a playful charm that makes the actual Bush more likable. Watching the sketches, it is clear that Carvey is having a good time playing the part, which gives the impression a softer edge than Chevy Chase's Ford or Alec Baldwin's Trump. While the impression is excellent, what makes it significant is how Bush himself reacted to it.

Most presidents have accepted satiric takes as part of the job. They might not like it, but for the most part, they have endured them. Bush, on the other hand, much like Carvey, seemed to relish the impression. He didn't love all comedy about him, he had a rather famous spat with *Doonesbury* cartoonist Gary Trudeau, but he did love Carvey's loving impersonation. Bush began adopting Carvey's catchphrases as a way to earn laughs himself,[37] and even famously invited Carvey to the White House to cheer up his staff after losing the 1992 election. Both men saw their relationship as essential to the health of the nation, with Bush commenting at the 1992 event that "The fact that we can laugh at each other . . . is a very fundamental thing."[38] Yet again, we see the president defending satire's role in America. It is the freedom to criticize our leaders that makes America great. Bush, like many before and after, is using the concept of political satire to spread American values.

By the time Bush left office, there was a new standard for both presidential sketch comedy as well as presidential identity. What began with Meader's impression of JFK was solidified with Carvey's Bush – the conflation of identity between comic and president. People began to see Carvey's Bush as an authentic and real representation. People began assigning Carvey's catchphrases to Bush, to the point that Bush had to stop using his "a thousand points of light" phrase because Carvey's Bush had rendered it a mockery. What set Bush apart from his predecessors was that he was an active participant. He didn't merely good-naturedly laugh at Carvey, he joined in. This active participation worked to build a friendship between the two men, but it also worked to soften the bite of Carvey's impression. Carvey's Bush also set a new standard for *how* to satirize a president. By focusing mainly on personality and physical/vocal quirks, the policy would take a back seat to personality. As Jeffrey P. Jones argues, there is a definite shift toward an "emphasis on physical or phonetic resemblance that focuses on the politician's presentation of self."[39] This positioning is due to Carvey's performance as much as Bush's policies. The portrayal was as much about Carvey as Bush, turning Carvey into the premiere sketch comedian of the time.

A Break of Safe Satire

The 12 years of Reagan and Bush satire was tame compared to what came before and after. There was almost a holding period of biting satire. The tumult of the 1960s and the shock and cynicism of Watergate left many wanting a sense of normalcy. Much like the 1950s, the 1980s seemed to be an era of normalcy. With the fall of the Soviet Union, the Iran-Contra affair, and the AIDS epidemic, that's a façade, but satirists mirrored the national mood of conservatism in the 1980s. Neither president faced harsh satiric criticism. Even lightning rod political issues often escaped a strong satiric response. The Supreme Court confirmation hearings of Clarence Thomas in 1991 are an excellent example. The hearings were national news, airing on network television and captivating the nation. Thomas, who was accused of sexual harassment by Anita Hill, was eventually confirmed after a bitter partisan fight that Thomas famously described as a "high tech lynching."[40] Rather than satirize Thomas or explore the allegations brought by Hill, *SNL*'s sketch framed Thomas as bad at picking up women. The senators questioning him alternate between asking Thomas for dating advice and giving Thomas their own advice. For instance, Phil Hartman's Ted Kennedy asks Thomas, "Have you ever tried coming out of the bathroom nude and acting like you didn't know someone was there? That works, too."[41] As Allison Yarrow argues, the sketch is problematic for numerous reasons, mainly because the joke is that sexual harassment is funny. Likewise, she argues that by removing Hill from the sketch – she is in the opening moments and then literally dismissed – the sketch ignores the seriousness of sexual harassment. She argues, "they spend the whole sketch mocking sexual harassment, and conflating it with failed dating." Summing up the sketch, but also the entire *SNL* era, writer Jim Downey said, "We try to be funny first and foremost. We don't mind if the work also makes some important points, but we're ostensibly trying to be funny. . . . It just seemed like a nice, funny take on the thing. Like a silly idea. We, generally speaking, prefer silly to, like, angry and preachy."[42] *SNL*'s "silly" response to the hearings serves as an illustrative sketch of the show's attitude toward political sketch comedy of the time. Its "silliness" partly demonstrates why Reagan and Bush received relatively little harsh comedic treatment. Americans wanted silly satire, not angry satire.

As the 1990s began, there was a sense of stagnation setting in, yet the country didn't feel like it was going off course. John Lopez argues that

> there was an air of bland, reassuring consensus underscored by light dissatisfaction. We didn't want to rock the boat too much, just giggle at our aging elders – the greatest generation who didn't quite get it anymore. You could appreciate Bush Senior's deep understanding of government while still suspecting his hand at the helm shook a little more than was ideal.[43]

It was safe to laugh at a "Mastermind" Reagan, or a dorky Bush wildly gesticulating. In part, the safe nature of the satire reflects the country's relative stability. As Sophia McClennen argues, "Robust satire is often a sign of crisis and the ability to share and consume it is a sign of a free society.... We see satire emerge when political discourse is in crisis and when it becomes important to use satirical comedy to put political pressure on misinformation, folly, and the abuse of power."[44] Carvey's Bush perfectly encapsulated a time when even though the president wasn't wildly popular, there was not a great deal of unrest about it. Unlike the 1960s and 1970s, satire didn't need to defend American ideals from enemies foreign and domestic. Americans might not have been thrilled with the state of the country by 1992, but they were okay with it. Americans didn't want radical change, so the era's satire was relatively light. The next two occupants of the White House would not be so lucky.

Notes

1. "Inaugural Address," *The Reagan Foundation*, 21 January 1981. www.reaganfoundation.org/media/128614/inaguration.pdf.
2. Qtd. in Margaret Chadbourn, "Anniversary of Ronald Reagan's Attempted Assassination," *ABC News*, 30 March 2016. https://abcnews.go.com/News/anniversary-ronald-reagans-attempted-assassination/story?id=38031365.
3. Peter M. Robinson, *Dance of the Comedians: The People, the President, and the Performance of Political Standup Comedy in America* (Amherst: University of Massachusetts Press, 2010), 204.
4. "How Good a President?" *Newsweek*, 27 August 1984, 31.
5. Qtd. in Joan A. Lowy, *Pat Schroeder: A Woman of the House* (Albuquerque: University of New Mexico Press, 2003), 10.
6. Similar complaints would later be lodged by critics of Barack Obama and Donald Trump.
7. Jules Feiffer, "You Can't Beat Reagan at Satire," *The Washington Post*, 24 May 1981. www.washingtonpost.com/archive/opinions/1981/05/24/you-cant-beat-reagan-at-satire/b54892af-2c87-4e1a-93e5-2afe6538e7ba/?utm_term=.e2df734ddef1.
8. Qtd. in Todd Purdum, "S.N.L.: The Skyscraper of Satire," *Vanity Fair*, 29 April 2011. www.vanityfair.com/news/2011/04/todd-purdum-saturday-night-live-201104.
9. Qtd. in Tom Shales and James Andrew Miller, *Live From New York: An Uncensored History of Saturday Night Live* (Boston: Little, Brown and Company, 2002), 223.
10. Qtd. in Shales and Miller, 223.
11. Qtd. in Shales and Miller, 274.
12. Dennis Perrin, "'Fridays': The 'SNL' Ripoff That Nearly Surpassed the Original," *Vulture*, 31 January 2012. www.vulture.com/2012/01/fridays-the-snl-ripoff-that-nearly-surpassed-the-original.html.
13. Perrin.
14. "The Ronald Reagan Mic Drop Moment at the 1984 Debate," *NBC News*, 22 September 2016. www.youtube.com/watch?v=22Lr4fgSFAY.
15. Patrick A. Stewart, "Presidential Laugh Lines: Candidate Display Behavior and Audience Laughter in the 2008 Primary Debates," *Politics and the Life Sciences* 29, no. 2 (2010), 56.
16. Lesley Stahl, *Reporting Live* (New York: Touchstone, 1999), 257.
17. "President Reagan, Mastermind," *Saturday Night Live*, 4 October 2013. www.youtube.com/watch?v=b5wfPlgKFh8.

18. Neel Burton, "The Meaning of Nostalgia," *Psychology Today*, 27 November 2014. www.psychologytoday.com/us/blog/hide-and-seek/201411/the-meaning-nostalgia.
19. "Altered Statesman," *Fridays*, 27 February 1981. www.youtube.com/watch?v=JJCSRYzzEM.
20. "That Darned Reagan," *Fridays*, 23 January 1981. www.youtube.com/watch?v=5gQejSbrEfg.
21. "The Ronnie Horror Picture Show, *Fridays*, 12 December 1980. www.youtube.com/watch?v=hupJFbKIIpc.
22. Frederick M. Winship, "Reagan Satire Opens Off-Broadway," *United Press International*, 3 October 1984. www.upi.com/Archives/1984/10/03/Reagan-satire-opens-off-Broadway/9195465624000/.
23. Qtd. in Winship.
24. Frank Rich, "Stage: Partisan Revue, 'Rap Master Ronnie,'" *New York Times*, 4 October 1984. www.nytimes.com/1984/10/04/arts/stage-partisan-revue-rap-master-ronnie.html.
25. Terry Atkinson, "Television Reviews: Cinemax's Grades Slump with 'Rap Master Ronnie,'" *Los Angeles Times*, 12 February 1988. www.latimes.com/archives/la-xpm-1988-02-12-ca-28768-story.html.
26. Qtd. in Aimee Ortiz, "Jim Morris, The Other Bush Impersonator, Recalls 41," *Boston Globe*, 4 December 2018. https://www2.bostonglobe.com/opinion/2018/12/04/jim-morris-other-bush-impersonator/Lqq1hN4Mfn4TR7chlDpYHK/story.html.
27. "ABC Campaign '88," *Saturday Night Live*, 8 October 1988. www.nbc.com/saturday-night-live/video/abc-campaign-88/n9702.
28. Qtd. in Shales and Miller, 347.
29. Sarah Mervosh, "How George Bush Befriended Dana Carvey, the 'S.N.L.' Comedian Who Impersonated Him," *The New York Times*, 1 December 2018. www.nytimes.com/2018/12/01/arts/george-bush-dana-carvey.html.
30. Qtd. in Shales and Miller, 347.
31. "Presidential Address: Bush's First 100 Days Cold Open," *Saturday Night Live*, 22 April 1989. www.nbc.com/saturday-night-live/video/presidential-address-bushs-first-100-days-cold-open/2859810.
32. "George Bush Taxes Cold Opening," *Saturday Night Live*, 19 May 1990. www.nbc.com/saturday-night-live/video/george-bush-taxes-cold-opening/n9730.
33. David Sims, "Dana Carvey's George H.W. Bush Was an All-Time Great *SNL* Impression," *The Atlantic*, 3 December 2018. www.theatlantic.com/entertainment/archive/2018/12/dana-carveys-george-h-w-bush-impression-saturday-night-live/577186/.
34. "Bush Cold Open," *Saturday Night Live*, NBC, 15 December 1990. www.nbc.com/saturday-night-live/video/bush-cold-open/n9998.
35. William Hughes, "George H.W. Bush Has Died, but Pop Culture's Impression of Him Lives on," *The A.V. Club*, 1 December 2018. https://news.avclub.com/george-h-w-bush-has-died-but-pop-cultures-impression-1830789538.
36. "Bush Cold Open," *Saturday Night Live*, 10 November 1990. www.nbc.com/saturday-night-live/video/bush-cold-open/n9968.
37. Bush gave the commencement address at my alma mater, Monmouth College, in 2000 and uttered numerous Carvey catchphrases to the delight of the audience.
38. Mervosh.
39. Jeffrey P. Jones, "With All Due Respect," in *Satire TV: Politics and Comedy in the Post-Network Era* (New York: New York University Press, 2009), 43.
40. "Flashback: Clarence Thomas Responds to Anita Hill," *CNN*, 13 April 2016. www.youtube.com/watch?v=ZURHD5BU1o8.

41. "Cold Open," *Saturday Night Live*, 12 October 1991. www.nbc.com/saturday-night-live/video/cold-opening/n10108.
42. Qtd. in Travis M. Andrews, "SNL's 1991 Clarence Thomas Sketch Resonates Today: But Is It Problematic in the #MeToo Era?" *The Washington Post*, 27 September 2018. www.washingtonpost.com/news/arts-and-entertainment/wp/2018/09/27/snls-1991-clarence-thomas-sketch-resonates-today-but-is-it-problematic-in-the-metoo-era/.
43. John Lopez, "And Now, Ladies and Gentlemen, a Message from the 'Saturday Night Live' President of the United States," *Grantland*, 25 August 2014. http://grantland.com/hollywood-prospectus/saturday-night-live-president-impressions/.
44. Qtd. in Matthew Swayne, "Satire Is as American as Apple Pie," *US News and World Report*, 30 January 2015. www.usnews.com/news/blogs/at-the-edge/2015/01/29/satire-is-as-american-as-apple-pie.

CHAPTER 6

The Clintons

Much like the election of John F. Kennedy marked a generational shift in leadership in 1960, the election of Bill Clinton in 1992 signaled a new era in American politics. Like JFK, Clinton was young, charismatic, and, at least by political standards, cool. He was the first president to grow up in the postwar boom, coming of age alongside the growth of sketch comedy on television. As such, Clinton was especially adept at using TV and its entertainment value as a way to enhance his appeal. He was one of the first presidents to appear on a late-night television talk show, famously playing the saxophone in 1992 on *The Arsenio Hall Show*. If the initial problem with George H.W. Bush was that there wasn't anything to grasp onto to satirize him, Bill Clinton represented the opposite problem. The voice, the slick-talking, the womanizing, the scandals, his "I feel your pain" persona, and voracious appetite for food and women all became staples of Clinton satire and omnipresent in 1990s American popular culture. Like Kennedy, nearly everyone had a Bill Clinton vocal impression. His slow somewhat sly slightly raspy Southern drawl echoed across America. During Clinton's second term (and well beyond), it was nearly impossible to avoid Monica Lewinsky jokes. He was the perfect president for the newly dominant personality-driven satire, and everyone got in on the jokes. One study about political humor found that between 1992 and 2012 Clinton was the butt of the joke more so than any other president, with the authors noting that "Clinton personally accounted for nearly one out of ten jokes about politics and political affairs over the entire two decades of our study [1992–2012]."[1]

Part of the reason there were so many jokes is because the Clinton presidency existed in scandals. From Gennifer Flowers to Paula Jones to White House travel to Whitewater to Monica Lewinsky: the Clintons were constantly under investigation. Thanks to a robust economy and his political skill and charm, Clinton only got more popular with Americans as his scandals deepened. Just the second president to ever be impeached, Clinton's popularity rating actually *increased* as a result of his impeachment, with Democrats gaining seats in the 1998 midterm elections. The Monica Lewinsky scandal captured the nation's almost undivided attention. His affair with Lewinsky, a 22-year-old White House intern, was uncovered in part through two other investigations: his affair with Paula Jones and Whitewater. Linda Tripp, a confidant of Lewinsky who had been recording their phone conversations and convinced Lewinsky not to dry-clean the infamous blue dress, discovered an affidavit in connection to the Paula Jones case in which Lewinsky swore that she did not have a relationship with Clinton. Tripp gave the affidavit to Kenneth Starr, who was the independent counsel investigating Whitewater (and several other matters). Clinton denied the affair, emphatically stating, "I did not have sexual relations with that woman, Miss Lewinsky." Clinton found himself in trouble when it became clear that was not true – perjury was one of the articles of impeachment. Clinton testified before a grand jury as part of Starr's investigation and was notoriously evasive. When asked if he had a relationship with Lewinsky, he defended telling his top aides and the American public that nothing was going on between him and Lewinsky by saying, "It depends on what the meaning of the word 'is' is." Speaking to the American people directly that evening, August 17, 1998, Clinton admitted to the relationship, then called on the country to move on from the scandal. He implored Americans to let it go: "This matter is between me, the two people I love most – my wife and our daughter – and our God. I must put it right, and I am prepared to do whatever it takes to do so."[2] Americans did not let it go, the media continued its Lewinsky frenzy, Clinton was impeached (but not convicted in the Senate), and comedians of all stripes began a relentless onslaught of blowjob jokes. Clinton's own words became a significant source of the comedy – a clear marker of the satiric shift to amplifying the real in the absurd rather than vice versa. There was no need to make the Clinton–Lewinsky scandal absurd because it was doing that just fine on its own. The best satire of the Clinton years worked to amplify the real behind the ridiculous, yet much of the Clinton satire focused on the absurd itself, repeating jokes about Clinton's sexual exploits.

His various scandals impeded his legislative agenda, but so too did the emergence of conservative talk radio and Fox News, both of which used Clinton's shortcomings as weapons against his policy agenda. Newt Gingrich launched his "Contract With America" ahead of the 1994 midterm elections, laying out a national conservative plan that helped Republicans win considerable gains in Congress. Despite that, in 1996, Clinton became the first Democrat to win two terms in a generation, beating Bob Dole rather handily. Even though the drumbeat from Gingrich and conservative media was that Clinton was wildly radical, his policy agenda was decidedly centrist. He was a "new" Democrat, legislating from the middle. His few forays into what would be considered staunchly liberal policy, namely his 1994 healthcare plan headed by Hillary Clinton, were massive political failures. Yet neither personal scandal nor political losses stuck to Clinton in terms of his popularity. Like Reagan, he seemed to be covered in Teflon, emerging from every new battle more and more popular. His "Slick Willy" persona came to define his satiric persona, a larger than life character who could charm his way into, and out of, anything.

The 1992 Election

Some election years are better than others for satirists. The 1992 election proved to be exceptionally fertile ground. The patrician Bush was facing off against the young Southerner with a penchant for women – a tremendous comedic contrast.

What tipped the scales to make this one of the exceptional election cycles for satire, and arguably helped tip the scales for Clinton's victory, was the emergence of third-party candidate H. Ross Perot. An eccentric billionaire from Texas, Perot threw a wrench into the political world when his third-party candidacy became a viable challenge to the two-party system. Perot was the most successful third-party candidate since Theodore Roosevelt in 1912, and even though he never had a realistic path to the White House, he did win nearly 20 million votes, just under 19% of the popular vote (Clinton won 43%, Bush 37%). A former Republican, Perot ran as an Independent with a conservative economic message, mostly railing against the North American Free Trade Agreement (NAFTA) and warning the rising national debt was "destroying the country." His policies were incredibly vague, but he was a magnet for people disenfranchised by the system and worried about America's increasingly global economy. He was also a comedy magnet. He seemed like a sketch comedy invention. He was short, brash, politically unpolished, and spoke in a rapid Texas accent that was unmistakable. In hindsight, his candidacy was a roadmap for a future eccentric billionaire with a distinct accent intent on disrupting the system: Donald Trump. Democratic strategist James Carville summed it up, saying, "If Donald Trump is the kind of Jesus of the disenchanted, displaced non-college white voter, then Perot was the John the Baptist of that sort of movement."[3] Like Trump, Perot had an outsized personality, was a master of television, and wasn't afraid to say controversial things.

The combination of Bush, Clinton, and Perot was the stuff of sketch comedy dreams. According to Al Franken, when he showed a tape of Perot to Lorne Michaels and Dana Carvey before Perot was nationally known, Carvey remarked, "Oh my God, he's a fully formed three-dimensional comic character!"[4] In one of the first sketches featuring Carvey's Perot, Perot offers to pay for all the damage done during the Los Angeles riots and then offers to be president for free, but only if he gets a cut of the country's economic growth: if it hits 3% growth he gets $1 billion, 4% and he gets $20 billion, and if it gets to 5% he gets $50 billion – "everybody's happy."[5] Perot reportedly called Carvey to congratulate him on the impression, allegedly trying to get Carvey to stump for him: "Tell you what we do. You get on that costume and makeup and go around the country. Then they'll be two of me! Cover twice the territory!"[6] With Perot, it was not entirely clear if he was joking or serious. He probably would have welcomed Carvey stumping for him across the country. Carvey certainly helped expose Americans to Perot, undoubtedly helping Perot gain visibility and publicity for his message. While Carvey was obviously mocking Perot, given the platform of *SNL* at the very least his impression made Perot more well-known. The biggest obstacle to any third-party candidate is exposure. Perot bought large chunks of air time on television to do political infomercials, but arguably Carvey's impression did more to make Perot a household name than anything.

Thanks to his ad buys, *SNL* exposure, and message that resonated with disaffected Americans, Perot gained momentum as the election neared. As absurd as he seemed, Perot became a serious contender, one without a clear path to victory, but a candidate that was going to impact the outcome of the election. As he became more and more popular, *SNL* continued to mine his character for material. The October 3, 1992, cold open featured a paid address from Perot, which were common in reality, in which Carvey's Perot satirizes the comedic take on Perot's appearance:

> I want to focus on the issues in this campaign, but seems these people in the press want to focus on my business practices or some fella I might have fired or my physical appearance ... my ears maybe. I got funny ears, fine. Let's have a debate on my ears, is that what you want? Here's the deal on my ears: large, oversized lobs filled with wax and covered with thousands of spiky hairs. Are you happy? You got your lead story? You go do your story on that, I'm going to talk about real issues.

He then goes on to talk about the numerous stories and jokes about his height. "Go write your midget article while I save this country from ruin." He then details his draconian plans to cut the deficit, including an 8:45 p.m. curfew, a 4:45 a.m. national wake-up siren, and a single style of shoe for all Americans.[7] Here we have an absurd real-life character played on a comedy show complaining about how the real Perot was being satirized on comedy shows. It's a self-critique of the way the news media and comedians focus so much on his personality quirks rather than his policy vision. As big of a joke as Perot was to many comedians, he had a serious impact on the election and is responsible for bringing the national debt into the political conversation.

When Perot picked Admiral James Stockdale as his running mate, it was a gift from the satiric gods. Stockdale was rough around the edges, appeared to know almost nothing about the issues, and was terrible on television – his famous debate answer, "Who am I? Why am I here?" became the stuff of comedic legend. The Perot–Stockdale ticket featured much more *SNL* airtime than any previous third-party candidacy. "Joyride With Perot" in October 1992 featured the two men out on a country road taking a long ride. As Perot reminisces about the campaign, Stockdale (Phil Hartman) blurts out debate phrases and nonsequiturs, while his face and eyes continuously twitch. When Perot turns to the election and the perception that Stockdale was dragging down the ticket, Perot references Stockdale's terrible performance during the vice presidential debate, saying, "When you were quiet there for an hour, that was world-class."[8] As Perot continues to go over the litany of Stockdale's debate missteps, Perot pulls over the car and tells Stockdale to take a look at a deer in the distance. When Stockdale gets out, Perot pulls away, leaving Stockdale behind. Suddenly we see Stockdale chasing down the car before hopping back in. The two were like an old vaudeville duo, who happened to be running for president in real life.

With the emergence of Perot, the 1992 debates proved to be thoroughly bizarre. *SNL*'s debate sketch is one of its very best. Featuring Carvey as both Bush and Perot,[9] and Phil Hartman as Clinton, it manages to encapsulate the absurdity of the 1992 election cycle perfectly. Aired on October 10, 1992, the sketch is more a showcase of Dana Carvey than biting political satire. Clinton spends most of the debate deflecting questions about Arkansas and its backward ways. He continually cites statistics that Arkansas is on the rise, such as, "When I started as governor we were 50th in adult literacy, and last year I'm proud to say we shot ahead of Mississippi. That's right, we're number 49, and we're closing in fast on Alabama – watch out Alabama, we've got your number!" Bush retorts that while on a fishing trip to Arkansas he was "chased and assaulted by a couple of inbred mountain people." Bush continues to rail against Arkansas, attempting to be forceful and stern but coming off as out of touch and weak. Perot hammers the national debt, his signature issue, stating, "Can we talk about the deficit? While we've been here jabbering, our deficit has increased by half-a-million dollars. That's enough to buy a still and a new outhouse for every family in Little Rock."[10] The debate ends with each candidate looking at the other and imagining what they really look like: Bush sees Clinton as a weed-smoking hippie; Clinton sees Bush as an older woman in pearls; and the two see Perot as a munchkin from *Wizard of Oz*. All three candidates had distinct personality quirks, leading to *SNL* zeroing in almost exclusively on personality-based satire. The distinctive characters were part of it, but it was also a reflection of Americans' attitude – they didn't want angry satire. They wanted silly satire, and the addition of Perot pushed it to the forefront.

Carvey's Bush put policy-through-personality satire out in front, but it was the 1992 election with Bush, Clinton, and Perot that solidified this new satiric approach to the presidency. Seth Meyers, commenting about the 2004 and 2008 elections, summed up the transition, saying "It helps us when the D.C. characters are bigger because, as actors, we have to play those people, and just like with any impression, it helps if the target is just bigger, with funnier things about them. We don't do policy pieces as well. We do sort of big character pieces well."[11] With Bush, Clinton, and Perot, the show had three big characters to play with and were only beginning to realize the comedic depth that Clinton would provide. Clinton went on to win the 1992 election, though because of Carvey's mastery of the two losing candidates, Bush and Perot continued to make appearances on *SNL* post-election, with Carvey's Bush returning when George W. Bush won the White House eight years later.

Sketch TV Beyond *Saturday Night Live*

Clinton sketches were a regular feature on *SNL* (described in more detail below), but Clinton was the first president to find himself satirized on numerous television sketch comedy shows at the same time. Thanks to the emergence of cable television, a splintering media market, and the past success of *SCTV*, *Fridays*, and *The Kids in the Hall*, sketch comedy was no longer limited to Saturday nights on NBC. Clinton comedy found its way to virtually all of the sketch comedy shows that emerged in the 1990s. None of these sketches were as influential as Phil Hartman's or Darrell Hammond's *SNL* Clinton, but they do speak to the omnipresence of Clinton humor, the evolution of Clinton's sketch persona, and the vast cultural footprint of presidential sketch comedy. Second City likewise had a creative rebirth in the 1990s that reflected the growing Gen-X aesthetic – "steeped in irony, detachment, and a sense of dread" – and helped reassert its satiric muscle and influence.[12] The 1990s proved to be a fertile combination of new sketch comedy outlets, a new generational outlook, and an ideal sketch comedy target.

In Living Color and *MADtv*

In the late 1980s and into the 1990s, Fox sat on the outside of the three big network stations – ABC, CBS, and NBC. The network made a concerted effort in the 1990s to attract younger viewers as a way to bolster its standing and increase revenue. They bought the rights to broadcast NFL games beginning in 1994, became a player in late-night talk shows with *The Late Show with Joan Rivers* (1986-1987), the ill-fated *Chevy Chase Show* (1993), and *The Arsenio Hall Show* (1989-1994). They joined the sketch comedy ranks in 1990 with the critically acclaimed *In Living Color* (1990-1994), followed by *MADtv* (1995-2009). Both shows challenged *SNL*'s dominance and featured outsized characters and catchphrases that became fixtures of 1990s America.

In Living Color was more focused on satirizing American culture and race in the 1990s than doing traditional political sketch comedy. The show certainly was political, taking on stereotypes about African Americans and turning them on their head. The show was at the satiric forefront of commentary on Rodney King and the L.A. riots. King had been dragged from his car and beaten by the LAPD. The assault was caught on video and stunned many white Americans who couldn't conceive of the police in that manner. When an all-white jury acquitted the officers, Los Angeles erupted into riots. *In Living Color* addressed the riots numerous times, including in one sketch featuring David Alan Grier as Rodney King and Jim Carrey as Reginald Denny, the white truck driver pulled from his vehicle and beaten on live television. The two implore viewers to "stay in your car," as their physical tics – King's face twitches and sways and Carrey's eyes are crossed – act as a reminder of the violence and anger at the heart of the riots. The show proved to be a way to process the massive riots. As Amanda Nell Edgar argues, "And for some of us distanced both proximally and culturally from the Uprising, the parody not only made sense through our understanding of the real – the real made sense through the lens of the parody. This complex interplay fused together my memory of the comic signifier and the tragic signified forever."[13] Grier's repetition of King's own plea – "Can't we all just get along?" – was funny and a gut punch. The show dealt with the situation much more effectively, and frequently, than *SNL*.

In Living Color was a master of social satire, but they didn't do a ton of traditional political satire. That said, the show did feature several Bill Clinton sketches, though unlike *MADtv* and *SNL*, they weren't recurring. The first, "Humpin' Around," aired two days before the 1992 election. Clinton's sexual proclivities were a fairly steady ingredient in Clinton comedy, and "Humpin' Around" is no exception. Clinton is played by Jim Carrey (billed at the time as James Carrey) in a relatively broad impersonation. A detailed Clinton impression is not the point of the sketch; after all, the real Clinton didn't break into choreographed dance very often. The sketch begins as a final press conference before the election, where Clinton tells the American people that Bush "has proven we can't believe anything he says." A reporter asks how the American people can trust Clinton, especially given his affairs, at which point Clinton throws aside the microphone and a music video breaks out, complete with MTV-style credits in the lower-left-hand corner of the screen (the song is on the record "Too Much Lust to Trust," released by Infidelity Records). Set to the beat of Bobby Brown's number-one hit of the same name, Clinton dances and gyrates across the stage complete with a saxophone solo, with the show's iconic Fly Girls dancing behind him. The lyrics satirize Clinton's womanizing and reflect the raunchier nature of *In Living Color* compared to the relatively staid *SNL*:

> When you trust someone
> And then you say he lied.
> You believe it was Gennifer Flowers,
> And you claim that I am not qualified
> Because I work that booty for hours.
> I'm not a draft dodger.
> No, not like that fool Quayle.
> No, don't believe the thing they say.
> (Spoken) I'm not an adulterer (wink), and I did not inhale (chokes).
> So vote for me on election day!
>
> (Chorus) Get up off my back.
> Let me blow my sax.
> Ain't nobody humpin' around.
> Ain't nobody humpin'.
> I'm not a gigolo.
> I never had a ho.
> Ain't nobody humpin' around.[14]

The song hits all of the high notes about Clinton during the election cycle – his womanizing, his famous statement that he tried marijuana but did not inhale, and his saxophone. It also showcases him as young and fresh. The lyrics make fun of Clinton, but it is clear that Clinton is actually being presented in a positive light. The song is encouraging you to vote for Clinton despite his shortcomings. In this way, the sketch is representative of most Clinton satire. It highlights his womanizing, but does so in a way that presents his exploits as overblown, and rather than criticize him, they celebrate him. The treatment of Clinton's womanizing is a clear reflection of sketch comedy's historic male perspective.

Three days before Clinton's inauguration in 1993, *In Living Color* did another song sketch, "The Capital Hillbillies." Using the theme song from *The Beverly Hillbillies*, the song tracks Clinton's journey from Arkansas to the White House.

Stepping out of a Clampett-style shack, Jim Carrey's Clinton appears dressed as Jed Clampett, complete with shotgun, while the song plays:

> Come and listen to a story 'bout a man named Bill,
> Hick Razorback with a destiny to fill.
> But 20 years before he would take the oath and freed,
> He dodged Vietnam and he toked a little weed.
> Reefer, that is. Mary Jane. Didn't inhale.
>
> The next thing you know Bill's the head of Arkansas,
> Fiddlin' with the budget and a honey from Yee-Haw (Gennifer Flowers enters and sits on Bill's lap).
> Said "Hey Bill, you should be the Chief Exec,"
> So he balanced off the ticket with another redneck.
> Gore, that is. Senator. Tennessee.

After a shot of the Clinton's in the Clampett's rickety truck driving into Washington, with Hillary driving and Bill playing the jug, the song continues.

> So now it's time to say goodbye to Bush and all his kin,
> So take that dog and Millie too, 'cause Bill's a swearin' in.
> He better work some miracles on this economy,
> And not do to the country what he does to Hillary.
> Gennifer, too. Take your clothes off.
> Y'all come again now, ya hear.[15]

The sketch is an obvious play on Clinton's Arkansas upbringing, with plenty of jokes about his relationship with Gennifer Flowers and the tension between him and Hillary. Clinton himself recalled his childhood in Hope, Arkansas, regularly on the campaign trail, using it to evoke his rural roots and ingrained hard work – his version of the Stage Yankee character. It also was one of the many contrasts between Clinton and the patrician Bush and the cultural change that was coming to Washington, D.C. It evoked Tyler's 1787 play *The Contrast*, pitting the rural hillbilly Clinton as superior to the aristocratic Bush. Furthermore, the sketch is an excellent example of the use of pop culture on *In Living Color*. The show regularly used pop culture as a way to satirize pop culture, creating numerous song parodies, and often presenting "black" examples of white television shows, such as "Tales From the Crib," "The Homeboy Shopping Network," and "East Hollywood Squares."

When *In Living Color* left Fox, the network ultimately replaced it with *MADtv*, which featured a heavier dose of Clinton sketches. *MADtv* was big and brash, but not quite as sophisticated in its satiric take on American culture. As such, their satire of Clinton doesn't go much beyond an oversexualized Clinton. Played by a few different cast members over the years, the most notable and longest-lasting

Clinton was played by Will Sasso, who didn't join the cast until 1997, the beginning of Clinton's second term. Clinton comedy had been on the show, but it wasn't until Sasso took on the role that it became a recurring sketch. Sasso's Clinton works harder to be an impression than Carrey's, though while Sasso has a distinct Clinton voice, many of the other mannerisms and appearance of the president are broad. Sasso's Clinton is an excellent character sketch as his Clinton has a distinct point of view pushed to comic extremes; however, it is not a great example of presidential satire. Much of the humor relies simply on an oversexualized Clinton in situations where Sasso can heighten that aspect of Clinton's character. The character is big and broad, and the same is true about the content of the sketches. The first Sasso/Clinton sketch is a fictional sequel to the movie *Liar Liar* (in which, ironically, Jim Carrey plays a lawyer who cannot lie). In the sketch, Clinton is unable to lie and admits to a whole slew of wrongdoings. A month later in November 1997, Sasso's Clinton and Nicole Sullivan's Hillary Clinton have a town hall turn into an episode of *The Jerry Springer Show*. JFK's ghost visits Clinton in a March 1998 sketch. After Clinton swears he'll never have sex again, JFK (played in a very generic manner by Chris Hogan) appears to tell him that he must sleep with as many women as possible. The two presidents swap as many sex jokes and double-entendres as possible, such as Clinton's "Ask not what your country can do for you, but who in your country you can do." Again, we see Clinton's affairs as laughing matters and nothing more. The Clinton sketches continue in this vein for several seasons – make as many sex jokes as possible, present Hillary as an unlikable wife, and then make more sex jokes. Even sketches that don't rely on sex jokes, such as the rather clever sketch featuring Clinton taking a job as Nurse #2 on *General Hospital* post-presidency, undercut more subtle humor and rely on easy sex jokes for laughs.

The Dana Carvey Show

Both of Fox's sketch shows found a natural audience. The same was not true of ABC's *The Dana Carvey Show*. When Carvey left *SNL*, it was a massive comedy moment. How would *SNL* replace the iconic and versatile Carvey? And what would be the comedian's next move? – a question so prevalent in American pop culture that made its way to the cover of *Rolling Stone*. Carvey turned down movies and an offer to take over David Letterman's late-night slot, opting to bring sketch comedy to primetime network television. Carvey and *SNL* writer Robert Smigel teamed up and began pitching their idea to the various networks, including HBO. They opted for ABC, despite Carvey's misgivings and desire to go to HBO, because ABC offered them a lucrative deal and a slot after *Home Improvement*, the number-one show on television. Carvey assembled what many have viewed as the greatest comedy talent collection since *Your Show of Shows* historic writers' room. Robert Smigel, Louis C.K., Charlie Kaufman, Jon Glaser, Robert Carlock, Bob Odenkirk, and Dino Stamatopoulos were all part of the creative team and writing staff, while the cast featured Bill Chott, Heather Morgan, Chris McKinney, and a couple of unknown Steves from Second City – Steve Carell and Stephen Colbert. It seemed like a masterpiece waiting to happen, but instead turned into one of the most fabulous flops in sketch comedy history, lasting only seven episodes. ABC thought they were getting the premiere sketch comedy talent to do something akin to *The Carol Burnett Show* with regular appearances by Carvey characters like the Church Lady, but Carvey's aesthetic was closer to the irreverent, absurdist nature of *Monty Python*, only with a harder edge. Instead of Dean Martin's and Jerry Lewis's mainstream sensibility and charm, ABC got Ernie Kovacs pushing the boundaries and experimenting with the medium. Carvey wanted to blow up the system, but instead, his show imploded.

Many factors led to the show's downfall, but one of the biggest was its placement as a primetime network show. Carvey desired to bring sketch comedy back to its primetime roots, having grown up in an age where sketch comedy variety shows were more common (this is also why each episode had a different sponsor as an homage to shows like the *Colgate Comedy Hour*). But unlike the broad appeal and variety nature of those earlier shows, Carvey's show was not primetime friendly. Much like *The Richard Pryor Show* two decades before, the content was not well suited to primetime. While being slotted directly after Tim Allen's *Home Improvement*, a traditional sitcom about a typical American man obsessed with power tools and sports trying to balance his masculinity with his domestic responsibilities, seemed like a great lead-in due to its huge audience, the contrast in content was a recipe for disaster. *Home Improvement*, like many of ABC's shows at the time, was a family-friendly show, one meant to be watched by parents and their children. It was a comedy, but it also dealt with weightier issues. For instance, one of the *Home Improvement* lead-in episodes featured one of Allen's sons on the show facing a life-threatening medical diagnosis – not precisely the ideal lead-in for an absurdist sketch comedy show looking to blow up the establishment. The show's very first sketch also set the show on a collision course with cancellation, and it was the show's one sketch featuring Bill Clinton.

There was a lot of internal debate about whether they wanted to start the series with an offbeat presidential sketch. Viewers tuning in would love to see Carvey-as-Clinton, but the content of the sketch was hardly reminiscent of Carvey's Bush sitting in the Oval Office directly addressing the American people. Ultimately, they decided to go with the sketch, which sent *Home Improvement* viewers running for their remotes. Carvey's Clinton appears in the Oval Office to talk about the upcoming 1996 election, and everything seems normal, aside from Clinton wearing what appears to be a rather broad suit jacket. He laughs about the quality of the potential candidates and relishes his chances of winning a second term. So far so good – ABC is getting the Carvey that was an *SNL* star. But then it takes a turn. He announces that he's locked Hillary away in another room to keep her out of the picture for his next term. The show was overwhelmingly white and male, with Heather Morgan appearing mostly as wives and girlfriends, and in this case, given a nonspeaking role of a woman locked in a cage. By 1996, Hillary Clinton-as-demon jokes were common, so while portraying Hillary in this manner is certainly problematic and indicative of the show's lack of diversity, it was unfortunately not an uncommon depiction. He then declares that with Hillary out of the picture, he will be both the father and mother to the country. Then things get weird. Clinton announces he's taken estrogen therapy to develop the ability to breastfeed. A baby is brought on, and Clinton unbuttons his shirt and begins breastfeeding. Then the show boldly declares that it is not going to be Carvey repeating his *SNL* hits. Clinton stands up and fully opens his shirt to reveal eight working nipples. Real puppies and kittens are brought on and begin to drink actual milk from Clinton's teats. Within three minutes, it was clear that ABC wasn't getting another Carol Burnett. According to real-time ratings, "in the first few minutes the show lost millions of *Home Improvement* viewers who had hung around to check it out."[16] Clinton then turns to reveal that he's had a hen's bottom added to his body so that he can keep eggs warm while he's in the Oval Office. Reflecting on the sketch, Smigel said,

> The president breast-feeding was probably the worst decision I've ever been involved in. . . . I was so stupid. I didn't even watch *Home Improvement*. I should've taken a second to watch five minutes of it. I'd heard Tim Allen had done coke and gone to jail. Then, about five shows into it, after a horrendous ratings drop-off, with every week getting worse and worse, I finally tuned in to *Home Improvement*. I was absolutely mortified. Not just for myself, but for the audience to whom I'd subjected *The Dana Carvey Show*.[17]

Smigel added, "What a huge mistake. I mean we literally killed our show in the first five minutes."[18]

In hindsight, it's clear that all Carvey had to do was a typical Clinton impression, and the show perhaps would have had a different fate. Instead, they came out guns blazing, and seven episodes later, the show was off the air. Despite its incredibly short run, the show became hugely influential in the sketch comedy world. Sketches like "Stupid Pranksters," "Waiters Who Are Nauseated by Food," "Germans Who Say Nice Things," "The Ambiguously Gay Duo," and "Maine Skinheads" all exemplified the offbeat sensibility that would come to dominate non-*SNL* sketch comedy. "Grandma the Clown," a sketch featuring an older woman with a walker dressed like a clown to entertain children, is the perfect example. In one sketch, she has a banana cream pie on her walker that is going to be smashed in her face. Only in this version, the pie is very slowly raised by a hand on a spring to gently touch Grandma the Clown in the face, at which point it slowly goes back down. Grandma the Clown has virtually no reaction aside from a soft moan, and then she stares off in the distance for 15 seconds before the sketch ends.[19] Not exactly The Church Lady or Hans and Franz, but its comic aesthetic provided a blueprint for the slew of non-network sketch comedy shows that would appear over the next two decades. Ironically absurd comedy was all the rage within the comedy community, but it had not yet gained a mainstream audience.

Mr. Show

Had Dana Carvey taken his show to HBO, it probably would have looked a bit like *Mr. Show*. Featuring David Cross and Bob Odenkirk (Odenkirk had worked on virtually every essential 1990s sketch show, including *SNL* and *The Dana Carvey Show*), *Mr. Show* proved that an offbeat sketch comedy show could be a hit under the right circumstances. Mixing live sketches with pre-taped bits, often with interweaving themes and cuts, the show became the standard-bearer for alternative comedy. It was a 1990s version of *Monty Python* mixed with an anti-*SNL* bent that came together in a low-budget manner on cable television, a show that grew in popularity and influence long after it left the air. Much more interested in characters and subverting traditional sketch comedy structure and style, *Mr. Show* did little in the way of direct political satire, though it is rife with cultural commentary. The one obvious example was the 1998 sketch "Marty Farty," a satiric take on the country's obsession with the Monica Lewinsky scandal.

Its style is indicative of the show – it is ridiculous with everything played utterly straight, almost deadpan, allowing the absurdity of the situation to provide the humor. It at first appears to be just a silly fart joke sketch, but is a deeply satirical look at the country and media's obsession with the Monica Lewinsky scandal. In the sketch, President Truman Theodore "Two-T" Fruitty, who vaguely resembles Clinton, has farted during a diplomatic gathering. Framed as an international news report, the sketch begins with news stories about a major monsoon in Myanmar, the Japanese government devaluing the yen, and the American president farting. Rather than covering the first two much more significant stories, the remainder of the news report focuses on the fart, which, "Despite the president's quick and adamant denial, the fart has captured the outrage and imagination of an entire nation." A quick montage of comic responses – including a joke from *The Chris Rock Show* and a parody of The Capital Steps song parodies, satirizes the comic reactions to the Lewinsky scandal. The president eventually issues a solemn rhyming fart joke apology, echoing Clinton's real apology, saying,

> My fellow Americans, tonight I am prepared to accept full responsibility for my actions. One week ago, Marty Farty threw a party and everyone was there. I, Two-T Fruitty, let a beauty and everyone went out for air. Now it is time to stop the attacks, the finger pointing, the giggling. For now, this matter should be between me, my wife, my pants, and our god.[20]

The sketch ends with reactions from children around the world, who all take turns laughing about farts. As Randall Colburn argues, "By anchoring [the sketch] on the flimsiest, most juvenile of jokes, the writers created a sketch that flays the mainstream media's approach to the Lewinsky scandal without ever having to mention a blowjob, let alone a cigar."[21] The sketch is illustrative of Clinton comedy. The satire is not aimed at Clinton or his behavior; instead, it targets the media's coverage of the scandal. The press made the scandal into a circus and satirizing the media's treatment of the scandal was important, but again, Clinton mostly avoids any critique. It is not his behavior that is presented as offensive; it is the media's coverage of his behavior that is absurd.

This layering of seemingly stupid, juvenile, and silly jokes with biting satire became a hallmark of the show. It set the standard for cultural commentary via sketch comedy outside of the *SNL* universe. *The Dana Carvey Show* and *Mr. Show* reflected a new trend that sketch comedy didn't necessarily have to engage with political content to be funny or popular. Whereas *SNL* and Second City made their mark through political and cultural satire, sketch comedy's new wave was moving more toward ironically detached sketch comedy. Again, we see comedy being used as a way to assert identity. The new generation sought to define themselves by laughing at a different type of comedy than their baby boomer parents. They grew up under Reagan, disaffected by the nation's conservatism. Rather than turn to activism as their parents had, this generation detached. Their comedy didn't need to directly address the presidency; instead, they sought to satirize the culture produced by the presidency. *SNL* continued to make politics and the president a major focus, but other shows no longer saw the presidency as an essential component of their content. Even Second City was moving toward a more Gen-X aesthetic.

The Return of Second City – *Piñata Full of Bees*

During the 1980s and into the early 1990s, Second City was seen more as a tourist destination than the cutting-edge satirical theatre it once was. Much as *SNL* is continually depicted as "not as good as it used to be," Second City likewise found itself repeatedly declared dead or in decline. In a review of 1988's *Kuwait Until Dark; or, Bright Lights, Night Baseball*, one reviewer summed up Second City at the time:

> In the end, my ambivalence persists. I don't know. I guess I'm hungry for something spicier. Even when it's good, this is cafeteria food. What happened to Second City's reputation for cut-and-slash satire? Are they consciously appealing to an upscale audience by hanging back and pulling their punches? Is this the gentrification of Second City? Have they become, God forbid, an institution?[22]

Longtime Chicago theatre critic Jack Helbig likewise commented on Second City of the 1980s, saying, "the Second City of the 80s perfected the corporate comedy revue, absolutely free of satire and controversy, capable of entertaining the most philistine of audiences without a single challenge to their values or wit."[23]

That all changed in 1995 with the cult-classic revue *Piñata Full of Bees*. The sketch revue form was tired, and *Piñata* eschewed it in favor of a darker, edgier style. The revue replaced the piano with rock music, the traditional sketch with interconnected scenes. There were no blackouts, and all of the costume and prop changes happened in full view of the audience. Directed by Tom Gianas and featuring Adam McKay, Rachel Dratch, Scott Adsit, Scott Allman, Jon Glaser, and Jenna Jolovitz, the revue suddenly made Second City hip and relevant again. Audiences were slow to build for the show, but critics loved it. The *Chicago Tribune* said, "The whole revue is fresher, feistier, more invigorating and scarier – a leap forward in style that manages miraculously to breathe new life into some of the troupe's cherished themes from the past."[24] It wasn't just the format that changed, but the material as well, which was darker and more intertwining than typical Second City shows.

The *Chicago Reader* lauded the new form, but said the real breakthrough was the material itself, calling it

> easily the funniest and most intelligent, surprising, and creative stuff Second City has done in a long time.... Second City proved a long time ago that a comedy troupe can survive and even thrive (thanks to tourists, conventioneers, and suburbanites) long after its artistic death. Now they're showing that there's artistic life after death.[25]

In the improv set after the revue, the cast did one of the most notorious bits in Second City's history – "The Clinton Assassination."

As is typical with Second City, after the two-act sketch revue, there is the third act of improvised scenes as well as new and developing sketches that are being tried out in front of an audience for the next show. *Piñata* was all about breaking expectations and destroying Second City norms, so they had the idea that they would interrupt the show to announce the assassination of Bill Clinton. Scott Adsit stepped onstage during another sketch and whispered into one of the player's ears, causing the scene to end and the players to exit the stage. Adsit then stepped forward and somberly announced that Clinton had been assassinated. He said, "We're going to bring out a TV and you can watch the coverage here with us or you can go home, but the show is over."[26] The audience was stunned and silent, evoking the same atmosphere that hung in the theatre after Kennedy's assassination. The cast wheeled on a television, which played sports bloopers. Adsit and the other cast members gathered around and then just started laughing at the tape. Audiences often walked out, not knowing what was real. Adam McKay, who many credited as the driving artistic force behind the revue, later commented on the bit:

> And you know, that's the kind of thing you do when you're twenty-five or twenty-six. Now that I'm a forty-four-year-old, I think, You can't do that. What happens if someone starts sobbing? What happens if.... There are too many *what ifs*. But at twenty-six, you're not quite that compassionate. I'll now bump into members of the improv group and say, "Can you believe we did that?" But that was part of the process. We were pushing things as far as they could go. And the only reason I accept it now is that there was real satire there: entertainment and silly pop culture trumping real information. But we probably should have popped it. There probably should have been some reveal at the end. Something to clue the audience in to the fact that what they had just seen was staged.[27]

One thing was for sure; Second City was back. Given television's reach and the emergence of internet and web-based comedy, stage revues were less potent and nationally relevant but proved fertile ground for Clinton humor. Most important, Second City continued to be hugely influential training for later television satirists like Tina Fey, Amy Poehler, and Stephen Colbert. The reemergence of Second City, as well as the new Gen-X comic aesthetic of shows like *Mr. Show*, were ushering in a new type of offbeat sketch comedy, yet they were still playing second fiddle to *Saturday Night Live*.

Saturday Night Live

Carvey's Bush and the gift of the 1992 election helped reestablish *SNL* as the nation's leading satiric voice. Like with George H.W. Bush, the defining feature of *SNL*'s Clinton sketches was personality satire. Unlike with Bush, however, the friendliness of the satire quickly wore off. While Bush was an out-of-touch nerd, Clinton was a salacious figure who couldn't be trusted. Most Clinton sketches were hard on the president, but rarely did they delve into policy. Instead, they aimed at his personal failings, mostly involving his libido or appetite (and often both). On the whole, they were more nuanced than those of *MADtv*, with considerably more layered impersonations. Initially played by Phil Hartman and later by Darrell Hammond, the *SNL* Clinton was hypersexualized, but he was also always playing politics. He was never simply a man who couldn't control his urges. Instead, he was an often-brilliant man who was brought down by his inability to control his impulses. His intelligence and slick-talking was both the source of his success and his greatest weakness. Again, the satiric depictions largely avoid condemning his sexual proclivities. Instead, they are a result of his positive qualities pushed a bit too far. When he seemingly "got away with it," *SNL*'s Clinton became more dangerous and dark.

One of the earliest and most iconic Clinton sketches featured Phil Hartman's Clinton on a morning jog when he stops at a McDonald's. Aired a month after the election in December 1992 and before Clinton officially took office, it set up the character traits that helped Clinton win the White House but would prove to be his ultimate weakness. In the sketch, Clinton and his two Secret Service agents enter the restaurant, having only gone "three blocks." Encouraging Clinton to eat a healthier diet and take better care of himself, the agents prod Clinton to continue running. He assuages them, and they tell Clinton not to say to Mrs. Clinton that they allowed him to stop for fast food, to which Hartman's Clinton responds, "Jim, let me tell you something: There's going to be a whole bunch of things we don't tell Mrs. Clinton." From there, Clinton makes his way from table to table, charming each customer along the way. He stops at the first table to greet a mom and her new baby, Shakira. Clinton instantly responds, "Shakira, that means African princess, doesn't it? . . . She certainly is beautiful enough to be a princess." As the new mom beams and the crowd is impressed, he immediately shifts gears, "Say, you gonna finish these fries?" He eats the fries and makes his way to the next table where he meets a hardware store owner and his son. Again, Hartman's Clinton displays the one-on-one charm and policy knowledge that made Clinton such a great candidate. He charms the man and his son while pitching his idea of a network of community banks that will lend money to small businesses to help spur economic growth. Then he eats the son's untouched pickles, before telling the small business owner, "I'm going to wake up every morning, thinking about you." Next, he tackles the high cost of college . . . and a McLean burger and milkshake.

Clinton eats an Egg McMuffin as he explains why he supports intervention in Somalia. He demonstrates how Somalian warlords are intercepting food sent by an international coalition – by stealing and eating everyone's food. It's both funny and a fantastic performance by Hartman (eating while acting being one of the most underappreciated performance skills). His Clinton is at ease with people, making every person he meets feel like they are the only ones in the world. He's quick on his feet and has seemingly endless knowledge about all matters of political and international affairs. In short, he's beguiling.[28]

It is probably the nicest of the *SNL* Clinton sketches, poking fun at his appetite and smooth-talking, but ultimately showing him as a nimble and deft politician. Like the earlier Bush sketches, most of the critique is about Clinton's personality; his shortcomings are sources of humor rather than scorn. This particular sketch focuses on Clinton's personality because it happened before Clinton even officially took office, but even after his presidency had seen major legislative defeats, most satire continued to focus on his outsized personality. In part this is due to the lingering "Dana Carvey effect" and the immense success of his Bush impersonation. It also is in part due to the way the media covered Clinton – his personality and sexuality were always front and center. While his healthcare plans were roundly defeated, he was again embroiled in personal scandals, which were often covered much more extensively than his policy efforts. Truth be told, it was also *easier* to make fun of Clinton's personality than it was to satirize his healthcare policy. A charming slick talking womanizer is easier to satirize than a president who can't pass healthcare reform.

The largely rosy and benign image would change as Clinton's presidency wore on, amplified by the country's changing landscape and by *SNL*'s new Clinton, Darrell Hammond. With a strong economy, Clinton sailed to reelection in 1996, despite the government shutdown of 1995–1996 that grew out of the Republican movement that was hell-bent on stopping Clinton's agenda, outlined in Newt Gingrich's famous 1994 Contract With America. Yet for all the effort expelled to impede Clinton's agenda, even more was spent trying to tarnish Clinton personally. The strategy to attack his character as the best way to oppose his plans worked, and it is telling that so much about Clinton's presidency was about his personal shortcomings. Clinton's impeachment was not over legislative or political matters. It was because he lied about an affair. Despite Republican opposition to Clinton's agenda, much like Clinton satire, even his political opponents were more interested in taking down and exposing Clinton the man than Clinton the legislator. Hammond's Clinton seized on this atmosphere, playfully bouncing back and forth between a rascally teenager and a power-hungry man testing the limits of his power.

One of *SNL*'s all-time best impressionists, Hammond didn't take naturally to Clinton. As Hammond reflected, "I went about three months before I ever got a handle on him. He was the hardest thing I've ever done, and then my instinct told me: He's doing John Kennedy. He's doing John Kennedy! So I learned Clinton by practicing JFK's inaugural address in a southern accent."[29] Hammond developed the physical ticks of Clinton while doing stand-up at the Comedy Cellar in New York. Among the many combinations he tried out was the pursed thumb coupled with biting his lower lip – it killed and became Hammond's signature physical gesture to signify Clinton knew he was "getting away with it," depending on what the definition of "it" is. Hammond's Clinton presents a duality, but rather than the duality representing Hammond and Clinton, the duality here is between Clinton the politician and Clinton the womanizing frat boy. Nearly every sketch exploits the tension of this duality for humor. Hammond signaled this duality with his lip-biting thumb gesture, an example of what Brecht called "gestus." The physical gesture is a signal from the actor as a form of commentary on the character. In this case, the gestus is Clinton the frat boy signaling through Clinton the politician that he's "getting away with it."

Along with a distinct impression, Hammond had the good comedic fortune of playing Clinton during his tumultuous second term (and well beyond). As Clinton's scandals mounted and his dirty laundry (no pun intended) was aired for all Americans to see, Hammond's Clinton became decidedly darker than Hartman's. Hammond pulled back some of the façade, showing that Clinton's charm was dangerous and a weapon that the president freely utilized to get what he wanted, whether political or sexual. Hammond's Clinton willingly and knowingly pushed the boundaries of acceptable behavior, showing a president that was not spurned by his scandals but driven and inspired by them. Hammond's Clinton was also a nearly weekly presence, with Hammond eventually appearing in more than 90 sketches as Bill Clinton over almost three decades, by far the most any one person has portrayed a president on the show.

Hammond's Clinton was partly annoyed by the Lewinsky scandal, but also weirdly proud of it. He relished the image of himself as a ladies' man, even if that image was destroying his presidency. In "Deposition Cold Open," Clinton addresses the nation about the release of Paula Jones's deposition to the media. Rather than refute the 700-page report's accounts, Clinton is enthralled, saying, "My fellow Americans, I have read this document cover to cover, and folks: (thumb) it's good stuff. I mean, it's hotter than hell! And the best part is, it's all about me." He goes on to read sections of the report, damning passages that detail him sexually assaulting women, but rather than deny or apologize, he slams the book closed, pounds his fist on the desk, and exclaims, "Now that is hot! Jackie Collins my ass! . . . And I actually did all that. I mean, 'I didn't' [bites his lower lip]." Rather than try to keep the public from reading the deposition, Clinton announces that he's releasing it as a romance novel, *Deposition*.[30] The sketch perfectly captures Hammond's take on Clinton, which is further solidified in "Linda Tripp Cold Open." Aired the day after the Senate acquitted Clinton, Hammond's Clinton appears in the Rose Garden to address the nation. With his thumb out, he says, "I. Am. Bulletproof." Then turns to walk away, but returns to say, "Next time you best bring kryptonite [thumb-lip gesture]."[31] Hammond's Clinton was hypersexualized like other sketch comedy Clintons, but there were layers to his portrayal that do not exist in the other "horny Clintons." As John Lopez argues,

> Hammond played Clinton like an alto sax on *Arsenio*. He rocketed beyond the cliché of the Southern politician and sculpted a gleefully unapologetic

hound dog armed with epic charisma. If anything, his impression captured how Clinton's personal faults actually worked like a snake charmer's flute: They only made us love him more.[32]

Clinton became the perfect foil for personality-driven satire. Virtually none of his scandals were actually about policy – they were all about his character. That allowed *SNL* to go hard at Clinton the man without worrying about satirizing his politics or alienating viewers. They didn't have to worry about the intricacies of healthcare policy or criminal justice reform or the global economy. The Soviet Union was gone, and there was relative harmony domestically. Given the circumstances, they could simply make fun of Clinton having sex. His scandals were easy to understand, unlike say Iran-Contra, so there was a very low point of entry for viewers. Clinton's treatment compared with Ford's is illuminating. The Ford sketches painted the president in a negative light, but they were, in hindsight, much less prevalent than Clinton's sketches. Yet, they impacted Ford much more so than Hammond impacted Clinton. Even though there were significantly more Clinton sketches, they were not as detrimental as Ford sketches. Yes, the novelty of Ford's portrayal was influential, but Ford sketches were much more about his policy and positioning as president, while Clinton's were about sex. They didn't question Clinton's legitimacy to be president. Ford was presented as not the "real" president, whereas they teased Clinton for having affairs. Clinton sketches satirized things everyone agreed were bad, like infidelity, so *SNL* and others did not need to worry about ostracizing or offending viewers. They could attack Clinton, in part, because many Americans continued to separate Clinton's extramarital behavior from his performance as president. His approval rating going up after impeachment proves as much. Viewers could laugh at jokes about Clinton's scandals and still like President Clinton. The same was not true of Ford. Clinton satire was inherently conservative, making fun of his "bad behavior," while also excusing it. Americans liked Clinton, by and large, so satire reflected the nation's mood. It is fair to ask, however, especially in light of Ford's treatment, had satire taken a more critical approach to Clinton would it have affected public opinion. One thing is certain: Hillary Clinton did not receive the same friendly-mean treatment of her husband.

Hillary Clinton

While Bill Clinton tried to usher in a new style of government, his wife, Hillary Rodham Clinton, attempted to redefine the role of First Lady. Hillary Clinton was not interested in baking cookies. Instead, she wanted to lead an overhaul of the healthcare system. Her assertive style and refusal to be placed into a domesticated position did not sit well with a lot of people, especially conservatives who viewed the First Lady as a ceremonial position. They felt the First Lady should be seen and not heard. This misogynist attitude was fairly widespread, and cast her in a negative light – an image that for some stuck with Hillary for the remainder of her career. With a career that spans decades in public life, including two campaigns for president, Hillary Clinton has been pilloried in sketch comedy almost as much as her husband. Though she's spent nearly three decades as a character on various sketch shows, she was hardly the first First Lady satirized on *SNL*. In its very first season, "Not for First Ladies Only," Gilda Radner, as Barbara Walters (Barbara WaWa), is interviewing Betty Ford and Rosalyn Carter in the lead up to the 1976 election. The sketch is satirizing the very traditional role of First Lady that Hillary would later challenge, with Jane Curtin's Betty Ford remarking that she's a great First Lady because "I'm the kind of person you can't picture going to the bathroom."[33] Nancy Reagan was in several sketches about the Reagan presidency, but no First Lady appeared in more comedy sketches than Hillary Clinton. Her sketch comedy footprint spans decades as well as numerous positions and points of view – from First Lady to senator to presidential candidate.

Hillary's sketch comedy image, much like her accent, transformed over the decades. Initially, she was a nagging and shrill wife who didn't know her place in the White House hierarchy (or a woman's place in general). In a 1993 cold open sketch, Jan Hooks's cold, calculating, and intimidating Hillary Clinton is discussing the impending healthcare reform bill with a weak Bill (Hartman). When Bob Dole (Dan Aykroyd) enters, the two butt heads as he asks her to leave the room. She responds, "I happen to be co-president of the United States." Dole tells Hillary to be quiet, saying,

> Hillary, why don't you give it a rest? [The audience applauds.] No one elected you to a damn thing. Now last year, you made fun of women who made cookies. Well, let me tell you something, my wife, Elizabeth Dole, the best secretary of transportation this country ever had, she ran the bus of this country for four years, and they ran on time. She'd come home every night and still had time to bake me a batch of cookies. So why don't you run along and whip up a batch of chocolate chip, oatmeal raisin, macaroons, marshmallow treats, or whatever you're making and keep your nose out of things you know nothing about. [The audience applauds.]

The two then begin to physically spar, with Dole telling Bill, "You stay out of this Bill. I'm doing something you should have done a long time ago [the audience applauds]."[34] To some, she was everything wrong with the feminist movement – as evidenced both by the sketch itself and its reception by the studio audience. While the studio audiences' dislike of Clinton is apparent, so, too, is the overwhelming misogyny of this particular sketch, evident in so much of Hillary's sketch persona. In this sketch, much of the humor relies on Bob Dole beating up Hillary, with the implication that had Bill been more physically dominant, Hillary wouldn't be "so out of control." Rather than resist the stereotypical role of the First Lady, the sketch reinforces it, thereby criticizing Clinton not for her policy, but for the audacity of stepping out of line. The audiences' laughter – and even cheers – demonstrates the importance laughter plays in articulating our values at any one point in time. In this case, the sketch demonstrates the rampant misogyny of the time and the way many Americans viewed the role of First Lady, and of women in America. The

2016 campaign proved that we hadn't traveled very far from 1993, but the cheering of domestic violence to remind a woman of "her place" highlights the many challenges Hillary Clinton faced, as well as female satirists. The sketch reeks of male privilege and demonstrates yet again how important the satirist is in the satire.

Sketch comedy about presidents has historically taken a male perspective. JFK's affairs were ignored, while Clinton's were weirdly celebrated. Meanwhile, early Hillary sketches positioned her as extremely unlikeable, even going so far as to show her grating personality as the *cause* of Bill's infidelity. Audiences sympathized with Clinton – "With a wife like that, of course he cheated." She was seen and projected as a liability to Bill, to the point that in *The Dana Carvey Show* sketch Hillary is literally locked away to protect Bill. The misogyny obviously put Hillary in a negative light, but importantly, that negative impression haunted her as she herself sought higher office. The 2016 campaign coverage, especially from the news media, continued to play on the image of Hillary as an out-of-control feminist, with reporters repeatedly asking if America was "ready" for a female president. The "Lock Her Up" chants at Trump's rallies echo the laughter of the above *SNL* sketch. Even before she sought the presidency, she was routinely cast as an impediment to Clinton's personal happiness and political success.

Though Hillary was hardly seen as sympathetic, ironically, by the end of Clinton's term, it was Bill who became seen as a liability to Hillary's future political aspirations. The first shift in her sketch comedy persona came after the Lewinsky scandal, as Clinton's presidency neared its end. She was still wooden, but she was also no longer going to sit in her husband's shadow. "A Message From Hillary Rodham Clinton" (2000) sums up this nontransition well. The sketch is a public service announcement for Clinton's campaign for New York's open Senate seat. The sketch pushes Hillary's new image as someone unable to connect with regular people, and let's say, less than trustworthy, as she tries to describe her typical female roles and her nonexistent history of being a New Yorker. "Bill and I are here in my favorite room of the new house, the kitchen. I can't wait to prepare some food dishes in this kitchen. Such as salads and toast. Because I love cooking for my family." Delivered in a wooden tone by Ana Gasteyer, the sketch then displays the next phase of Hillary sketches: dealing with being overshadowed. Bill Clinton looms in the background throughout, with Hillary scolding him for trying to steal her spotlight. Gasteyer's Clinton then runs down the differences between the old Hillary and the new Hillary: "The old Hillary was dykey and threatening. The new Hillary is motherly and warm. The old Hillary was driven by blind ambition and fueled by rage over her wasted potential and her husband's chronic skank-pronging." Hammond's Clinton then pops back into frame, with his signature thumb and lip-bite, silently mouthing "thanks" to the crowd.[35] The sketch is less a transition for Hillary, and more of a transition for Bill, from president to husband. Yet, there is no "old Bill, new Bill." He is assumed to remain the oversexualized Clinton. It is Hillary who has to change her image. She is still presented in unflattering terms, and he is still presented relatively positively. In fact, we see here the root of many of her later image problems that surfaced in 2016. She had to combat the persona, perpetuated by sketch comedy, of her being a bloodthirsty, ruthlessly ambitious, personally emotionless, feminist monster. *SNL* and sketch comedy were hardly the only ones pushing this persona, but they certainly contributed to its impact.

Both Clintons popped up in sketches throughout the George W. Bush presidency, but Hillary once again was front and center during the 2008 presidential election, where she was in a fierce Democratic primary battle with Barack Obama. Played during this period by Amy Poehler, Hillary's sketch persona was contrasted with Obama, and then against Tina Fey's Sarah Palin (explored in the next chapter). Poehler's Clinton was stoic and severe, but also calculating and petty. There was a rage simmering behind Poehler's Clinton. The anger behind the smile stemming from Clinton's image as being overlooked and in the shadows, first to Bill, then to Obama, then to Palin, and finally to Trump. Poehler's rage also stems from the aforementioned Hillary persona perpetuated by the media and comedians. There is an empathy to Poehler's portrayals that was absent earlier Hillary sketches. In part, that is due to Amy Poehler. It is also in part due to the changes to *SNL*'s writing staff. Tina Fey became the show's first female head writer in 1999, and though she was gone by 2008, the show had hired Paula Pell, and later still Sarah Schneider. All three women influenced the changing sketch comedy portrayals of Hillary. It's important to note that the female writers didn't just instantly make Hillary likeable; in fact, many of the Hillary sketches feature a highly unlikeable Clinton. What changed was that she was no longer presented as unlikeable simply because she was a feminist.

Rather than a Hillary who needs to be locked away because she's a feminist, this incarnation of Hillary is frustrated by the media's inability to celebrate her experience. In "3 AM Phone Call," a Clinton campaign ad features Hillary talking Obama through the many problems of his imagined presidency. Riffing on an actual campaign ad released by Hillary's campaign that evoked the Cold War and asked who voters wanted to answer the call when a crisis hit, the ad was both tone-deaf and, frankly, disturbing. The main thrust of Hillary's campaign was to tout her experience in contrast with Obama's relative lack of experience.[36] The *SNL* sketch begins with Poehler's Clinton: "I'm Hillary Clinton, and I approved this unfair and deceptive message." In the ad, it is Fred Armisen's Obama calling Hillary because he's hapless and helpless. Clinton has to talk Obama through his meltdown, from a nuclear crisis with Iran to helping him with the White House furnace (a traditionally male responsibility). Clinton, who is in a nightgown and facial cream, calmly talks Obama through his various issues. Obama responds, "Once again, I am amazed by the range and depth of your experience. I would gladly trade all of my superficial charm and rock star appeal for even a part of it." Poehler's Clinton appears at the end of the ad and appeals for voters to write and call the Democratic National Committee and tell them, "Wait. We've changed our minds."[37]

Later in the election cycle, the contrast between Hillary and Sarah Palin became sketch comedy gold. "Sarah Palin and Hillary Address the Nation" has become legendary, mostly because of Fey's Palin – "I can see Russia from my house!" But it is also an excellent depiction of Clinton and the 2008 election. For instance, the purpose of the address is meant to respond to sexism in the campaign and the media's coverage of the two, to which Clinton responds, "An issue I am frankly surprised to hear people suddenly care about." Palin is completely uninformed, and Clinton silently fumes as Palin displays her complete lack of knowledge about the issues and the very different ways the media have covered the two women. By the end of the sketch, the rage beneath Poehler's Clinton lashes out:

> Nooo! Mine! It's supposed to be mine. I'm sorry, I need to say something. I didn't want a woman to be president. *I* wanted to be president, and I just happened to be a woman. I don't want to hear you compare your road to the White House to my road to the White House. I scratched and clawed through mud and barbed wire, and you just glided in on a dog sled wearing your pageant sash and your Tina Fey glasses!

Palin does pageant poses throughout Clinton's speech, then returns to say that her campaign represents that anyone can be president, all you have to do is want it, which pushes Clinton over the edge. Poehler's Clinton laughs through her pain and anger, "You know Sarah, looking back, if I could change one thing, I probably should have *wanted it more*." She then rips off a chunk of the podium. "In conclusion, I invite the media to grow a pair. And if you can't, I will lend you mine."[38] The sketch demonstrates the growing frustration in Poehler's Clinton. Importantly, rather than solely laugh at her anger, the sketch *explains* her anger. It doesn't excuse it, but it examines why Hillary is so angry, an element that would become the backbone of Kate McKinnon's Clinton.

By the 2016 presidential election, Hillary had become a wooden yet highly ambitious figure, a woman with a ruthless ambition stuck behind a front of inauthentic empathy. There was deep seething anger beneath McKinnon's Clinton, a woman who can't articulate her message and whose most significant flaw is wanting to be president too much. As Matthew Love argues, "Kate McKinnon's Hillary impression accomplishes something that no previous attempt has: It peels back the veil of the reserved, measured candidate to reveal a woman animated by an ambition so intense it's prepared to consume her body and soul."[39] McKinnon's Clinton is willing to do anything to become president, including taking on her major rival's policies. In "Hillary Clinton Campaign Ad," she attempts to connect with millennial voters by taking on Bernie Sanders. Rather than critique his plans, she becomes him, using his talking points, and taking on his voice and appearance. By the end, she is full-on Bernie, with the tag line "Feel the Bern. For her." McKinnon, in full Bernie Sanders costume, closes the ad, "I'm whoever you want me to be, and I approve this message."[40] The ambition and overlooked motifs run through nearly all of McKinnon's Clinton sketches. She tries to restrain her overt ambition, fuming that she is not being taken more seriously against Bernie Sanders in the primary and that voters do not see what she sees as her obvious superiority to Trump in the general election. In a debate sketch between Hillary and Trump, McKinnon summed up Hillary's popularity:

> Listen, America, I get it: you hate me. You hate my voice, and you hate my face. Well, here's a tip: If you never want to see my face again, elect me president,

and I swear to God I will lock myself in the Oval Office and not come out for four years. But if you don't elect me, I will continue to run for president until the day I die. And I will never die.[41]

As had become the custom, Clinton herself even appeared in a sketch, playing a bartender opposite McKinnon's despondent Hillary Clinton. The sketch itself is somewhat unremarkable aside from the real Hillary doing a passable Donald Trump impression, but her very presence on the show, and that of many other politicians over the years, shows just how influential sketch comedy and *SNL* have become in the world of presidential politics. Perhaps the ultimate sign of the evolution of Hillary's *SNL* portrayals came the Saturday after she lost the election. McKinnon's Clinton somberly, and quite beautifully, performed Leonard Cohen's "Hallelujah."[42] It was a touching moment and a sincere tribute from McKinnon to Clinton, one that would have been unthinkable in 1992.

Where Are the Right-Wing Satirists?

The Clintons have been in the crosshairs of satirists and sketch comedy for three decades, yet most of that satire is coming from what many would consider to be liberal outlets like *SNL*. Inevitably, when talking about political satire, the question about conservative satire emerges: where is it? Shouldn't the Clintons have been the perfect targets for the right-wing satirist? Yet there was very little satire from a conservative bent. There might not have been a lot of conservative-based satire, but there was a mountain of conservative criticism. A variety of factors have led to the contemporary lack of conservative satire, but one of the most obvious is the aims of satire – to take down the status quo. Alison Dagnes argues in her book on conservative humor *A Conservative Walks Into a Bar*,

> Conservatism supports institutions and satire aims to knock these institutions down a peg. . . . The very nature of satire mandates challenges to the power structure, targets across the board, and an ability to take a nuanced or relativist examination of an issue in order to make the joke, and this falls squarely into the tool belt of liberalism.[43]

While conservatives tend to represent the status quo and defend institutions, liberals tend to champion the disenfranchised. It can be difficult to make jokes about marginalized groups without punching down and coming across as mean or arrogant. There also tend to be fewer comedians who identify as conservative, and there is a built-in history of 20th-century American satire leaning left. The emergence of *SNL* and later *The Daily Show* established the leading voices in sketch comedy and satiric news as liberal-leaning.

There is no shortage of outrage on the right. While some liberals tend to express their anger through comedy (and others through *Portlandia*-style liberal self-mockery), the principal outlet for conservative outrage has been AM radio and Fox News. While liberals have Jon Stewart and John Oliver, conservatives have Rush Limbaugh and Sean Hannity, and before them, Ronald Reagan. The emergence of conservative talk radio became the primary outlet for the type of energy many satirists have put into sketch comedy or satiric news. On the right, that energy first went into talk radio and then into Fox News. Ronald Reagan became a conservative radio star in the 1970s, railing against taxes, welfare, communism, and the Carter administration. As Kevin Kruse and Julian Zelizer argue, "Like many conservatives of the decade, Reagan used this medium both to express his arguments and expand his constituency, circumventing the seeming liberal dominance of the mainstream press and presenting the country with a political perspective that contrasted sharply with the Democratic dominance in Washington."[44] Conservative on-air personalities became stars, like Reagan and Bob Grant, and later Rush Limbaugh, who became a national sensation by decrying the foulness of the Clinton presidency day-in, day-out on the airwaves.

In 1987, *Meredith Corp. v. FCC* ruled that the Federal Communications Commission (FCC) had no obligation to adhere to the "fairness doctrine," and with the support of now President Reagan, they ended it. The policy was based on the idea that the three major networks were "public trustees" licensed by the government and therefore had an obligation to serve the public interest by airing multiple perspectives on issues. Never rigidly enforced, the doctrine did keep overtly political opinion–based shows off the air. With the advent of cable television and a growing number of channels, the idea that the three networks were the sole source of information was losing steam. Conservatives, likewise, continued to complain about what they saw as a liberal bias among the mainstream media. FCC Chairman Dennis Patrick called the ruling a "cause for celebration."[45] The Democratic Congress tried to pass a new version of the fairness doctrine, but Reagan vetoed the bill. The media landscape completely changed, as "suddenly, there were new possibilities on television and radio, as hosts could now openly make political arguments from one side of the spectrum with no requirements for balance."[46] With the fairness doctrine long gone and apparent demand for more conservative content, in 1996 Rupert Murdoch and Roger Ailes launched Fox News. The network became hugely popular as its conservative stars took to the airwaves to rail against the Clintons. Under its slogan "Fair and Balanced," it took precise aim at what it considered to be the liberal media. Its pundits – Bill O'Reilly front and center – became national stars. Stephen Colbert would later satirize O'Reilly and Fox News on *The Colbert Report*, but where's their satire?

As Dannagal G. Young argues in *Irony and Outrage*, there is no conservative satire because talk radio and Fox News *are* conservative satire. They don't take the same tactics or even actually employ satire, but they are serving a similar function. Numerous social science studies have shown that liberals' and conservatives' brains react differently, with liberals more attuned to irony, and conservatives more attuned to straightforwardness and an acute sense of danger. Conservatives want to protect establishments and institutions under real or perceived threats – as seen in Nixon's objections to *The First Family*. The audiences of both liberal satire and Fox News are more similar than they first appear. Obviously, they are different audiences. An Ohio State study found that many conservatives did not realize that

The Colbert Report was satiric. They didn't know that Colbert was playing a satiric version of an over-the-top, trust-your-guts-not-facts right-wing commentator . . . they just thought he was an over-the-top, trust-your-guts-not-facts right-wing commentator.[47] Colbert's performance of Colbert is a key moment in satire's blurring of absurdity and reality, as, too, is the many conservatives who missed the blurring and simply took it as real. His "real" self is separate from the character, but he never breaks character on screen. Some would likewise think there was a blurring of absurdity and reality when Trump took office, that his often-outlandish behavior was an act. But unlike Colbert, there was no performer behind the clown. Trump simply was absurdity.

While it is true that liberal and conservatives care about different issues, hold different political beliefs, often argue about basic facts, and scoff at the other's choice of political punditry, they share many similarities. Both are interested in politics, both have a strong sense of civic engagement, and both lack faith in the government as a whole. Liberals lack confidence in Republicans, and conservatives lack trust in Democrats. The hosts of the various shows, likewise, act in similar ways for their very similarly dissimilar audiences. They work to galvanize their audiences around particular issues, often encouraging their viewers to enact change. They likewise have a distrust of the mainstream media. Jon Stewart rose to fame on *The Daily Show* for his attacks on CNN just as much as he did for his take on the Bush White House. The entire Fox News network operates on the belief that the mainstream media is heavily biased toward liberals and cannot be trusted.[48]

The power and influence of right-wing talk shows, both radio and television, has been profound. Commentators like Limbaugh and Hannity are not just influencing voters, they are influencing policy, and even the presidency. President Donald Trump regularly talks with Sean Hannity from the Oval Office. Trump watches *Fox & Friends* every morning, often tweeting policy ideas and proposals only minutes after they have aired on the show. Hannity and other Fox News personalities even attend Trump rallies. Trump's embrace of Fox News isn't surprising, nor is their embrace of him. Part of Trump's own appeal is that he sounds a lot like a conservative talk radio figure. He's loud, bombastic, and unapologetic. He vows to fight the Democrats and reestablish the voice of the "forgotten" conservative voter. As Brian Rosenwald argues in *Talk Radio's America*:

> Yet if Trump, at least initially, appeared ideologically problematic, stylistically he was perfect for conservative media. Hosts had long decried political correctness and yearned for a blunt-speaking Republican who would eschew niceties and norms, take the gloves off, and pummel the hated Democrats and mainstream media. Hosts wanted a politician who sounded like them and voiced the grievances they had long stoked and aired, but which the establishment largely ignored. In this respect Trump was their man. . . . The mainstream press latched onto the most outlandish and unusual elements of the address [Trump's presidential announcement], framing them as disqualifying. But conservative media personalities understood what the rest of the press didn't: Trump's shocking language was not disqualifying; it was appealing.[49]

Trump's performance was Trump's reality, a reality television star who was always in performance mode. His absurdity wasn't a hindrance, it was his greatest asset. He would become the perfect president to bring absurd reality to fruition by essentially playing the part of Stephen Colbert minus the irony.

As the new century neared, Americans had grown further apart. The Clinton presidency was a mixture of highs and lows – and a lot of blowjob jokes. The economy was booming, but many on the right felt Clinton had deeply tarnished the presidency. Clinton was popular with the American public but was just the second president ever to be impeached. With the emergence of cable television and conservative media, there were more and more outlets for people to voice more and more opinions. Personality-driven satire had taken hold, and the absurdity of the Clinton White House and the amplification of it by 24-hour cable news made humor rely less on finding the absurd and more on finding the reality within a growingly ridiculous world. Luckily for sketch comedy, the next president would prove almost as deep of a well of satiric material as his predecessor.

Notes

1. S. Robert Lichter, Jody C Baumgartner, and Jonathan S. Morris, *Politics is a Joke! How TV Comedians are Remaking Political Life* (Boulder, CO: Westview Press, 2015), 51–52.
2. "President Bill Clinton," *CNN.com*, 17 August 1998. www.cnn.com/ALLPOLITICS/1998/08/17/speech/transcript.html.
3. Qtd. in Galen Druke, "Long Before Trump, There Was Ross Perot," *FiveThirtyEight.com*, 24 October 2016. https://fivethirtyeight.com/features/long-before-trump-there-was-ross-perot/.
4. Al Franken, "My 10 Favorite 'Saturday Night Live' Political Sketches," *The Washington Post*, 22 October 2016. www.washingtonpost.com/lifestyle/al-franken-my-10-favorite-saturday-night-live-political-sketches/2016/10/17/56e9d5be-8739-11e6-92c2-14b64f3d453f_story.html?utm_term=.3a2ac93d1bdb.
5. "Perot Cold Opening," *Saturday Night Live*, 9 May 1992. www.nbc.com/saturday-night-live/video/perot-cold-opening/2868125.
6. Qtd. in Franken.
7. "Cold Opening," *Saturday Night Live*, 3 October 1992. www.nbc.com/saturday-night-live/video/cold-opening/n10287.
8. "Joyride with Perot," *Saturday Night Live*, 24 October 1992. www.nbc.com/saturday-night-live/video/joyride-with-perot/n10313.
9. The Perot bits were prerecorded, with David Spade acting as Perot's body double during the performance.
10. "Bush-Clinton-Perot Debate Cold Opening," *Saturday Night Live*, 10 October 1992. www.nbc.com/saturday-night-live/video/bush-clinton-perot-debate-cold-opening/n10302.
11. Qtd. in Todd Purdum, "S.N.L.: The Skyscraper of Satire," *Vanity Fair*, 29 April 2011. www.vanityfair.com/news/2011/04/todd-purdum-saturday-night-live-201104.
12. Rich Cohen, "Why Generation X Might Be Our Last, Best Hope," *Vanity Fair*, 11 August 2017. www.vanityfair.com/style/2017/08/why-generation-x-might-be-our-last-best-hope.

13. Amanda Nell Edgar, "A Reflection on Rodney King and the Poignancy of Satire," *Antenna*, The University of Wisconsin, 2 July 2012. http://blog.commarts.wisc.edu/2012/07/02/a-reflection-on-rodney-king-and-the-poignancy-of-satire/.
14. "Humpin' Around," *In Living Color*, 1 November 1992. www.youtube.com/watch?v=g6TFGrCp9Zg&list=RDg6TFGrCp9Zg&index=1.
15. "The Capital Hillbillies," *In Living Color*, 17 January 1993. www.youtube.com/watch?v=XbjDCWjYVfM.
16. Ian Crouch, "The Unfortunate Genius of 'The Dana Carvey Show,'" *The New Yorker*, 23 October 2017. www.newyorker.com/culture/culture-desk/the-unfortunate-genius-of-the-dana-carvey-show.
17. Kliph Nesteroff, *The Comedians: Drunks, Thieves, Scoundrels and the History of American Comedy* (New York: Grove Press, 2015), 344.
18. Qtd. in Mike Ryan, "Teats Out: An Oral History of the Rise and Fall (and Rise) of 'The Dana Carvey Show,'" *GQ*, 8 August 2011. www.gq.com/story/dana-carvey-oral-history-dana-carvey-show.
19. "Grandma the Clown," *The Dana Carvey Show*, 23 April 1996. www.youtube.com/watch?v=AsOPbrBNsfs.
20. "Marty Farty," *Mr. Show*, 7 December 1998. www.youtube.com/watch?v=TiJ2n65Ryas.
21. Randall Colburn, "Mr. Show's Top Twenty Sketches," *ConsequenceOfSound.Net*. https://consequenceofsound.net/2013/07/mr-shows-top-20-sketches/full-post/.
22. Tom Boeker, "Kuwait Until Dark: Or, Bright Lights, Night Baseball," *Chicago Reader*, 9 June 1988. www.chicagoreader.com/chicago/kuwait-until-dark-or-bright-lights-night-baseball/Content?oid=872320.
23. Jack Helbig, "The Gods Must Be Lazy, or, There's More to Life Than Death," *Chicago Reader*, 23 March 1989. www.chicagoreader.com/chicago/the-gods-must-be-lazy-or-theres-more-to-life-than-death/Content?oid=873566.
24. Sid Smith, "In 'Pinata,' Troupe Takes Daring Step, Breaks Out of Second City Mold," *Chicago Tribune*, 23 June 1995. www.chicagotribune.com/news/ct-xpm-1995-06-23-9506230221-story.html??dssReturn=true.
25. Jack Helbig, "Pinata Full of Bees," *Chicago Reader*, 6 July 1995. www.chicagoreader.com/chicago/pinata-full-of-bees/Content?oid=887869.
26. Qtd. in Mike Thomas, *The Second City Unscripted: Revolution and Revelation at the World Famous Comedy Theater* (Evanston, IL: Northwestern University Press, 2009), 215.
27. Qtd. in Mick Sacks, *Poking a Dead Frog: Conversations with Today's Top Comedy Writers* (New York: Penguin Books, 2014), 122–123.
28. "Bill Clinton at McDonald's," *Saturday Night Live*, 5 December 1992. www.nbc.com/saturday-night-live/video/bill-clinton-at-mcdonalds/n10361.
29. Qtd. in Tom Shales and James Andrew Miller, *Live From New York: An Uncensored History of Saturday Night Live*, (Boston: Little, Brown and Company, 2002), 450.
30. "Deposition Cold Open," *Saturday Night Live*, 14 March 1998. www.nbc.com/saturday-night-live/video/deposition-cold-open/n11094.
31. "Linda Tripp Cold Open," *Saturday Night Live*, 13 February 2009. www.nbc.com/saturday-night-live/video/linda-tripp-cold-open/n11205.
32. John Lopez, "And Now, Ladies and Gentlemen, a Message From the 'Saturday Night Live' President of the United States," *Grantland.com*, 25 August 2014. http://grantland.com/hollywood-prospectus/saturday-night-live-president-impressions/.
33. "Not for First Ladies Only," *Saturday Night Live*, 30 October 1976. www.nbc.com/saturday-night-live/video/not-for-first-ladies-only/3004182.

34. "Dole/Clinton Cold Open," *Saturday Night Live*, 15 May 1993. www.nbc.com/saturday-night-live/video/doleclinton-cold-open/n10444.
35. "Clinton Cold Opening," *Saturday Night Live*, 12 February 2000. www.nbc.com/saturday-night-live/video/clinton-cold-opening/n11305.
36. LatinXTC, "Hillary and Her 'Red Phone,'" 29 February 2008, www.youtube.com/watch?time_continue=6&v=kddX7LqgCvc.
37. "3 AM Phone Call," *Saturday Night Live*, 8 March 2008. www.nbc.com/saturday-night-live/video/3am-phone-call/n12207.
38. "Sarah Palin and Hillary Clinton Address the Nation," *Saturday Night Live*, 13 September 2008. www.nbc.com/saturday-night-live/video/sarah-palin-and-hillary-clinton-address-the-nation/n12287.
39. Matthew Love, "The 10 Best *Saturday Night Live* Sketches About Hillary Clinton," *Vulture.com*, 27 October 2016. www.vulture.com/2016/10/hillary-clinton-best-snl-sketches.html.
40. "Hillary Campaign Ad," *Saturday Night Live*, 13 March 2016. www.youtube.com/watch?v=O3iBb1gvehI.
41. "Donald Trump vs. Hillary Clinton Debate Cold Open," *Saturday Night Live*, 1 October 2016. www.youtube.com/watch?v=-nQGBZQrtT0.
42. "Election Week Cold Open," *Saturday Night Live*, 12 November 2016. www.nbc.com/saturday-night-live/video/election-week-cold-open/3424949.
43. Alison Dagnes, *A Conservative Walks into a Bar: The Politics of Political Humor* (New York: Palgrave Macmillan, 2012), 6.
44. Kevin Kruse and Julian Zelizer, *Fault Lines: A History of the United States Since 1974* (New York: W.W. Norton and Company, 2019), 98.
45. Bob Davis, "FCC Abolishes Fairness Doctrine, Arousing Debate," *Wall Street Journal*, 5 August 1987.
46. Kruse and Zelizer, 152.
47. H.L. LaMarre, K.D. Landreville and M.A. Beam, "The Irony of Satire: Political Ideology and the Motivation to See What You Want to See in The Colbert Report," *The International Journal of Press/Politics* 14, no. 2 (2009), 212–231.
48. Dannagal Goldthwaite Young, *Irony and Outrage: The Polarized Landscape of Rage, Fear, and Laughter in the United States* (Oxford: Oxford University Press, 2019).
49. Brian Rosenwald, *Talk Radio's America: How an Industry Took Over a Political Party That Took Over the United States* (Cambridge: Harvard University Press, 2019), 228–229.

CHAPTER 7

Dubbya

There is only one president in American history with a one letter nickname: W (properly pronounced as "Dubbya") – George W. Bush. Winning one of the closest and most controversial elections in history (and cementing Florida's legacy as, well, Florida), Bush assumed the White House with a robust economy, but a deeply divided electorate. During his eight years in office, the United States would suffer its worst terrorist attack in history, launch two foreign wars, and turn a budget surplus from the Clinton administration into the country's worst economic meltdown since the Great Depression. Bush came into office as a "compassionate conservative," promising a new kind of Republican leadership that married personal responsibility with a commitment from the state. Bush summed up his philosophy, saying, "It is compassionate to actively help our fellow citizens in need. It is conservative to insist on responsibility and on results. And with this hopeful approach, we can make a real difference in people's lives."[1] Bush's new Republican philosophy quickly faded. For most of his term, there was an intensification of the so-called culture wars, with issues like gay marriage deeply dividing the country. After 9/11, the nation bounced between fear and intense patriotism during Bush's first term, and between malaise and outrage during his second. In the immediate wake of 9/11, Bush seemed like the ideal leader to galvanize the nation. The brief national unity soon faded, however, and a harder satiric front arose in opposition to the Bush White House.

Every president carefully crafts a public persona, but Bush took his to an extreme. The hard-partying patrician son of a president educated at Yale and Harvard, Bush was hardly an "everyman." Yet, he and his team worked hard to turn him into a rough-and-tumble, no-nonsense, straight-shooting-from-the-gut cowboy from Texas, strongly evoking the Yankee and Frontier types that have long symbolized Americanness. He bought his now-famous Crawford ranch in 1999, which would become the "Western White House," where he would clear brush and host foreign dignitaries. He was a "compassionate conservative," who pledged to restore honor to the White House despite his shaky record with drugs and alcohol (though he was completely clean by the time he was a politician and had no "personal" scandals while in office). He served in the Texas Air National Guard during Vietnam, but his spotty attendance records led to questions about if he went AWOL and actually fulfilled his military obligations. Despite this history, he became a strong military leader who would end up casting aspersions on John Kerry's decorated Vietnam service in the 2004 election. He was wildly unpopular but became the first Republican to win a second term in 20 years. He was a mess of competing ideas, images, and personas – an excellent combination for sketch comedy.

If Clinton was the first president to deal with the emergence of cable television and a splintering media landscape, Bush's presidency oversaw the explosion of the internet and a further and more specialized media tailored to individualized audiences. News and entertainment no longer had to find a mass audience. Instead, the opposite became true. Niche shows of all stripes found their target audiences. The three big networks still held power, but they did not completely dominate the news or entertainment market. Americans no longer communally got their news and information from national sources. Americans could now easily and readily seek out news and entertainment explicitly tailored to their tastes and worldview. Rather than receiving the facts from the news media, Americans could now easily go find news media to support their views. With this massively expanded news world came an expanded distrust of the "mainstream media." Fox News exploded on the right, and while MSNBC is the closest news equivalent on the left – and it is not nearly as partisan or loose with facts – the shows that gained the most traction with liberal viewers were *The Daily Show* and *The Colbert Report*. Fox News, MSNBC, *The Daily Show*, and *The Colbert Report* all played to different, but relatively homogeneous, audiences that shared a common suspicion of the media.

Beyond these major players, hundreds of smaller shows and thousands of websites catered to audiences more eager to hear what they wanted to hear than have their worldview challenged. Facts began to give way to feelings. Reality gave way to the absurd. A senior advisor to Bush (who many believe to be Karl Rove) summed up the new world with what has come to be known as the "reality-based community." Speaking in 2004 to journalist Ron Suskind, the aide said:

> People like you are still living in what we call the reality-based community. You believe that solutions emerge from your judicious study of discernible reality. That's not the way the world really works anymore. We're an empire now, and when we act, we create our own reality. And while you're studying that reality – judiciously, as you will – we'll act again, creating other new realities, which you can study too, and that's how things will sort out. We're history's actors, and you, all of you, will be left to study what we do.[2]

The technological advances and expansion of sources had profoundly changed the exchange of information – both in *how* we received news as well as *what* we received. While news had always been somewhat manufactured and biases have always existed, there was now a full-on assault on the very idea of objective truth. Evoking Jonathan Swift's essay "The Art of Political Lying," which warned of the dangers of how quickly a lie can spread, this senior advisor knew that framing the story was more important than telling the truth about a story. Donald Trump would push this to an even further extreme, continually lying and letting the lies and the truth coexist as *equal* possibilities. By the time political opponents and the news media had sorted out reality from fiction, the false story had already taken hold, and especially with Trump, several new false stories had since been introduced. As the new century began, the media, the presidency, and satirists, were all waging a war over constructing reality. But before Dubbya could take office and change reality, he'd first need to win a historically close and fraught election.

The 2000 Election – Lockbox vs. Strategery

The 2000 election coverage was one of *SNL*'s best. Darrell Hammond, perhaps *SNL*'s greatest pure impressionist, took on the stodgy and dry Al Gore, as Will Ferrell began crafting what would become an iconic George W. Bush. Hammond's Gore and Ferrell's Bush were funny in different ways. Hammond's Gore was arrogant, monotonous, and impatient; Ferrell's Bush was still in the aimless Texas frat boy phase, though the seeds of the cocky, straight-shooting, dimwitted Bush were there. They played against and off of one another brilliantly. It helped *SNL* that neither Bush nor Gore was a nationally known political figure. Even though Gore was the sitting vice president, he existed from the start of the Clinton presidency in Clinton's gigantic shadow. Bush was the governor of Texas and certainly had name recognition thanks to his father, but his character was virtually unknown. In political circles, it was Bush's brother Jeb dubbed the "heir apparent," not his hard-partying older brother. *SNL* is usually at its best when it gets to help craft the narrative about a candidate, when the sketches work to shape a politician's persona rather than reflect it. The 2000 election presented them with two contrasting comic foils with distinct personality quirks and little national recognition: a perfect comedy cocktail.

The first debate in any presidential cycle is one of the most critical moments of the campaign. John Buell argues that "For many citizens, the first televised debate is their only political participation."[3] Voters often encounter candidates outside of sound clips and ads for the first time in debates, with the first debate garnering more viewers than subsequent debates. It is a chance for the candidates to pitch themselves and their message while contrasting themselves against their opponent. It is an essential step in crafting their persona and message. When a "new" president is to be elected (there is no incumbent running), the stakes are higher, as both candidates often have less national recognition. Not only is the actual debate a colossal moment in the campaign, but so too is the spin, which has become increasingly more and more important. Many Americans do not watch the debate and rely on media reports to help form their opinions. In an age of 24-hour news and viral videos, the media spin has come to dominate the debate cycle. *SNL*'s debate sketches may not be news (though many viewers do learn about the candidates and the issues), but it certainly is part of the spin cycle.

The first debate in 2000 was no different. What was unusual was the outsized impact of *SNL*'s sketch debate. Aired on October 7, 2000, the sketch etched a persona of each man that stuck through the election. In part, this influence is attributable to the nature of the 2000 election. The economy was strong, and both candidates positioned themselves as the best suited to keep the good times rolling. Neither candidate wanted to make massive policy changes. Therefore, the election came down to the personalities of the two men – who would you rather have a beer with? There were undoubtedly policy differences between them, but for many, the election was as much about character as policy. This atmosphere allowed for their sketch impressions to have an outsized impact since *SNL* impressions tend to be better at capturing personality than policy. The *SNL* debate kicked off with Hammond's Gore talking about Bush's tax plan, with a painfully slow and erudite answer about his famous "lockbox" to protect Social Security and Medicare. His sighs, snail's pace, and arrogance are all equally off-putting, amplifying the real Gore's debate performance. Ferrell's Bush responds, "I don't know what that was all about. But I will say this: Don't mess with Texas." Bush later furrows his brow and answers a question with, "Pass." Bush is distracted at times, staring at the lights in his own little world. Meanwhile, Gore continues to drone on and on about his lockbox. Reflecting the real Gore's performance in the first debate, Gore later jumps in on a question to Bush about prescription drug costs, saying, "I'd like to interrupt here and answer that question as if it were my turn to speak." He then goes on to talk in excruciatingly slow detail about a senior and her litany of medical issues. When the moderator asks each candidate to sum up their candidacy in a single word, Bush replies with the now-iconic "Strategery," while Gore, you guessed it, answers, "Lockbox."[4] The two words became synonymous with each candidate, and the sketch impressions drew rave reviews. Gore's aides reportedly made the real Gore watch the sketch to see its devastating take on the candidate, hoping the real Gore could loosen up for the remaining debates. Gore attempted to adapt his performances in the next two contests in part based on the sketch, which led the public to mistrust him – they weren't sure who the "real" Al Gore was. Bush, meanwhile, came off as uninformed but likable. Lorne Michaels said of the sketch, "You know, 'strategery' seems to sum up a view of George Bush that made him more human, I think. I think people knew people like George Bush. They didn't, so much, [know] people like Al Gore. He seems like the kid in class you didn't like so much."[5] The sketch reflected the Americanness at the heart of Royall Tyler's 1787 play *The Contrast*. Gore is the educated elite you can't trust, while Bush is the stupid but honorable Stage Yankee. Bush represented the common man against Gore's intellectual elitism, and as we've seen, Americans almost always identify with the common man.

SNL's first debate sketch was so influential that some think it swayed the election. As noted, Gore's team immediately reacted to the impression, which made them look weak and unsure of their candidate. Hammond certainly reflected flaws in Gore's debate performance, but he was comedically amplifying them. Gore tried to correct a sketch comedy impression of him, which in itself is excellent fodder for sketch comedy, but not so great for a presidential candidate. Ferrell's Bush, in contrast, was certainly not flattering, but it made him likable. That likeability has led some to argue, including *SNL* cast member Horatio Sanz, that it helped the real Bush capture the White House. And maybe it did. The election, after all, ultimately came down to 537 votes in Florida. There was a ridiculous and messy recount, highlighted by ballot irregularities and hanging chads. The Supreme Court eventually called off the recount, effectively handing Bush the presidency. With Florida, Bush won the Electoral College by five votes, though he narrowly lost the popular vote to Gore.

With such a razor-thin margin, it is not inconceivable to think that Ferrell's fun-loving Bush, who was undoubtedly more attractive than Hammond's devastatingly arrogant and tedious Gore, helped swing a few votes. Hammond's Gore was prissy and lectured the American people. He was pompous and dismissive. Hammond's sighs alone were enough to make you dislike Gore. By contrast, Ferrell's Bush was at the very least fun. He might not be that bright, but you didn't actively dislike him after sketches. If anything, he became oddly endearing, evoking long-standing traits of Americanness embedded in the Yankee character type. Hammond's Gore also literally impacted the real Gore, whose team tried to make over Gore's presentation. If anything, the fact that *SNL* made the Gore team reevaluate itself points to the power of Hammond's satiric take. Mike Ryan argues, sort of tongue-in-cheek but mostly not, that Hammond's Gore was "the most important political impression ever done on the show and probably changed the course of human history."[6] That might be going a touch far, but it arguably did more to sway public opinion than any impression since Gerald Ford. In an election that hinged on personality and likeability, Hammond's impression undoubtedly hurt Gore. There are thousands of factors that influence an election, but in such a close election it is fair to say that *SNL* contributed to Gore losing the White House.

It also is perhaps the last time that the general public viewed *SNL* as politically "neutral," hitting both parties in equal measure. Longtime political sketch writer James Downey commented about the 2000 debate sketch, saying it was "perfectly even handed. I think maybe some people were used to a more traditional approach where we're only rough on Republicans – at least really rough."[7] None other than Rudy Giuliani commented on the fairness of the show, something that after his work in the Trump White House seems unconscionable: "They've made fun of me or made fun of basically my heroes or the Republicans that I like, I know they've made equal fun of Democrats, so it doesn't offend me.... They made equal fun of Gore and Bush, so I think politically it ends up a wash."[8] Why did *SNL* and other political satire "turn left?" First, one could argue that satire did not turn left, but let's take that as accurate. The 9/11 attacks, Bush's foreign policy, the continued rise of Fox News, and the growing divide between liberals and conservatives on social issues all pushed satire to appear more "left-leaning." It's perhaps more accurate to note that satire seemed anti-Republican during this time because Republicans were in power, and satire always takes aim at power. It's also true that satire didn't necessarily take a sharp turn left; instead, its teeth became much sharper in the wake of 9/11 as the country moved right.

9/11 – Can We Be Funny?

After the 9/11 terrorist attacks, *Vanity Fair* editor Graydon Carter announced, "I think it's the end of the age of irony." Carter was not alone in pronouncing the death of irony. Roger Rosenblatt declared in *Time* that "One good thing could come from this horror: it could spell the end of the age of irony."[9] Irony did not die, but there certainly was a lack of comedic response to the attacks. Comedy Central pulled reruns of its short-lived sitcom about Bush, *That's My Bush!* Syndicated humor columnist Dave Barry wrote, "No humor column today.... I don't want to write it, and you don't want to read it."[10] Nearly every late-night host delivered sincere and heartfelt monologues void of anything remotely comic. Many of them apologized for being comics, vowing to be more earnest and sincere. At the same time, they also celebrated satire and its relationship to power. Stewart most fully defended satire in his first *The Daily Show* opening monologue since the attacks, saying,

> Even the idea that we can sit in the back of the country and make wisecracks . . . but never forgetting the fact that it is a luxury in this country that allows us to do that. That is . . . a country that allows for open satire. And I know that sounds basic and sounds as though it goes without saying, but that's really what this whole situation is all about. It's the difference between closed and open. It's the difference between free and burdened. And we don't take that for granted here.... Our show has changed. I don't doubt that. What it's become, I don't know.[11]

Stewart evokes the central tenets of Americanness in his defense, arguing that satire is central to freedom of speech and vital to our democratic process. He calls it a luxury, but not in the sense that it is something we don't need. Instead, he is celebrating the luxury of its purpose being vital to Americans' sense of self. *SNL* returned on September 29, bringing "America's Mayor" Rudy Giuliani onto the stage to give the show his blessing to continue making jokes. Lorne Michaels asks Giuliani, "Can we be funny?" To which Giuliani replies, "Why start now?" The exchange was a funny, self-deprecating joke. It also worked to help reinforce the idea Stewart and others spoke about – the very nature of political satire and its role in a healthy democracy. Would it still be okay to satirize the powerful? The show asked America's second-most-prominent political leader at the time to sanction satire – and of course, he did, because political satire is fundamental to America's identity.

Only one major outlet responded satirically: *The Onion*, with the famous September 26, 2011, issue "Holy Fucking Shit: Attack on America." They were supposed to release a new issue on September 11, their first from their new home in New York, but instead postponed publication. Stephen Thompson, founder and editor of *The Onion*'s *A.V. Club*, said, "There will be humor, but not now.... We're not feeling especially relevant right now. What are we going to say? 'Ooh, that Osama bin Laden, he'll be the victim of our rapier wit!' "[12] What they did release was "especially relevant" and would provide a comedic roadmap for responding to 9/11. With stories like "U.S. Vows to Defeat Whoever It Is We're At War With," *The Onion* ironically used irony to satirize the overwhelming sincerity of the response to 9/11: "Not Knowing What Else to Do, Woman Bakes American-Flag Cake."

The issue captured the feeling of the nation. Sincerely reflecting on the mood, *The Onion* ironically reflected that mood better than any other satiric outlet, in the process illustrating just how different the world had become. By ironically juxtaposing a meaningless act like baking a cake with Americans deep sense of pain, loss, and helplessness, *The Onion* helped the nation (and comedians) begin to process the attacks. Not to use *The Onion*'s own satiric true-but-not-really-true-but-actually-true aesthetic, the issue unquestionably is one of the most critical comedic documents in American history.

SNL would do something similar in the "Short Shorts for the USA" sketch on October 6. In the sketch, an office has relaxed the dress code to allow for shows of patriotism. Will Ferrell's character comes to a meeting in a crop top USA shirt and American flag thong underwear to display his patriotism. Ferrell's coworkers are wearing flag pins, flag ties, and the like, but he's taken his patriotic display to an absurd extreme. When the boss pushes back, Ferrell's character responds, "Am I missing something? Do you *not* want me to be patriotic?" When he's eventually kicked out of the meeting, he says, "Just remember this: The US of A is the greatest country on the face of the earth. And for that I will make no apologies." The meeting then bursts out into chants of "USA! USA! USA!"[13] The sketch reflects the country's patriotic surge after the attacks. In hindsight, the sketch reads as a satiric critique on the dangers of excessive patriotism, but at the time it was a reflection of the country's mood.

Following *The Onion*'s lead, it would take a year or so for satire to regain its footing after 9/11, but what emerged was powerful. The age of irony was hardly over – it was just beginning. At the same time, the respite of satire proved to be a consequential break. To be fair, Carter and Rosenblatt were not saying humor was dead. They were referencing the hollow blank-irony that recycled pop-culture tropes to satirize pop-culture tropes, the *South Park* aesthetic that caring about anything was uncool, and arguing that type of irony would no longer suffice in a post-9/11 world. Comedy in the 1990s, as noted in the Introduction, was very often stupid and crude. Pop culture celebrated *The Jerry Springer Show* and the dumb antics of comedies like *Ace Ventura: Pet Detective*. The social commentary and satirical edge of comedy from the 1970s was long gone. Carter and Rosenblatt wanted people to believe again in broad ideas about America and the world – though a sincere belief in those broad ideals without any satiric check also proved dangerous. Bush and others would respond to 9/11 with sweeping metanarratives about American greatness against "the Axis of Evil." Countries were either "with us or against us." With the momentary "pause" on political satire and irony, those messages resonated strongly with Americans. As AJ Aronstein argues, the combination of sweeping generalizations and a lack of irony was dangerous: "Irony was supposed to take the teeth out of claims like 'America is the greatest country in the world,' not necessarily because they should feel untrue to people, but because when shouted loudly enough they are used to deceive and manipulate."[14] Irony's job is to make such sweeping generalizations laughable, and in the immediate aftermath of 9/11, irony fell down on the job.

But it would get back up and then some. What emerged over the next 18 months was closer to what Zoe Williams described in an impassioned essay about irony in *The Guardian* in 2003:

> The end of irony would be a disaster for the world – bad things will always occur, and those at fault will always attempt to cover them up with emotional and overblown language. If their opponents have to emote back at them, you're basically looking at a battle of wills, and the winner will be the person who can beat their breast the hardest without getting embarrassed. Irony allows you to launch a challenge without being dragged into this orbit of self-regarding sentiment that you get from Tony Blair, say, when he talks about "fighting for what's right." Irony can deflate a windbag in the way that very little else can.[15]

The Daily Show and later *The Colbert Report* would lead the charge of "deflating windbags." Stewart was correct on 9/11: *The Daily Show* had changed. What is clear is that in the aftermath of the attacks is that satire became more serious and sincere. Satire's job had changed. No longer was it going to suffice to make Monica Lewinsky jokes and make fun of Bush mispronouncing words. In the eyes of many political satirists, the very future of democracy was at stake. The content of *The Daily Show* illustrates this shift, moving from its origin as entertainment gossip to viable political news, with several studies finding *The Daily Show*'s content to be as substantive as traditional news programs.[16] The failure of satire to immediately respond to 9/11 caused satirists to double down on their critical role when satire did reemerge. Comedy's long-standing position of being a check on power resurfaced, and in some cases, more effectively than the traditional news media's role in calling truth to power. Satire's democratic responsibility returned in full force.

Sketch TV Beyond *Saturday Night Live*

Dubbya would find himself ridiculed and satirized across a wide range of mediums. Elizabeth LeCompte credited Bush for fostering "the rise of political satire as an art form again."[17] He was depicted in sitcoms like *Family Guy*, *South Park*, and *The Simpsons*, among many others. He even had sitcoms solely dedicated to him, like the aforementioned *That's My Bush!* and the animated series *Lil' Bush*. His likeness appeared in countless movies, from Oliver Stone's biopic *W.* (2008), smoking cocaine-laced marijuana in *Harold & Kumar Go to White Castle* (2008), to playing the fool front man to Vice President Dick Cheney's mastermind in *Vice* (2018). Michael Moore's 2004 anti-Bush documentary *Fahrenheit 9/11* won the Palme d'Or at the Cannes Film Festival and is the highest-grossing documentary of all time. Bush became a star on the animated web videos of JibJab, singing a parody of "This Land" with John Kerry during the 2004 election that became a viral sensation. Like all presidents, he was a regular feature in editorial cartoons and was mocked on a nightly basis by late-night comedians. *The Onion* aimed at Bush from the very beginning, with the January 2001 story "Our Long National Nightmare of Peace and Prosperity is Finally Over." Nearly all of the Dubbya portrayals are negative, veering between Bush being very stupid to Bush the cocaine-snorting party animal.

He was likewise a focal point of satiric news, with Stephen Colbert taking it a step further by rebuking the president – who was sitting just mere feet from the comedian – during the 2006 White House Correspondents Dinner. In one of the most iconic moments of political satire, Colbert lambasted Bush while pretending to support him:

> I stand by this man. I stand by this man, because he stands for things. Not only for things, he stands on things, things like aircraft carriers and rubble and recently flooded city squares. And that sends a strong message, that no matter what happens to America, she will always rebound with the most powerfully staged photo-ops in the world. . . . I'm sorry, I've never been a fan of books. I don't trust them. They're all fact, no heart. I mean, they're elitist, telling us what is or isn't true or what did or didn't happen. Who's Britannica to tell me the Panama Canal was built in 1914? If I want to say it was built in 1941, that's my right as an American! I'm with the President. Let history decide what did or did not happen. He believes the same thing Wednesday that he believed on Monday, no matter what happened Tuesday. Events can change; this man's beliefs never will.[18]

Colbert's comments link to the reality construction inherent to the Bush White House. It also points to the importance of partisanship over truth. Colbert's critique aims at Bush's, and conservative media's, unerring belief in everything they believe to be true. Even if facts say otherwise, like the lack of weapons of mass destruction in Iraq, Bush and conservative media continued to propagate their constructed reality. Donald Trump, again, would push this tactic to an absurd level, but we see here a core issue that satirists have been fighting for most of the 21st century – how do they get people to believe facts?

Chappelle's Show – "Black Bush"

Comedian Dave Chappelle's sketch comedy show *Chappelle's Show* set a new standard for dealing with race via comedy. Despite its relatively short two-plus season run, the show produced numerous sketches about race and America that were both smart and funny. The very first episode featured "Frontline: Clayton Bigsby," a mock news story about a blind white supremacist who doesn't know that he's black. The sketch masterfully exposes the learned nature of racism and set the no-nonsense tone for the show. "Reparations" imagines a world where African Americans are paid reparations for slavery, while "The Wayne Brady Show" takes on black masculinity, with Wayne Brady saying one of the show's most iconic lines: "Is Wayne Brady going to have to choke a bitch?" Countless other sketches examined race, like "Mad Real World," "Racial Draft," and the highly controversial

"The Niggar Family." Chappelle didn't directly take on traditional politics much, instead working more with social satire regarding race and culture in America. Still, he did do one incredibly influential (and perhaps prescient) sketch about Dubbya – "Black Bush."

The final sketch in the show's last full season, aired only months before Barack Obama's now-famous 2004 Democratic National Convention keynote speech, imagines a world where George W. Bush is black. The central premise is that a black president could never get away with the things the Bush administration was getting away with, namely blatantly lying about the Iraq War, because a black president would be held to impossibly high standards. Chappelle is not the first African American sketch comedian to imagine a black presidency. In 1977, Richard Pryor's "First Black President" portrayed a similar scenario. The sketch takes place at a press conference, in which Pryor plays a very reserved and restrained president. As the questions go on, he becomes more and more stereotypically black, ultimately attacking a reporter for disrespecting his mother.[19] Coupled with Pryor's *SNL* "Word Association" sketch, the message is clear – "No matter how African-Americans look, no matter what they achieve, they'll always look the same in the eyes of white people – or at least some of them."[20] Pryor's sketch evokes the duality inherent in *Key & Peele*'s later "Luther" sketches about Obama. Both Pryor and Key and Peele satirize the different standards placed upon black men in power and the incredible burden on them to not display stereotypical "black behavior." "Black Bush" plays on a similar assumption, but rather than resist the stereotypes of black men being unable to handle authority, it relishes in the stereotype (which is the premise for a much less nuanced 2007 *Mind of Mencia* sketch about the first black president).[21] Rather than try to hide and mask his race, Black Bush celebrates it.

"Black Bush" not only satirizes stereotypes about African Americans as a way to mock Bush, but it also is a deft piece of political satire, dismantling the Bush administration's involvement in the Iraq War. Black Bush states that the area is ripe for regime change, but the real reason he's going to war is that "he tried to kill my father." When a reporter asks about the United States going to Iraq for oil, Black Bush responds with mock shock and outrage, playing dumb: "What? Huh? Oil? Who said something about oil, bitch? You cookin'? Oil? . . ." He looks at his cabinet before pushing over the water pitcher on the table and running out of the room. Black Bush trashes the UN for not having an army and celebrates the "coalition of the willing," which is a very unimpressive list of countries. He admonishes the UN, telling them to "Go sell some medicine, bitches. I'm trying to get that oil . . . (coughs)." Black Bush, like the real Bush, lands a plane on an aircraft carrier and delivers a self-congratulatory speech in front of the infamous "Mission Accomplished" banner. When the press begins to question Black Bush about the uprisings in Iraq, he responds, "You always trying to distract motherfuckers with things like the war, and skirt all the real issues: gay people are getting married folks!"[22] The Bush administration similarly took a hard turn away from the war in the lead up to the 2004 election, preferring to focus on culturally divisive issues like gay marriage to steer clear of talking about the growingly disastrous Iraq War.

"Black Bush" was one of the earliest sketches to satirize the Bush administration's handling of the Iraq War. It worked on multiple levels, not only satirizing race in America, but also the political machinations that led the country into what many have come to feel was an unjustified war. It is reflective of the satiric tension after 9/11 in terms of policy and personality. With Clinton, satiric sketch comedy and the presidency had tipped almost exclusively toward personality. As the Bush presidency wore on, more and more sketch comedy began tipping toward policy. The work on *The Daily Show* and *The Colbert Report* were leading this transition, but it is worth noting that Chappelle's sketch is almost exclusively about Bush's policy. Chappelle makes zero attempt to impersonate Bush, in some ways completely excluding Bush's personality from the sketch to focus on Bush's policies within the context of systemic and institutional racism. The only personality satire is about how a black president would be treated much differently than a white president, which in itself is arguably more a form of policy satire than personality satire. "Black Bush" is also a prime example of finding the absurd within the real. Bush's behavior is shown to be absurd within the post-9/11 American reality by pointing out the concrete actions the administration took throughout the build-up and early execution of the war, including the inherent absurdity of Bush's "Mission Accomplished" moment. It also imagines an "absurd" reality – a black president then flips the absurdity on its head by showing that what's truly absurd is what Bush is "getting away with" in terms of the Iraq War.

Not only does the sketch demonstrate a harder satiric bite, it also was rather prescient – but not about Obama. Part of what makes the sketch so impactful is what has happened since it aired. In the spring of 2004, a black president seemed years away. Thankfully, when Obama did take office in 2009, he broke many of the stereotypes associated with a black president. At the same time, the major premise of the sketch played out during Obama's tenure: a black president was held to a higher standard than a white president, which is further explored in the next chapter. But "Black Bush" seems to have less in common with Obama than it does with his successor – Donald Trump. When Trump took office in 2017, he seemed to be playing out many of the tropes satirized in "Black Bush," namely a president who would say and do whatever he wanted whenever he wanted. He would clearly state his aims and never apologize, even when the answers were not "politically correct." He surrounded himself with unqualified friends and family and similarly attacked the press. He clearly crafted policy that benefited him and his entourage, blatantly lying to the public about all of it. Both Black Bush and Trump said whatever was on their mind, both demeaned the UN for not having an army, and both threw traditional presidential decorum out the window. Most important, it was Donald Trump who made the country confront race and racism in ways that the first black president did not.

Sketch comedians have imagined an African American president for decades. For white comedians throughout American history, the idea of a black man as president was seen as humorous, playing on classic comic tropes of incongruity and superiority. The famous minstrel song "When a Coon Sits in the Presidential Chair," written by Irving Jones in 1898–1899, ridicules the spectacle and debasement a black president and his followers would bring to the White House. The idea of a black man in authority, let alone as president, is so absurd in the song as to be funny. For centuries, a black man as president was seen as ridiculous – and therefore hilarious – and allowed white people to feel a sense of superiority over stereotyped black characters. White America has historically used comedy about black people in positions of authority and power as a justification to *exclude* African Americans from positions of authority and power by depicting them as unable to handle those positions successfully. While the end result is laughter, the impetus is often fear. Most prominent in minstrel shows, Eric Lott argues that blackface and the stereotypes associated with it stem from white audiences' fear: "They are afraid of black groups, mobs rising up and taking the power."[23] Blackface and its influence on comedy can be seen in the ways it works to make white audiences feel superior. It takes the threat of black people in power and ridicules it in an attempt to neutralize that fear. The comic tropes of blackface and minstrel did not go away in the 19th century, remaining staples of American comedy. Erica R. Edwards argues in "The Black President Hokum" that "the terror of black electoral representation gave 'birth' to American film," with this fear at the heart of D.W. Griffith's *The Birth of a Nation* (1915).[24] Chappelle's sketch is working within this context to both reinforce the idea of a black man being unfit to be president, but more importantly, by deconstructing that myth by contrasting it against the "acceptable" behavior of white presidents that would be deemed "unacceptable" by a black president. Chappelle was using a long-standing tradition of comedy within marginalized groups, Ralph Ellison's famous advice, "Change the joke and slip the yoke."[25] In so doing, he was satirizing race relations. Chappelle was also navigating a "dilemma" in African American comedy, as Mel Watkins argues, first confronted by the blackface minstrel actor Billy Kersands, "the conflict between satirizing social images of blacks and contributing to whites' negative stereotypes of blacks in general."[26] Though executed brilliantly in "Black Bush," that dilemma, which came to a head in the "Pixie" sketch outlined in Chapter 1, ultimately led to Chappelle leaving *Chappelle's Show* after the second full season.

MADtv

Much like *MADtv*'s portrayal of Clinton, their George W. Bush was funny, but not terribly layered. Several actors played Bush on the show, including Will Sasso, but Frank Caliendo's impression is by far the most frequent and successful. Caliendo's impression of Dubbya is perhaps the best of all sketch comedians in terms of straight impersonation. He looks and sounds just like Bush. Caliendo masterfully takes on Bush's furrowed brow, machine-gun laugh, and physical mannerisms. Many of the sketches rely heavily on Caliendo's technical skill, and the comedy derives almost exclusively from Caliendo's mimetic ability. It is by all accounts a much more accurate impression than Will Ferrell's. There is little satire, however, beyond "Bush is stupid." In "George Bush at the Rusty Miller Show," Bush is fielding questions from a studio audience. When asked why Bush has focused on Iraq instead of Osama bin Laden, Bush responds, "Listen here's the deal: you gotta stop terrorism. Sodama bin Laden, this guy, he must be stopped. We went to Iraq-istan, and we stopped Hussein from sodomizing us."[27] The question provides a perfect opportunity to satirize the Bush administration's conflation of Iraq and 9/11, but instead of digging into that aspect of the issue, the answer veers toward Dubbya mispronouncing words. In "Goodnight America Late Night Tonight Show," Dubbya hosts a late-night style show as a way "to improve his improval rating." Once again, Caliendo's Bush is magnificent, but the humor relies on "Bush is stupid." Doing a Jay Leno–style headlines bit, Bush shows the headline, "Poll: Bush Worst President Ever." Caliendo's Bush then responds, "They spelled pole wrong, they forgot to put the 'e' at the end. Whoever did this was a child that was left behind."[28] Bush gave comedians plenty of material to fill "Bush is stupid" sketches, and that was an obvious through-line for nearly all Bush sketch comedy, but the best Bush satire went well beyond Bush's pronunciation problems. Unlike Chappelle, *MADtv*'s Bush satire is exclusively personality, which in light of the satiric shift taking place makes their satire unusually tame.

Robot Chicken

W was roasted on network television, across cable, and even Cartoon Network via its evening programming for adults, Adult Swim. Dubbya found himself being mocked regularly on the stop-motion animation series *Robot Chicken*. Created by Seth Green, who voices Bush, and Matthew Senreich, the show is a pop-culture mashup loosely based on the action-figure magazine *ToyFare*. The show features a series of short independent sketches that put two pop culture things together into one quick sketch. The humor comes from the discrepancy of the mashup, often putting childhood toys or action figures into adult situations, such as the Nintendo characters Mario and Luigi traveling to Vice City from the video game *Grand Theft Auto*. The show occasionally did a fully themed episode, such as "Robot Chicken: Star Wars," which was an entire episode dedicated to mashing up *Star Wars* and current pop culture. Dubbya found his way into the episode via "Jedi in Chief," in which Bush discovers that he has Jedi powers. Adorned in his famous "Mission Accomplished" flight jacket, Dubbya uses his new Jedi powers to convince his wife Laura to have a threesome with Condoleezza Rice. He then throws Bill Clinton's car into a pond outside of a McDonald's, and uses his lightsaber to write "W was hear" on the Lincoln Memorial. Lincoln comes to life, and the two have a lightsaber battle, with Dubbya slaying Lincoln: "That'll teach you, George Washington!" Bush then cuts off his daughter Jenna's finger in a mashup of the famous Darth Vader–Luke Skywalker "I am your father" scene. Dubbya then wakes up in the Oval Office, unsure if it was all just a dream.

Up until this point the sketch is a pretty standard take on "Bush is stupid and immature," but when an aide tells the president that they still haven't found any weapons of mass destruction, Bush tries to use his Jedi powers, telling the aide, "You have found weapons of mass destruction." It doesn't work, but Bush doesn't realize it because he then asks the aide to bring him a taco, and the aide does – a callback to the very first joke ever aired on the series in which Bush delivers a short campaign commercial, declaring "Tacos rule!"[29] The end bit is a clever mashup satirizing the way the Bush administration essentially tried to Jedi mind trick the country into thinking there were weapons of mass destruction in Iraq by endlessly repeating the claim. By 2007 when the sketch aired, it was apparent that the claim was a complete lie.[30] In "George W. Gremlin," Bush is given a mogwai and immediately does everything he's not supposed to do with it – feed it past midnight, get it wet, etc. Before he knows it, the White House is overrun with gremlins wreaking havoc. Rather than try to fix the situation, Dubbya joins in the revelry. Eventually, one of the gremlins grabs the nuclear launch codes from Bush's pocket and initiates a nuclear holocaust.[31] Nuclear weapons again pop up in "Captain Texas is Coming," in which Dubbya imagines himself as a comic book superhero saving the world from terrorism and throwing nuclear missiles at all of America's enemies, including the sun, which is how Dubbya proposes to end global warming.[32] The sketches all illustrate the humor on the show and the way it used "Bush is stupid" as the centerpiece of its satire. Nearly every Dubbya sketch featured a quick turn at the end that put a bite onto the satire. In "Jedi," we see that Bush lied us into war, while in "Gremlin" Bush's stupidity and immaturity is juxtaposed with the immense power he wields over the entire world. *Robot Chicken* sketches are certainly not dripping with biting satire, but they do move beyond the simple "Bush is stupid" through-line of *MADtv*. Furthermore, it demonstrates the pervasiveness of Bush satire.

SNL – Will Ferrell . . . and Everybody Else

A kindred spirit to Chevy Chase's Gerald Ford, Ferrell's Bush is arguably the most iconic of *SNL*'s presidential sketch impressions. After all, he is the only cast member to do a one-person Broadway show as the president, 2009's *You're Welcome America. A Final Night With George W. Bush*. While Ferrell's Bush is the most recognizable of the *SNL* impressions, he only impersonated Bush for a few short years before leaving the show in May 2002. Chris Parnell, Darrell Hammond, Will Forte, and Jason Sudeikis all donned the Texas accent, but they have become mere footnotes to Ferrell. Forte later admitted that he didn't want to do Bush because Ferrell's impression was so resonant: "I didn't want to see anybody else come in and do George Bush after Will Ferrell did it. It was almost like somebody coming in and taking over the role of Church Lady. That's Dana Carvey; nobody else can do Church Lady."[33] Ferrell himself didn't think much of the role when he first got it, thinking that Al Gore was more likely to win and that his Bush would be a short-lived character. Of course, Bush won, and as Ferrell noted in an interview after Bush left office,

> There was this incredible combination of insane news events that he had to deal with and obviously some poor decisions on his part, along with his type of personality and the fact that he kind of can't speak properly. That, you know, makes for a wonderful kind of comedic stew.[34]

As with Chase's Ford, Ferrell's Bush is not a good impression in terms of straight accuracy. Caliendo's Bush is much more accurate, but Ferrell, like Chase, seemed to capture the nature of Bush better than anyone else. There was plenty of "Bush is stupid" in Ferrell's impersonation, but ultimately, he was able to marry Bush's intelligence with his policy. Ferrell's Dubbya walked the very fine line between a moron and lovable buffoon, but unlike many other Bush impressions Ferrell's managed to show the impact of Dubbya's frat-boy persona. Ferrell demonstrated better than others that if Dubbya is as dumb as everyone says, then it stands to reason that the policy choices and decisions that he makes for the country will have a disastrous outcome. What makes Ferrell's Bush so good – and perhaps an indictment of all of us – is that this devastating satiric take is delivered through a Bush that is highly likable.

Ferrell's Bush might have made the actual Bush more likable, but it provided opponents of the Bush administration a cathartic release during what they saw as troubling times. As John Lopez argues:

> as the goodwill that Bush's post-attack leadership earned him was burned away in the fires of Iraq, Ferrell's impersonation soldiered on. It was both tonic and scourge. All the underlying angst of the Iraq war, America's ballooning cultural excess, and the foreboding of an inevitable headache to come was sublimated into a Dionysian release of gallows laughter at our nation held hostage by Bush's buffoonery. Ferrell's Bush gave us emperor-has-no-clothes moments upon moments until we ultimately realized we were really laughing at ourselves.[35]

As Lopez argues, though Ferrell only played Bush for three seasons, there was a noticeable shift in Ferrell's portrayal. The "strategery" Bush of the election continued for a short while but soon gave way to the 9/11 Bush, only to be replaced by a Bush consumed by his idiocy. The clear through-line of Ferrell's Bush was digging just below the "Bush is stupid" trope to unearth a more profound critique of Bush's presidency.

The April 7, 2001, cold open helps to illustrate how Ferrell's Bush moves beyond "Bush is stupid." On April 1, 2001, Bush faced his first international affairs test. A U.S. Navy EP3 surveillance aircraft collided in midair with a Chinese fighter jet in what came to be called the Hainan Island incident. The pilot of the Chinese plane was killed, and the U.S. aircraft was forced to land. The 24 crew members were interrogated and held by Chinese officials, who demanded an apology from the United States. Many in the Bush administration wanted to respond with force, but Bush sought a more conciliatory diplomatic approach. The United States issued a vaguely worded document – the "Letter of Two Sorries" – where the United States said it was "very sorry" about the pilot's death and "very sorry" there was not clear verbal clearance to enter Chinese airspace. The vague letter allowed both sides to claim victory. The Chinese claimed it was an apology by the United States, while the United States claimed it was not an apology. Many saw the letter and the "two sorries" as weak on the part of the United States and a rebuke of Bush's pledges to take a tougher stance with China than President Clinton, though not escalating militarily with China certainly was not a bad idea.

When the sketch aired, the letter was still being written and negotiated, so Ferrell's Bush took the negotiating into his own hands. In the sketch, Ferrell uses Bush's "stupidity" as an explanation for the looming "bad" deal. He announces that "I made a bold decision to meet with the Chinese President Jiang Zemin alone, one-on-one, no Dick Cheney. No state department officials, no military advisers, no international law specialists, no China scholars, no translators." Ferrell's Bush states that the two men hashed out an agreement in less than 20 minutes, a deal in which "the United States government sincerely, profusely, and abjectly apologizes to China for this incident. It was entirely our fault, and we did a bad thing." Bush further announces that the North Koreans will be dismantling and examining the plane, which will then be sold to Libya to help fund the Palestine Liberation Organization. The Chinese will be allowed to keep photocopies of all classified documents, but will not share the photocopies with Iran or Iraq, "although sharing photocopies of photocopies is permitted. Provided they are readable – I fought hard for that one." Bush continues as the list of American concessions continues to grow: the 24 Americans will be allowed to return to America to reunite with their families before being returned to China and forced labor camps, where they will be joined by Secretary of State Colin Powell, who will resign his position and head to China. The list goes on and on, with more and more ludicrous concessions to the Chinese, while the only thing Bush seems to get is an agreement from the Chinese: "Don't mess with Texas."[36] The terrible deal, which to some, was not much different than the real deal, is importantly a *policy result* of Bush's stupidity. The sketch plays on the cliché of "Bush is dumb," but moves beyond it to show how that can influence Bush's performance as president and, in this instance, America's standing in the world.

Bush's character would stay true to the "Bush's stupidity is endearing but dangerous" caricature of the previous seasons, but take a patriotic turn following the 9/11 attacks. Much like the real Bush, Ferrell's Bush talks tough about fighting terrorism, and his Texas-spun wisdom and shoot-from-the-gut mentality serve him well in the immediate months after 9/11. In the October 6, 2001, cold open, for instance, Ferrell's Bush is still not the brightest, but his patriotic, in-charge demeanor outweighs it. Bush's stupidity is lovingly displayed as power. His empty catchphrases suddenly imbued with patriotism. From the Oval Office, Ferrell's Bush declares to Osama bin Laden, "Buddy, you screwed up big time. Guess what amigo? I'm comin' to getchya. You see, you made a big mistake. If you had any brains, you would have challenged me to a game of Scrabble." Bush goes on to relish in freezing bin Laden's assets, and declares, "Make no mistake. We're coming for you bin Laden. I'm gonna make you my own personal 'Where's Waldo?' And unlike those frustrating Waldo books, I'm gonna find ya. Maybe not today, maybe not tomorrow. But *maybe* tomorrow."[37] The sketch is an excellent example of the country – and comedy – rallying around Bush in the wake of 9/11. He's still presented as an intellectual lightweight, but rather than being an impediment, his Stage Yankee "wisdom" will somehow help him to win the war on terror.

The two personas would come together during early 2002, Ferrell's last year on the show. In the May 11, 2002, cold open, Bush has his daily briefing with Secretary of State Condoleezza Rice (Maya Rudolph) and Vice President Dick Cheney (Darrell Hammond). Bush starts the sketch with a pep talk for himself: "They will not make you look stupid. They will not make you look stupid. They will not make you look stupid." Naturally, as the sketch goes on, Bush looks stupid. Rice and Cheney go through the numerous foreign policy issues that face the administration, with Bush struggling with names, places, and positions of international allies and adversaries. Bush can't recognize or remember the leaders of Palestine, Yemen, Saudi Arabia, Syria, Egypt, or Jordan, often confusing them with fictional characters, like Queen Amidala from *Star Wars* or the Fremen people from the novel *Dune*. As Bush struggles, he asks, "Do I get to talk with someone today with the name Smith or Jones or Cooper or Knievel?" Bush goes on to lament, "What happened to us? Sure we have a war on terror, that's great. But we used to have domestic issues. I used to work a regular six-hour day." Cheney responds, as if to a toddler, "It's a complex world, sir." Bush replies, "It's a complex world? Try telling that to those boys and girls out on the South Lawn playing Little League baseball. They don't think it's a complex world. And this might come as a big surprise to y'all, but I also don't think it's a complex world." Cheney and Rice laugh, and Cheney responds, "Sir, I'm not surprised by that at all."[38] The sketch does an excellent job of demonstrating just how unprepared Bush was to take on the war on terror, and even eight months after 9/11, he is still struggling with basic facts about the Middle East. In retrospect, the sketch is even more damning of Bush than it was at the time, as Bush's missteps in the Middle East mounted during his time in office and have continued long after he left.

It took a few years for Ferrell's Bush to come full circle, but he did in 2009's Broadway production *You're Welcome America. A Final Night With George W. Bush*. Directed by Adam McKay (who would later write and direct the highly critical *Vice* about Dick Cheney), the show opened shortly after Bush left office, and became both a cathartic and traumatic experience. Anderson Tepper summed up the conflicting experience for many:

> Ferrell's Bush is a swaggering, petulant wise-ass; a spliff-smoking pseudo-Texan with only a limited, child-like grasp of language and politics. How easy it was to laugh at Ferrell's caricature in the early years of the Bush presidency; how hard to reconcile the buffoonery with the global mess and destruction that defined his final days. For one night, though, it's a relief to give in to the dark humor of it all – the inane nicknames, the cock-eyed cast of characters (from Cheney to Condi), the malapropisms, lies, and manipulations. If ever there was any argument for the therapeutic effects of laughing to keep from crying, this is it.[39]

The show reflects the evolution of Ferrell's Bush, beginning with some well-worn Bush-isms, but ending with some incredibly targeted satiric barbs. It also represents the Brechtian aspects of Ferrell's Bush. By the time of this show, audiences were well aware of Ferrell's opinions on Bush, allowing the audience to lay that additional subtext onto the performance.

The final act of the show starts with Bush's "Mission Accomplished" aircraft carrier moment, complete with Ferrell in Bush's signature flight suit. From here, the show takes a decidedly darker turn. Bush steps off the Oval Office desk, and while bragging about the success of the war, "It truly was – Mission Accomplished. Even though 98.3 percent of all casualties, including civilians, have occurred after that speech was made." For the remainder of the show, Ferrell excoriates Bush's legacy, taking on the failures at home and abroad. Ferrell's Bush turns introspective, reflecting on the tremendous human cost of the Iraq War in a way the actual Bush never did publicly:

> Has the war weighed heavily on me? Sure it has. I think about it every day. Do I cry about it? Yeah, without a doubt. I cry a lot. I feel for the families who have lost loved ones. I cry for the parents who have lost a son or daughter. I cry for the kids who never get to know their mom or dad. I also feel for the hundreds of thousands of Iraqi civilians who've lost their lives. I lot of this crying is done alone. 'Cause I'm the one who made the call, and I must live with that. So at this moment in time, I'd like to honor all of those who've died as a result of this war with a moment of silence.

The audience is silent throughout Bush's reflection, and rather than release the tension with a new Bush bit, Ferrell's Bush fields a call from former FEMA Director Michael Brown, who oversaw the administration's disastrous response to Hurricane Katrina. Bush famously defended Brown during the disaster: "Brownie, you're doing a heck of a job." Ferrell's Bush digs into the situation, going over Brown's lack of qualifications and how New Orleans is still trying to recover with little help from the government:

> It's funny, you would've thought after my initial mess-up that I would've dedicated more of my second term just to checkin' in on New Orleans . . . I know, but I DIDN'T! You hit the nail on the head Brownie, Americans do have short attention spans. No, it's great. You can just half-ass shit, and it doesn't matter.

The laughter here is uncomfortable because a very hard truth is evident – Bush wasn't up to the job.

The two episodes reflect Ferrell's attitude toward Bush, and is a prime example of how Brechtian acting technique works in sketch comedy. In the first, he displays the pathos and regrets he believes Bush owes the country. The audience reads both Ferrell's take and the real Bush's actions here, with the satire existing in the distance between the two. In the second, he mirrors the assuredness and cockiness of the real Bush, bragging in the face of disaster. Ferrell's Bush continues to wear the stupid-but-cocky hat as he does an interactive bit with the audience where Ferrell's Bush gives audience members Bush-style nicknames. He runs down the long list of Bush's accomplishments, including, "We also tripled the deficit, sanctioned torture, and illegally wiretapped Americans months before 9/11. But on the downside, we did oversee the collapse of the entire world economy . . . so . . . mas or menos." Reflective on the real Bush, the show ends with Ferrell's Bush running down a litany of America's worst presidents to prove that he wasn't so bad. Rather than apologize and show the regret Ferrell clearly thinks Bush owes to the country, Bush ends the show with his signature cockiness and its titular phrase, "You're welcome America."[40]

The 2009 Dubbya portrayed by Ferrell encapsulates the life cycle of Ferrell's Bush – from bumbling frat-boy moron to one of the worst presidents in history. Yet, Ferrell's Bush remains highly likable. When he's reflecting on the Iraq War, rather than only being a searing satiric critique, it also acts as a moment of catharsis – for both the audience and Bush's legacy. Because Ferrell had become so closely associated with Bush, it is easy to imagine that Ferrell is giving voice to the actual Bush's inner thoughts. In this way, it is the epitome of Brechtian acting. Yet, Ferrell's Bush also shows the limits to this style. In his sillier moments, Ferrell's Bush is simply another in a long line of overgrown man-child Ferrell characters – Ron Burgundy in *Anchorman* (2004), Ricky Bobby in *Talladega Nights* (2006), Chazz Michael Michaels in *Blades of Glory* (2007), Buddy in *Elf* (2003), Frank in *Old School* (2003), and Brennan Huff in *Step Brothers* (2008). All of these characters are versions of Bush (and Ferrell's comic persona): they are stupid but lovable, overly cocky for no apparent reason, and their combination of arrogance and stupidity drives their actions, with often disastrous results. Yet, like with Bush, we *like* these characters. Ferrell is, in some ways, the exception to Dubbya satire. While Stewart and Colbert and other sketch comedians clearly show a dislike for Bush, there is, intentional or not, a charming quality to Ferrell's Bush that makes the sketches funnier, but also works to make the real Bush more likable. Ferrell's likeable Bush simultaneously excoriated Bush's legacy while rehabilitating Bush's legacy. Ferrell is obviously not the only reason that Bush's image has softened since he left office, time and Trump are more culpable, but Ferrell's imprint on Bush reflexively made the man more likeable, and made Americans more willing to forgive and forget Bush's transgressions.

While the Broadway show was supposed to be Ferrell's goodbye to the character of Dubbya, he has returned several times to *SNL*, most notably in 2018 when Ferrell hosted. Ferrell's likable Bush was a welcome sight on *SNL*, which had become home for Alec Baldwin's miserable Trump. Audiences loved Baldwin's portrayal, but it didn't make Trump more likable. As the Trump presidency wore on, Bush's presidency was remembered in more halcyon ways. Bush's approval ratings hit all-time highs in early 2018, as Ferrell's Bush says, "Donnie Q. Trump came in, and suddenly I'm looking pretty sweet by comparison." Ferrell's likable Bush pushes back on that narrative, saying, "I wanted to address my fellow Americans tonight and remind you guys that I was really bad. Like historically not good. . . . Don't forget, we're still in two different wars that I started. Hey, what has two thumbs and created ISIS – this guy." He goes over some of Bush's "greatest hits" like the stock market losses, before going on to share the similarities between himself and Trump, "We both won the election despite losing the popular vote, though back in my day we didn't let Russians rig our elections, we used the Supreme Court like Americans."[41] The 2018 Dubbya sketch is a crystal-clear illustration of the shift in sketch comedy toward the real in the absurd. Ferrell is just listing out the "accomplishments" of the Bush presidency as satire. He includes some mispronounced words for good measure, but the majority of the humor in the sketch relies on remembering that Bush was a lousy president. The sketch acts as a reminder to not get caught up in the day-to-day absurdities of the Trump administration by recognizing the genuine consequences of the Bush administration.

Despite Bush's pledge of "compassionate conservatism" and the brief national unity following 9/11, the Bush years further polarized a growingly divided nation. Fox News and conservative media became less concerned with objectivity and more concerned with defending the president. Meanwhile, liberal satirists led by Jon Stewart and Stephen Colbert began attacking the president not just for his personality, but for his policy, and doing it with sharper teeth than had been seen in a generation. The rise of this satiric authenticity galvanized the left, but also worked to deepen the red state–blue state divide. As Bush left office, the country was embroiled in two foreign wars and facing the worst economic crisis in nearly a century. As the housing bubble burst, banks nearly collapsed, and the stock market crashed, America seemed headed in the wrong direction. The next president, like Ronald Reagan before him, promised a new morning in America with a pledge of "Yes, we can!"

Notes

1. "Fact Sheet: Compassionate Conservatism," *Office of the Press Secretary, The White House*, 30 April 2002. https://georgewbush-whitehouse.archives.gov/news/releases/2002/04/20020430.html.
2. Qtd. in Ron Suskind, "Faith, Certainty and the Presidency of George W. Bush," *New York Times*, 17 October 2004. www.nytimes.com/2004/10/17/magazine/faith-certainty-and-the-presidency-of-george-w-bush.html.
3. John Buell, "Presidential Debates as Corporate Circus," *Bangor Daily News*, 10 October 2000, 1.
4. "First Presidential Debate: Al Gore and George W. Bush," *Saturday Night Live*, 7 October 2000. www.youtube.com/watch?v=zDgRRVpemLo.
5. Qtd. in William Horner and Heather Carver, *Saturday Night Live and the 1976 Presidential Election: A New Voice Enters Campaign Politics* (Jefferson, NC: McFarland & Co. Inc., 2018), 6.
6. Mike Ryan, "What Was the Most Damning 'SNL' Political Impression Ever?" *Uproxx.com*, 5 April 2016. https://uproxx.com/tv/snl-trump-bush-gore/.
7. Qtd. in Tom Shales and James Andrew Miller, *Live From New York: An Uncensored History of Saturday Night Live* (Boston: Little, Brown and Company, 2002), 449.
8. Qtd. in Shales and Miller, 449.
9. Roger Rosenblatt, "The Age of Irony Comes to an End," *Time*, 24 September 2001. http://content.time.com/time/magazine/article/0,9171,1000893,00.html.
10. "Humor Muted on Late-Night Shows," *USA Today*, 17 September 2001. https://usatoday30.usatoday.com/life/enter/tv/2001-09-17-late-night-humor.htm.

11. "September 11, 2001," *The Daily Show with Jon Stewart, Comedy Central*, 20 September 2001. www.cc.com/video-clips/1q93jy/the-daily-show-with-jon-stewart-september-11 – 2001.
12. "Humor Muted on Late-Night Shows."
13. "Short Shorts for the USA," *Saturday Night Live*, 6 October 2001. www.nbc.com/saturday-night-live/video/short-shorts-for-the-usa/2872698.
14. AJ Aronstein, "Comedy After 9/11: Sincerity and Irony," *Vulture.com*, 8 September 2011. www.vulture.com/2011/09/comedy-after-911-sincerity-and-irony.html.
15. Zoe Williams, "The Final Irony," *The Guardian*, 27 June 2003. www.theguardian.com/theguardian/2003/jun/28/weekend7.weekend2.
16. Jeffrey P. Jones, "'Fake' News Versus 'Real' News as Sources of Political Information: The Daily Show and Postmodern Political Reality," in *Politicotainment: Television's Take on the Real*, ed. Kristina Riegert (New York: Peter Lang, 2007), 129; Julia R. Fox, Glory Koloen and Volkan Sahin, "No Joke: A Comparison of Substance in *The Daily Show with Jon Stewart* and Broadcast Network Television Coverage of the 2004 Presidential Election Campaign," *Journal of Broadcasting & Electronic Media* 51, no. 2 (2007), 213.
17. Qtd. in Lionel Shriver and Naomi Wolf, "One Book Fair, Hours of Satire, and the Dixie Chicks – Bush's Cultural Legacy," *The Guardian*, 30 October 2008. www.theguardian.com/world/2008/oct/31/george-bush-usa-culture.
18. Stephen Colbert, "Stephen Colbert at The White House Correspondents Dinner," *C-SPAN*, 29 April 2006. www.youtube.com/watch?v=CWqzLgDc030.
19. "First Black President," *The Richard Pryor Show*, 1977. www.youtube.com/watch?v=RvehAOCNwp8.
20. David Peisner, *Homey Don't Play That! The Story of In Living Color and the Black Comedy Revolution* (New York: Atria/37 INK, 2018), 49.
21. "Black President," *Mind of Mencia*, 8 July 2007. www.cc.com/video-clips/ixup5p/mind-of-mencia-black-president.
22. "Black Bush," *Chappelle's Show*, 14 April 2004. www.youtube.com/watch?v=9DLuALBnolM.
23. Qtd. in "Unmasking the Racist History of Blackface," *CBSnews.com*, 28 October 2018. www.cbsnews.com/news/history-of-blackface-unmasking-the-racism-reignited-by-megyn-kelly-controversy/.
24. Erica R. Edwards, "The Black President Hokum," *American Quarterly* 63, no. 1 (2011), 36.
25. Ralph Ellison, "Change the Joke Slip the Yoke," *Partisan Review* 25, no. 2 (1958), 212–222.
26. Mel Watkins, *On the Real Side: A History of African American Comedy* (Chicago: Lawrence Hill Books, 1999), 114.
27. "Rusty: Presidential Questions," *MADtv*, 12 March 2005. www.youtube.com/watch?v=Qw_lGRzInxc.
28. "Goodnight America Late Night Tonight Show Show," *MADtv*, 12 November 2005. www.youtube.com/watch?v=K1901OlQMIU.
29. "Junk in the Trunk," *Robot Chicken*, 20 February 2005. www.adultswim.com/videos/robot-chicken/junk-in-the-trunk.
30. "Jedi in Chief," *Robot Chicken*, 17 June 2007. www.youtube.com/watch?v=bfiaGungQsg.
31. "George W. Gremlin," *Robot Chicken*, 2 September 2007. www.youtube.com/watch?v=zh0bXxr7bu0.
32. "Captain Texas Is Coming," *Robot Chicken*, 5 October 2008. www.youtube.com/watch?v=fieDBw6Qppw.

33. Qtd. in Josef Adalian, "How Each Era of *SNL* Has Ridiculed American Presidents," *Vulture.com*, 2 June 2017. www.vulture.com/2017/06/snl-how-each-era-has-ridiculed-american-presidents.html.
34. Qtd. in Neal Justin, "Will Ferrell Takes a Final Shot at George W. Bush," *The Orange County Register*, 13 March 2009. www.ocregister.com/2009/03/13/will-ferrell-takes-a-final-shot-at-george-w-bush/.
35. John Lopez, "And Now, Ladies and Gentlemen, a Message From the 'Saturday Night Live' President of the United States," *Grantland.com*, 25 August 2014. http://grantland.com/hollywood-prospectus/saturday-night-live-president-impressions/.
36. "President Bush Cold Opening," *Saturday Night Live*, 7 April 2001. www.nbc.com/saturday-night-live/video/president-bush-cold-opening/n11454.
37. "Bush Cold Opening: Message to Bin Laden," *Saturday Night Live*, 6 October 2001. www.nbc.com/saturday-night-live/video/bush-cold-opening-message-to-bin-laden/2860776.
38. "Cold Opening: George W. Bush," *Saturday Night Live*, 11 May 2002. www.nbc.com/saturday-night-live/video/cold-opening-george-w-bush/n11600.
39. Anderson Tepper, "Will Ferrell's 'You're Welcome America: A Final Night With George W. Bush," *Vanity Fair*, 26 January 2009. www.vanityfair.com/news/2009/01/will-ferrells-youre-welcome-america-a-final-night-with-george-w-bush.
40. *You're Welcome America. A Final Night With George W. Bush*, HBO, 14 March 2009.
41. "George W. Bush Returns Cold Open," *Saturday Night Live*, 27 January 2018. www.nbc.com/saturday-night-live/video/george-w-bush-returns-cold-open/3658037.

CHAPTER 8

Obama

Barack Obama assumed the presidency amidst a global financial meltdown known as the Great Recession. The housing bubble burst; the financial sector, banks, and stock market were in free fall; the American auto industry was near collapse; and America was entangled in two sprawling foreign wars. When Obama left office eight years later, he had overseen the longest period of sustained job growth in U.S. history. Obama's job numbers and the overall economic recovery were impressive, but two things defined his time in office. On the policy front, Obama worked to pass comprehensive healthcare reform through the Affordable Care Act, also known as Obamacare. On the personal side, Obama is the country's first African American president. Sketch comedians have imagined an African American president for decades. Initially, the incongruity of a black man as president was humorous. In the 1960 election, many Americans were struggling with the idea of a Catholic as president. The idea of an African American president was inconceivable. Jim Crow laws were still in effect, and it wouldn't be until the 1964 Civil Rights Act and the 1965 Voting Rights Act that segregation was outlawed. Even today, many barriers make simply voting as a minority troublesome, let alone running and winning the highest office in the land.

When Obama was elected, many prematurely declared it the end of racism, seeing his presidency ushering in a new post-racial America. The post-racial myth was pushed by both liberal and conservative pundits, arguing that Obama's ascendancy, much like Flip Wilson's, was proof that African Americans had achieved racial equality, despite mountains of evidence to the contrary. Historically ridiculed in American comedy, a black president became in more recent popular culture mythologized as America's savior, the only person who can bridge America's racial past. Erica Edwards argues that there is an inherent duality to the mythology: "The invention of the black president as messianic figure who embodies the nation's most sacred ideals of liberty, brotherhood, and equality, while either banishing the threat or fulfilling the promise of black social protest."[1] Obama would simultaneously always be "too black" and never "black enough." He would be responsible for ending racism while being responsible if he didn't end racism. He would likewise face a burden no other president has faced: he would be representative of ALL black people. His every move scrutinized like no other president – from criticism for wearing a tan suit to the profoundly racist "birther" movement that claimed Obama was born in Kenya. He was put in the impossible position of a systemically racist country using him as proof of the country's lack of racism. The rise of the Tea Party, "birtherism," and the 2016 election of Donald Trump, a leading proponent of "birtherism," all proved that America was anything but post-racial.

Obama's election did signal a new era in politics, however short-lived. His message of hope and unity, embodied in the "Yes, we can!" mantra of his campaign, gave new confidence to liberals disheartened by the Bush years. The passage of Obamacare likewise marked a milestone in Democratic politics, becoming the first comprehensive healthcare bill to be passed after generations of Democrats had failed to enact reform. The passage of Obamacare, along with a healthy dose of racism, though, led to the rise in 2009–2010 of the Tea Party, an ultraconservative branch of the Republican Party that sought lower taxes, lower government spending, and a lower national debt (at least while Obama was president). Behind the Tea Party movement, Republicans retook control of the House of Representatives with its largest midterm election victory in nearly a century, eclipsing even the 1994 Republican wave. Suddenly, Obama faced a Republican-controlled Congress who vowed never to compromise. In the words of Senate Majority Leader Mitch McConnell, "The single most important thing we want to achieve is for President Obama to be a one-term president."[2] As a result, despite all the promises of hope, change, and unity, the majority of Obama's two terms in office saw deepening partisan divides and a further fractioning of the American electorate.

For satirists, though, Obama was a respite. He was friends with Jay-Z and Beyoncé, a celebrity in his own right. In short, he was cooler than other presidents. After the dizzying Bush years, comics saw Obama as an opportunity to take their foot off the pedal. He lacked the scandals of Nixon and Clinton (and later Trump), didn't have any signature catchphrases, and his most striking vocal quality was slow and melodic. *SNL* producer and writer Jim Downey remarked on the difficulty of satirizing Obama, saying, "If I had to describe Obama as a comedy project, I would say, 'Degree of difficulty, 10 point 10 . . . with Obama, it was the phenomenon – less about him and more about the effect he had on other people and the way he changed their behavior."[3] Obama and the movement around him were certainly not easy targets, but race played a major factor in satirists' inability to effectively target Obama. The overwhelming whiteness of mainstream American comedy had difficulty grappling with Obama's race, frequently pretending it didn't exist or that attacks against him, like "birtherism," weren't based on race. We see here again evidence of satire's conservative nature. The privileged viewpoint of white male heteronormativity simply was not capable of satirizing Obama as both president and a black man. It is not a coincidence that *Key & Peele* was one of the only mainstream satiric voices that was able to craft a cogent and effective satiric take on Obama.

Obama's race undoubtedly impacted his satiric treatment, but there were other factors beyond race that contributed to the lighter treatment he received. First and foremost, Obama was hilarious, perhaps our funniest president. Like both JFK and Reagan, Obama's wit endeared him to Americans and worked to stave off other comedic voices, with his wit working to advance his agenda and stifle his critics. Obama was the first sitting president to appear on a late-night talk show, regularly making appearances, especially near the end of his second term. He did "Slow Jam the News" on *The Tonight Show With Jimmy Fallon*, read mean tweets on *Jimmy Kimmel Live*, and underwent a post-presidency job interview on *The Late Show With Stephen Colbert*. *The Late Show*'s head writer Opus Moreschi said of Obama,

> A lot of politicians are so eager to win over an audience that they'll tell a joke and then look around the room, laugh, then see if anyone's laughing.... They're too eager for the room to love them. [Obama] can play it cool, have a slow burn, and nail a good punch line. The fact that he's the president is actually kind of infuriating, frankly. He should pick a lane.[4]

Obama's monologues at the White House Correspondents Dinner regularly brought down the house, including an appearance with Keegan-Michael Key's "Luther the Anger Translator," only in this version it was the real Obama who needed to be calmed down.[5] He likewise regularly appeared on satiric news programs, from *The Daily Show* to *Full Frontal*. He even showed up on off-the-radar type of shows like Zach Galifianakis's *Between Two Ferns*, and ahead of a trip to Cuba, Obama appeared in a sketch on the Cuban sketch show *Vivir del Cuento* with Luis Silva.[6] And like any middle-aged man, he was also quick with "dad jokes," like his final Thanksgiving turkey pardon, when he told his daughters, "What I haven't told them yet is we are going to do this every year from now on. No cameras, just us, every year. No way I'm cutting this habit cold turkey."[7] He likewise participated in the various memes that surrounded his administration, most notably with the immensely popular "Thanks Obama" meme that blamed pretty much anything on Obama.

Obama also used his wit to take on his opponents, including the now infamous 2011 White House Correspondents Dinner, when he roasted Donald Trump, who was in attendance and had been leading the racist "birther" movement. Commenting that the matter was over, Obama said it would allow Trump to focus "on the issues that matter, like, did we fake the moon landing? What really happened in Roswell? And where are Biggie and Tupac?" Obama didn't stop there, further lambasting Trump's claim to fame, *Celebrity Apprentice*:

> We all know about your credentials and breadth of experience ... just recently, in an episode of *Celebrity Apprentice* at the steakhouse, the men's cooking team did not impress the judges from Omaha Steaks. And there was a lot of blame to go around. But you, Mr. Trump, recognized that the real problem was a lack of leadership. And so ultimately, you didn't blame Lil' Jon or Meatloaf. You fired Gary Busey. And these are the kind of decisions that would keep me up at night. Well handled, sir. Well handled.[8]

Many, including the *New York Times*, point to this moment as pivotal to Trump's run for the White House in 2016. The *Times* said of the evening:

> That evening of public abasement, rather than sending Mr. Trump away, accelerated his ferocious efforts to gain stature within the political world. And it captured the degree to which Mr. Trump's campaign is driven by a deep yearning sometimes obscured by his bluster and bragging: a desire to be taken seriously.[9]

While Trump's intentions are speculative, Obama's wit served him well.

At times, Obama was funnier about Obama than many satirists. Obama was funny and that helped blunt satire aimed at him, but his light satiric treatment was due more so to the ideological alignment between satirists and Obama, who saw the new president as a welcome reprieve from Bush. Lionel Shriver seemed to sum up the attitude of many, saying that "Obama could be terrible for the arts. Why, when there's barely an artist in the States who doesn't support him? Art thrives on resistance. There's nothing more arid, more enervating, more stultifying, or more utterly uninspiring than getting your way."[10] Early Obama satire was fawning, a reaction both to the failures of Bush as well as the promise of Obama. *The Onion*'s November 4, 2008, headline, "Black Man Given Nation's Worst Job," summed up much of the satiric mood in November 2008:

> In his new high-stress, low-reward position, Obama will be charged with such tasks as completely overhauling the nation's broken-down economy, repairing the crumbling infrastructure, and generally having to please more than 300 million Americans and cater to their every whim on a daily basis. As part of his duties, the black man will have to spend four to eight years cleaning up the messes other people left behind.[11]

In his 2018 show *Tambourine*, Chris Rock likewise tied Obama's popularity to Bush's failures: "Bush was so bad he gave us Obama. You forget that shit, don't ya? Bush was so bad that people said, 'Hey, maybe this black guy has the answers.' I think people overlook George Bush's contributions to black history."[12] JibJab released an Obama video, "He's Barack Obama," that featured the new president as a superhero who comes to save the day. The video slightly satirizes the mythology that Obama will be able to fix all of the nation's problems, while also suggesting that Obama will be able to solve a lot of the nation's problems.[13]

Second City's 2007 revue "Between Barack and a Hard Place" likewise satirized the glowing coverage of the Illinois senator, with the *Chicago Tribune* calling it "the funniest Second City show in years" (Michelle Obama agreed, reportedly laughing throughout when she saw the show).[14] The show both poked fun at the glowing coverage of Obama, but also his everything-to-everyone persona for many liberal Americans. The opening of the show featured each cast member stepping forward to announce themselves as Obama:

> "Hello, African-Americans, I am Barack Obama," says Amber Ruffin, the revue's only black member. "Hello, white male Americans," says Brian Gallivan,

"I am Barack Obama." "Hello, American women, I am Barack Obama," says Molly Erdman. Ithamar Enriquez greets "Hispanic slash Latino Americans," Joe Canale greets gay ones and then Brad Morris concludes, "Shalom, Jewish-Americans." We are all Barack Obama.[15]

Another sketch in the revue, "Killer," imagines "Sillary Tinton" trying to hire a hitman to assassinate Obama, but no one will take the job. When yet another says no, "Sillary" says, "You are the 11th assassin I've talked to, and they've all said the same thing. What is it with this guy?" The assassin, who earlier stated his affinity for Obama, replies that Obama is "just the right amount of black." Cast member Brad Morris commented on the sketch, saying, "That's a line that to me is pretty on the mark for a lot of Americans. It's really close to saying, 'That's a black person I feel comfortable with.' And the fact that we're still having that conversation in America right now is something to play with, too."[16] The Second City's next revue, *America: All Better!*, likewise paints Obama as America's savior, though it has moments of pessimism, such as when Anthony Leblanc says, "Hope Obama doesn't fuck it up!" The majority of the show is fawning over the optimism of Obama's presidency. As Albert Williams writes, "But for all the Obama allusions, political satire doesn't figure all that heavily here . . . *America: All Better!* focuses primarily on how average folks are handling a world of unprecedented possibilities and challenges, paradoxes and conundrums, economic downturns and emotional upticks."[17] Yet again, satire was mirroring the American reflection from the White House. As with Kennedy and Reagan, a majority of Americans liked his message of hope and his vision for a unified America. But like those before him, before Obama could make America "all better," he had to win an election.

The 2008 Election – Overshadowed by Tina Fey

The 2008 election was surprisingly low-key in terms of sketch comedy. There weren't any great Obama or John McCain impressions, in part because neither man was easy to mock. That is, of course, until McCain nominated Alaska Governor Sarah Palin as his running mate. Palin was a perfect sketch comedy storm for *Saturday Night Live*: she was virtually unknown, had a distinct vocal accent, and had a penchant for gaffes. The fact that former cast member Tina Fey just so happened to look precisely like Palin was the icing on the cake. Though *SNL* only aired a handful of sketches with Fey as Palin, it arguably is the most impactful political impression in the show's history. When Palin first emerged, she was wildly popular, seen as a potential saving grace to McCain's flagging candidacy. Her folksiness and colloquialisms – a clear link to the Stage Yankee persona so fundamental to American identity – endeared her to many Americans. That popularity soon waned, as she struggled in several national interviews, most notably in her *CBS Evening News* interview with Katie Couric, often rambling and having difficulty even naming a single newspaper that she read. The interview was a disaster for the Republican ticket, and *SNL*'s sketch satirizing the conversation became one of its very best.

What is notable about the sketch is the undeniable shift to pointing out the real in the absurd, as Fey's Palin uses Palin's own words numerous times throughout the sketch. The interview itself was so ridiculous that there was little to exaggerate. Instead, the most effective satire was simply repeating reality, as Fey said, "shining a light on it." Fey further elaborated on the impression, saying, "We went into it wanting to make sure that we were very fair. That we weren't just swinging, throwing punches. That we focused on what *seemed true* about the situation."[18] For instance, here is an excerpt from the actual interview about Palin's claim that Alaska's proximity to Russia gives her foreign policy experience:

Couric: You've cited Alaska's proximity to Russia as part of your foreign-policy experience. What did you mean by that?

Palin: That Alaska has a very narrow maritime border between a foreign country, Russia, and on our other side, the land – boundary that we have with – Canada. It, it's funny that a comment like that was – kind of made to cari – I don't know. You know. Reporters –

Couric: Mocked?

Palin: Yeah, mocked, I guess that's the word, yeah.

Couric: Explain to me why that enhances your foreign policy credentials.

Palin: Well, it certainly does because our – our next-door neighbors are foreign countries. They're in the state that I am the executive of. And there in Russia –

Couric: Have you ever been involved with any negotiations, for example, with the Russians?

Palin: We have trade missions back and forth. We – we do – it's very important when you consider even national security issues with Russia as Putin rears his head and comes into the air space of the United States of America, where – where do they go? It's Alaska. It's just right over the border. It is – from Alaska that we send those out to make sure that an eye is being kept on this very powerful nation, Russia, because they are right there. They are right next to – to our state.[19]

Compare the real interview to *SNL*'s:

Couric (Amy Poehler): On foreign policy, I want to give you . . . one more chance . . . to explain your claim that you have foreign policy experience, based on Alaska's proximity to Russia. What did you mean by that?

Palin: Well, Alaska and Russia are only separated by a *narrow* maritime border. [She holds up her hands.] You've got Alaska here, and this right here is water, and, then, that up there is Russia. So we keep an eye on them.

Couric: And how do you *do* that, exactly?

Palin: Every morning, when Alaskans wake up, one of the first things they do is look outside and see if there are any

Russians hanging around. If there are, you gotta go up to them and ask, "What are ya' doing here?" And if they give you a good reason —they can't – then, it's our responsibility to say, you know, "Shoo! Get back over there!"

Again, when asked about the economic meltdown and the proposed $700 billion bailouts, the similarities between the real interview and *SNL*'s are eerie. First, the actual interview:

Couric: Why isn't it better, Governor Palin, to spend $700 billion helping middle-class families, who are struggling with health care, housing, gas and groceries, allow them to spend more and put more money into the economy instead of helping these big financial institutions that played a role in creating this mess?

Palin: That's why I say, I, like every American I'm speaking with, we're ill about this position that we have been put in where it is the taxpayers looking to bail out, but ultimately, what the bailout does is help those who are concerned about the healthcare reform that is needed to help shore up our economy, helping tho – it's got to be all about job creation too, shoring up our economy, and putting it back on the right track, so healthcare reform and reducing taxes and reining in spending has got to accompany tax reductions and tax relief for Americans. And trade, we've got to see trade as opportunity, not as – competitive – scary thing, but one in five jobs being created in the trade sector today, we've got to look at that as more opportunity. All those things under the umbrella of job creation. This bailout is a part of that.[20]

And *SNL*:

Couric: Sen. McCain shut down his campaign this week, in order to deal with the economic crisis. What's your opinion of this potential $700 billion bailout?

Palin: Like every American I'm speaking with, we are ill about this! We're saying, "Hey! Why bail out Fannie and Freddie, and not *me*?" But ultimately, what the bailout does is help those that are concerned about the healthcare reform that is needed to help shore up our economy. To help, um – it's gotta be about job creation, too. Also, about shoring up our economy, and putting Fannie and Freddie back on the right track. And, so, healthcare reform and reducing taxes and reining in spending, 'cause, Barack Obama, you know? You know, we've got to accompany tax reduction, and tax relief for Americans. Also, having a dollar value meal at restaurants – that's gonna help. But, one in five jobs being created today, under the umbrella of job creation. That, you know, also. . . .[21]

While the *SNL* interview certainly has more jokes, it is remarkably similar to the original, working to demonstrate how unqualified Palin was, not through exaggeration but by merely repeating Palin's own words. The two quotes are so similar that the fact-checking site Snopes actually ran a comparison of the two and had to debunk Fey's quotes as real Sarah Palin quotes. Though they noted: "Admittedly, this portion of the comedy skit hewed so closely to reality that dismissing it as satire might be considered misleading, as without close reading the [SNL] transcript offered above is difficult to tell apart from a genuine transcript of Governor Palin's interview with Katie Couric."[22] We see here a clear example of the absurdity of reality overtaking the absurdity of sketch comedy. Palin's own performance was so absurd, and Fey's near-verbatim repetition so effective, that people assumed everything Fey said was a direct Palin quote, no matter how ridiculous it may have been because the real Palin said so many ridiculous things. There was no need to exaggerate reality in this case because the reality was already absurd.

Fey's satiric takedown of Palin led to what has been deemed "The Tina Fey Effect." In part, Fey's feelings about Palin helped lead to the effect. Fey made it clear that she thought Palin was unfit, refusing to share the stage when the real Palin made a cameo on *SNL* for fear of there being any hint of an endorsement. Fey's Palin again highlights the Brechtian dual-presentation acting style inherent in political sketch comedy. Audiences read Fey's own opinions about Palin onto the performance, deepening the satiric take, and for those opposed to Palin's candidacy, deepening their enjoyment of the sketches. Their almost identical appearance was also part of the appeal. They looked *so much* alike that it was hard to believe any of it was real. As such, Fey's Palin is also an excellent example of the emerging need for satiric authenticity. With the deepening divides in American life and politics, it has become more effective if we know how the satirist feels about the person, rather than merely attacking them as a way to keep a check on power. People liked Fey's Palin not only because it was an excellent impersonation, but because it demonstrated that Fey was on their side. Similarly, conservatives disliked the sketch because they saw Fey's personal opinions about Palin as illustrating *SNL*'s liberal bias. This alienation effect shows one of the potential limits of satiric authenticity. When the audience reads the satirists personal opinions onto the sketch, does it then immediately discount the sketch for half of the audience.

With satiric authenticity there is an obvious question: does it just make liberals feel good? According to a study in *Public Opinion Quarterly*, the answer is a resounding "no." Jody Baumgartner, Jonathan Morris, and Natasha Walth found in "The Fey Effect" that Democrats were not swayed, mostly because they already had a negative perception, but interestingly found that younger Republicans and Independents were less likely to vote for McCain–Palin. They write,

> Using panel data of young adults surveyed in the late stages of the 2008 presidential campaign, we find that those who saw Tina Fey's impersonation of Sarah Palin on *Saturday Night Live*'s (*SNL*) skit of the vice-presidential debate displayed steeper declines in approval for Palin than those who saw debate

coverage through other means. Interestingly, this "Fey Effect" spilled over into vote intention, and was most pronounced among self-identified Republicans.[23]

As John Lopez writes, "Beneath the surface mockery of *faux*-folksiness, Fey had an agenda: Get this person off the political stage. And if any comedian has ever had any real impact on politics, it has to be Tina Fey."[24] Satire, specifically sketch comedy, has not always had a direct impact on politics and politicians. It has certainly helped to shape public perceptions and opinions, and as noted throughout has galvanized supporters, but it has not always had a palpable effect on voters. Tina Fey's Sarah Palin, however, like Chase's Ford and Hammond's Gore, is one of the clearest examples of satire not just "making liberals feel good," but an example of the inherent power of satire and sketch comedy.

SNL's Race Problem

Obama's popularity among liberal satirists was a contributing factor to his relatively light satiric treatment, but it would be naïve to ignore race. The vast majority of mainstream Obama satire tried to avoid it at all costs. When satirists did comment on race, they often did it clumsily, such as the July 21, 2008, cover of *The New Yorker*. The cover, meant to mock right-wing fear-mongering about the Obamas, instead ignited a controversy. Obama and First Lady Michelle Obama appear as versions of the worst stereotypes about them. He is dressed in traditional Muslim clothing, while she is dressed like a Black Panther with a rifle slung over her shoulder. As they fist bump, behind them, an American flag burns in a White House fireplace. *New Yorker* editor David Remnick defended the cartoon, arguing that "the intention is to satirize not Barack Obama and Michelle Obama, but, in fact, to hold a pretty harsh light up to the rumors, innuendos, lies about the Obamas that have come up – that they are somehow insufficiently patriotic or soft on terrorism." He went on to note, "Satire doesn't run with subtitles. . . . A satirical cartoon would not be any good if it came with a set of instructions."[25] The satire was unclear, as many in the right-wing media had been literally depicting the Obamas in that way, so it read less as a satiric take and more of an amplification of the stereotypes, one of the pitfalls of verbatim satire.

Quite simply, American mainstream comedy is overwhelmingly white and male. Nearly every late-night and satiric news host has been a white male, with mostly white male writers' rooms. *SNL* is no different, with very few cast members or writers of color in its five-decade run. The show even addressed its lack of diversity in a 2013 sketch featuring Jay Pharoah as President Obama and host Kerry Washington as Michelle Obama . . . and several other black women. Since the show had no black women in the cast, Washington had to exit and reenter to have more than one black female character in the sketch. During one of her costume changes, the following announcement is made:

> The producers of *SNL* would like to apologize to Kerry Washington for the number of black women she will be asked to play tonight. We made these requests both because Ms. Washington is an actress of considerable range and talent and also because *SNL* does not currently have a black woman in the

cast. As for the latter reason, we agree this is not an ideal situation and look forward to rectifying in the future . . . unless, of course, we fall in love with another white guy first.[26]

To further drive home the point during another Washington costume change, six white male cast members enter to play Matthew McConaughey. The sketch is funny and shows *SNL*'s awareness of the problem, but doesn't do much actually to address the issue. This overwhelming whiteness both at *SNL* and in mainstream comedy, in general, contributed to many either being unable or unwilling to criticize the first African American president.

Saturday Night Live's first Obama, Fred Armisen, wasn't even black. Leading into the 2008 election, *SNL* was on hiatus thanks to an industrywide writers' strike. The strike gave the show several months in which to find a suitable actor to play Obama, and in the end, Lorne Michaels opted for Armisen, who is of German, Venezuelan, and Korean heritage. Michaels said the show auditioned several actors for the role, but that Armisen was the best Obama: "When it came down to it, I went with the person with the cleanest comedy 'take' on Obama. . . . It's not about race."[27] In the sketch, which satirizes the glowing media coverage of Obama versus Hillary Clinton, played marvelously by Amy Poehler, Armisen darkens his skin and takes on the understated and reserved mannerisms of Obama.[28] Armisen's impression didn't wow the critics, but the casting choice caused controversy. Reflecting the mood of many, Maureen Ryan wrote in the *Chicago Tribune*, "Call me crazy, but shouldn't 'Saturday Night Lives' fictional Sen. Barack Obama be played by an African-American? . . . They couldn't find an African-American performer who was funny enough to play the junior senator from Illinois? They couldn't find one in New York? Not anywhere in the country? Really?" Summing up the controversy, Ryan continued, "But mainly, I find 'SNL's' choice inexplicable. Obama's candidacy gives us solid proof of the progress that African-Americans have made in this country. I guess 'SNL' still has further to go on that front."[29] America had progressed faster than satire. The country had elected its first African American president, but *SNL* didn't have the appropriate cast to play the new First Family: a sobering reality about the state of satire. Despite the controversy, Armisen would play Obama for three seasons, and while *SNL* has begun to address its lack of diversity, the show remains predominantly populated by white comedians. Reflecting Brecht's dual performance, it became impossible for audiences not to read Armisen's non-blackness, and *SNL*'s overall diversity problems, onto the impression.

On its own merits, Armisen's Obama is similar to the show's satiric take on Obama: bland. He does a solid mimetic impression of Obama, but there isn't much to grasp onto, and there is little in the way of meaningful satire. Shortly after Obama's election, Armisen played Obama in a sketch about Obama keeping his cool, in which Armisen does an understated rhyme set to jazz:

I keep it cool.
I take my kids to school.
I don't lose my temper. It's my only rule.
I keep it cool.[30]

218 *Obama*

The sketch isn't terribly funny and the satire is pretty much missing. The sketch's whole point is that Obama is planning to be bipartisan and work with people who either opposed him, like Senator Joe Lieberman, or who ran against him, like Senators Hillary Clinton and John McCain. Not exactly comic gold. The most glaring omission in the sketch and *SNL*'s Obama satire is the failure to address *why* Obama keeps it cool, something so fundamental to understanding Obama's presidency that *Key & Peele* would place it at the heart of their Obama satire.

It's telling that one of the better Obama sketches is "Cosby Obama," where the Obama family morphs into the Huxtable family from *The Cosby Show* to help sell Michelle Obama's campaign against childhood obesity. Armisen's Obama takes on the traits of Cliff Huxtable from the show, making him more fun and dynamic than usual.[31] The sketch does not hold up well due to the sexual crimes of Bill Cosby, but it is one of the more dynamic Armisen-as-Obama sketches, mostly because Armisen isn't mimicking Obama. While Fey's Palin worked because she hewed so closely to Palin, Armisen's Obama failed because he hewed so closely to Obama without capturing the president's essence, showing the limits of a verbatim satiric take. Armisen's Obama was ultimately dull, as Jason Zinoman wrote in 2011 in the *New York Times*, *SNL* "still has not figured out how to make Barack Obama funny. In its long history of mocking presidents, no impression has made less of one."[32] The *Wall Street Journal* wasn't much kinder, saying, "I think it's written right in the U.S. Constitution somewhere that Fred Armisen's impression of President Barack Obama isn't very funny."[33] *SNL*'s Obama simply lacked a point of view. Undoubtedly this is related to *SNL*'s lack of diversity and historic privileging of white male heterosexual identity. *SNL* largely ignored one of the central tensions of Obama's presidency, and one that is at the heart of the much more successful Obama on *Key & Peele*, which is the relationship between race and the unreasonable expectations placed on Obama. He was not simply playing it cool, he *had* to play it cool to avoid falling into negative stereotypes about black male aggression. *SNL* never investigated the layers of Obama's "cool," ultimately making its impression toothless and bland. Comedy's role in the fabrication and dissemination of racial stereotypes demeaning African Americans was something *SNL* should have addressed, but instead ignored.

In part to begin addressing its lack of diversity, *SNL* brought on Jay Pharoah as a featured player in 2010, the first African American man hired by the show since Kenan Thompson in 2003. Pharoah was hired, in part, or at least gained notoriety, for a video showcasing his Barack Obama impression.[34] Rumors immediately began swirling that Pharoah would take over Obama, though it would be two years before he eventually became the commander in chief. Michaels reportedly felt that the enormity of playing the president would be too big a burden to place on a new cast member. In an interview before Pharoah's 2012 debut as Obama, Michaels admitted the show's satiric take was lacking, saying, "So far we haven't found it."[35] When Pharoah did take over, it was greeted enthusiastically by critics. The *A.V. Club* welcomed the shift with the following satirically non-satiric headline, "*Saturday Night Live* Gives Job of Playing Barack Obama to Actual Black Man."[36] Armisen introduced Pharoah's Obama in the September 15, 2012, cold open, announcing, "It is my distinct honor to introduce the president of the United States – I wouldn't want his job, right? Ladies and gentlemen, President Barack Obama." Pharoah was welcomed with thunderous applause, showcasing his Obama's signature "uauahhh" sound between thoughts. The sketch itself goes harder after Republican nominee Mitt Romney (Jason Sudeikis) for being out of touch – "I understand the hardships facing ordinary Americans. For example, this summer one of my horses failed to medal at the Olympics."[37] Pharoah didn't have the same controversy hanging over his Obama for obvious reasons, and by the time Pharoah stepped into the *SNL* Oval Office in 2012 the celebrity of Obama had begun to wane. He was still popular, but the great idealism of his election had faded away – the inconsistency of "The Great American Joke" had worn off, but the satire did not get much more pointed. Even with 2012 being an election year, *SNL*'s Obama satire failed to take off. Pharoah's Obama was a solid technical impression, a step up from Armisen's, but it too lacked any defining characteristic in terms of a satiric take.

The lack of a clear satiric take on Obama led *SNL*'s Obamas, both Armisen and Pharoah, to play the straight man to more interesting characters. Poehler's Hillary Clinton, Dwayne "The Rock" Johnson's "The Rock Obama," Jason Sudeikis's Joe Biden and Mitt Romney, and others. Comedically this often made the sketches funnier, but satirically it weakened an already weak take on the president. The "Healthcare.gov Meeting Cold Open" is an excellent example. The sketch features a rotating cast of new, exaggerated, and exciting characters, from the Pope to Justin Bieber, parading in as Obama stands idly by. There is some light satire about Obama's use of social media to spread the word about Obamacare, including his appearance on *Between Two Ferns*, but mostly it is an opportunity to showcase the characters *other than* Obama.[38] An earlier sketch about Obamacare similarly featured a series of "regular" people talking about Obamacare, including a cameo from Jesse of *Breaking Bad*, who explains that Walter White had to cook meth and kill people because he didn't have Obamacare.[39] The rollout of Obamacare was a disaster for the Obama administration and put the future of the Affordable Care Act in serious jeopardy, but rather than satirize that immense failure, the sketch mines other characters for comedy. A sketch about the government sequester, a huge spending cut forced on Obama by the Republican congress, likewise features Obama introducing a series of *other* characters to talk about the sequester, this time highlighted by the Village People.[40] One sketch that does satirize Obama effectively scrutinizes his reliance on using executive orders, "How a Bill Does Not Become a Law." Yet it, too, still draws much of its humor from other characters. A parody of the *Schoolhouse Rock!* cartoon, Kenan Thompson dressed as a "Bill," and Bobby Moynihan dressed as a smoking "Executive Order," provide the majority of the comedic moments.[41] In nearly all these sketches, there is little satire, and Obama plays second fiddle. Pharoah himself had some sharp criticism for *SNL* when he left the show, saying, "If you really noticed, for the last year and a half, they didn't do any Obama sketches at all. I was like, 'Just let me do my character, and we'll be fine.' They didn't want to do that. . . . No disrespect to them, but I kind of feel like they gave up . . . gave up on the Obama thing. . . . I think it was just a whatever attitude."⁴² To be frank, due to the show's historic lack of diversity, *SNL* wasn't capable of presenting a nuanced satiric take on Obama.

Key & Peele

While *SNL* struggled to satirize Obama, another show provided a much clearer, albeit still positive, satiric take on Obama: *Key & Peele*. *SNL* was ill-suited to satirize Obama, while Key and Peele were the perfect satirists. Before Keegan-Michael Key and Jordan Peele teamed up for their own show, they were cast members on *MADtv*. The show brought both Key and Peele in to audition as *MADtv* was looking to add a single African American male cast member, again, comedy has a diversity problem, but *MADtv* hired them both after seeing how well they worked together. And while Peele would play Obama on their show and Key would famously become Luther the Anger Translator, on *MADtv* it was Key who played Obama, though it was Peele who auditioned for *SNL* during the aforementioned writers' strike, in part to play Obama (Donald Glover was also among those auditioned). Peele was offered a job, not necessarily Obama, but when *MADtv* didn't let him out of his contract, Michaels went with Armisen (again, comedy has a diversity problem). Key's impression, dubbed "Fauxbama," is not a particularly good or mimetic impression. The impression lives in the *MADtv* world of parody, and for Obama, song parody in particular. Satirizing the race between Hillary Clinton and Obama, *MADtv* parodied Rihanna's "Umbrella," featuring Hillary (Nicole Parker) lusting for Obama: "I just want to be under Barack Obama-bama-bama-bama."⁴³ The 2008 sketch "Obama and Oprah" is another excellent example. A parody of Flo Rida's "Low," the sketch features Obama paying tribute to the woman who made his candidacy possible: "Now I would not be standing here, mesmerizing you with my inspirational and contagious joie de vivre, if it were not for the efforts of one woman. She is responsible for everything I have achieved. And no, I am absolutely not speaking about my wife." Key's Obama then sings:

> Let me tell you about her.
> I was a big-eared senator
> Without a chance in hell.
> Then the Queen of the world
> Put you under her spell.
> She took control,
> I think you know,
> Talkin' 'bout Oh Oh Oh Oh Oh Oh O-prah.

Oprah, played by Daheli Hall, enters, and the song parody continues. Like the *SNL* Obama sketches, Oprah is the real star of the sketch. The sketch becomes less about Obama and more about the cultural and political power Oprah wields, essentially crediting her with turning the junior senator from Illinois into the president.⁴⁴

The duo left *MADtv* in 2009 and later reunited in 2011–2012 to bring *Key & Peele* to Comedy Central. The show was seen by many as a follow up to *Chappelle's*

Show due to its format and the fact that both shows featured African American men (yes, sketch comedy has a lot of work to do in terms of diversity). Though it existed for a time in the former's shadow, eventually *Key & Peele* came to be regarded by many as the best sketch comedy show on television. The show focused mostly on popular culture, often viewing it through a lens of race and stereotypes. Commenting on their "fit" within sketch comedy, Peele said,

> One of the things that has made our show relevant, it's a very in-between show for in-between times. There are things that, plain and simple, haven't changed. There are things that we have to address that are different – we have a president of color now. Being mixed-race ourselves, we take advantage of sketch being able to go all different places.[45]

While *SNL* was having a non-African American playing the country's first African American president, Key and Peele were satirizing race in nuanced and hilarious ways.

Their five-season run is filled with smartly layered satire about race – "Auction Block," "Soul Food," "East/West College Bowl," and "Negrotown," to name but a few.[46] In "Confederate Reenactors," the duo go to a Civil War reenactment. The sketch opens with a Southern general opining about "the Southern way of life – a way of life so pure and beautiful, that no man or government can take this away from us." Then Key and Peele show up as slave-reenactors. The general responds, "How many times do I have to tell people? Just because we're dressed like Confederate soldiers does not mean we're pro-slavery. We're just here to preserve the pure and beautiful slice of Southern history." Key and Peele continue their over-the-top stereotyped reenactment, angering the general to the point where he stops just short of calling them the n-word, at which point Key and Peele drop their charade and rob the soldiers.[47] The sketch deftly satirizes the long-held notion of the "Southern way of life" and how proponents claim it has nothing to do with racism, when in fact, the entire point of the Confederate Army was to preserve slavery. The "how" of the satire is just as relevant here, as Key and Peele take on minstrel stereotypes to satirize white nostalgia. As E. Alex Jung writes, it's "a performance aware of the fact that everything is performance. . . . When Key and Peele go from playing slaves to robbing Confederates, it's a smart turn. They're performing yet another, more modern stereotype – that of the black criminal – and mocking the idea that there is any inherent truth to that stereotype."[48] There are *multiple* layers of dual performance in the sketch. The duo presents the layers of historical reenactment that works to "preserve" the past by revising it; the duality of performing minstrel stereotypes and black masculinity; the duality of contemporary black men playing on historic tropes about black masculinity that we pretend no longer exist but are embedded in American culture; the duality of whiteness inherent in the "Southern way of life"; and many more.

They similarly take on stereotypes about black male identity and the performance of blackness in "Playing a Thug." The duo are portraying gangster stereotypes in a film. The white director, played by Colin Hanks, lauds the performance of Key's Nigel, a classically trained British actor who has no real "authenticity."

The director then turns to Peele's character Antoine, telling him that the director doesn't "believe" the performance. Antoine is essentially playing an autobiographical character, but it is not authentically black enough for the Hollywood depiction of blackness the director wants. The sketch ends with each actor taking turns punching the director, with Antoine's violence still critiqued as not coming from a real place.[49] This sketch likewise demonstrates the way the show takes on minstrel stereotypes and the idea that blackness is something to be performed for white audiences. The notion of "blackness" and specifically black male identity is shown to be a constructed white definition that black men have been expected to perform for centuries.

One of the most famous sketches from the series, "Substitute Teacher," likewise plays with ideas about race and normalcy. In the sketch, Mr. Garvey, an African American inner-city teacher, is now a substitute in a white suburban school. During the morning attendance, Mr. Garvey has difficulty pronouncing the students' names, like "Jay-kwel-en" for Jacqueline, "D-Nice" for Denise, and "A-A-Ron" for Aaron. The sketch on one level makes Mr. Garvey the butt of the joke, as his identity as an African American inner-city teacher makes him the clear outsider. On a deeper level though, the sketch demonstrates the constructed nature of racial power structures and the historic presentation of whiteness as "normal."[50] Comedy Central's majority white audience will laugh at the mispronunciation of the typical names, but there is also a critique of that audiences' assumptions of normal. The joke that Mr. Garvey should know these names suddenly takes on a layered meaning when you examine the cultural assumptions that make white names normal and black names abnormal. A white teacher mispronouncing a black student's name is considered acceptable, but Mr. Garvey mispronouncing white students' names is laughable. The sketch is also an example of the show's dual consumption and the shifting media landscape of the post-network era. Many *Key & Peele* sketches are consumed online as single videos, rather than as part of an entire episode. Viewers regularly engaged with sketches online, then went to watch the show.

These sketches and many more approach race in ways that the much more conservative *SNL* could not. Moreover, and more importantly, they approached race in ways that *SNL* could not even conceive of due to its historic white male perspective. *Key & Peele*'s treatment of race demonstrates once again the inherent importance of the satirist's identity. As outlined in Chapter 1, historically African American satirists and comedians have been able to much more effectively discuss and critique race relations in America. Similarly, from Fanny Fern to Tina Fey, women have provided much more nuanced and effective critiques about gender. As is also evident in Chapter 1, too often throughout comedy's history satire about race and gender has come from a white male perspective that has been intentionally *detrimental* to the identity and agency of marginalized groups. *SNL*'s take on Obama was not intentionally detrimental, but their inability to satirize him points to the incredible importance of a diversity of satiric voices to effectively challenge and define the American presidency and the American identity.

"Luther the Anger Translator"

The duo is probably most well-known, particularly within the world of political sketch comedy, for their take on Obama – "Luther the Anger Translator." The pair did several other Obama sketches, such as "Obama's Meeting with Republicans," in which they satirize Republican's opposition to anything Obama proposes, including when he suggests Republican ideas.[51] But those all take a back seat to Luther. The recurring sketches feature Jordan Peele as Obama and Keegan-Michael Key as Luther, who expresses the anger beneath Obama's calm exterior, a sort of subtext translator to express how Obama *really* feels. The sketch was part of the original pilot of the show, and became a sort of "eureka moment" for them, as Peele said, "Anytime there's something that's out there that no one's discussing, it's a golden opportunity. It fit perfectly in that category – what can *Key & Peele* do that no one else can do?"[52] The answer: effectively satirize Obama.

The sketches are also a prime example of pointing out the real within the absurd. The whole point of the sketches is to say what Obama really feels, as Peele explains, Obama "couldn't come off like an angry black man, especially early on, so what Luther says are things that ring true to us."[53] Aside from the fact that Peele does a much more natural Obama than either Armisen or Pharoah, the satiric take is much clearer and working on multiple levels. In the first "Luther" sketch, Obama talks about a range of issues, including the strain between him and the Tea Party:

Obama: I just want to say to my critics, I hear your voices and I'm aware of your concerns.
Luther: So maybe you could chill the hell out for like a second, then maybe I could focus on some shit. You know?
Obama: That goes for everybody, including members of the Tea Party.
Luther: Oh, don't even get me started on these mother-fuckers right here!
Obama: I want to assure you we will be looking for new compromises with the GOP in the months ahead.
Luther: You know these mother-fuckers are gonna say "no" before I even suggest some shit.

Throughout, Obama remains cool and collected, diplomatically addressing a wide range of issues, while Luther seethes with anger. Obama addresses Iran and North Korea in terms of nuclear weapons in very couched terms, then Luther exclaims, "Mahmoud, Kim-Jong! I think I already done told both y'all: 86 your shit, bitches! Or I'm gonna come over there and do it FOR Y'ALL!"[54] Importantly, Obama often reins in Luther, completely in control of Luther's raging excesses. Obama never loses control (except when the real Obama did a bit with Luther at the White House Correspondents Dinner), allowing Luther to vent his frustrations, but never letting Luther take control. Luther might be saying what Obama is thinking, but Obama is hyperaware that even his inner monologue needs to be constrained to maintain his authority and his image. The sketch moves beyond the conventional take of "Obama is calm." More importantly, it exposes both what he is thinking as well as *why* he is so careful with his public perception. Key explained that the character arose from their frustration about the lose-lose situation Obama faced: "If he gets angry, he's the angry black man. If he doesn't say anything, he's uppity or ineffectual. The guy couldn't win. So that's where this raging id standing next to him, of Luther, was founded."[55] That "raging id" takes the satire to another level.

The sketches also took on Obama's successes, showing how even those had to be couched in their delivery. In another "Luther" sketch, Obama talks about why voters should choose him in 2012, highlighting his job creation numbers and the fact that he killed Osama bin Laden:

Obama: What has changed in the last four years?
Luther: Who killed Osama bin Laden?
Obama: What has my administration accomplished?
Luther: Did we accomplish killing America's biggest enemy? Check. Did that. Boom!
Obama: In 2011 alone, we created more jobs than George W. Bush did in all eight years of his office.
Luther: Except for Osama bin Laden hunter, because that job don't exist anymore because I went over there and I killed him in his face![56]

As Aisha Harris argues, "By poking fun at the President's need to remain palatable and 'safe' to mainstream America in order to steer clear of preconceived notions about how black men are supposed to act, Key and Peele make a far more interesting point than *SNL* ever has with its rather bland take on Obama's 'cool.'"[57] Luther satirizes what is at the heart of Obama's presidency – the historic, contradictory, unfair, and often unrealizable expectations placed upon black men, up to and including the president of the United States.

The "Luther" sketches became a recurring bit for the duo, with even Obama getting in on the act when Key portrayed Luther with the actual Obama at the White House Correspondents Dinner in 2015. The sketches are also an excellent illustration of the growing importance of satiric authenticity. As noted, the character was created out of Key and Peele's own frustrations with the way Obama was being treated, and the ways in which African American men have been stereotyped and portrayed in comedy and the media. That frustration is palpable in every "Luther" sketch, as is their own admiration of Obama. Nowhere is that more overt than in "Obama and Luther's Farewell Address." Filmed two years after *Key & Peele* left the air, it was aired in January 2017 after Donald Trump was elected and meant to mimic Obama's actual farewell address. According to Key, the sketch was written by former executive producer and writer Jay Martell, "for his [Martell] catharsis." Shown on *The Daily Show*, the sketch is dripping with anger and sadness that the man responsible for bringing the racist birther issue to the forefront and who ran on a campaign of intolerance would now be succeeding the country's first black president.

The sketch begins with Obama asking Luther to be on his best behavior. Obama goes on, "Since we last spoke, the country has voted for a new president." There is a pause and then the camera jumps back and forth between the two men as they silently try to conceal their feelings until Luther bursts out, "TRUUMMMP!" He jumps around, the anger pouring out of his every limb, "How did this happen, man!?!" He then kicks away a Trump balloon that briefly floats on screen. Luther continues ranting, as Obama maintains a dignified tone:

Obama: It's more imperative than ever that we move on as a country united.
Luther: United in the fact that we can't fucking stand each other.
Obama: Even as the country adopts new policies on trade, immigration –
Luther: New policy! The only good immigrant is a smoking hot white one!
Obama: Who plagiarizes speeches.
Luther: Oohhh. [Looks around as a call back to a recurring bit on the show.] I said biiiitttcchh.
Obama: I have greatly enjoyed my time as your president.
Luther: Except when um, let me think let me think, when Republicans wouldn't let me do shit, and then that one dude said I wasn't born here and then y'all elected him. So you know what? Didn't love that part so much. So pretty much the beginning the middle and the end sucked!

The sketch continues, taking aim at the very real fears of many surrounding the then impending Trump presidency:

Obama: I assure you, that if he succeeds, we all succeed.
Luther: Unless he succeeds with all the shit he promised to succeed with. In that case, we're fucked.

Harkening to Obama's actual farewell address, Obama continues:

Obama: To all of you out there who are afraid your way of life is under attack, remember that progress isn't always a straight line.
Luther: No, 'cause sometimes it's a line that goes like this [he points straight up], and then goes straight down for four fucking years!

After Luther tries to book a hotel for four years in Sweden, Obama wraps up:

Obama: In summation, thanks America. It's been real. It's been good. But it ain't been real good.
Luther: Apparently, orange is the new black. Good luck with your healthcare, assholes.[58]

Foreshadowing much of the comedy of the Trump era, the sketch makes no bones about its position. There is a precise point of view: Trump is terrible. There is anger but also a sadness beneath the sketch. Obama puts on a dignified face to try and help a man whose entire political career is based on a racist conspiracy theory about Obama and whose agenda is to systematically dismantle and erase Obama's legacy. Peele's "It ain't been real good" lands perhaps harder than anything. The hope and optimism the left had for Obama in 2008 was replaced with disappointment in his second term, and Obama throws that back in their faces, as Obama expresses *his* disappointment, and even betrayal, at this final, though ultimately predictable, insult to his legacy.

While satire was relatively easy on Obama, conservative media more than made up for it. They heavily pushed the birther conspiracy theory, even well after it was debunked, and Obama was forced to produce his long-form birth certificate. Fox News and other outlets did their very best to blame everything on Obama (the genesis for the "Thanks Obama" memes), and to make controversies out of anything – like Obama using Dijon mustard rather than yellow mustard; the "terrorist fist jab" referencing Obama fist-bumping with Michelle after a 2008 speech (also referenced in the infamous *New Yorker* cover); having a binder clip on the 2011 American Jobs Act paperwork; or having the audacity to wear a tan suit. During an August 2014 press conference, Obama decided to wear a tan suit, and the internet and cable news went wild – with one conservative commentator saying, "This proves he's a Marxist."[59] Fox News was hardly the only station dedicating wall-to-wall coverage of the nonincident. The degree to which the suit captured the news cycle is telling and harkens to *Key & Peele*'s main satiric point about the outsized behavioral expectations placed upon Obama. As Elena Hilton writes in *Esquire*, "that the tan suit is one of Obama's most memorable controversies speaks volumes about how much we expected of him while he was in office."[60] The media spent days covering the "controversy," arguably spending more time dissecting the intricacies of the suit and its meaning than they would five years later when Special Counsel Robert Mueller released his report on Russian interference and the Trump campaign in the 2016 election. They certainly spent more time on it than they spend discussing Trump's ill-fitting suits and overly long (and taped) red ties.

Given the unbelievable scrutiny Obama was under, the tan suit coverage is both laughable and awful. Every move Obama made was picked apart by conservative media, yet he left the office with zero scandals. That's not to say everything Obama did was great or that he didn't make any mistakes – he did. Still, the ferocity with which any little thing could become a national news story is undoubtedly an underappreciated facet of the Obama presidency. The level of decorum Obama kept throughout his presidency is quite simply remarkable, a feat that is both illuminated and celebrated by the "Luther" sketches. Yet, what makes the sketches work so well is that they also point out the long history of racism that made Obama's steel public exterior necessary in the first place – including the central role satire played in creating and propagating racist stereotypes. Obama keeping it cool is amazing, but inherently tragic – a reminder of the work America still must do to reach the promised post-racial society of Obama's presidency. When compared to the nearly daily scandals of the Trump presidency and the virtual pass he receives compared to the outrage over a tan suit, the hypocrisy is striking and startling . . . which leads us to the unexpected presidency of Donald J. Trump.

Notes

1. Erica R. Edwards, "The Black President Hokum," *American Quarterly* 63, no. 1 (2011), 33.
2. Qtd. in Andy Barr, "The GOP's No-Compromise Pledge," *Politico*, 28 October 2010. www.politico.com/story/2010/10/the-gops-no-compromise-pledge-044311.
3. Qtd. in Jamie Fuller, "Sarah Palin Is Not Impressed by the Idea That Tina Fey Sunk Her in 2008," *The Washington Post*, 20 August 2014. www.washingtonpost.com/news/the-fix/wp/2014/08/20/dont-include-sarah-palin-on-a-list-of-people-who-thought-tina-feys-impression-of-her-was-a-big-deal/.
4. Qtd. in Dave Itzkoff, "It's Late Night with President Obama," *The New York Times*, 7 November 2016. www.nytimes.com/2016/11/08/arts/television/its-late-night-with-president-obama.html.
5. "Slow Jam the News with President Obama," *The Tonight Show with Jimmy Fallon*, 9 June 2016. www.youtube.com/watch?v=ziwYbVx_-qg&feature=youtu.be. "Mean Tweets – President Obama Edition," *Jimmy Kimmel Live*, 12 March 2015. www.youtube.com/watch?v=RDocnbkHjhI&feature=youtu.be; "Stephen Helps President Obama Polish His Resume," *The Late Show with Stephen Colbert*, 18 October 2016. www.youtube.com/watch?v=aRQLU3IwNYs&feature=youtu.be. "President Obama's Anger Translator at White House Correspondents Dinner," 25 April 2015. www.youtube.com/watch?v=G6NfRMv-4OY&feature=youtu.be; "Obama Out," White House Correspondents Dinner, 30 April 2016. www.youtube.com/watch?v=NxFkEj7KPC0.
6. "President Barack Obama," *Between Two Ferns, Funny or Die*, 13 March 2014. www.youtube.com/watch?v=UnW3xkHxIEQ&feature=youtu.be; "Pánfilo habla con Obama," *Vivir del Cuento*, 19 March 2016. www.youtube.com/watch?v=umxRCqd6bdI&feature=youtu.be.
7. Qtd. in Shelby Slauer, "21 Jokes Obama Made in Office That Had His Daughters Cringing," *Business Insider*, 2 August 2018. www.businessinsider.com/dad-jokes-obama-2018-8.
8. "C-SPAN: President Obama at the 2011 White House Correspondents' Dinner," *C-SPAN*, 30 April 2011. www.youtube.com/watch?v=n9mzJhvC-8E.
9. Maggie Haberman and Alexander Burns, "Donald Trump's Presidential Run Began in an Effort to Gain Stature," *The New York Times*, 12 March 2016. www.nytimes.com/2016/03/13/us/politics/donald-trump-campaign.html?_r=0.
10. Lionel Shriver and Naomi Wolf, "One Book Fair, Hours of Satire, and the Dixie Chicks – Bush's Cultural Legacy," *The Guardian*, 30 October 2008. www.theguardian.com/world/2008/oct/31/george-bush-usa-culture.
11. "Black Man Given Nation's Worst Job," *The Onion*, 4 November 2008. https://politics.theonion.com/black-man-given-nations-worst-job-1819570341.
12. Chris Rock, *Tambourine*, Netflix, 2018. https://www.netflix.com/title/80167498.
13. "He's Barack Obama," *JibJab*, 19 June 2009. www.youtube.com/watch?v=kVFdAJRVm94.
14. Chris Jones, "'Between Barack' Funniest Second City Show in Years," *The Chicago Tribune*, 24 March 2007. www.chicagotribune.com/entertainment/chi-0703230372mar24-story.html.
15. Qtd. in Sid Smith, "2nd to None," *The Chicago Tribune*, 20 May 2007. www.chicagotribune.com/news/ct-xpm-2007-05-20-0705180369-story.html.
16. Qtd. in David Schaper, "The Second City Skewers Obama and Clinton," *National Public Radio*, 1 March 2008. www.npr.org/templates/story/story.php?storyId=18557995.

17. Albert Williams, "Is It Funny Yet?" *The Chicago Reader*, 18 December 2008. www.chicagoreader.com/chicago/is-it-funny-yet/Content?oid=1103919.
18. Qtd. in Katherine Schaffstall, "Tina Fey 'Relieved' She's No Longer on 'SNL' Amid 'Ugly' Political Climate," *The Hollywood Reporter*, 18 April 2019. www.hollywoodreporter.com/news/tina-fey-snl-ugly-political-climate-show-sways-viewers-1203101. Emphasis mine.
19. "Palin on Foreign Policy," *CBS Evening News*, 25 September 2008. www.youtube.com/watch?v=nokTjEdaUGg.
20. Qtd. in James Rainey, "Palin Is Talking More, But If She's Lucky, Few Are Listening," *Los Angeles Times*, 26 September 2008. www.latimes.com/archives/la-xpm-2008-sep-26-na-onthemedia26-story.html.
21. "CBS Evening News: Katie Couric Interviews Sarah Palin," *Saturday Night Live*, 27 September 2008. www.nbc.com/saturday-night-live/video/couric – palin-open/n12311.
22. David Mikkelson, "Katie Couric Interview," *Snopes.com*, 1 October 2008. www.snopes.com/fact-check/katie-couric-interview/.
23. Jody C. Baumgartner, Jonathan S. Morris and Natasha L. Walth, "The Fey Effect: Young Adults, Political Humor, and Perceptions of Sarah Palin in the 2008 Presidential Election Campaign," *Public Opinion Quarterly* 76, no. 1 (Spring 2012), 95–104.
24. John Lopez, "And Now, Ladies and Gentlemen, a Message from the 'Saturday Night Live' President of the United States," *Grantland.com*, 25 August 2014. http://grantland.com/hollywood-prospectus/saturday-night-live-president-impressions/.
25. Qtd. in "'New Yorker' Editor Defends Obama Cover," *All Things Considered, National Public Radio*, 14 July 2008. www.npr.org/templates/story/story.php?storyId=92529393.
26. "Black Women on SNL and in the White House," *Saturday Night Live*, 4 November 2013. www.youtube.com/watch?v=0tgQlcJ0QYg.
27. Qtd. in Paul Farhi, "Did 'SNL' Go Beyond the Pale with Fauxbama?" *The Washington Post*, 29 February 2008. www.washingtonpost.com/wp-dyn/content/article/2008/02/28/AR2008022803988_2.html.
28. "Democratic Debate," *Saturday Night Live*, 23 February 2008. www.nbc.com/saturday-night-live/video/democratic-debate/n12190.
29. Maureen Ryan, "'SNL' Can Do Better Than Armisen's Obama," *The Chicago Tribune*, 27 February 2008. www.chicagotribune.com/news/ct-xpm-2008-02-27-0802250142-story.html.
30. "Obama Plays It Cool," *Saturday Night Live*, 6 December 2008. www.nbc.com/saturday-night-live/video/obama-plays-it-cool/n12381.
31. "Cosby Obama," *Saturday Night Live*, 18 February 2012. www.nbc.com/saturday-night-live/video/cosby-obama/n13405.
32. Jason Zinoman, "Comedians in Chief Musn't Be Prudent," *The New York Times*, 5 December 2011. www.nytimes.com/2011/12/05/arts/television/comparing-fred-armisens-snl-obama-to-dana-carveys-bush.html?_r=1&.
33. Christopher John Farley, "Should Jay Pharoah Be the Next President of the United States of 'SNL'?" *The Wall Street Journal*, 26 September 2010. https://blogs.wsj.com/speakeasy/2010/09/26/should-jay-pharoah-be-the-next-president-of-the-united-states-of-snl/.
34. "Best Obama Impression Ever from 'Jay Pharoah' What's Knockin Wednesday's on Hot 91," 25 June 2009. www.youtube.com/watch?v=SkZgHjmBlvE.
35. Bill Carter, "Open Season on Politicians at 'SNL,'" *The New York Times*, 12 September 2012. www.nytimes.com/2012/09/13/arts/television/saturday-night-live-parodies-presidential-campaign.html.

36. Sean O'Neal, "*Saturday Night Live* Gives Job of Playing Barack Obama to Actual Black Man," *The A.V. Club*, 12 September 2012. https://news.avclub.com/saturday-night-live-gives-job-of-playing-barack-obama-t-1798233359.
37. "Obama vs. Romney Cold Open," *Saturday Night Live*, 15 September 2012. www.nbc.com/saturday-night-live/video/obama-vs-romney-cold-open/n27667.
38. "Healthcare.gov Meeting Cold Open," *Saturday Night Live*, 30 March 2014. www.nbc.com/saturday-night-live/video/healthcaregov-meeting-cold-open/2768597.
39. "Obamacare Cold Open," *Saturday Night Live*, 28 September 2013. www.nbc.com/saturday-night-live/video/obamacare-cold-open/n41321.
40. "Sequester Cold Open," *Saturday Night Live*, 2 March 2013. www.nbc.com/saturday-night-live/video/sequester-cold-open/n33493.
41. "How a Bill Does Not Become a Law," *Saturday Night Live*, 22 November 2014. www.nbc.com/saturday-night-live/video/how-a-bill-does-not-become-a-law/2830152.
42. Qtd. in Elizabeth Wagmeister, "Jay Pharoah Disses 'Saturday Night Live' After Firing: 'I'm Not a Yes N– ,'" *Variety*, 14 April 2017. https://variety.com/2017/tv/news/jay-pharoah-snl-fired-diss-interview-1202030820/.
43. "Under Barack Obama," *MADtv*, 24 November 2007. www.youtube.com/watch?v=FOTAfGuLA-0.
44. "Obama and Oprah," *MADtv*, 28 December 2008. www.youtube.com/watch?v=1XtO13Ejoqg&list=RD1XtO13Ejoqg&start_radio=1&t=15.
45. Qtd. in Lew, "'Key & Peele' Talk Sketch Comedy, Race and 'Fargo' With Patton Oswalt," *Variety*, 9 June 2014. https://variety.com/2014/scene/news/key-peele-talk-sketch-comedy-race-and-fargo-with-patton-oswalt-1201217112/
46. "Auction Block," *Key & Peele*, 14 February 2012. www.youtube.com/watch?v=zB7MichlL1k. "Soul Food," *Key & Peele*, 1 February 2012. www.youtube.com/watch?v=3zDHSLDY0Q8. "Substitute Teacher," *Key & Peele*, 17 October 2012. www.youtube.com/watch?v=Dd7FixvoKBw. "East/West College Bowl," *Key & Peele*, 20 September 2012. www.youtube.com/watch?v=gODZzSOelss. "Negrotown," *Key & Peele*, 6 May 2015. www.youtube.com/watch?v=Rg58d8opQKA.
47. "Confederate Reenactors," *Key & Peele*, 26 September 2012. www.cc.com/episodes/rh8n7f/key-and-peele-obama-college-years-season-2-ep-202
48. E. Alex Jung, "*Key & Peele* Knew How to Tell a Race Joke," *Vulture*, 9 September 2015. www.vulture.com/2015/09/key-peele-knew-how-to-tell-a-race-joke.html
49. "Playing a Thug – Uncensored," *Key & Peele*, 4 December 2013. www.cc.com/video-clips/8oygnl/key-and-peele-playing-a-thug – uncensored
50. "Substitute Teacher Pt. 1," *Key & Peele*, 17 October 2012. www.cc.com/video-clips/w5hxki/key-and-peele-substitute-teacher-pt – 1
51. "Obama's Meeting with Republicans," *Key & Peele*, 28 February 2012. www.cc.com/video-clips/tnawa2/key-and-peele-obama-s-meeting-with-republicans
52. Qtd. in Lew.
53. Qtd. in Elahe Izadi, "The Most Memorable Comedy Moments of the Obama Presidency," *The Washington Post*, 3 September 2016. www.washingtonpost.com/entertainment/the-most-memorable-comedy-moments-of-the-obama-presidency/2016/09/02/0c655342-6880-11e6-99bf-f0cf3a6449a6_story.html.
54. "Obama's Anger Translator – Meet Luther (Uncensored)," *Key & Peele*, 11 January 2012. www.youtube.com/watch?v=-qv7k2_lc0M&feature=youtu.be.
55. Qtd. in Michele Moses, "Keegan-Michael Key on Playing Obama's 'Anger Translator,'" *The New Yorker*, 27 October 2016. www.newyorker.com/culture/new-yorker-festival/keegan-michael-key-on-playing-obamas-anger-translator.

56. "Luther the Anger Translator," *Key & Peele*. www.comedycentral.com.au/key-and-peele/videos/key-peele-103#key-and-peele-103-act-3.
57. Aisha Harris, "TV's Best Obama Impression Isn't on *SNL*," *Slate.com*, 17 September 2012. www.slate.com/blogs/browbeat/2012/09/17/snl_obama_by_jay_pharoah_vs_key_peele_saturday_night_live_has_catching_up_to_do_.html.
58. "Obama and Luther's Farewell Address," *The Daily Show*, 5 January 2017. www.cc.com/video-clips/7pxts9/the-daily-show-with-trevor-noah-keegan-michael-key–a-farewell-address-from-president-obama-s-anger-translator.
59. Qtd. in Jake Woolf, "Barack Obama's Tan Suit 'Controversy' Is Now Three Years Old," *GQ*, 29 August 2017. www.gq.com/story/barack-obama-tan-suit-anniversary.
60. Elena Hilton, "Four Years Later, I Still Can't Stop Thinking About Obama's Tan Suit Controversy," *Esquire*, 29 August 2018. www.esquire.com/style/a22862882/obama-tan-suit-anniversary/.

CHAPTER 9

Donald J. Trump

The Obama presidency proved to be the comedic eye of the storm between two satirically charged administrations. If Dubbya's presidency reignited political satire, Trump's would push it to its limits. Obama's presidency was supposed to change politics forever, but instead, the political world changed on June 16, 2015, when Donald Trump descended an escalator at Trump Tower in New York City to announce his bid for the presidency. Instead of a promise of hope and change or a new morning in America, Trump railed about all the failures of America, warned that the country was in trouble, and proclaimed the American Dream dead. He declared his American vision almost immediately by attacking immigrants: "When Mexico sends its people, they're not sending their best. They're not sending you. They're sending people that have lots of problems, and they're bringing those problems with us. They're bringing drugs. They're bringing crime. They're rapists. And some, I assume, are good people."[1] He immediately asserted his view of American identity by vociferously and forcefully declaring who counted and who did not, with whiteness central to his vision of Americanness. He promised to "Make America Great Again" by repealing Obamacare and building a wall – "I would build a great wall, and nobody builds walls better than me believe me, and I'll build them very inexpensively. I will build a great, great wall on our southern border, and I will have Mexico pay for that wall."[2] His nostalgic calls to "make America great again" were based on his vision of a "lost" America, and it was clear who he saw as the victims.

Trump's announcement was so bizarre, so brazen, and so out of step with the norms of political and personal decorum that the news media and the Democratic National Committee (DNC) treated him as a joke. The DNC responded to Trump's announcement with a tongue-in-cheek reply: "[Trump] adds some much-needed seriousness that has been previously lacking from the GOP field, and we look forward to hearing more about his ideas for the nation."[3] It's easy to see why he was treated as a joke. Trump was a New York icon, known mostly for his braggart persona and larger-than-life personality. A self-proclaimed successful businessman with a string of failed product lines and casinos (and multiple bankruptcy filings), his greatest claims to fame were a book he didn't write, *The Art of the Deal*, and *The Apprentice*, a reality television show in which he fired people. His only political experience was in leading the racist conspiracy theory that Barack Obama was born in Kenya. Mix in his overwhelming narcissism – "I'm really rich," "I will be the greatest jobs president that God ever created," and of course his promise that Mexico would pay for a border wall – and it is easy to see why so many thought he was not a serious candidate. What the media and the DNC didn't count on was that reality had shifted so close to absurdity that half of the country did not see Trump as a joke. They took his absurdities, inherent contradictions, and ridiculous statements at face value – they saw no hyperbole in his hyper-hyperbolic statements, with the punchline being him winning the presidency. With Trump stepping into the Oval Office, absurdity had become reality.

Trump's presidency thus far has been marked by division, rising partisan tensions, and a whirlwind of scandals. From the infamous *Access Hollywood* tape, to paying porn star Stormy Daniels to remain quiet about an affair in the lead up to the 2016 election, to possible collusion with Russia and his odd public subservience to Vladimir Putin, to the unprecedented number of affiliated Trump administration officials who have resigned due to any number of issues/scandals (including multiple federal indictments and several prison sentences), to his lackadaisical response to a white nationalist rally in Charlottesville, to his unprecedented financial conflicts of interest, to his fake university, to his fine for misusing charity money, to his impeachment over his infamous call with Ukraine, to the multiple sexual assault and rape accusations, to the 30 other scandals (to whatever happened yesterday), there is a constant swirl of activity surrounding Trump that can be difficult to navigate. Trump himself often adds fuel to the fire through his favorite communication tool – Twitter. FDR had "Fireside Chats," JFK introduced the power of television to the presidency, Ronald Reagan perfected the sound-bite speech, and Obama opened up the possibilities of the internet and social media, but Trump's use of Twitter to convey personal thoughts, attack opponents, spread false information, and unveil policy decisions is unprecedented. Those policy matters have likewise been highly contentious and polarizing. From a Muslim ban barring entry to the United States for anyone from specific Muslim countries, to his array of immigration policies, including family separation and child detention centers (and the revelation that the architect of those policies, Stephen Miller, is documented spreading white nationalist propaganda), to massive tax cuts for corporations and the wealthiest Americans, to major foreign policy decisions such as his sudden troop withdrawal from Syria, to his trade war with China, to repeated efforts to repeal healthcare coverage, to just plain absurd moments such as the nonsense "Covfefe" tweet and the administration's insistence that it actually had a secret meaning[4] . . . nearly every Trump policy (or tweet) immediately causes sharp divisions, only to be replaced, sometimes minutes later, by a new policy or tweet that causes even sharper divisions.

How Do You Satirize a Living Parody?

Perhaps the only thing everyone can agree on is that the Trump presidency produces news like no other.[5] Every day seems to have 15 different news cycles. For instance, on the same day that Trump agreed with a commentator that called him "King of Israel," adding that Jews "love him like the second coming of God," he later stated when discussing a trade deal with China, "I'm the Chosen One," and "joked" in front of a veterans group that he might give himself the Medal of Honor.[6] On top of all that, the following headlines appeared: "N.R.A. Gets Results in One Phone Call With the President," "Trump Accuses Jewish Democrats of 'Disloyalty,' Inciting Fierce Backlash," "Mr. Trump also canceled a meeting with Denmark over its refusal to sell Greenland. The rare snub drew condemnation," and "New Rule Would Let U.S. Hold Migrant Families Indefinitely." To be clear, *all* of this happened in about 36 hours. In any other presidency, these events would be the events of an entire term. Not to mention that many of these headlines, like buying Greenland or the NRA swaying the president with one phone call, would be headlines in *The Onion*. Under Trump, they are in the *New York Times*, further proof that reality had become absurd.[7] The *Boston Globe* actually did run a fake front page to warn about Trump in April 2016, imagining what the headlines might be in April 2017: "Deportations to Begin," "Markets Sink as Trade War Looms," "New Libel Law Targets 'Absolute Scum' in Press."[8] They weren't far off; in fact, they were pretty spot on. While Democrats and the news media warned about the potential dangers of a Trump presidency, they didn't predict the *speed* of the news. The combination of absurd stories, seemingly unthinkable policy – like kidnapping and caging immigrant children – and the ridiculous speed of it all became overwhelming for many, further fueling the move to absurdity becoming the new normal. The only thing that could be anticipated in Trump's presidency was that there was nothing that was outside the realm of possibility – no matter how ridiculous.

Fueling all of the absurdity, from policy to the flurry of activity, was Trump's personality. An unapologetic narcissist, the most important thing for Trump was that everything was about Trump – and that everything be presented in a positive light. This tension created numerous real-life moments that a generation earlier would have been found on a sketch comedy show but were now part of presidential politics. In an interview with *Face the Nation*, when asked about humility, Trump responded, "I do have, actually, much more humility than a lot of people would think."[9] The man who puts his name in gold letters on everything he owns bragging about how much humility he has should be a classic sketch comedy take on his character, instead it is an example of the real Trump creating an un-ironic absurd reality. An earlier interview with Bloomberg's *With All Due Respect* provides another example of Trump's absurd reality. At a campaign stop, Trump said that the Bible was his favorite book, which surprised most people since Trump rarely talks about religion. As such, the interviewers wanted to contextualize the quote. This was not a "gotcha" interview by any stretch of the imagination. If anything, the interviewers go out of their way to help Trump. The transcript reads like a sketch:

Mark Halperin: I'm wondering what one or two of your most favorite verses are and why?

Trump:	I wouldn't want to get into it because, to me, that's very personal. You know, when I talk about the Bible, it's very personal, so I don't want to get into verses.
Mark Halperin:	There's no verse that means a lot to you that you think about or cite?
Trump:	The Bible means a lot to me, but I don't want to get into specifics.
Mark Halperin:	Even to cite a verse that you like?
Trump:	No, I don't want to do that.
Mark Halperin:	Are you an Old Testament or New Testament guy?
Trump:	Probablyyyy . . . equal. I think it's just an incredible, the whole Bible is incredible. I joke, very much so, they always hold up *The Art of the Deal*, I say it's my second favorite book of all time.[10]

Watching the clip, it is painfully evident that Trump's favorite book is not the Bible and that he's never read it. None of that would matter if Trump hadn't (1) said it was his favorite book, and then (2) doubled down on the lie. That sort of hypocrisy is usually ripe for political satire, but because Trump's performance was so painfully bad, it almost became impossible to satirize the situation. It would be challenging to mock his blatant lie more effectively than having a Trump character say that he likes the Old and New Testaments "Probablyyyy . . . equal." Seth MacFarlane, the creative force behind *Family Guy*, commented, "This could be a Brian/Stewie exchange."[11] How do you satirize a narcissist more effectively than having him say people don't realize just how much humility he really has? In both cases, the truth is sitting in plain sight during the *real* interview; everyone pretending it is not, makes it absurd. There is no need for a satirist to point out the truth because it is already so obvious.

Because of moments like the Bible interview (or any of hundreds of other examples, like thinking Frederick Douglass is still alive), many people have argued that Trump would be/has been great for comedy. In "Making America Laugh Again: The Yuge Bump for Political Comedy," Dean Obeidallah argues that Trump has been great for comedy: "Whatever your thoughts about President Donald Trump's impact on America, no one can deny that he's truly made one sector of America great again: Political comedy."[12] There certainly has been a massive uptick in the *amount* of political comedy since Trump's election, as well as the amount of material Trump has provided comedians. Late-night shows, *SNL*, and satiric news are thriving in terms of sheer numbers. Trump's election likewise has reignited the satiric teeth that dulled during Obama's tenure, but the comedy itself has not always been that great, in part because Trump himself isn't a layered comedic target. If satirists didn't quite know how to tackle Obama, the opposite has been true with Trump: nearly everyone has the same satiric take. He's been in the national spotlight for decades, and much of the humor about him centers on the same things: his accent, his hair, his long red ties. As Jesse David Fox argues, "Trump is a bad subject for comedy: He's shallow and played out, and already what people

Donald J. Trump 235

expect from the comedy about him is bad."[13] Jokes about him are omnipresent, with almost everything he does immediately followed by a flurry of jokes on social media.

When coupled with the speed of news in the Trump era, it has been tough for comedy about Trump to take hold. As Patton Oswalt jokes in his stand-up special *Annihilation*:

> People tell me, "You comedians must be so happy. Trump is president. All this free material." You know what, yes, there is a lot of material, but there is too fucking much. It's exhausting. Being a comedian while Trump is president is like, imagine there's like an insane man on the sidewalk, just shitting on the sidewalk and yelling about Hitler. So you're looking at him and immediately think of the funniest joke about shitting on the sidewalk, and you turn to tell it to a bunch of people, and behind you he's taken the shit and made a sombrero out of it. So you turn and you tell your amazing shitting on the sidewalk [story] and everyone goes, "Oh. . . . turn around, he made a sombrero out of it. Do a sombrero joke." Ah, fuck! I can make fun of the shit he did the last couple of days, but by the time it airs, you guys are going to be like, "Wait what was that again?"[14]

Comic Sara Schaefer illuminates another factor influencing Trump comedy: anger and distance. In an op-ed, she writes:

> I was talking about this to my friend, fellow comedian Nikki Glaser, and we both agreed that in many ways, we're too angry and scared to find the funny in Donald Trump's rule. For me, dark material has to incubate for a really long time before it can make its way to the stage. (To give you an idea, it took me a decade to be able to find a way to write jokes about my mom's death.) Comedians are now struggling to get the distance needed to make something awful hilarious.[15]

The vast amounts of material, the speed of news, the fully formed Trump persona, and the un-ironic presentation of absurdity from Trump himself have made satirizing Trump much more complicated than many thought when he was elected. Speaking about the difficulty satirizing Trump poses, Wanda Sykes says, "You would think, 'Oh boy, there's so much to make fun of,' but really I can't write anything funnier or more ridiculous than what Trump actually says. . . . It's like doing a parody of a parody."[16] Trump's world is so absurd that pointing it out isn't funny, instead, as Schaefer argues, it just makes people angry. Trump has tipped satire's inherent balance between anger and laughter almost exclusively to anger. For those opposed to Trump, his persona and policies and myriad of "comic" moments aren't funny, they are cause for genuine concern and outrage.

The absurdity and rapidity of Trump's news cycle and the outlandishness of so much of the world around Trump makes writing satire extremely difficult.

Jay Martel, a writer for *Key & Peele* and *Alternatino With Arturo Castro*, argues that "Our present moment is so relentlessly off-kilter that crazy, heightened satire written a year ago will be upstaged by reality when it plays on television today."[17] Martel points to the *Alternatino* sketch "The White House Rewrites the Poem on the Statue of Liberty" as a prime example. The sketch imagines a world where the White House aims to rewrite Emma Lazarus's iconic *The New Colossus* poem on the Statue of Liberty to the point that all that remains of the poem is "Keep your wretched refuse."[18] As Martel writes, "we thought that the concept of government officials setting out to rewrite Emma Lazarus poem on the Statue of Liberty was unlikely enough to be clearly satirical while also giving us a chance to comment on the callousness of Trump's immigration policies." And it was, until two weeks after the sketch aired, the satiric absurdity turned into reality. Ken Cuccinelli, acting director of U.S. Citizenship and Immigration Services, actually did offer a rewrite of the poem during a CNN interview, "Give me your tired and your poor *who can stand on their own two feet and who will not become a public charge*."[19] The satiric idea became a reality. Sketch comedy was no longer more exaggerated or absurd than reality. In a similar situation, *Alternatino*'s sketch "ICE Response to All that Negative Press" speaks to the Trump administration's policy of separating families and detaining children in inhumane and unsanitary conditions. The sketch posits that ICE will begin to hold children as "cage-free," likening the detention facilities to a chicken farm.[20] The Trump administration's policy was already in effect when the sketch aired, but as Martel says, "the idea was that the policy we were mocking was so horrible (children had already died) that it would almost certainly be brought to a stop before the show was produced and aired."[21] Instead of ending the policy, Republican officials doubled down on it. They began visiting the detention centers to point out that things weren't completely terrible, doing so in a way that is eerily close to the satiric exaggeration of Castro's character in the sketch. As Martel points out, one of the major challenges of comedy under Trump is, "How do you heighten a situation for comic effect in a world that's grown more outrageous than anyone can imagine?"[22]

The administration's policies, coupled with Trump's almost never-ending un-ironic parody moments, make satirizing him more difficult than any previous president. For instance, in late September of 2019, Democrats announced they were launching a formal impeachment inquiry. Days before, a whistleblower complaint alleged Trump withheld congressionally approved military aid to Ukraine, vowing to release it only if the Ukrainian president agreed to open an investigation into potential 2020 rival Joe Biden. Trump went on the offensive, tweeting an attack on the "LameStream media" and the House Intelligence Chair Adam Schiff, a frequent Trump target:

> To show you how dishonest the LameStream Media is, I used the word Liddle', not Liddle, in discribing (sic) Corrupt Congressman Liddle' Adam Schiff. Low ratings @CNN purposely took the hyphen out and said I spelled the word little wrong. A small but never ending situation with CNN![23]

Only days after the greatest threat to his presidency, Trump is tweeting about the spelling of his schoolyard nicknames for his political opponents. Merriam-Webster, perhaps the most unlikely of Trump critics, tweeted an hour later, saying:

For those looking up punctuation early on a Friday morning:

A hyphen is a mark – used to divide or to compound words.
An apostrophe is a mark ' used to indicate the omission of letters or figures.[24]

What is there left to say? First, everyone knows it's "Lil'" or "Li'l," but it is absurd that the president is facing impeachment and is complaining about nicknames, and he's doing it by misspelling words and confusing punctuation. How does a satirist make this moment more ludicrous?

As more and more news comes out about Trump's call with Ukraine, often because Trump himself admits to the deeds, the absurdity continues. Days after the "Liddle Controversy," Trump tweeted a meme featuring a Nickelback song to defend himself (Nickelback themselves being a long-standing meme/joke), only to have the meme taken down after Nickelback complained about copyright infringement. John Oliver summed it up best: "Twitter removed one of the president's memes because Nickelback complained. That's a sentence that somehow suggests the news is now being written by an algorithm designed to generate random shittiness." He went on to explain that Trump not only asked Ukraine to investigate Joe Biden, but also asked China to investigate – on live television from the White House lawn. Oliver brought everything full circle at the end of the show by stating that "not every foreign government will be as brave and willing to stand up to Trump as fucking Nickelback."[25] Days later, the White House then sent Congress a letter essentially declaring that Trump can't be impeached because he does not want to be impeached because if there is impeachment in the House, he might be impeached. And that came only hours after the Department of Justice argued in court that the grand jury evidence from the Mueller Report shouldn't be handed over to Congress because the grand jury ruling in Watergate that turned over grand jury information led to Nixon resigning. To which the presiding judge responded, "Wow, OK. As I said, the department is taking extraordinary positions in this case."[26] And that was followed by Trump's personal lawyer Rudy Giuliani arguing on Twitter that the accused in the Salem Witch Trials had a fairer shake than Trump (because the Salem Witch Trials are a shining example of judicial fairness), and then followed *that* up with "Ah, the Soviet Union had trials with anonymous, unnamed witnesses. Welcome to McCarthy II."[27] How is a satirist to respond?

These types of occurrences are literally never-ending. During a press conference after Trump's controversial move to withdraw U.S. troops from northern Syria, Trump declared, "When I took over our military, we did not have ammunition. I was told by a top general, maybe the top of them all, 'Sir, I'm sorry sir, we don't have ammunition.'"[28] Obviously, the military did not run out of ammunition. He then took to Twitter to defend his Syria withdrawal, citing his "great and unmatched wisdom."[29] Trump *then* wrote the following letter to Turkish President Erdogan:

Dear Mr. President:

Let's work out a good deal! You don't want to be responsible for slaughtering thousands of people, and I don't want to be responsible for destroying the Turkish economy – and I will. I've already given you a little sample with respect to Pastor Brunson.

I have worked hard to solve some of your problems. Don't let the world down. You can make a great deal. General Mazloum is willing to negotiate with you, and he is willing to make concessions that they would never have made in the past. I am confidentially enclosing a copy of his letter to me, just received.

History will look upon you favorably if you get this done the right and humane way. It will look upon you forever as the devil if good things don't happen. Don't be a tough guy. Don't be a fool!

I will call you later.[30]

The letter reads like something in *The Onion*. Several news outlets had to confirm with the White House that the letter was, in fact, real. MSNBC's Nicole Wallace said the letter is "so weird we had to check with the White House to make sure it's real. . . . And it is."[31] *New York Times* White House correspondent Katie Rogers similarly tweeted, "Felt the need to ask WH if this is actually real and it is."[32] Let that sink in.

Not every Trump un-ironic parody moment involves impeachment or disastrous national security decisions. During a trip to the National Museum of African American History and Culture, Trump was given a tour by Lonnie G. Bunch III, founding director of the museum. According to Bunch,

> The president paused in front of the exhibit that discussed the role of the Dutch in the slave trade. . . . As he pondered the label I felt that maybe he was paying attention to the work of the museum. He quickly proved me wrong. As he turned from the display he said to me, "You know, they love me in the Netherlands." All I could say was let's continue walking.[33]

What is a satirist supposed to do with a statement like that? How do you make a joke about someone who sees an exhibit about one of the world's most massive atrocities and says that the Dutch love him? A satirist would clearly see that Trump's visit to the museum was a public relations stunt, as his actions obviously demonstrate his lack of interest toward ending institutional racism, and his past statements show his ignorance about much of American history. A satiric sketch might have a sketch-Trump say "The Dutch love me," when confronted with slavery's past, but when the real Trump says it, what is a comedian left to say?

In the same week that his Dutch comments made national news, he used a Sharpie to alter a picture of Hurricane Dorian's path to include Alabama. Trump had tweeted Alabama was in the storm's path, but when no predictive models showed that to be accurate, Trump took his signature Sharpie and drew a circle around Alabama (not to mention that he used a black Sharpie to extend a white circle, because, of course he did). When confronted about the hand drawn alteration to the map, he pretended he hadn't done it – how do you make that moment funnier? To pile on the absurdity, the National Oceanic and Atmospheric Administration (NOAA) publicly backed Trump. Despite all evidence, the agency was given a directive to "only stick with official National Hurricane Center forecasts if questions arise from some national level social media posts which hit the news this afternoon." The directive clearly about Trump's tweets was issued after a National Weather Service office in Birmingham, Alabama, contradicted the president by saying Alabama would "NOT see any impacts from the hurricane."[34] How do you satirize ordering a weather service to lie to protect the president's ego? That's already a farcical situation. How do you mock something as stupid and simple as Trump using the wrong color Sharpie so that his addition looks like a toddler added it to the map? How do you satirize these moments when they happen every single day?

The humor magazine *McSweeney's* kept a cataloged list of Trump's missteps through October of 2018 – "Lest We Forget the Horrors: A Catalog of Trump's Worst Cruelties, Collusions, Corruptions, and Crimes."[35] And it's not satiric or embellished. It's a literal list of Trump's "horrors." In any other presidency, this list would have been a joke, or listed faux horrors, like President Obama wearing a tan suit. *McSweeney's* similarly ran Donald Trump's remarks at a Black History Month celebration as a humor column. "My Very Good Black History Month Tribute to Some of the Most Tremendous Black People" is literally an unedited, verbatim transcript of what Trump said at the event, because there is no way to better capture the ridiculousness of what he actually said than to just repeat what he actually said.[36]

As impeachment hearings escalated in October 2019, *The Onion* published a similar story that listed out Trump's absurd moments in office. Rather than make them up, they cataloged real un-ironic parody events:

> WASHINGTON – Imploring Americans to take a moment to recall jovial incidents such as tweeting "covfefe" instead of "coverage" or when he touched that strange glowing orb during a visit to Saudi Arabia, U.S. president Donald Trump, increasingly cornered by House impeachment proceedings, called upon the nation Friday to remember "all the good times." "Come on, guys, wasn't that fun when I got in that really huge truck or did that photo op with the taco bowl?" said the 45th commander in chief of the halcyon days when he was attacked by a bald eagle, insulted the appearance of Ted Cruz's wife, or threw paper towels to Puerto Rico rescue workers, spiraling into an ever-deeper panic as he realized the gravity of the investigation into his diplomatic misdeeds in Ukraine. "I feel like everybody is just focusing on the negative

here. Don't forget, we've had a lot of great laughs together, like when that lawn mower kid came to the White House or when I looked up at a solar eclipse without the glasses. Boy, wasn't that a real hoot? I mean, how can you not remember the fast food banquet, or when my butt looked big in that one picture? Doesn't that count for anything? That was classic Trump." At press time, the American public sighed deeply in fond remembrance of all the good times they'd shared together as support for impeachment dropped to 0%.[37]

These three stories are clear-cut examples of absurdity becoming reality, and unfortunately, these moments have almost entirely taken over reality – Trump simply is absurdity incarnate.

The above examples point to an aspect of Trump satire that has been largely ineffective. Trump satire has failed under Trump in creating overarching narratives. The *McSweeney's* list and *Onion* article try to piece together the big picture, but most satire, including sketch comedy, has been so hyper-responsive to the day-to-day insanity of Trump that they often go from one absurd story to the next. Satire is not alone in this, as the news media has likewise failed to make broader connections between Trump scandals, sometimes overlooking an issue because seemingly every day there is a new issue. For instance, Trump was fined over $2 million for misusing money from the Trump Foundation for personal and political business.[38] In other words, he committed fraud by embezzling money from his charity for personal use. That story would take down any other president and likely land them in jail. With Trump, it was barely a blip – there was not even a mention of it on the next episode of *Saturday Night Live*. There are many similar examples. Ignoring this scandal is all the more egregious because Trump made Hillary Clinton's association with the Clinton Foundation a fundamental issue during the 2016 campaign. Despite no evidence of wrongdoing, Trump hammered Clinton for an improper relationship with her charity. Similarly, he hammered her (with an enormous assist from the news media) over her private email server, which famously received more coverage than any other issue in the 2016 campaign. His own use of an unsecured cellphone and the revelation of many administration officials using private email in the White House, including his daughter Ivanka, was again but a blip. Sketch comedy and satirists (and the news media) failed to connect anything in an overarching narrative. The charity fraud is part of a string of fraud, from Trump University to decades of tax fraud, to fraudulent loan documents, to the fraud of lying two dozen times a day, to the fraud at the heart of the Mueller investigation and the Ukraine bribery and extortion scandal. Satire has yet to connect the dots, instead chasing the day-to-day absurdity. Part of satire's job is to speak the truth others are not. As the news media chases story to story, satire should be filling in the gap and articulating the historic proportions of fraud and criminality of the Trump White House. Instead, it has allowed Trump's own chaos to continue to control the truth and the news cycle by responding to everything he does and never contextualizing it for Americans.

The absurd reality goes deeper than Trump, however, because without his audience (or base) playing along with him, it would all fall apart. Half of the country, and nearly every congressional Republican, takes his absurdity at face value. The key to "Sharpie-gate" (and soooooo much more), is that so many people go out of their way to prove the obvious falsehood is true. They disbelieve the facts or simply choose to ignore the incident altogether. A satirist needs a target and an audience, but when the audience doesn't care, how does a satirist work? The satiric triangle breaks down. Do you just "continue walking"? During the 2016 election, *The Daily Show* aired several segments with Jordan Klepper interviewing Trump supporters. While liberal audiences delighted in the cognitive dissonance, obvious contradictions, and inherent flaws in Trump supporters support of Trump's policies, the Trump supporters themselves didn't seem to care, nor did the millions who would go on to vote for Trump.[39] For example, a Trump supporter wearing a misogynistic shirt about Hillary Clinton talks to Klepper about the American principle of respecting women, causing Klepper to comment, "We don't even see the irony." No, the man does not. The Trump era has seen the breakdown of the satiric triangle between satirist–target–audience. Begging the question, can you satirize a target if (half) the audience isn't present? Can you satirize the target if the target doesn't realize he's being satirized? To further complicate the matter, how do you satirize a living parody? How do you satirize a movement that doesn't care? Satirists are still grappling with these questions in the age of Trump, but one of the most prominent tactics, as seen in the *McSweeney's* essay, has been through satiric authenticity.

Purposeful Absurdity vs. Satiric Authenticity

Trump purposefully creates chaos and absurdity within the news cycle. He is a master at self-promotion and controlling a media cycle. Love him or hate him, it is undeniable that he has faced numerous scandals, any one of which would have consumed any other presidency. With Trump, oftentimes those scandals don't even last a week. Part of that is due to the media's failures in covering Trump – continually switching topics as Trump himself constantly introduces new things to debate. Part of it is Trump's media strategy – the continual chaos makes it difficult to focus on anything. At the heart of this strategy is deceit. Trump lies at an unprecedented clip. Between his January 20, 2017, inauguration and May 5, 2019, reporter Daniel Dale tracked Trump's lies for the *Toronto Star* (he was later hired by CNN to follow Trump's lies). According to Dale, "Donald Trump has said 5,276 false things as U.S. President," further arguing that "the sheer frequency of Trump's inaccuracy is a central story of his presidency."[40] By October 2019, nearly 1,000 days into his presidency, the *Washington Post* counted 13,435 "false or misleading claims."[41] By January 20, 2020, the three year mark of his presidency, the number had risen to 16,241.[42] Trump frequently lied during the campaign and kicked off his presidency by sending out Press Secretary Sean Spicer to lie about the size of Trump's inaugural crowd. Despite indisputable photographic evidence to the contrary, Spicer aggressively declared, "This was the largest audience to ever witness an inauguration – Period!"[43] The moment was initially treated humorously, but ultimately signaled that the administration would not be dealing in truth.

Kellyanne Conway doubled down on the administration's lie and defended Spicer's claim, saying the next day during a combative interview on *Meet the Press*, "You're saying it's a falsehood. And they're giving – Sean Spicer, our press secretary, gave alternative facts."[44] The lies would continue nearly every day, from big lies such as saying the Mueller Report "totally exonerated" the president when it says the exact opposite, to small lies like lying about the time, claiming a 2:40 p.m. speech was being given at 11 a.m. The defense and dismissal of the lies likewise continued, such as during an August 2019 interview where Trump's 2020 Campaign National Press Secretary Kayleigh McEnany had the following exchange with CNN's Chris Cuomo:

Cuomo: You don't think this President has lied to the American people?
McEnany: Let me finish, Chris.
Cuomo: You –
McEnany: No, I don't think the President has lied.
Cuomo: – have to answer that question, first.
McEnany: I don't think the President has lied.
Cuomo: He has never lied to the American people?
McEnany: No, I don't think the President has lied.[45]

As Trump continues his historically paced lying, the media struggles to cover his lies. Some spend hours and days fact-checking in vain, others repeat Trump's lies in their headlines with no context, and others began to accept the lies as par for the course. The purposeful absurdity breeds mistrust with the media, destabilizes the truth, and distracts from the corruption and scandals of the Trump administration. The satiric response to this absurdity is twofold – (1) point out the real and find the truth, and (2) full-fledged satiric authenticity.

The George W. Bush presidency saw satire turn more critical, and some would argue angrier or meaner. Jon Stewart and Stephen Colbert became immensely popular during Bush's presidency because audiences felt like the two comedians "were on their side." As satire began to turn more toward the left as Bush's presidency wore on, viewers began to demand an authenticity on behalf of the satirist. When Trump took office, after the satiric lull of the Obama presidency, it was no longer enough to point out the foible; audiences wanted to know that satirists were on their side in what the left began to view as a battle between right and wrong and the future of democracy. Audiences craved satirists who weren't just making jokes, but who were genuinely part of the fight against Trump. Mark Boukes and colleagues argue that the most effective contemporary satire happens when satirists do "not provide too many discounting cues but make clear that although they bring their message in the form of a joke, they are serious about the content."[46] *The Tonight Show* host Jimmy Fallon faced a huge liberal backlash after the now infamous September 2016 interview in which Fallon messed up Trump's hair. Fallon thought the moment would be silly and innocuous, but it turned into a flashpoint. The segment caused immediate outcries from liberals accusing Fallon of "normalizing" Trump and his radical rhetoric with the stunt. *The Tonight Show*'s ratings took a hit, with Colbert's and Jimmy Kimmel's more politically charged late-night shows gaining in the ratings. Fallon himself later said in a 2018 interview that he regretted the moment, saying, "Looking back, I would do it differently." Trump then responded via tweet, saying, "Be a man Jimmy!"[47] The initial moment proved to be a turning point in the comedy world, one where audiences demanded that comedians take sides. Johnny Carson hosted *The Tonight Show* for a generation and never revealed his political leanings, but by 2016 revealing personal politics had become a requirement. One sketch comedy actor who benefited from picking a side was Alec Baldwin. He became popular not just because he was doing a funny impersonation of Trump on *SNL*, but also because the audience knew, to put it mildly, that Baldwin did not personally agree with Trump. Earnest pleas became normal for satirists, from Jimmy Kimmel, Samantha Bee, John Oliver, and even Jon Stewart. Trump himself exacerbated this need for satiric authenticity as he actively sought to divide the nation with polarizing policies and personal behavior. From Muslim bans to child detention centers on the border to his interactions with foreign dictators to his daily Twitter barrage – Trump continually pitted Americans against one another. Rather than try to keep up with Trump's chaos, many satirists choose instead to focus on clearly articulating their opposition to Trump in a big-picture sense.

Wanda Sykes sums up the satiric authenticity that audiences crave in the very first line of her 2019 *Not Normal* stand-up special, saying, "So, let me just start by saying, if you voted for Trump and you came to see *me* – you fucked up again."[48] The audience cheers throughout the line, reveling in their shared dislike of Trump. One of the obvious examples of satiric authenticity in sketch comedy is the multitude of celebrity cameos on *SNL* to play various people in the Trump universe: Matt Damon as Brett Kavanaugh, Melissa McCarthy as Sean Spicer, Scarlett Johansson as Ivanka Trump, Ben Stiller as Michael Cohen, and Robert De Niro as Robert Mueller, to name but a few. Here we clearly see the influence of Brecht's idea of the actor and character both being portrayed in the scene. In each instance, the audience enjoys the celebrity cameo because it is quite often clear that the celebrity is signaling their own dissatisfaction with the Trump administration. Kate McKinnon's turn as pretty much everyone in Trump's universe – Jeff Sessions, Kellyanne Conway, Lindsey Graham, Rudy Giuliani, Betsy DeVos, Laura Ingraham, Wilbur Ross – likewise signals to the audience a "friendly" take, as McKinnon both played and openly supported Hillary Clinton on the show (and plays 2020 rival Senator Elizabeth Warren). Audiences seemed to take particular delight in De Niro, the most outspoken critic of the celebrity cameo group, playing Special Counsel Mueller, projecting De Niro's criticisms of Trump onto Robert Mueller.

Johansson's turn as Ivanka in "Complicit" is one of *SNL*'s best sketches on Trump-world. A perfume commercial parody, the sketch satirizes the mythology that Ivanka would somehow be a check on her father's worst impulses, which for those on the left proved to be flagrantly wrong: "A woman like her deserves a scent all her own. She's beautiful. She's powerful. She's – complicit." It continues, delivering its satiric tagline, "Complicit: the fragrance for the woman who could stop all this, but won't."[49] Damon's Kavanaugh is a clear example of the real in the absurd.

The vast majority of the sketch features a slightly exaggerated Damon repeating much of Kavanaugh's own aggressive, emotional, and partisan opening testimony from his actual confirmation hearing. It likewise includes an almost verbatim repeat of Kavanaugh's contentious exchange with Senator Amy Klobuchar (played by *SNL* alum Rachel Dratch) that revolved around blacking out from drinking too much. That's right. The actual Supreme Court hearing saw a man who now sits on the highest court asking a sitting U.S. Senator if she had ever blacked out from drinking after she asked him if *he'd* ever blacked out from drinking. Rather than try to amplify it, or Kavanaugh's emotional tirade of an opening statement, *SNL* just repeated them.[50] The actual President Trump was reportedly most rattled by Melissa McCarthy's aggressive portrayal of Sean Spicer.[51] Not because of the searing portrayal of an outwitted and overmatched Spicer, but for a much stupider reason. As *Politico* reported, "More than being lampooned as a press secretary who makes up facts, it was Spicer's portrayal by a woman that was most problematic in the president's eyes, according to sources close to him."[52] A woman playing Spicer made him appear weak in Trump's eyes, which was in Trump-land a more egregious error than pointedly lying to the American public. Trump's sexist and stupid objection points to the satiric problem – even when the satiric take is clear and clean (and funny), if the target misses the point, does it matter?

Satiric authenticity can be taken a step further into what Don Waisanen calls "advocacy satire." Beyond revealing their personal political beliefs, advocacy satire overtly calls for action. All satire inherently asks something of its audience, but rarely contains a direct appeal. The satirist traditionally has worked under the assumption that by revealing a truth or vice, the audience will recognize it and work toward it. Waisanen defines advocacy satire as "the use of political humor to take action on behalf of disadvantaged individuals or groups, lending force to their voices by making a direct intervention into public affairs." Satirists are now not just seeking to expose the truth; they are themselves actively working toward solutions. Rather than sitting on the edges and commenting from an outsider perspective, instead, "comedians are now engaging in actions in the public interest – the kinds of actions that were formerly the exclusive preserve of lobbyists, movement leaders, investigative journalists, and others."[53] Jon Stewart advocating for 9/11 first responders; Stephen Colbert creating a super PAC to draw attention to campaign finance reform; Stewart and Colbert's political rally, the "Rally to Restore Sanity and/or Fear"; Hasan Minhaj doing a deep dive into student loan debt on his show *Patriot Act* and then going to testify before Congress about the issue; John Oliver paying off $15 million in medical debt for 9,000 people; or Oliver's staff writing a children's book – *A Day in the Life of Marlon Bundo* – as a way to counteract Mike Pence's anti-LGBTQ work, with the show donating the profits of the parody book to the Trevor Project and AIDS United. While satiric authenticity has been near-universal in the age of Trump, not every satirist has risen to the level of satiric advocacy. Nevertheless, its emergence points to the foundational shift in political satire and the role of the satirists within not just the world of comedy, but the world of politics.

Sometimes, though, satiric authenticity (or advocacy) does not work. Often within satiric authenticity, there is more authenticity than satire, what Ross

Douthat derided in the *New York Times* as "less comics than propagandists – liberal 'explanatory journalists' with laugh lines."[54] As the Trump presidency has worn on, more and more comedians are ditching the satire in favor of outright authenticity. An obvious example is Jimmy Kimmel's entrance into the Obamacare debate, delivering a heartfelt and emotional opening monologue in the wake of Republican attempts to dismantle Obamacare.[55] His continued sincere championing of Obamacare on his show, in interviews, and via social media won him widespread support, but that's not always the case – the most obvious example being Samantha Bee calling Ivanka Trump on *Full Frontal* a "feckless cunt." Responding to the Trump administration's immigration policies regarding separating children from their parents, Bee reacted to Ivanka Trump tweeting a picture of her son, "You know, Ivanka, that's a beautiful photo of you and your child, but let me just say, one mother to another, do something about your dad's immigration practices, you feckless c–!"[56] The audience cheered, but Bee immediately found herself in hot water. She later apologized for using the c-word, but not the intent behind what she said. The incident points to the heart of much satiric authenticity under Trump – sometimes, there's no joke. Sometimes it's just commentary without comedy. Dannagal Young said of the incident, "There was no incongruity in what she did. . . . I don't care she's used the c-word a bunch. I care that she, like, didn't make a joke."[57] One of the flaws of satiric authenticity, or only outrage, is that it strips satire of a critical component – it doesn't allow the audience to make connections and draw conclusions. Young further argues, "When satire is doing a good job, it's not just punching up. It's reminding us of our complicity. . . . Outrage tells you, 'Here is the thing, here is the thing that's bad, here is the thing that's good. . . . It says exactly what it should conclude. You don't have to draw conclusions."[58] Satire, it seems, had shifted almost completely to anger.

Even when there is comedy, such as on *Last Week Tonight With John Oliver*, the comedy is there to support the genuine issues Oliver addresses on the show, which are quite often at odds with Trump's policy agenda. Whatever Oliver might say, *Last Week Tonight* is an investigative journalism program that happens to be funny as well. Indeed, Oliver does not fit the bill of a traditional journalist – he has no press credentials or access – but his work is being consumed as news by many viewers. More importantly, his work is influencing viewers in ways that go beyond traditional news sources. As Amy Becker argues, "viewing political comedy engenders greater cognitive engagement and information seeking behavior, encouraging viewers to connect the dots between the comedy they view and what they already know from traditional news sources." Furthermore, she argues that "exposure to political satire not only encourages knowledge gain and learning, but also encourages viewers to participate in the political process."[59] Viewers are not simply tuning in to gain new information, they are actively seeking avenues for political advocacy and activism.

Oliver's 2014 segment about net neutrality is an excellent example of Oliver's mixture of investigative journalism, satiric authenticity, and satiric advocacy. In the piece, Oliver combines jokes about obtaining coyote urine and *Caillou* with the real issues surrounding the fight for net neutrality protections. Oliver presents a wealth of information about the subject, much as an investigative journalist would do, while also making direct appeals about the importance of the issue (satiric authenticity). At the end of the segment, Oliver turns to satiric advocacy:

> The FCC are literally inviting internet comments at this address. . . . And at this point, and I can't believe I'm about to do this, I would like to address the internet commenters out there directly. (Sigh.) Good evening monsters. This may be the moment you've spent your whole lives training for. You have been out there ferociously commenting on dance videos with adorable three-year-olds, saying things like, "Everyone could dance like this little loser after 1 week of practice." Or you've been polluting *Frozen*'s "Let it Go," with comments like "ice castle would give her hypothermia and she dead in an hour." Or, and I know you've done this one, commenting on a video of this show, saying, "Fuck this asshole anchor . . . go suck ur presidents dick . . . ur just friends with the terrorists xD." . . . But this is the moment you were made for commenters. Like Ralph Macchio, you've been honing your skills, waxing cars and painting fences. Well, guess what, now it's time to do some fucking karate. For once in your life, we need you to channel that anger, that badly spelled bile that you normally reserve for unforgivable attacks on actresses you seem to think have put on weight, or politicians that you disagree with, or photos of your ex-girlfriend getting on with her life, or non-white actors being cast as fictional characters. And I'm talking to you. . . . We need you to get out there and for once in your lives focus your indiscriminate rage in a useful direction! Seize your moment my lovely trolls. Turn on caps lock and fly my pretties![60]

Not only is the segment an example of changing satire, but it was also effective. The FCC comments site crashed after the episode from the flood of visitors and commenters. Furthermore, a study from the University of Delaware's Center for Political Communication[61] found that Oliver's show did more than any news outlet in swaying public opinion: "Exposure to his show had the strongest impact of all of the news media outlets we asked about. . . . We did not find any effects of exposure to CNN, MSNBC, newspapers – none of those things were related to public opinion on net neutrality."[62] Oliver similarly merged satiric authenticity and satiric advocacy with his November 2019 episode on the 2020 U.S. Census. The episode explained the census, outlined Republican attempts to undermine the census, and articulated why people should participate in the census. Oliver gave one final reason that people should fill out their census data: "It would probably really irritate [Trump]. Because, think about it, his administration already clearly think that certain people don't count, so what better way to get back at him than to make sure that you do and make the census count you."[63] Both episodes advocate for viewers to take action, and while the net neutrality issue implicitly implies a resistance to Trump, the census episode explicitly connects advocacy with authenticity – it literally asks viewers to take action to "stick it" to Trump.

Michelle Wolf's highly controversial 2018 White House Correspondents Dinner appearance provides another example, though with a decidedly different outcome than Oliver's net neutrality and census battles. Wolf went after the Trump administration as any good satirist would, but was attacked after the performance by both liberals and conservatives. The performance was so contentious that moving forward they canceled the traditional comedian appearance and replaced it with an appearance by a historian. Wolf told a wide range of jokes, including about Democrats: "It is kind of crazy that the Trump campaign was in contact with Russia when the Hillary campaign wasn't even in contact with Michigan." Jokes about CNN, MSNBC, and others were overshadowed by Wolf's comments about then Press Secretary Sarah Huckabee Sanders:

> And of course, we have Sarah Huckabee Sanders. We are graced with Sarah's presence tonight. I have to say I'm a little star-struck. I love you as Aunt Lydia in *The Handmaid's Tale*. Mike Pence, if you haven't seen it, you would love it. Every time Sarah steps up to the podium I get excited, because I'm not really sure what we're going to get. You know, a press briefing, a bunch of lies or divided into softball teams. "It's shirts and skins, and this time don't be such a little b–, Jim Acosta!" I actually really like Sarah. I think she's very resourceful. Like she burns facts, and then she uses that ash to create a perfect smoky eye. Like maybe she's born with it, maybe it's lies. It's probably lies. And I'm never really sure what to call Sarah Huckabee Sanders, you know? Is it Sarah Sanders, is it Sarah Huckabee Sanders, is it Cousin Huckabee, is it Auntie Huckabee Sanders? Like, what's Uncle Tom but for white women who disappoint other white women? Oh, I know. Ann Coulter.[64]

The response was immediate, with many outraged that Wolf had made fun of Sanders's looks, even though that's not what Wolf said. It's telling that the outrage wasn't about the fact that Sanders lies, which she admitted in an FBI deposition, but was framed as an unfair personal attack about her appearance.[65] Maggie Haberman of the *New York Times* summed up the outrage in a tweet, saying, "That @PressSec sat and absorbed intense criticism of her physical appearance, her job performance, and so forth, instead of walking out, on national television, was impressive."[66] The Sanders backlash was another flashpoint for satire in the age of Trump. Wolf revealed a truth about the administration – it lies all the time and Sarah Huckabee Sanders's job seems to be to reinforce the president's lies. Wolf's joke was met with outrage, not because the claim was untrue, but because to admit that it *was* true would be to expose the deceit of the administration. That would admit that the Trump presidency was indeed unlike any presidency in modern history and an existential threat to the future of American democracy. To admit the press secretary purposefully lies on behalf of the president – despite the mountains of evidence – would be admitting to the fundamental breakdown of the foundational trust between Americans and the government that has been slowly eroding since the Kennedy assassination and the Watergate break-in.

It likewise demonstrates one of the major pitfalls of satiric authenticity. When the audience demands a satirist "be on their side," the other side can choose to ignore the satirist as biased. Whether their satiric authenticity is intentional or not – Wolf was likely selected because of her prior position as a *Daily Show* correspondent – the perception can lessen the impact. The Wolf situation also showcases the limits of satire in the Trump era. When presented with the truth, the response was to vilify the satirist rather than the target. It hardly mattered that what Wolf said about Sanders was true – Sanders did lie as press secretary. But when satire is seen as only coming from liberal "explanatory journalists," conservatives immediately push back against it regardless of merit as part of the partisan political divide. The conservative pushback further deepens the demand for satiric authenticity on the left, thus perpetuating the cycle.

On the flip side, many of Trump's strongest proponents point to Trump's authenticity as central to his appeal. Despite the evidence and the absurd amount of lies, his non-political correctness and outright racism/sexism/xenophobia/narcissism/lack of empathy, all read to his supporters as authentic. He's not just another politician trying to spin them. Instead, he's telling it like it really is. It's why his support among his base has virtually stayed unchanged no matter what new scandal erupts or new disparaging tweet the president sends out into the world. His lying has *become* his authenticity – the ultimate proof that the absurd has overtaken the real.

The Codependency of Trump and *SNL*

Trump comedy is everywhere, but during the campaign and early days of his presidency, *SNL* was the heart – mostly because of Trump himself. Trump, as a character, had appeared on the show for decades, not as a politician, but as a real-estate/reality television celebrity. Trump first hosted the show in 2004, and then again in November 2015 after announcing his candidacy. The show was *SNL*'s highest-rated episode in four years but was controversial. The episode received mostly poor reviews, with Joe Berkowitz writing in *Vulture*, "Not only was Trump not funny during his meager 12 minutes of screen time on *Saturday Night Live*, he proved to be a black hole of comedic antimatter through which no humor could escape."[67] The sketches were relatively listless, Trump himself is not a great comedic performer, and the atmosphere of Trump's worldview combined to make it an awkward evening. The "White House 2018" sketch is a good example. It imagines the "yuge" success of Trump's presidency. The economy is booming, China has capitulated in the trade war, the Syrian crisis is solved, Omarosa is a principal advisor, and everyone is happy. Even the president of Mexico (played by Beck Bennett – see *SNL*'s diversity issues) gives Trump a check for the border wall. The sketch might work if it weren't unintentionally dystopic – for many, the success of a Trump presidency based on his racist and xenophobic campaign rhetoric would be terrifying. In the end, Trump breaks the fourth wall to directly address the audience, stating, "I said to the writers of this sketch, 'Keep it modest.'"[68] The audience is silent. As time has worn on, more and more people associated with the show have looked back at the episode with regret. Some claimed it helped get Trump elected, which might be a stretch, but it was not an especially good look for a show that prides itself on speaking truth to power. Former cast member and previous *SNL* Trump Taran Killam talked about the experience with NPR, saying:

> It was rough. It was not enjoyable at the time and something that only grows more embarrassing and shameful as time goes on. I don't necessarily put so much weight into [the idea of] Trump hosting *SNL* helping him become president, but there's definitely something where it normalizes him and makes it OK for him to be part of the conversation. And I don't think the intention of having him on was ever politically based. But I don't think it was considered – the implications that it had then and could have moving forward. And I think looking back . . . there's nothing good I can take from that week.[69]

Trump was never going to be a typical host, but nobody yet knew just how differently he would engage with satire. The hosting appearance began a kind of codependent relationship between the two New York icons.

While most modern presidents have laughed along with their comic portrayals or ignored them, Trump continually criticizes them. Perhaps Trump thought the show would go easy on him after his appearance, though it's hard to imagine given the show's history that he'd be unprepared for them to go after him. Yet, in his own way, his criticism of Baldwin and *SNL* is his version of playing along. If there's anything Trump understands, it is television ratings. His constant criticism of *SNL* brings attention to the show, developing a feedback loop. *SNL* makes fun of Trump; everyone goes to Twitter to see how Trump responds; then everyone tunes in to *SNL* the next week to see how they'll respond; and on and on. Trump's first response to the show came in October 2016, just weeks before the election. *SNL* had aired its take on the nasty second presidential debate, and Trump was not happy. The sketch took numerous shots at Trump and his performance. Responding to an African American audience member's question about being a president for all Americans, Baldwin's Trump rambles about violence in inner cities, before pivoting to Hillary: "Speaking of black men, you know who else should be in jail? Hillary Clinton. She's committed so many crimes; she's basically a black."[70] Trump took to Twitter at 7 a.m. to lambast the show, saying, "Watched Saturday Night Live hit job on me. Time to retire the boring and unfunny show. Alec Baldwin portrayal stinks. Media rigging election!"[71] Trump's responses are unprecedented and give an outsized importance to *SNL*'s portrayals. By responding to the sketches, Trump elevates the sketches to the level of presidential interaction, ironically giving them more importance as he tries to deflate the satiric take. His continual responses, however, have worked to dull Baldwin's impact. Amy Becker found in a study that "viewing Trump's Twitter response accusing *SNL* of media bias inoculates viewers against Baldwin's anti-Trump satire that is present in the original skit."[72] The sketch–Twitter war was only beginning.

Trump's response kicked off a codependent loop between *SNL* and Trump. The November 19, 2016, cold open, "Donald Trump Prepares," was met with more disdain from the new president-elect. The sketch presented a Trump entirely in over his head and totally unprepared to make good on the many promises he made on the campaign trail, including a secret plan to defeat ISIS, bringing back coal jobs, deporting 11 million immigrants, repealing Obamacare, and more.[73] Trump again took to Twitter, calling the show a "totally one-sided, biased show – nothing funny at all. Equal time for us?" Alec Baldwin added to the loop, responding to Trump via Twitter in a thread, "You know what I would do if I were Prez? I'd be focused on how to improve the lives of AS MANY AMERICANS AS POSSIBLE." Baldwin went on offering advice, closing the thread, "You want more advice, call me. I'll be at SNL."[74] The complete absurdity of the president-elect of the United States sparring with a sketch comedy show was just getting started. In "Classroom Cold Open," *SNL* mocked Trump's excessive use of Twitter, including a case earlier in the week where he retweeted a high school student. The sketch breaks the fourth wall to point out that what might seem absurd, the president of the United States retweeting a 16-year-old as "proof" in a political argument, actually happened, with Baldwin's Trump saying, "I really did retweet him. Seriously. This is real." Kate McKinnon's Kellyanne Conway likewise addresses the camera, "He really did do this." As Trump continues to marvel about how cool this kid seems, his advisors plead with him to pay attention. Conway responds, "There is a reason actually that Donald tweets so much. He does it to distract the media from his business conflicts and all the very scary people in his cabinet." Trump immediately contradicts her, saying, "Actually, that's not why I do it. I do it because my brain is bad."[75] The real Trump responded *within the hour*, of course via Twitter, saying, "Just tried watching Saturday Night Live – unwatchable! Totally biased, not funny and the Baldwin impersonation just can't get any worse. Sad."[76]

The week before Trump's inauguration, *SNL*'s cold open "Donald Trump Press Conference" continued the loop by satirizing Trump's bizarre press conference earlier in the week. The actual press conference was wide-ranging and rambling, with plenty of unreal moments, from the clearly fake file folders that "proved" Trump was divesting from his businesses to the fallout from the publication of the Trump–Russia dossier known as the Steele dossier. Released in full by *Buzzfeed*, the unsubstantiated intelligence report detailed several troubling bits of intelligence surrounding Trump and Russia, including the now-infamous "pee tape." The dossier alleged that while in Moscow in 2013 the Russian government had taped Trump in a hotel room where he hired prostitutes to pee on a bed that the Obamas reportedly slept in during a state visit. The claim is unsubstantiated. Yet, former FBI Director James Comey said in a 2018 interview, "I honestly never thought these words would come out of my mouth, but I don't know whether the current President of the United States was with prostitutes peeing on each other in Moscow in 2013. It's possible, but I don't know."[77] At the real press conference, Trump attacked *Buzzfeed*:

> I think it was disgraceful, disgraceful that the intelligence agencies allowed any information that turned out to be so false and fake out. I think it's a disgrace. And I say that and I say that. That's something that Nazi Germany would have done and did do. It's a disgrace. That information that was false and fake and never happened got released to the public, as far as Buzzfeed,

which is a failing pile of garbage, writing it, I think they're going to suffer the consequences.[78]

The *SNL* sketch made numerous pee-tape jokes, with Baldwin's Trump responding to a question about the tape:

> Guys, no no, I do not want to talk about the pee-pee. I want to talk about what is really important, which is jobs. Okay, because I am going to bring back a thick stream of jobs back in this country. The biggest, strongest, steadiest stream you've ever seen. This country will be literally showered with jobs because I am a major whiz at jobs. This will be a golden opportunity for me as president to make a big splash. Now who's in? I know you're-in (sounds like "urine"). You're-in, you're-in, you're-in.

Reflecting the sheer absurdity of the press conference and Trump's impending presidency, the sketch opens with Trump saying, "I'd like to start by answering the question on everyone's mind. Yes, this is real life, this is really happening."[79] Trump himself responded, again via Twitter, ".@NBCNews is bad but Saturday Night Live is the worst of NBC. Not funny, cast is terrible, always a complete hit job. Really bad television."[80] The tweet is telling, as Trump works to conflate *SNL* with NBC's news department, working to lump them both into his ever-growing "fake news" category. Thomas Gallagher argues this is part of Trump's strategy to link not only *SNL* to "fake news," but also to blunt harsher satiric takes on Trump from *The Daily Show*, *Full Frontal*, or *Last Week Tonight* by focusing all of his attention on the milder *SNL* criticism. As Gallagher writes:

> When Trump promoting *Saturday Night Live* as the official comedic program of the opposition during his transition is combined with the reality of Trump blatantly promoting Fox News as a legitimate source of news while attacking opposing figures and outlets like NBC News during his presidency, one can see how Trump can take hold of the news cycle with just a social media account to both encourage supporters to ignore various news outlets critical of him and trust those favorable to him – and to drive some opponents to focus on material they believe personally irritates the president, even if that material is less harmful to the president's image than other, more overlooked comedic material.[81]

Trump would occasionally respond to the show or Baldwin after becoming president. In March 2018, he lashed out at Baldwin, who had said in an interview that playing Trump was agony: "Alec Baldwin, whose dying mediocre career was saved by his terrible impression of me on SNL, now says playing me was agony. Alec, it was agony for those who were forced to watch. Bring back Darrell Hammond, funnier and a far greater talent!"[82] Aside from his vendetta with Baldwin, Trump also worked to further tie the show to "fake news," even threatening to take the show to court. After the December 2018 "It's a Wonderful Trump Cold

Open" imagined *It's A Wonderful Life*–style world where Trump didn't exist,[83] the president responded, "A REAL scandal is the one sided coverage, hour by hour, of networks like NBC & Democrat spin machines like Saturday Night Live. It is all nothing less than unfair news coverage and Dem commercials. Should be tested in courts, can't be legal? Only defame & belittle! Collusion?"[84] The tweet demonstrates Trump's assault on not only freedom of the press, but freedom of speech. If the reality–absurdity continuum needed further proof, the sitting president of the United States threatening to forgo the Constitution to punish a sketch comedy show for making fun of him should tip the scales.

Trump's work to make *SNL* synonymous with "fake news" points to the power of comedy, and his understanding of *SNL*'s ability to influence public opinion. It also points to Trump's exploitation of *SNL*'s perceived bias. As Outi Hakola argues, "Some American viewers might already have felt that *SNL* was not representing their values, but treating them as outcasts. By claiming on Twitter that *SNL* was being biased, Trump created his own 'in-group,' which shared with his intended audience the feeling of not-belonging." Hakolo further articulates that "This action correlates with what in humor studies is called reverse discourse, where racist humor, for example, encourages a counter-strategy in the form of laughing back."[85] When combined with the show's clear preference for Clinton, Trump was able to use *SNL*'s impersonation as a way to portray *himself* as the victim of a rigged and fake media, conflating sketches with *all* negative news coverage. While most presidents at least publicly laughed off impersonations in an attempt to inoculate against and blunt future satiric criticism, Trump publicly fought back by victimizing himself. Trump not only worked to make himself the victim, he projected that victimization onto his base, telling them that by targeting him, the "elites" were also targeting – and mocking – them. For his base, Trump threatening to take *SNL* to court was evidence that he was on their side, willing to stand up for them and fight against a perceived rigged system that's inherently biased against their conservative viewpoint. Rather than seeing his feud with *SNL* as ridiculous, they saw it as galvanizing.

It can be argued, though, that Baldwin's Trump is not a great impression. It relies heavily on the stock tropes about Trump: his pursed mouth, hand movements, vocal inflections, extreme narcissism, etc. It does not reveal anything about Trump that we did not already know, as Jesse David Fox argues, "Baldwin's [Trump] just reflects back, thoroughly and confidently, what everyone already thinks about Trump."[86] Baldwin's Trump does reflect satire in the age of Trump, comedy that is more about rallying supporters than revealing truth. Baldwin's Trump has done a great job of generating huge ratings and lots of attention. There are undoubtedly good satiric jabs at Trump, but what is interesting is that the best satiric takes on *SNL* have been less about Trump and more about Trumpism, such as the aforementioned "Complicit" and "Black Jeopardy" (see Introduction). The "Voters for Trump Ad" is another good example. It parodies a typical campaign ad, with "real" people giving their reasons for voting for Trump, from his job creation history to writing the book on negotiating. As the ad goes on, each "real" person is revealed to be a white nationalist – one man is wearing a Nazi armband, a woman is ironing her KKK robe, another man is burning books. The sketch takes on the false narrative that Trump voters have "economic anxiety" and posits that Trump's openly racist rhetoric is what is really drawing people to support him.[87] Part of why the sketch works is because it is not satirizing Trump or even Trump supporters. Instead, it is criticizing the news media that was going out of its way to downplay Trump's blatant racist appeals. In this case, the satire is working to reveal the truth. Much like "Black Jeopardy," the ad is satirizing the world of Trumpism rather than Trump himself.

"Election Night," aired just days after Trump's surprise win, again satirizes the world around Trump, this time focusing on the naivety of white liberals. In the sketch, a group of white liberals gathers to watch the election returns, continually making arguments about how Hillary will win, while Dave Chappelle's character continues to remind them that America is not the liberal bastion the white characters are imagining. When Kentucky goes to Trump, a white character exclaims, "Of course he won Kentucky, I mean that's where all the racists are." Chappelle responds, "All of 'em are in Kentucky?" As the night goes on, and it becomes clear that Trump is going to win, the white characters melt down. Chris Rock shows up for no real reason, and he and Chappelle are the only two in the room not surprised at all by the results. When it becomes abundantly clear Trump will win, a white character comes to a realization: "Oh my God, I think America is racist." Chappelle's character reacts with mock sincerity: "Oh. My. God. You know I remember my great-grandfather told me something like that, but he was a slave." After Trump's win is officially announced, the white characters are all depressed, with one saying, "God, this is the most shameful thing America has ever done," to which Rock and Chappelle just laugh.[88] The sketch mirrored the dual experience of election night for many Democratic voters, with white liberals expressing shock that "America could do something like this," or perhaps the eponymous Facebook post "This is not the America I know," or "We're better than this." For marginalized groups, the election was hardly a shock, nor was the "revelation" that America is racist. Leslie Jones commented about the sketch, saying, "It's like we've been living in this world forever, and you all just woke up to it."[89] "The Bubble" continues the white liberal theme, imagining a world where progressives can move to a "planned community of like-minded free thinkers – and no one else!"[90] The sketch satirizes the inability of many progressives to understand that half of the country voted for Trump to the point that it was literally a shock to them that he won. It certainly plays on the long-standing trope of liberal bubbles where progressives pretend like the rest of the country doesn't exist. The sketch also satirizes the hypocrisy of the open-mindedness of progressives, proclaiming that you can join them so long as you agree with them.

So Much Trump

There is Trump comedy everywhere. One study found that in the 2016 election, including the primaries, late-night comedy lobbed more jokes at Trump (1,105) than at Hillary Clinton (314) and Bernie Sanders (302) combined.[91] The trend did not stop after the election. Even *SNL* devotes more time to Trump than to other presidents. While the show usually dials back the political sketches after elections, Trump sketches have been a near constant. As the above study demonstrates, nearly every late-night host and satiric news host does some version of a Trump impression or a nightly/weekly monologue that almost always prominently features Trump. Comedy Central created the Trump-centric show *The President Show*. Featuring Anthony Atamanuik's spot-on impression, the show imagines Trump as the host of a late-night style talk show hosted in the Oval Office, with Mike Pence acting as his Ed McMahon. Reflecting the tone of the show, Atamanuik described his Trump impression, acknowledging the physical aspects, but pointing more toward the inner workings of the president: "It's about turning off any sense of empathy. Turning off any sense of curiosity or intellect and running purely on survival. And how do I survive moment to moment? I think the main thesis of doing Trump is 'I don't care.'"[92] The show is a mixed bag in terms of Trump satire, often displaying the same types of Trump jokes as every other American, but occasionally digging a little deeper into Trump's psyche.

The show also features the comic return of Kathy Griffin, who was shunned by the entertainment world after she posted a photo of her holding a Donald Trump severed head. Even more intense than Samantha Bee's "feckless" moment, Griffin was immediately lambasted by nearly everyone. Her career was deemed over. For good measure, she was also put on the federal "no-fly list" for two months and investigated by the Secret Service and the Justice Department. She did return, though, after two years in comedic exile, with a stand-up tour and a spot as Kellyanne Conway on *The President Show*. In the sketch, Conway takes Trump's challenge to defend the worst people in history, for instance: "At the end of the day, [Jeffrey Dahmer] is just a foodie. A salt-of-the-earth, a flesh-of-the-human kind of guy. And our workforce could use more Americans with that kind of appetite for life."[93] Our neighbors to the north have had no shortage of Trump comedy, mostly laughing at Americans, like a sketch on *22 Minutes* about the border crisis that Canadians are facing as Americans try to move north, including Melania Trump and Hillary Clinton.[94] Second City Toronto's *Everything Is Great Again* likewise mocks Americans and reimagines the border crisis as refugees from Michigan fleeing to Canada because their "country has been torn apart."[95] Second City stages across America have likewise poured on the Trump comedy, with hundreds of smaller sketch companies and theatres doing the same. There is so much comedy about Trump, and yet, so much of it feels the same. The same voice, the same expressions, the same take on his presidency.

At the same time, there is a small but growing movement of comedy expressly void of Trump. *South Park* famously said they would no longer talk about Trump, while many stand-ups and sketch shows pretend he's not there. Seth Meyers's Netflix special *Lobby Baby* (2019) straddles the line, providing viewers with an opt-out button that allows them to skip the special's Trump jokes. In an interview, Meyers, a fierce Trump critic, said, "It dawned on me that because it was on Netflix, there would be this opportunity to put in technology that would allow people to skip it. It was a way to build in the response to anyone who would say, 'Oh, let me guess there's going to be jokes about the President.' "[96] While Meyers is allowing viewers to opt-out, other comics are doing their best to avoid Trump all together. Netflix's *I Think You Should Leave* celebrates the weird and absurd through short idiosyncratic sketches that have absolutely nothing to do with politics in any way, shape, or form. As Dom Nero writes, "*I Think You Should Leave* shows that sketch comedy need not directly unpack the news of the day to still supplement the cultural discourse. Tim Robinson's sketches skewer today's hive-mind attitude, capturing the frantic nature of our internet brains through consistently funny group scenes."[97] In "Focus Group," a focus group is giving recommendations on a car. Most members are giving common suggestions, but one older man keeps giving absurd ideas like "a good steering wheel that doesn't fly off your hand while you're driving." As the sketch continues, the focus group respondents rally to the man's side as he begins to bully the everyman, "Paul."[98] It is a good example of the humor on the show, yet in the age of Trump, even an utterly apolitical sketch still has a Trump spin. As Nero later writes, in the sketch,

> it's the selfish, mischievous idiot who the rest of the group sides with – not the polite dude who's just trying to maintain decency. This nuanced spin on sketch tradition makes the show feel acutely relevant today, when some of society's dumbest and most awful members are also somehow our most powerful.[99]

It's nearly impossible to escape Trump's shadow.

HBO's hilarious *A Black Lady Sketch Show* likewise avoids Trump (at least as of this writing), while not ignoring the cultural ramifications of his election. The show openly tackles issues of race and gender, which have been exacerbated under Trump, but they make no effort to link the issues to Trump. The show is as apolitical as it can be in terms of traditional political sketch comedy (i.e., sketches about/featuring politicians). Yet the link to Trump is unavoidable. Even if he is not the source of the problem or the intended target, he's still there. Even when comics and satirists purposefully leave him out, his presence looms over the reception of the material. When Trump regularly attacks powerful women of color on Twitter (Congresswoman Maxine Waters, "The Squad" – Congresswomen Alexandria Ocasio-Cortez, Ilhan Omar, Ayanna Pressley, and Rashida Tlaib, among others), it becomes nearly impossible to not lay that cultural subtext onto a show produced by and featuring powerful women of color. There's been no other president who has had such a vast cultural or comedic footprint as Trump – he is omnipresent in everything that happens in America in a way that has simply never happened before. His excessive use of social media, coupled with the nonstop coverage of his every (mis)step, makes it nearly impossible to stay connected to the world but avoid Donald Trump. His absurd nature, detailed throughout this chapter, makes contextualizing the reality he's created nearly impossible. Satirists have pointed out that what is actually happening is absurd, imploring their audiences through satiric authenticity and advocacy satire to try and return us to "normal" . . . whatever that means.

Notes

1. Qtd. in Ian Schwartz, "Trump: Mexico Not Sending Us Their Best; Criminals, Drug Dealers and Rapists Are Crossing Border," *Real Clear Politics*, 16 June 2015. www.realclearpolitics.com/video/2015/06/16/trump_mexico_not_sending_us_their_best_criminals_drug_dealers_and_rapists_are_crossing_border.html.
2. Qtd. in John Santucci and Veronica Stracqualursi, "Donald Trump Announces 2016 Presidential Campaign: 'We Are Going Make Our Country Great Again,'" *ABC News*, 16 June 2015. https://abcnews.go.com/Politics/donald-trump-announces-2016-presidential-campaign-make-country/story?id=31799741.
3. Qtd in Santucci and Stracqualursi.
4. Jessica Estepa, "Covfefe, One Year Later: How a Late-Night Trump Tweet Turned into a Phenomenon," *USA Today*, 31 May 2018. www.usatoday.com/story/news/politics/onpolitics/2018/05/31/covfefe-one-year-anniverary-donald-trumps-confusing-tweet/659414002/.
5. It is very likely that between the writing of this in the summer/fall of 2019 and when you are reading it that Trump will have done 2,000 new things that have captured the media's attention.
6. Zachary B. Wolf, "Trump Is Either Trolling Everyone or Thinks He's Like a God," *CNN*, 22 August 2019. www.cnn.com/2019/08/21/politics/erratic-trump-god-complex/index.html.
7. Michelle Goldberg (@michelleinbklyn), "The Front Page of the NYT Right Now Looks Like One of Those Pre-election Parodies About What a Trump Administration Would Be Like," 21 August 2019, 10:45 am, Tweet. https://twitter.com/michelleinbklyn/status/1164186758646575105.
8. Eyder Peralta, "'Boston Globe' Runs Fake Front Page Detailing a Donald Trump World," *NPR*, 10 April 2016. www.npr.org/sections/thetwo-way/2016/04/10/473709316/boston-globe-runs-fake-front-page-detailing-a-donald-trump-world?t=1566399237074.
9. "Donald Trump: I Have 'More Humility Than You Would Think,'" *Face the Nation*, 2 February 2016. www.youtube.com/watch?v=tQkiawW6B9I.
10. Qtd. in Hunter Walker, "Donald Trump Just Dodged Two Questions About the Bible," *Business Insider*, 26 August 2015. www.businessinsider.com/donald-trump-refused-to-name-favorite-bible-verse-2015-8.
11. Seth MacFarlane (@SethMacFarlane), "This Could Be a Brian/Stewie exchange . . .," 22 August 2019, 1:36 pm, Tweet. www.businessinsider.com/donald-trump-refused-to-name-favorite-bible-verse-2015-8.
12. Dean Obeidallah, "Making America Laugh Again: The Yuge Trump Bump for Political Comedy," *CNN*, 19 July 2017. www.cnn.com/2017/03/16/opinions/snl-trump-bump-comedy-obeidallah-opinion/index.html.
13. Jesse David Fox, "Trump Is One of the Worst Things Ever to Happen to Comedy," *Vulture*, 21 December 2017. www.vulture.com/2017/12/donald-trump-jokes-bad-comedy.html.
14. Qtd. in Fox.
15. Sara Schaefer, "Why Trump Jokes Aren't Funny: American Stand-Up Sara Schaefer on Making Comedy in the Age of the 45th US President," *The Herald*, 29 July 2017. www.heraldscotland.com/opinion/15442379.why-trump-jokes-arent-funny-american-stand-up-sara-schaefer-on-making-comedy-in-the-age-of-the-45th-us-president/.

16. Qtd. in Terry Gross, "Wanda Sykes Loves Stand-Up: That's Where 'I Can Be Free,' She Says," *Fresh Air – NPR*, 1 August 2019. www.npr.org/2019/08/01/747103750/wanda-sykes-loves-stand-up-that-s-where-i-can-be-free-she-says.
17. Jay Martel, "Always Too Soon: Writing Sketch Comedy in the Trump Era," *The New Yorker*, 19 August 2019. www.newyorker.com/culture/cultural-comment/always-too-soon-writing-sketch-comedy-in-the-trump-era-alternatino-with-arturo-castro/amp.
18. "The White House Rewrites the Poem on the Statue of Liberty," *Alternatino with Arturo Castro*, Comedy Central, 24 July 2019.
19. Martel. Italics are mine.
20. "ICE Responds to All That Negative Press," *Alternatino with Arturo Castro*, Comedy Central, 25 June 2019. www.youtube.com/watch?v=jp_5WrJSb3A&feature=youtu.be.
21. Martel.
22. Martel.
23. Donald J. Trump (@realdonaldtrump), "To Show You How Dishonest the LameStream Media Is . . .," 27 September 2019, 7:02 am, Tweet. https://twitter.com/realDonaldTrump/status/1177539052683309056.
24. Merriam-Webster (@MerriamWebster), "For Those Looking Up Punctuation Early on a Friday Morning . . .," 27 September 2019, 8:32 am, Tweet. https://twitter.com/MerriamWebster/status/1177559300245471233.
25. Qtd. in Laura Bradley, "John Oliver Just Hopes Foreign Governments Are as Brave as 'Fucking Nickelback,'" *Vanity Fair*, 7 October 2019. www.vanityfair.com/hollywood/2019/10/trump-ukraine-impeachment-nickelback-john-oliver.
26. Qtd. in Charlie Gile and Associated Press, "Justice Department Asks Judge to Block House from Obtaining Mueller Grand Jury Material," *NBC News*, 8 October 2019. www.nbcnews.com/politics/trump-impeachment-inquiry/justice-department-asks-judge-block-house-obtaining-mueller-grand-jury-n1063856.
27. Qtd. in Bess Levin, "Rudy Giuliani: Those Witches in Salem Got a Fairer Shake Than Me and Trump," *Vanity Fair*, 8 October 2019. www.vanityfair.com/news/2019/10/rudy-giuliani-salem-witch-trials.
28. Qtd. in David Brennan, "Donald Trump's Claim That the Military Ran Out of Ammunition Is 'Not True,' House Armed Services Committee Member Says," *Newsweek*, 8 October 2019. www.newsweek.com/donald-trump-claim-military-ran-out-ammunition-not-true-house-armed-services-committee-member-says-1463749.
29. Donald J. Trump (@realDonaldTrump), "As I Have Stated Strongly Before . . .," 7 October 2019, 11:38 am, Tweet. https://twitter.com/realDonaldTrump/status/1181232249821388801.
30. "Read Trump's Letter to President Erdogan of Turkey," *The New York Times*, 16 October 2019. www.nytimes.com/interactive/2019/10/16/us/politics/trump-letter-turkey.html.
31. "This Letter Trump Sent to Erdogan Is 'So Weird We Had to Check with the White House to Make Sure It's Real," *MSNBC*, 16 October 2019. www.msnbc.com/deadline-white-house/watch/this-letter-trump-sent-to-erdogan-is-so-weird-we-had-to-check-with-the-white-house-to-make-sure-it-s-real-71409221925.
32. Katie Rogers (@katierogers), "Felt the Need to Ask WH If This Is Actually Real and It Is," 16 October 2019, 4:29 pm, Tweet. https://twitter.com/katierogers/status/1184567108853751809.
33. Qtd. in Peggy McGlone, "What Happened When Trump Visited the African American History Museum, According to Its Founding Director," *The Washington Post*, 31

August 2019. www.washingtonpost.com/entertainment/museums/what-happened-when-trump-visited-the-african-american-history-museum-according-to-its-former-director/2019/08/30/5471494e-cb5a-11e9-a1fe-ca46e8d573c0_story.html.
34. Andrew Freedman, Colby Itkowitz and Jason Samenow, "NOAA Staff Warned in Sept. 1 Directive Against Contradicting Trump," *The Washington Post*, 7 September 2019. www.washingtonpost.com/politics/noaa-staff-warned-in-sept-1-directive-against-contradicting-trump/2019/09/07/12a52d1a-d18f-11e9-87fa-8501a456c003_story.html.
35. Ben Parker, Stephanie Steinbrecher and Kelsey Ronan, "Lest We Forget the Horrors: A Catalog of Trump's Worst Cruelties, Collusions, Corruptions, and Crimes," *McSweeney's*, 5 November 2018. www.mcsweeneys.net/articles/the-complete-listing-so-far-atrocities-1-546.
36. Donald Trump, "My Very Good Black History Month Tribute to Some of the Most Tremendous Black People," *McSweeney's*, 1 February 2017. www.mcsweeneys.net/articles/my-very-good-black-history-month-tribute-to-some-of-the-most-tremendous-black-people.
37. "'What About All the Good Times?' Says Cornered President Calling on Nation to Remember Covfefe and the Saudi Arabia Orb," *The Onion*, 25 October 2019. https://politics.theonion.com/what-about-all-the-good-times-says-cornered-presiden-1839361527.
38. Michael R. Sisak, "Judge Fines Trump $2 Million for Misusing Charity Foundation," *The Washington Post*, 7 November 2019. www.washingtonpost.com/national/judge-fines-trump-2-million-for-misusing-charity-foundation/2019/11/07/b97db71a-01c3-11ea-8341-cc3dce52e7de_story.html.
39. "Putting Donald Trump Supporters Through an Ideology Test: The Daily Show," *The Daily Show*, 19 August 2016. www.youtube.com/watch?v=Y4Zdx97A63s.
40. Daniel Dale, "Donald Trump Has Said 5276 False Things as U.S. President," *Toronto Star*, updated 5 May 2019. http://projects.thestar.com/donald-trump-fact-check/.
41. Glenn Kessler, Salvador Rizzo and Meg Kelly, "President Trump Has Made 13,435 False or Misleading Claims Over 993 Days," *The Washington Post*, 14 October 2019. www.washingtonpost.com/politics/2019/10/14/president-trump-has-made-false-or-misleading-claims-over-days/.
42. Glenn Kessler, Salvador Rizzo and Meg Kelly, "President Trump Made 16,241 False or Misleading Claims in His First Three Years," *The Washington Post*, 20 January 2020. www.washingtonpost.com/politics/2020/01/20/president-trump-made-16241-false-or-misleading-claims-his-first-three-years/.
43. "Spicer: Inauguration Had Largest Audience Ever," *CNN*, 21 January 2017. www.cnn.com/videos/politics/2017/01/21/sean-spicer-donald-trump-inauguration-crowd-bts.cnn.
44. "Conway: Press Secretary Gave 'Alternative Facts,'" *NBC – Meet the Press*, 22 January 2017. www.nbcnews.com/meet-the-press/video/conway-press-secretary-gave-alternative-facts-860142147643.
45. Qtd. in Chris Cillizza, "The Trump Team Is Now Lying About Lying," *CNN*, 29 August 2019. www.cnn.com/2019/08/29/politics/donald-trump-kayleigh-mcenany-stephanie-grisham/index.html.
46. Mark Boukes et al., "At Odds: Laughing and Thinking? The Appreciation, Processing, and Persuasiveness of Political Satire," *Journal of Communication* 65, no. 5 (2015), 739.
47. Qtd. in Meagan Flynn, "'He Seriously Messed Up My Hair': Trump, Jimmy Fallon in Hair-Tousling Sequel," *The Washington Post*, 25 June 2018. www.washingtonpost.com/news/morning-mix/wp/2018/06/25/he-seriously-messed-up-my-hair-trump-jimmy-fallon-in-hair-tussling-sequel/.

48. Wanda Sykes, *Not Normal*, Netflix, 21 May 2019.
49. "Complicit," *Saturday Night Live*, 11 March 2017. www.nbc.com/saturday-night-live/video/complicit/3483871.
50. "Kavanaugh Hearing Cold Open," *Saturday Night Live*, 29 September 2018. www.nbc.com/saturday-night-live/video/kavanaugh-hearing-cold-open/3803621.
51. "Sean Spicer Press Conference," *Saturday Night Live*, 4 February 2017. www.nbc.com/saturday-night-live/video/sean-spicer-press-conference/3465162.
52. Annie Karni, Josh Dawsy and Tara Palmer, "White House Rattled by McCarthy's Spoof of Spicer," *Politico*, 6 February 2017. www.politico.com/story/2017/02/melissa-mccarthy-sean-spicer-234715.
53. Don J. Waisanen, "The Rise of Advocacy Satire," in *Political Humor in a Changing Media Landscape*, eds. Jody C. Baumgartner and Amy B. Becker (Lanham, MD: The Rowman & Littlefield Publishing Group Inc., 2018), 11–12.
54. Ross Douthat, "Clinton's Samantha Bee Problem," *The New York Times*, 21 September 2016. www.nytimes.com/2016/09/21/opinion/campaign-stops/clintons-samantha-bee-problem.html.
55. Raisa Bruner, "Read Jimmy Kimmel's Moving Healthcare Monologue That Everyone's Talking About," *Time*, 20 September 2017. https://time.com/4949522/jimmy-kimmel-healthcare-transcript/.
56. Qtd. in Erik Wemple, "'Feckless c–': Samantha Bee Apologizes for Misogyny That Delighted Her Audience," *The Washington Post*, 31 May 2018. www.washingtonpost.com/blogs/erik-wemple/wp/2018/05/31/feckless-c-samantha-bee-apologizes-for-misogyny-that-delighted-her-audience/.
57. Qtd. in Joanna Weiss, "How Trump Turned Liberal Comedians Conservative," *Politico*, 15 June 2019. www.politico.com/magazine/story/2019/06/15/trump-comedy-political-satire-daily-show-stewart-colbert-bee-227151.
58. Qtd. in Weiss.
59. Amy B. Becker, "Interviews and Viewing Motivations: Exploring Connections Between Political Satire, Perceived Learning, and Elaborative Processing," in *Political Humor in a Changing Media Landscape*, eds. Jody C. Baumgartner and Amy B. Becker (Lanham, MD: The Rowman & Littlefield Publishing Group Inc., 2018), 79–80.
60. "Net Neutrality," *Last Week Tonight with John Oliver*, HBO, 1 June 2014. www.youtube.com/watch?v=fpbOEoRrHyU.
61. Paul R. Brewer, Dannagal G. Young, Jennifer L. Lambe, Lindsay H. Hoffman and Justin Collier, "Seize Your Moment, My Lovely Trolls": News, Satire, and Public Opinion About Net Neutrality," *International Journal of Communication* 12 (2018), 1408–1430.
62. Brian Steinberg, "And Now This: John Oliver Just Might Be a Journalist," *Variety*, 16 February 2018. https://variety.com/2018/tv/news/john-oliver-journalist-hbo-last-week-tonight-1202702144/.
63. "Episode 30: November 17, 2019," *Last Week Tonight with John Oliver*, HBO, 17 November 2019.
64. "Michelle Wolf COMPLETE REMARKS at 2018 White House Correspondents' Dinner (C-SPAN)," *C-SPAN*, 28 April 2018. www.youtube.com/watch?v=DDbx1uArVOM.
65. Bess Levin, "Sarah Huckabee Sanders Tells Mueller Her Comey Firing Story Was Total B.S.," *Vanity Fair*, 18 April 2019. www.vanityfair.com/news/2019/04/sarah-sanders-mueller-report.
66. Maggie Haberman (@maggieNYT), "That @PressSec Sate and Absorbed Intense Criticism of Her Physical Appearance," 28 April 2018, 11:14 pm, Tweet. https://twitter.com/maggienyt/status/990428993542414336?lang=en.

67. Joe Berkowitz, "*Saturday Night Live* Recap: Donald Trump Is a Black Hole of Comedic Antimatter," *Vulture*, 8 November 2015. www.vulture.com/2015/11/saturday-night-live-recap-season-41-episode-4.html.
68. "White House 2018," *Saturday Night Live*, 7 November 2015. www.nbc.com/saturday-night-live/video/white-house-2018/2933531.
69. Qtd. in Sam Sanders and Brent Baughman, "Taran Killam Says 'There Was Never Any Common Ground' When Trump Hosted 'SNL,'" *National Public Radio*, 17 October 2017. www.npr.org/2017/10/17/558160262/taran-killam-says-there-was-never-any-common-ground-when-trump-hosted-snl.
70. "Donald Trump vs. Hillary Clinton Town Hall Debate Cold Open," *Saturday Night Live*, 16 October 2016. www.youtube.com/watch?v=qVMW_1aZXRk.
71. Donald J. Trump (@realDonaldTrump), "Watched Saturday Night Live Hit Job on Me," 16 October 2016, 7:14 am, Tweet. https://twitter.com/realdonaldtrump/status/787612552654155776?lang=en.
72. Amy Becker, "Trump Trumps Baldwin? How Trump's Tweets Transform SNL into Trump's Strategic Advantage," *Journal of Political Marketing* (2017), 1.
73. "Donald Trump Prepares Cold Open," *Saturday Night Live*, 19 November 2016. www.nbc.com/saturday-night-live/video/donald-trump-prepares-cold-open/3428575.
74. Qtd. in Halle Kiefer, "Alec Baldwin Replies to Donald Trump's Anti-*SNL* Tweet: 'Election Is Over,'" *Vulture*, 20 November 2016. www.vulture.com/2016/11/alec-baldwin-replies-to-donald-trumps-snl-hate.html.
75. "Classroom Cold Open," *Saturday Night Live*, 3 December 2016. www.nbc.com/saturday-night-live/video/classroom-cold-open/3435356.
76. Donald J. Trump (@realDonaldTrump), "Just Tried Watching Saturday Night Live," 4 December 2016, 12:13 am, Tweet. https://twitter.com/realdonaldtrump/status/805278955150471168?lang=en.
77. Qtd. in Stephen Collinson, "Comey Paints Unsparing Portrait of Trump in Devastating Tell-All Book," *CNN*, 13 April 2018. www.cnn.com/2018/04/13/politics/donald-trump-james-comey-book-revelations/index.html?sr=fbCNN041318donald-trump-james-comey-book-revelations0743AMVODtop.
78. "Transcript of President-elect Trump's News Conference," *CNBC*, 11 January 2017. www.cnbc.com/2017/01/11/transcript-of-president-elect-donald-j-trumps-news-conference.html.
79. "Donald Trump Press Conference Cold Open," *Saturday Night Live*, 14 January 2017. www.nbc.com/saturday-night-live/video/donald-trump-press-conference-cold-open/3454408.
80. Donald J. Trump (@realDonaldTrump), ".@NBCNews Is Bad but Saturday Night Live Is the Worst of NBC," 15 January 2017, 5:46 pm, Tweet. https://twitter.com/realdonaldtrump/status/820764134857969666?lang=en.
81. Thomas Gallagher, *The American Presidency and Entertainment Media: How Technology Affects Political Communication* (Lanham, MD: Lexington Books, 2017), 136.
82. Donald J. Trump (@realDonaldTrump), "Alec Baldwin, Whose Dying Mediocre Career Was Saved by His Terrible Impression of Me on SNL," 2 March 2018, 6:07am Tweet. https://twitter.com/realdonaldtrump/status/969529668234829825?lang=en. It is worth noting that in Trump's original tweet he misspelled "dieing," deleted the Tweet and resent it.
83. "It's a Wonderful Trump Cold Open," *Saturday Night Live*, 15 December 2018. www.nbc.com/saturday-night-live/video/its-a-wonderful-trump-cold-open/3847084.

84. Donald J. Trump (@realDonaldTrump), "A REAL Scandal Is the One Sided Coverage," 16 December 2018, 8:58 am, Tweet. https://twitter.com/realdonaldtrump/status/1074302851906707457?lang=en.
85. Outi J. Hakola, "Political Impersonations on *Saturday Night Live* During the 2016 US Presidential Elections," *European Journal of American Studies* 12, no. 12–2 (2017), 13.
86. Fox.
87. "Voters for Trump Ad," *Saturday Night Live*, 5 March 2016. www.nbc.com/saturday-night-live/video/voters-for-trump-ad/2997381.
88. "Election Night," *Saturday Night Live*, 12 November 2016. www.nbc.com/saturday-night-live/video/election-night/3424956.
89. Qtd. in Elahe Izadi, "SNL's 10 Best Political Sketches This Season – And 5 More That Have Nothing to Do with Trump," *The Washington Post*, 22 May 2017. www.washingtonpost.com/news/arts-and-entertainment/wp/2017/05/22/snls-10-best-political-sketches-this-season-and-5-more-that-have-nothing-to-do-with-trump/.
90. "The Bubble," *Saturday Night Live*, 19 November 2016. www.nbc.com/saturday-night-live/video/the-bubble/3428577.
91. S. Robert Lichter and Stephen J. Farnsworth, "Partisan Trends in Late Night Humor," in *Political Humor in a Changing Media Landscape*, eds. Jody C. Baumgartner and Amy B. Becker (Lanham, MD: The Rowman & Littlefield Publishing Group Inc., 2018), 51.
92. "Anthony Atamanuik of Comedy Central's 'The President Show' Discusses New Book," *The Hill*, 28 November 2018. https://thehill.com/hilltv/rising/418713-anthony-atamanuik-of-comedy-centrals-the-president-show-discusses-new-book.
93. Qtd. in Ryan Reed, "Kathy Griffin Makes TV Comeback as Kellyanne Conway on 'President Show'," *Rolling Stone*, 4 April 2018. www.rollingstone.com/tv/tv-news/kathy-griffin-makes-tv-comeback-as-kellyanne-conway-on-president-show-629343/.
94. "Mrs. Trump, This Is the Third Time This Week," *22 Minutes, CBC Comedy*, 27 February 2017. www.youtube.com/watch?v=zabXCwvFKYg&feature=youtu.be.
95. Qtd. in Max Fisher and Amanda Taub, "Canada's Comedy, the Voice of a Polite Nation, Rises in the Trump Era," *The New York Times*, 30 June 2017. www.nytimes.com/2017/06/30/world/canada/canadas-comedy-the-voice-of-a-polite-nation-rises-in-the-trump-era.html.
96. Qtd. in Frank Pallotta, "Seth Meyers' New Netflix Special Lets You Skip the Trump Jokes," *CNN*, 4 November 2019. www.cnn.com/2019/11/04/media/seth-meyers-skip-politics-button-netflix/index.html.
97. Dom Nero, "The New Golden Era of Sketch Comedy Embraces Diverse Voices and Weirdness," *Esquire*, 11 July 2019. www.esquire.com/entertainment/tv/a28340356/sketch-comedy-2019-golden-era-netflix-hbo-i-think-you-should-leave-alternatino/.
98. "Focus Group," *I Think You Should Leave, Netflix*, 2 May 2019. www.youtube.com/watch?v=8YDpvMYk5jA&feature=youtu.be.
99. Nero.

CHAPTER **10**

Conclusion

The use of comedy to criticize the government is as American as Ben Franklin. Yet, as we embark on a new era in American politics, the relationship between comedy and power is shifting and uncertain. Trump has changed the presidency itself, in some ways that are obvious (such as tweeting policy), and in others that it might take time to understand fully. As of this writing, Trump has been impeached, but still occupies the White House. By the time you are reading this, no scenario seems too absurd. Trump could be impeached again, he could have been removed from office, he could be impeached again while on trial in the Senate but not removed from office (and then impeached again), he could have won reelection in any number of likely or unlikely ways, or he could be serving his ninth term as King of America. Or, perhaps more likely, some combination of the three – like being impeached on election night because of his relationship with a Ukrainian comedian turned television president turned actual president only to reemerge on Christmas Day as part of a Republican coup to make him king.

One obvious change is the presidency's relationship to comedy. While most presidents have seen comedy either as a tool to help further their agenda (FDR, JFK, Reagan, Obama) or a thorn in their side (LBJ, Nixon), they all publicly tolerated the idea that comedians would make fun of them. Privately, perhaps not so much. Even though presidents sometimes bristle at comedy about them or put satirists on their "enemies list," most presidents have embraced humor and at least tacitly defended satirists' First Amendment rights to criticize the government. Those presidents have understood that making fun of our leaders as a form of criticism is a fundamental component of the American DNA. They further understand satire's and humor's capacity to help them while in office.

Trump has brought many things to the White House, but humor is not one of them. He's as unlikely to tell a joke as he is to take one good-naturedly. When he does "joke," it is often hostile, making fun of opponents and rivals like Barack Obama and Hillary Clinton, or taking mean-spirited jabs at critics like Rosie O'Donnell. Unlike the self-deprecating humor so effectively used by JFK, Reagan, and Obama, Trump tends to use ridicule to diminish his opponents, with his various derogatory Twitter nicknames the most obvious example. He also tellingly saves his most vicious and demeaning attacks for women and people of color. Trump regularly "jokes" at his rallies about how dishonest the news media is or about beating up protesters. While they're really more him complaining than joking, he's using the cover of humor to say often unacceptable things. The only time he seems to mention humor is when there is a backlash to something he's said – serving more than two terms, giving himself the Medal of Honor, referring to himself as the Chosen One, accusing Democrats of treason for not standing to applaud during his State of the Union address, inviting foreign countries to meddle in our elections, or dangling pardons for anyone willing to break the law to build his border wall, etc. – only then will he default to saying he was "joking." Instead of ignoring satiric takes like many of his predecessors, he amplifies them by responding negatively, aggressively, and *publicly* via social media – to the delight of his supporters. The public airing of his grievances sets Trump apart from other presidents. LBJ and Nixon both lobbied CBS in an attempt to control *The Smothers Brothers Comedy Hour*, but the majority of those efforts were behind the scenes. Not so with Trump, who has taken any criticism of him as "fake news," threatening on numerous occasions to "open up the libel laws."[1] By continually railing against the "fake" news media, of which he has lumped satiric comedy such as *SNL*, and questioning satirists' First Amendment right to criticize him by threatening to open the libel laws, Trump has fundamentally changed the relationship between satire and the state.

The days when Vaughan Meader's lighthearted JFK impression was edgy now seem antiquated and almost unbelievable – were we ever so naïve? Second City's playful Kennedy–Khrushchev press conferences satirized the Cold War and U.S.-Soviet relations, but that was back in the days when everyone agreed Russia was our enemy. The cultural shifts of the 1960s provided both the opportunity for satiric sketch comedy to flourish, but also revealed cracks in the American satiric voice – satire that both coalesced communities but represented fundamental differences among Americans. The political and social movements gave satire a harder edge and sharper teeth, fighting first against racism and inequality, then against the conservative backlash to the 1960s. Satirists still saw themselves mainly as speaking truth to power, rather than liberal or conservative, even though the majority of satire aimed at conservative ideas and persons. As the social battles of the 1960s gave way to the cynicism of the 1970s, satirists rightly laid claim to helping take down Richard Nixon (who tried to take them down first). While these satirists and others helped shine light on Nixon's shadows, rather than restore harmony, they fed American cynicism and distrust in the government. In the wake of Watergate, the emergence of *SNL* gave rise to the power of televised sketch comedy, as Chevy Chase's Gerald Ford worked to define Ford's public persona in a way few satirists ever had. Given *SNL*'s "brand-newness," the combination created a new pop-culture phenomenon – the *SNL* president. As the new wave of televised sketch comedy developed, there was a definite shift toward less policy satire and more personality-based satire. The best satiric depictions combined both, using personality as a way to satirize policy. Reagan's sleepy hands-off approach is just a façade for his secret arms deals. George H.W. Bush's nerdy persona a way to emphasize his lack of understanding of everyday Americans. Clinton's voracious appetite is for more than just Big Macs, while Dubbya's frat-boy stupidity demonstrates the dangers of a supremely confident but not necessarily competent president in the post-9/11 world.

The comedic atmosphere has changed as well, leading to a (temporary?) breakdown of the satiric triangle between satirist–target–audience. As cable news, the internet, and social media (and politicians) exacerbate the fractures in American life – race, gender, class, and politics – satire has become more ever-present in our lives. Political comedy is everywhere – on television, online, and on our phones – coming from any number of different satiric voices. This changing satire worked to show the absurdity of real life, with Tina Fey simply repeating Sarah Palin's words to devastating effect. The temporary lull of the Obama administration – the Obama memes seem as antiquated now as Meader's old comedy record – soon gave way to the meteoric rise of satiric authenticity and later advocacy satire. Satirists no longer solely took on the powerful – they needed to be on "our side." The Trump presidency has (thus far) deepened the divides in American life, and audiences have demanded that satirists take sides, and often, take real political action.

By taking sides, satirists are working to make real change, but are also forfeiting their objectivity. Taking sides has strengthened the liberal community, but further splits already deepening divides. One can certainly argue that the price of truth and preserving American democracy is worth the (temporary?) deepening of partisan divisions, but it has brought satire to a crossroads. When the country can't agree on facts or truth, with half the country ensconced in one media bubble and the other in another, how does satire break through? If the target and audience do not know, care, or realize they are being satirized, can satire affect any real change? Did satiric authenticity cause further divides, or is it a result of divides? The latter seems more likely. Still, it doesn't change the fact that Americans continue to grow further apart over fundamental issues. Those fights extend to the truth itself, which in some small part lies at the feet of satirists like Jon Stewart, who sowed mistrust in both conservative media like Fox News, as well as mainstream media like CNN.[2] Even though *The Daily Show* has increased political awareness among younger viewers, a study by Jody Baumgartner and Jonathan S. Morris found that the show "may have more detrimental effects, driving down support for political institutions and leaders among those already inclined toward nonparticipation."[3] With the turn to a more aggressive, personal, and Juvenalian type of satire, it is fair to ask if political comedy is engendering cynicism and breeding mistrust in our institutions more than it is revealing the truth or holding the powerful to account.

Yet, the opposite is just as plausible. Is satire, as Sophia McClennen and Remy Maisel argue, saving our nation? With the breakdown of truth and deepening divides, we've seen satire rise as a vital force in providing news and information. With satirists ever-growing role as comedy-journalists, there has been a marked rise in satiric authenticity. Comedians have laid bare their political beliefs to win new audiences and push for change. This fundamental shift in satire is still unfolding, and it remains to be seen if satirists will stay in the middle of the action or if they'll return to the role of outside commentator. As much as satire has changed, it also has remained the same. Have we really traveled very far from Vaughan Meader's vocal impression of JFK? On the surface, absolutely. Satire has become much more pointed, personal, and at times, nasty. Yet, the majority of Trump impressions rely mainly on a vocal impression of the president saying, "You're fired," or "China." Yet the best satire delves deeper, and that content has changed dramatically. While Meader put JFK into absurd circumstances to highlight truths about the man, Trump routinely puts himself into impossibly stupid situations leaving satirists with the job of satirizing the already ridiculous, fighting through the whirlwind to find reality. That reality has led to satiric authenticity, and often, advocacy. The rise of satiric authenticity has contributed to a surge in political advocacy and awareness, particularly among younger Americans. *The First Family* gave listeners a new insight into the humanity of JFK and let Americans feel like they were a part of the Kennedy mystique, but did little to affect political action or change. With Trump satire, satirists often give audiences tangible steps to resist the administration and fight for change. That is a dramatic transformation.

The (Not So) Changing Face of Satire

As the content of the satire has changed, so, too, has the satirist. Once the exclusive realm of white males, satire has begun to diversify in recent years. There is still a *long* way to go before sketch comedy practitioners and satirists more accurately reflect the American population. However, there has been a notable uptick in nonwhite-male satirists, though white men still dominate in terms of numbers. The lack of diversity on *SNL* helped precipitate a step toward more diversity across the comedy spectrum. As discussed in Chapter 8, the whiteness of the show was highlighted during Obama's presidency and forced the show to begin to address these issues in tangible ways. But it is about more than diversity for diversity's sake. The lack of diversity directly impacts the satire produced. Veronica Yang, director of the all-Asian sketch comedy group Model Majority, spoke about the importance of working in a diverse setting. She talked about the freedom it provides, saying, "Working with a group of fellow Asian Americans, rather than being a sole token member, allows for a freedom of expression and creativity many of us have never experienced before. This also allows us to write sketches with multiple Asian characters."[4] A white-male-heterosexual comedic aesthetic has historically dominated *SNL*, which has, intentionally or not, excluded numerous comedic voices. *SNL* is hardly alone. Second City and various improv comedy theatres have likewise have had issues with diversity and sexism.[5]

As outlined in Chapter 1, the vast majority of mainstream satire has come from a white-male-heterosexual perspective. The history of African Americans and comedy is one of immense pain and trauma, as humor worked for centuries to exclude and humiliate blacks, presenting them as not worthy of being American. As sketch comedy was gaining momentum on television, blacks were virtually nonexistent on American's television sets. After the cancellation of *Amos 'n Andy* in 1953, in part because of heavy pressure from the NAACP over the show's racial stereotypes, there was virtually no representation of African Americans outside of Bill Cosby as the costar of *I Spy* (1965–1968) and *The Flip Wilson Show* (1970–1974). That's it. While representation began to increase thanks to Wilson's success, it is difficult to overestimate the effect on identity that results from only two shows featuring black people over almost two decades. Women in comedy likewise had marginal representation in comedy, both pre- and post-television. They similarly have forever been pushing back against stereotypes, societal expectations, and negative assumptions by male comedians that women aren't funny. Fanny Fern's mid-19th-century columns feel eerily relevant and timely, as many of the sexist tropes she confronted then are still with us today. *SNL* has been foundational for political satire, but it also has been fundamental to the othering of satiric voices. With so many people never invited to sit at the table, it begs the question, what sketches have been left on the table because of those who were not allowed to sit there?

Tina Fey, who is considered the first woman to break through the boys' club of *SNL*, commented that it is still terribly difficult to be a woman in comedy, in part because interviewers continually ask about "if women are funny," or celebrate how great it is that one woman broke through the *SNL* male stranglehold. In talking about the press tour she did with Amy Poehler for their movie *Sisters* (2015), Fey said,

> Every single interviewer asked, "Isn't this an amazing time for women in comedy?" People really wanted us to be openly grateful – "Thank you so much!" – and we were like, "No, it's a terrible time. If you were to really look at it, the boys are still getting more money for a lot of garbage, while the ladies are hustling and doing amazing work for less."[6]

Part of this sexism is misogyny, but part of the sexism is a result of excluding women's voices from the comedy table. Fey further describes a table reading where she was pitching an *SNL* commercial parody about Kotex Classic pads. The male writers rejected the sketch on numerous occasions because they couldn't conceptualize it, and therefore they thought it wasn't funny. When Fey and the sketch's writer Paula Pell explained the joke, suddenly the men got it. For Fey,

> It was the moment I realized that there was no "institutionalized sexism" at this place – sometimes the guys just literally didn't know what we were talking about. In the same way that I was not familiar with the completely normal custom of pissing in jars, they had never been handed a bulging antique Kotex product by the school nurse.[7]

While the show's history does point to some institutionalized sexism, the more significant point shows how vital it is to have different voices equally represented at the comedy table. The men didn't find it funny because they had not been exposed to different comedic voices. The lack of exposure perpetuates a cycle of exclusion – by not being exposed to different voices, those voices then lack comedic authenticity, thereby allowing their continuous exclusion.

As *SNL* makes strides, it continues to shoot itself in the foot with issues of diversity, seemingly continually hiring white men with problematic comedic histories or Twitter feeds. The show hired Bowen Yang in 2019, its first-ever Asian American performer, and Chloe Fineman, a Groundlings alum with a penchant for celebrity impressions. It also hired Shane Gillis, a white male stand-up who has made racist jokes about Asian Americans and disparaging comments about women, going to the tried-and-true default of arguing men are funnier than women.[8] What makes the Gillis situation more complicated is that Gillis has a well-known and documented history of racist and sexist comments. He had been banned from performing at the Good Good Comedy Theatre in his hometown of Philadelphia,[9] and his offensive podcast comments from *Matt and Shane's Secret Podcast* are from as recent as 2018. It is not as though someone dug up 20-year-old comments (not to excuse those either, but there's always room for growth and change). Not to mention, there are thousands of very funny comedians without problematic diversity issues the show could have hired. After several days of public outcry, *SNL* parted ways with Gillis. Pointing to their own failures to properly vet the comedian, the show said in a statement, "We are sorry that we did not see these clips earlier, and that our vetting process was not up to our standard."[10] Much like the Kotex commercial, the lack of awareness is most striking. That *SNL* didn't even think to check Gillis's comedic history is shocking, especially considering *SNL* had gone through similar situations in the recent past.

One of the reasons *SNL* initially hired Gillis was for his "red state appeal," so while the show attempts to diversify, it also is working to regain its perceived objectivity on the political spectrum.[11] The situation also casts conservative comedians in a bad light, reflecting on conservative comedy as inherently racist when it is not. The case also reignited debates within the comedy community about pushing boundaries and "cancel-culture outrage." The #MeToo movement revelations about high-profile comedians like Louis C.K. have brought the sometimes-toxic male-dominated environment of comedy to the forefront. Most comedians agree that making racist and sexist jokes/comments is hardly pushing boundaries. But it does bring up important issues about taking risks and crossing lines (intentionally or not) that all comedians have to deal with, especially in political satire, and especially in an age with deep and sharp partisan divisions and a 24-hour news cycle. Many comedians condemned Gillis, but many others defended him. They didn't necessarily support what he said, but they defended his right to say it, arguing that comedians should push boundaries, even if it's offensive. The "too sensitive" card is frequently played in situations like Gillis's, with the argument being that comedy is supposed to make people uncomfortable, not make them feel good. The debate does illustrate the enduring conflicts over censorship and freedom of speech, but it also points to comedy's longstanding history of racism, sexism, and homophobia. The story of American comedy, like it or not, is one of laughing at others. It likewise highlights the positioning of American comedy as that of the straight white man, epitomized by *SNL*. It bears repeating that *SNL*, the leading satiric voice in the country, one with a problematic diversity history, would hire Gillis without even the most perfunctory of background checks is indicative of the systemic issues that still plague American comedy.

While the Gillis situation demonstrates the work still to do, perhaps most encouraging in terms of diversity is the growing lack of novelty surrounding any non-white-male performers. Celebrated as the first Asian American cast member on the show (and one of only a handful of LGBTQ performers in the show's history), Yang wasn't hired *because* of his identity. He was hired because he's funny (he was previously a writer on the show, a successful stand-up, one of Twitter's best lip-sync performers, cohost of the comedy podcast *Las Culturistas*, and more). Historically, a non-white-male performer would be pointed out for solely being a minority, proof of the show's commitment to diversity. Remember that Key and Peele auditioned *against* one another for *MADtv*'s one "black male" slot. The example of *The State*'s attempted transition to CBS from MTV found network executives pushing the 11-member all-white cast to hire ONE African American cast member to make the show diverse. The tokenism is worse when coupled with the network's allegedly appallingly racist rationale that lazy black viewers would like sketch comedy because of their short attention spans and the fact that they have nowhere to be in the morning. Historically, often being the only non-white comic also meant the performer would be expected to fulfill demeaning stereotypes in sketches for laughs. Similarly, non-white-male–centric shows have been dismissed as niche shows. In reviewing *The Big Gay Sketch Show* (2006–2010), Brian Lowry wrote in *Variety* that "Ultimately, it's another minor addition to the 'Every demographic will have its own cheap sketch show' trend."[12] As this review demonstrates, underrepresented performers still face numerous systemic issues, including from initiatives meant to increase diversity in comedy.

The diversity program through the Upright Citizens Brigade improv theatre in New York, one of the country's leading comedic training institutions, came under fire in 2015 for its lack of diversity. Writing for *Medium*, Oliver Chinyere said,

> UCB does not care about black people or minorities. It does, has done and will continue to do the bare minimum when it comes to maintaining diversity not unlike the entertainment industry at-large. As nine openings on house teams quietly came and went, not one POC was added, despite the fact that in the past year, two POC have stepped down. We are technically less diverse from a racial standpoint.[13]

Founded in the early 2000s, the CBS Diversity Sketch Comedy Showcase, meant to help underrepresented actors and writers gain exposure (and employment), has likewise faced diversity issues. While the program has had success – Kate McKinnon and Tiffany Haddish are alums – it also has significant problems. Director Rick Najera resigned amid sexual harassment allegations in 2017. Furthermore, participants also say "the program often leaves participants feeling dejected and bullied at the hands of leaders who view them stereotypically and insist that their work revolve around outdated racist, gender-based, or homophobic tropes."[14] When diversity initiatives are pushing stereotypes, it illustrates the profoundly entrenched problems that centuries of "othering" in comedy creates.

These systemic issues present significant barriers. Many satirists and comedians have worked outside of the system, which offers its own challenges and significant drawbacks, to gain some semblance of control. Resisting the niche label and pushing back against the historical trope of queerness being the joke in and of itself, Chicago's sketch comedy group GayCo, founded via Second City in 1996, follows its own motto of "Gay is the given, not the punchline."[15] On stage and online, the Native American sketch group The 1491s are using comedy to push back against a culture that tries to erase their existence. They are also a great example of 21st-century comedy. With no institutional comedy structure in place to showcase their work, the group got its start in 2009 by posting videos to YouTube. Their first sketch, "New Moon Wolf Pack Audition," imagines the casting call for *The Twilight* movie series. The sketch parodies the caricatured portrayal of Native Americans in film.[16] They have since created numerous viral sketches that helped the group gain national notoriety, including a 2014 appearance on *The Daily Show* in a segment exploring the racism behind Washington, D.C.'s football team's mascot. Member Bobby Wilson spoke about the group's aesthetic, saying,

> There's so much expectation put on indigenous people in the arts, especially in the media. It comes from a longstanding tradition of non-Native people, most often white men, writing stories for Hollywood and the stage. We're fighting those tropes. If they show up in our work, it's just to lampoon them.[17]

These examples all point to the impact and importance of showcasing and including multiple satiric voices and viewpoints.

While there is still progress to be made, there are more and more examples of underrepresented comedic voices being celebrated for their comedy rather than solely for their race. *A Black Lady Sketch Show* on HBO is a good example. Nearly every review of the show makes a note of the fact that the sketch show features four African American women – Robin Thede, Ashley Nicole Black, Quinta Brunson, and Gabrielle Dennis. Given sketch comedy's history, this is certainly noteworthy, but that is not the through-line of the story. The focus is more on the comedic content of the show. Yes, the race and gender of the creators' matters, but it is not the *sole* feature of a satirist. Nor do reviews treat the show as a "niche" show only appealing to African American viewers. In fact, for perhaps the first time in American history, the show's various points of view are catering to a mainstream audience (albeit a post-network audience that is inherently smaller). Still, mainstream is no longer synonymous with an assumed mostly white audience. Even more progressive shows on Comedy Central, like *Inside Amy Schumer* and *Key & Peele*, were explicitly marketed toward the network's targeted demographic of young white men. The network's audience is 60% men; as exec Brooke Posch notes, "Our ad buys are for men, so we can't lose them."[18] As progressive as those two shows were, they still needed to appeal to young white men. That demographic is still catered to, but it is no longer the only demographic that matters. Historically the perceived lack of an audience has kept networks from producing shows from nonmajority points of view. That mindset, of course, perpetuates a cycle: if you never produce shows from other points of view, then there will be no audience data to prove that those shows work, so networks can say there is no audience for the shows. The fallacy of that logic is evident in the wave of contemporary shows demonstrating the demand for diverse voices: *A Black Lady Sketch Show, Sherman's Showcase, Alternatino*, as well as more traditional sitcoms like *Atlanta, Insecure, Black-ish, Jane the Virgin, Empire, South Side, Fresh Off the Boat*, and many others, potentially signal the end of this cycle. Time will tell if this particular cultural moment will lead to more progress or is an outlier, but the trend is very encouraging for the future of American comedy.

Satire & The State

This all begs the questions raised at the beginning of the book – what's the point? Political satire via sketch comedy has fundamentally changed Americans' relationship with the presidency. Americans look to *SNL* and others to filter out the truth about our presidents. Trump's fixation on *SNL*'s depiction of him is proof of how vital the relationship between satire and the state is in America. As the country divides, Americans are turning to sketch comedy and satire more so than ever. Nearly every year after an election, *SNL*'s ratings fall and it produces less political content, but 2017 saw just the opposite, with the show staying with Trump and viewers tuning in for the communal experience. One of satire's strengths is building community, and *SNL* became such a place for liberals in the immediate aftermath of Trump's election, with its 2017 spring episodes hitting the show's highest Nielsen ratings in 24 years. Michael M. Grynbaum and John Koblin wrote of the "new" phenomenon: "Despite a dizzying array of new media choices, viewers are opting for television's mass gathering spots, seeking the kind of shared experience that can validate and reassure."[19] Americans, it seems, care more about political sketch comedy now than they have in a generation. If Americans didn't care about sketch comedy, then neither would the president. But Americans do care, and therefore so, too, do presidents. George H.W. Bush didn't go out of his way to become friendly with Dana Carvey out of the goodness of his heart or because he genuinely appreciated the impression. He did it because Carvey was taking over his public perception. Will Ferrell didn't get a Broadway show as George W. Bush because it was "all in good fun"; he got that show because Americans resonated with Ferrell's portrayal of Bush, peeling back the layers to delve into the flaws of the 43rd president. Satire about the president has become one of the ways Americans interact with the presidency.

Satire has importantly played an essential role in the creation and evolution of the American identity. One of the paradoxes of America is that while we openly celebrate our Americanness, we simultaneously can't agree on what that means. We love freedom but denied it to an entire race. We love liberty but denied it to a whole gender. The freedom and liberty promised *to* Americans and promised *of* America continue to this day to be unattainable for many. The tensions inherent in "The Great American Joke" have exacerbated, as more and more Americans demand the lofty language of our founding finally become a reality for the millions of Americans historically left out of the American story. The definition of American has changed over time and between communities. Even today, different people view American identity in different ways. We still can't agree on who constitutes "We the people."

Satire has been central to this identity creation. Satirists, for instance, have used comedy to assert their generational identities. The baby boomers used *SNL* to declare their more aggressive and confrontational comedic style from that of their parents and the 1950s variety shows. Boomers' Gen-X kids used a detached, ironic style seen in a variety of 1990s sketch shows to prove how out of touch their parents were, and the current "we care deeply but are simultaneously absurdly detached" comedy has defined millennials and Generation Z. Sketch comedy and satire go well beyond generational distinctions. We have laughed at otherness as a way to assuage white American notions about Americanness. We have used humor to assert our Americanness by laughing at those that are different from us. Americans made fun of the British and Europeans to distinguish the American character, creating a folksy vernacular that has become a signature of the American identity. We have also laughed at others as a way to demean and debase them – race matters in America and race matters in sketch comedy. As outlined above, satire is slowly becoming more diverse, and that is important for many reasons, including because race has historically been used to include or exclude people from the American identity. White Americans used humor to stereotype African Americans as less than, to show blacks' inferior nature as incapable of being American. That history is with us today.

We have also used satire to fight for social justice. Satire was a critical voice, for instance, during the Vietnam War and into Watergate. African Americans have likewise used humor to assert their own agency and authenticity, to take back control of their identities. As time wears on, one question that arises is what happens to the American identity as we include the voices of those we have long mocked and excluded. This question translates to comedy, as well. As more and more voices contribute to the lineage of American comedy, the ways we've used humor to define ourselves has changed. Richard Pryor redefined the American voice by reclaiming a voice long ridiculed in American comedy. Tina Fey likewise gave rise to a voice earlier articulated by Fanny Fern, satirizing the incongruities of sexism in America, a trope that has had an obvious connection to the presidency. As the American voice expands, we can see the direct translation to the White House.

The election of 2016 brought the battle over the "real" America to the forefront. The diverse coalition created by President Barack Obama in 2008 was at the heart of the election of Donald Trump eight years later. The great promise of Obama's election led to the premature declaration of a "post-racial" America. It was a promise that the American voice had finally begun to include those it had worked so hard to exclude. In hindsight, it is easy to see the naiveté of those assumptions, to laugh at the optimism of the early satire of Obama that celebrated him and his promise more than it criticized his flaws. We see a similar naiveté in the celebratory satire about JFK, followed by the intensely negative satire engendered by LBJ and Richard Nixon. The latter two presidents were seen as embodiments of what America did not want to be. As such, they were treated by satirists much more harshly than the American optimism inspired by JFK, Reagan, and Obama. Which again brings us back to the 2016 election. Trump's entire purpose was to undo the legacy of Obama, the promise of Obama, and that meant more than just reversing

Obama's policies. Trump's coalition used the presidency as a way to react against the emergence of diverse voices to assert what they saw as the historic white American identity. "Make America Great Again" is a thinly veiled slogan about what used to make America great in the false nostalgic reality of Trump – America's whiteness.

The past elicited by the slogan works to erase the modest gains in agency achieved by non-white people. Trump's America literally keeps track of who counts as American and who does not. It began by calling Mexicans rapists, was built on the promise of a wall to keep out brown people, perpetuated with a pledge to ban Muslims from entering the country, and cemented with the commitment to undoing the work of the nation's first African American president. Trump's mission to destroy Obama's legacy led Ta-Nehisi Coates to label Trump "The First White President." For Coates, Obama and Trump are intrinsically linked: "Trump truly is something new – the first president whose entire political existence hinges on the fact of a black president. And so it will not suffice to say that Trump is a white man like all the others who rose to become president. He must be called by his rightful honorific – America's first white president."[20] Throughout the campaign and during his presidency, Trump's message is clear – the primary factor for counting as American is skin color. His message resonated with many Americans.

During the GOP primary, Trump voters were much more likely to back race-based ideals of citizenship. In one poll of Republican voters, only 9% of voters supporting moderate John Kasich said European ancestry was an important component of being an American. Trump voters said European descent mattered at a clip over three times that of Kasich voters. When looking at voters from both parties in the 2016 primaries, Trump voters again stand out when weighing the importance of living in America for most of one's life and being born in America as central to one's Americanness. About 49% of Democratic voters said living in America for a majority of one's life was important, and 47% reported being born in America was important. Roughly 63% of Republican voters thought living here and being born here was important. Trump voters push those numbers even higher, with 69% supporting living here for a majority of one's life and 72% for being born in America as essential to American identity. While only one-third of Democrats thought being a Christian was fundamental to being an America, and slightly over half of Republicans did, nearly two-thirds of Trump voters saw Christianity as an important signifier of being an American. In analyzing the data, Lynn Vavreck said, "This context makes it easier to see why many people interpreted Mr. Trump's appeal to 'make America great again' as a call to exclude some groups of people from belonging of feeling like Americans."[21] Obviously, not every person who voted for Donald Trump did so because he appealed to a white American identity. There are many reasons to support a candidate, but the numbers and his rhetoric certainly lend credence to this perspective.

None of this is surprising. After all, Trump made his first real political noise supporting the racist "birther" movement, echoing centuries of racism that proclaims that black people can never be genuinely from America, and therefore never truly be Americans. Trump then demanded to see Obama's college grades, implying

Obama was not smart enough to have actually attained an Ivy League degree and that the only reason he was admitted to those schools was through "the fraud" of affirmative action (Trump had his lawyer send threatening letters to Trump's alma maters promising legal action if they released Trump's grades). He then argued that Obama's book *Dreams of My Father* must have been ghostwritten by a white man (ignoring the fact that Trump's *The Art of the Deal* was ghostwritten ... by a white man). Trump's troublesome relationship with race goes back decades. The U.S. government found that he worked to keep blacks out of his buildings, and he famously called for the death penalty of the Central Park Five – refusing to recant even after their exoneration. Unlike most politicians, he did not dilute his rhetoric while president. Say what you will about Trump, but he does not back away from his controversial statements. During the 2016 campaign and into the White House, he repeatedly referred to inner cities and life for African Americans as a dystopic hellscape, saying living in black America meant "Poverty. Rejection. Horrible education. No housing, no homes, no ownership. Crime at levels that nobody has seen. You can go to war zones in countries that we are fighting and it's safer than living in some of our inner cities."[22] Importantly, his descriptions of African American life in America were not meant to galvanize black people or an attempt to fight systemic racism. Instead, they were meant for white people who either feared black people or moderate white people who wanted to see Trump make an effort at outreach. The audience is eerily similar to the minstrel shows – whites who already thought blacks were inferior, or whites who needed to feel better about the systemic mistreatment of blacks without actually doing anything. Trump is not the first president to exploit such fears or make token outreach to minority voters, but he is the first contemporary president to do it so overtly. The examples are endless. Nativists and white nationalists have populated his campaign and White House staff, and he's defended neo-Nazis as "very fine people." When Trump tells four prominent congresswomen of color, three of whom were born in America, that "If they don't like it here, they can leave," it is abundantly clear who he thinks is "We the people."[23]

This is where satire steps into the mix. Much of the satire about Trump's presidency fights back against his American vision. The American president has come to reflect the American identity, and Americans have come to laugh at or with the president based on how they reflect that identity. From the Women's March held the day after Trump's inauguration, which is the largest single-day protest in American history, to the monologues of John Oliver, the resistance to Trump is based in his limited view of American identity. It rejects the idea that some people are "more" American based on the color of their skin or the ethnicity of their ancestors. The sheer amount of satire about Donald Trump is not merely a result of his outlandishness and absurdity. It is not just a result of him lying at historical rates. It is not just about him saying objectively bizarre and outlandish things, and it is not just about his policies or personal behavior: it is a reaction to and rejection of his definition of Americanness. Satirists push back against his assertion of American identity through satiric authenticity and satiric advocacy to literally fight back against his limited view of what it means to be an American. It is the action behind liberal mottos like "This is not who we are," and "We're better than this," that float between being proclaimed as statements and framed as nervous questions. The massive increase in satiric shows and audiences is proof of the *need* for satire in trying times. The recent inclusion of more diverse satiric voices has added to the satiric pushback. The voter survey mentioned above also found that "the nation as a whole is moving away from exclusionary conceptions of American identity even as Mr. Trump's strongest supporters hold on."[24] Part of the reason there has been such a strong satiric reaction to Trump is because, according to this survey and other data, the majority of Americans do not like the view of American identity being disseminated from the White House. At its core, the fierce satiric outpouring that defines Trump's presidency is a reaction to his notions of what it means to be an American. That reaction represents the vital importance of the relationship between satire and the state.

Will it work? Will satire fundamentally change or revert to prior forms when Trump leaves office? I don't know. But this much is certain, from King George III to Donald Trump to whoever follows Trump into the White House, America's leaders have and will always have to contend with Americans making fun of them. Satire may point out the negative, or reinforce the positive, but it is doing so to bring about political engagement, debate, and action – it is a call to democracy. Satire becomes more prevalent when tensions are at their highest; after all, when things are perfect, there's not much to be improved upon. But when things are not perfect, when the country is fractured and divided, when Americans can't seem to agree upon anything – that is when satire is needed most. The answer to the question of will satire heal our divides or exacerbate them seems to depend on each individual's positioning and view of the person in the White House. Yet, the best satire, like our best presidents, can begin to bridge the gap between what is and what ought to be.

Notes

1. Michael M. Grynbaum, "Trump Renews Pledge to 'Take a Strong Look' at Libel Laws," *The New York Times*, 10 January 2018. www.nytimes.com/2018/01/10/business/media/trump-libel-laws.html.
2. To be clear, most of it lies at the feet of Fox News.
3. Jody Baumgartner and Jonathan S. Morris, "*The Daily Show* Effect: Candidate Evaluations, Efficacy, and American Youth," *American Politics Research* 34, no. 3 (May 2006), 341.
4. Qtd. in "Q&A: Model Majority – 'Asian American 101'," *MagnetTheater.com*, 24 May 2019. https://magnettheater.com/2019/05/24/q-a-model-majority-asian-american-101/.
5. Amy Seham's *Whose Improv Is It Anyway?* details the problems of racism and sexism in improvisation.
6. Qtd. in Mary Kaye Schilling, "Tina Fey Goes to War," *Town & Country*, 1 March 2016. www.townandcountrymag.com/leisure/arts-and-culture/a5146/tina-fey-interview/.
7. Tina Fey, *Bossypants* (New York: Little, Brown, 2011).
8. David Sims, "*Saturday Night Live* Made a Mistake Hiring Shane Gillis," *The Atlantic*, 13 September 2019. www.theatlantic.com/entertainment/archive/2019/09/saturday-night-live-cant-ignore-its-shane-gillis-problem/598033/.

9. Good Good Comedy Theatre (@goodgoodcomedy), "We, Like Many . . .," 12 September 2019, 8:42 pm, Tweet. https://twitter.com/goodgoodcomedy/status/1172309623690289157.
10. Joe Otterson, "Shane Gillis Out from 'Saturday Night Live,'" *Variety*, 16 September 2019. https://variety.com/2019/tv/news/shane-gillis-saturday-night-live-1203337908/.
11. Joe Otterson and Michael Schneider, "'SNL' Sought Conservative Appeal with Shane Gillis Hire," *Variety*, 17 September 2019. https://variety.com/2019/tv/news/snl-conservative-shane-gillis-hire-1203339723/.
12. Brian Lowry, "The Big Gay Sketch Show," *Variety*, 16 April 2007. https://variety.com/2007/tv/reviews/the-big-gay-sketch-show-1200560107/.
13. Oliver Chinyere, "Why I'm Quitting UCB, and Its Problem with Diversity," *Medium.com*, 20 September 2015. https://medium.com/@ochinyere/why-i-m-quitting-ucb-and-its-problem-with-diversity-961f1195a790.
14. Maria Elena Fernandez, "CBS Diversity Comedy Showcase Has Been a Racist, Sexist, Homophobic Mess for Years, Participants Say," *Vulture*, 10 November 2017. www.vulture.com/2017/11/cbs-diversity-showcase-racist-sexist-homophobic-mess-participants-say.html.
15. Qtd. in Brianna Wellen, "GayCo Celebrates 20 Years of LGBTQ Revues," *Chicago Reader*, 10 October 2016. www.chicagoreader.com/chicago/gayco-20th-anniversary-sketch-comedy-second-city/Content?oid=23849634.
16. "New Moon Wolf Pack Audition," *The 1491s*, published 7 October 2013. www.youtube.com/watch?v=UqoNkAp0HXU.
17. Qtd. in Anne Hamilton, "A Troupe That Turns Tropes Into Takeoffs," *American Theatre*, 20 March 2018. www.americantheatre.org/2018/03/20/a-troupe-that-turns-tropes-into-takeoffs/.
18. Qtd. in Jason Zinoman, "Amy Schumer, Funny Girl," *The New York Times*, 18 April 2013. www.nytimes.com/2013/04/21/arts/television/amy-schumers-comedy-central-show-from-the-inside.html.
19. Michael M. Grynbaum and John Koblin, "For Solace and Solidarity in the Trump Age, Liberals Turn the TV Back On," *The New York Times*, 12 March 2017.
20. Ta-Nehisi Coates, "The First White President," *The Atlantic*, October 2017. www.theatlantic.com/magazine/archive/2017/10/the-first-white-president-ta-nehisi-coates/537909/.
21. Lynn Vavreck, "The Great Political Divide Over American Identity," *The New York Times*, 2 August 2017. www.nytimes.com/2017/08/02/upshot/the-great-political-divide-over-american-identity.html.
22. Qtd. in Osamudia James, "Trump Sees Black America as a Dystopian Hellhole: So Do Most White People," 26 August 2016. www.washingtonpost.com/posteverything/wp/2016/08/26/trump-sees-black-america-as-a-dystopian-hellhole-so-do-most-white-people/.
23. According to the U.S. Equal Employment Opportunity Commission, telling someone to "Go back where you came from" is illegal and a fire-able offense. www.eeoc.gov/eeoc/publications/immigrants-facts.cfm.
24. Vavreck.

Index

9/11 11, 13, 15, 20; and comedy, impact on 190–193; first responders 244; post- 64, 67–68, 186, 196, 198, 200–205, 264
1491s, The 71
1956–1957 Suez Crisis 49, 85
1964 Civil Rights Act 111, 208; *see also* civil rights movement
1965 Voting Rights Act 111, 208
1965 Watts riots 49
2011 American Jobs Act 226

Abbot, George 102
Abbott and Costello 36, 42, 140
Abbott, Bud *see* Abbott and Costello
ABC Network 163; *The Dana Carvey Show* 166–168; *Fridays* 142–143; *Politically Incorrect With Bill Maher* 67
ABC-Paramount Records 91
absurdist comedy 168, 205, 215
absurdity: and black humor 59; of Clinton White House 183; and Palin 13; and/of/in politics 47, 103, 117, 131–132; purposeful 241–248; and racism 39, 64; and/of Trump 81, 116, 182, 194, 232–243, 248, 250–252, 273; of war 103; of Watergate 117

absurdity and/in reality 12–14, 20, 84, 264; and Bush 196; and Clinton 183; and Palin 215; and satiric news 66–69; and Trump 182–183, 232–233, 236, 240, 251–252; and Watergate 117; and *What's Going on Here?* 53; *see also* reality and absurdity
Access Hollywood tape 232
Acosta, Jim 247
Addison, Joseph 25
Adsit, Scott 170–171
advocacy satire *see* satiric advocacy
Agnew, Spiro 123
Alexander, Andrew 141
Alk, Howard 82
Allen, Steve 46
Allen, Tim 167–168
All in the Family 64
Allman, Scott 170
Alternatino With Arturo Castro 70, 236
alternative comedy 169
"alternative facts" 6, 242
alt-right 65–66
American identity *see* national identity
Americanness 23; and blackness 27, 30, 36; in *The Contrast* (play) 25,

189; democratic ideals of 94; and the economy 35; of freedom of speech 191; and the frontier, idea of 186; and immigrants 37, 61; non- 47; paradoxes of 270; satire, importance to 270–271; and Twain 34; and vaudeville 36; and whiteness 231, 272–273; and Yankee character type 186, 190; *see also* national identity
Apprentice, The 231; *see also* Trump, Donald J.
Aristophanes 1
Arkin, Alan 83–84, 87
Armisen, Fred, as Obama 178, 217, 219–220, 223
Aronstein, AJ 192
Arsenio Hall Show, The 89, 158, 163, 174
Art of the Deal (Trump) 231
Atamanuik, Anthony 88, 254
Atlanta 270
authenticity *see* satiric authenticity
AV Club see Onion, The
"Axis of Evil" 192
Aykroyd, Dan 118, 123; "Bass-O-Matic" 128; as Carter 129–135, 141; as Dole 178

Baez, Joan 109
Baker, James 140
Baker, Russell 87
Baldwin, Alec, as Trump 1, 10, 125, 153, 204, 243, 249–252
Barnes, Clive 45
Barnum, P.T. 32
Baroness von Sketch Show 70
Barry, Dave 191
Barry, J.J. 109
Basie, Count 38
Baumgartner, Jody 16, 215, 264
Beard, Henry 58
Becker, Amy 245, 249
Bee, Samantha 69, 243, 245, 254
Belushi, John 18, 116–117, 129, 133
Bennett, Alan 50
Bennett, Beck 248
Benny, Jack 43
Ben Stiller Show, The 58
Berkowitz, Joe 248
Berman, Shelly 36, 48, 91
Bernstein, Carl 118

Between Two Ferns 210, 219
Beyoncé 4, 209
Bianculli, David 54, 109
Biden, Joe 68, 219, 236–237
bin Laden, Osama 191, 197, 201, 224
"birtherism" 209–210, 224, 226, 272
Birth of a Nation, The (Griffiths) 197
Black, Ashley Nicole 269
blackface 5, 11, 27, 36–37, 51, 64, 197; *see also* minstrelsy
Black-ish 270
Black Lady Sketch Show, A 70, 255, 269–270
Blair, Tony 68, 193
Bland, James 28
Blankfield, Mark 143
blank parody *see* parody
Blaustein, Barry 141–142
Bleyer, Archie 91
Bolke, Bradley 91
Booker, Bob 90
Boran, Arthur 89
Bowen, Roger 82–83
Brady, Wayne 194
Brecht, Bertolt 10; acting technique 203–204; Brechtian ideas and theory 16, 44, 82, 123–124, 243; and Ferrell's Bush 202; and Fey's Palin 215; "gestus" 174
British Satire Boom 52
Brossart, Naomi 90
Brown, Bobby 164
Brown, James 61
Brown, Michael (FEMA Director) 203
Browne, Charles Farrar 24, 32–33, 139
Bruce, Lenny 47–49, 57, 91, 97–98, 109
Brunson, Quinta 269
Bryan, William Jennings 31, 42
Buchwald, Art 12
Buckley, William F., Jr. 113
Buell, John 188
Bunch, Lonnie, III 238
Bunker, Archie (character) 65
Burnett, Carol 52, 54–57, 167–168
Bush, George H.W. 2, 3; Carvey's impression of 15, 19–20, 142, 149–153, 161, 172–173; and Clinton 158–162, 167; and Reagan 137–155; and *Saturday Night Live* 126; "thousand points of light" 153
Bush, George W. 2, 4, 10; and 9/11 67–68, 190–193; 2000 election 188–190; "Black

Bush" 64, 194–197; and Colbert 69; "Dubbya" 186–205; *MADtv* 197–198; presidency of 13, 182; *Robot Chicken* 198–199; and *Saturday Night Live* 178, 199–205; "Yankee" persona of 26

cacography 25, 27
Caesar, Sid 44
Caliendo, Frank 197–198, 200
Cambridge, Godfrey 2, 86
Candide 34
Carell, Steve 166
Carlin, George 48, 56–58, 109
Carlock, Robert 166
Carol Burnett Show, The 52, 55–57, 167
Carrey, Jim 149, 163, 165–166
Carson, Ben 68
Carson, Johnny 46–47, 115, 118, 122; political neutrality of 243; as presidential impersonator 139–140; and *Saturday Night Live* 132; see also *Tonight Show, The*
Carter, Bill 192
Carter, Graydon 190
Carter, Jimmy 15, 68, 122–135, 181; and Bush 149–150; and *Fridays* 146; and Iran hostage crisis of 1980 137; and *Saturday Night Live* 140, 143
Carter, John 40
Carter, Rosalyn 134, 176
Carter, Tron (character) 64
cartoons *see* political cartoons
Carver, Heather 122
Carvey, Dana 142, 270; as Church Lady 152, 167–168, 199; as George H.W. Bush 2–3, 15, 19, 149–153, 155, 172; as Hans from Hans and Franz 152, 168; as Perot 160–162; see also *Dana Carvey Show, The*
Carville, James 160
Casey, William 145
Castro, Arturo 70, 236
Castro, Fidel 82, 85, 87, 91
Cavalcade of Stars 44
Caufield, Rachel Paine 3
CBS 18, 53–54, 163; *Celebrity Talent Scouts* 88; and censorship 109; *The Ed Sullivan Show* 52–53; *Evening News* 212; and presidential impressions, banning of 89; *The State* 268; and Vietnam War 106
CBS Diversity Sketch Comedy Showcase 268

"CBS Evening News: Katie Couric Interviews Sarah Palin" sketch *see Saturday Night Live* (SNL)
censorship 41, 44, 48, 54–55; of Bruce 109; and free speech 58, 267; network 60, 63; and *Saturday Night Live* 141; and the Smothers Brothers 106–108
Central Park Five 273
Chaplin, Charlie 42
Chappaquiddick 58; *see also* Kennedy, Ted
Chappelle, Dave 11, 29, 194
Chappelle's Show 60, 62–64, 70; "Black Bush" 194–197; and *Key & Peele* 220–221
Charles, Larry 143
Chartoff, Melanie 146
Chase, Chevy 116–117, 133, 135, 153; *National Lampoon's Vacation* film series 57; as Reagan 143; *Saturday Night Live*, departure from 133; *see also* Ford, Gerald
Cheney, Dick 193, 201–202
Chesterton, G.K. 12
Chevy Chase Show 163
China 8, 111, 201, 237; trade war with 232–233
Chinyere, Oliver 267
Chitlin' Circuit 37–39, 74
Chonin, Neva 69
Chott, Bill 166
Chris Rock Show, The 169
Christie, Chris 68
civil rights movement 43, 48–49, 53, 55, 62, 101, 119; and the Kennedy administration 86; and Reagan 148
Civil War (American) 30–31, 102; reenactors 221
Cleese, John 9
Cleveland, Grover 42
Clinton, Hillary 16, 19, 159, 165, 254; and *The Daily Show* 68; as demon 167; as First Lady 175–180; and Gasteyer 177; and Hooks 176; and McKinnon 179–180, 243; misogyny directed toward 32, 175–177, 241, 249; and Poehler 178, 217; as presidential candidate 32, 178, 220, 240, 247, 253; and *Saturday Night Live* 252–253; as Senator 218; and Sullivan 166; and Trump 262

Clinton, William ("Bill") 158–183, 186; 1992 election 159–162; and Bush 198, 201; and cable television 187; and Carrey 163, 165; and *The Daily Show* 68; and Gore 188; and Hartman 12; and Hope 42; humor about 82; and *MADtv* 197; and Obama 209; and Sasso 166; and satire 110, 196; and *Saturday Night Live* 118, 126, 149, 162; sex scandal 13, 15, 80; and *The Tonight Show* 47
Close, Del 85, 117
CNN 47, 182, 241, 246–247, 264; Cuccinelli 236; Cuomo 242; Dale 241
Coates, Ta-Nehisi 272
Cochran, Johnny 13
Cohen, Leonard 217
Cohen, Michael 243
Colbert Report, The 5, 24, 68–69, 181–183, 187, 193
Colbert, Stephen 13, 24, 35, 69; on Bush 149, 194, 204–205; as "Colbert" 68; and Second City 166, 171
Colburn, Randall 169
Cold War 12–13; and Bush (H.W.) 149; and Clinton (Hillary) 178; and Johnson 105; and Kennedy 36, 81, 84, 87, 94, 101–103, 114; and Reagan 138–139, 146
Colgate Comedy Hour, The 43, 133, 167
Collins, Jackie 174
comedy: 1970s 57, 79; 1990s 192; absurdist 168; alternative 169; American 6, 23, 26–28, 30–40, 79; and American identity 58; black 38, 60, 197; and boomers 58–59, 170; British 50–51; and Bush 149; and Clinton 166; cynical turn in 98; diversity problem of 20, 220; and free speech 45; hipster 70; improvisational 45; and Kennedy 80–82, 87, 95, 97–98; liberal or conservative 16–20; male perspective of 164; outsider 58; physical 43; political 16, 109; and politics 41, 71; and power 197; power of 69; and the presidency 149; and race 49, 70, 194; satirical 155; stand-up 44, 47–48, 58, 70; and the state 127; surreal 70; and television 44, 46, 97; variety show 58; verbatim 14; visual 43; and Watergate 115, 117–119; *see also* sketch comedy

comedy albums 91, 103–104; "Cohen on the Telephone" sketch 36; *The First Family* (1962) 12, 87–98, 102–104; *Here Comes the Bird* 103; *I Am the President* (1969) 114; *Is It Something I Said?* (1975) 60; *LBJ in the Catskills* 103; *LBJ Menagerie* 103; *Meet the Great Society* 103; *The Missing White House Tapes* (1974) 116–117; and Nixon 110, 113–114; *Richard Nixon: A Fantasy* (1973) 114; *Richard Nixon Superstar* (1971) 114; and Watergate 115
Comedy Bang! Bang! 70
Comedy Cellar 173
Comedy Central: *Chappelle's Show* 64; *Inside Amy Schumer* 70, 269; *Key & Peele* 220, 222, 269; *Politically Incorrect With Bill Maher* 67; *The President Show* 254; *That's My Bush!* 191
Comey, James 250
Committee, The 103, 105–106, 110
"compassionate conservativism" 186, 205
Compass Players, The 9–10, 44–46, 79, 82–83, 103
Confederacy/Confederates 30, 221
conspiracy/conspiracy theories 110, 148, 225–226, 232
Conway, Kellyanne 6, 242–243, 250, 254
Conway, Tim 55
Coolidge, Calvin 40, 42, 89, 94
Cook, Peter 50, 82
corruption 27, 50; and Nixon 123; political 2, 31, 34, 143; and *The Simpsons* 65; and *South Park* 66; and Trump 242
Cosby, Bill 59, 62, 265
"Cosby Obama" 218
Cosby Show, The 218
Costello, Lou *see* Abbott and Costello
Coullet, Rhonda 116–117
Coulter, Ann 67, 247
Couric, Katie 13–14, 212–215
Cronkite, Walter 98, 133
Cross, David 168
Crystal, Billy 142
Cuban Missile Crisis 85, 91, 103
Cuccinelli, Ken 236
Cull, Nicholas 92
culture wars 186
Cuomo, Chris 242

Curtin, Jane 18, 55, 176
Cusack, Joan 142
c-word 245; *see also* Bee, Samantha

Dagnes, Alison 180
Daily Show, The 2, 13, 67–69; and 9/11, 191, 193; and Bush 196; and liberals 187; and Obama 224; Sahl's influence on 48; and Stewart 182; and Trump 241, 248, 251
Dale, Daniel 241
Damon, Matt 243–244
"Dana Carvey effect" 173
Dana Carvey Show, The 62, 166–170, 177
Dance of the Comedians see Robinson, Peter M.
Daniels, Stormy 232
Dante Alighieri 1
Darden, Severn 83–84
Darling, Joan 83, 86
David, Larry 143, 147
"David S. Pumpkins" 4; *see also* Hanks, Tom
Davis, Jefferson 30
Davis, Tom 118, 141
Day, Amber 17
Democratic National Committee (DNC) 42; 1972 break-in 111; and Clinton (Hillary) 178; and Kennedy 93; and Trump 231–232
Democratic National Convention 108, 195
De Niro, Robert 243
Dennis, Gabrielle 269
Denny, Reginald 163
DeVos, Betsy 243
Dole, Bob 159, 176
Dooley *see* Mr. Dooley
Doud, Earle 90
Douglas, Michael (writer) 126
Douglass, Frederick 27
Doumanian, Jean 61, 141, 143
Douthat, Ross 244–245
Downey, Jim 141, 154, 190, 209
Downey, Robert, Jr. 142
Dratch, Rachel 9, 170, 244
Dr. Strangelove 3
Dubbya *see* Bush, George W.
DuBois, W.E.B. 10, 37
Dudley, Sherman 39, 50
Dukakis, Michael 149
Duncan, Andrew 45, 82, 84
Dunne, Peter Finely 24, 35–36

Ebersol, Dick 61, 141–143
Edgar, Amanda Nell 163
Edison, Thomas 42
Ed Sullivan Show, The 43, 91, 97
Edwards, Erica R. 197, 208
Eisenhower, Dwight D. 43, 52, 79, 87, 91
Eisenhower, Mamie 39
Ellison, Ralph 197
Erdman, Mollie 212
Eric Andre Show, The 70
Ernie Kovacs Show, The 44

Fahrenheit 9/11 193
"fairness doctrine" 181
"fake news" 59, 69, 251–252
Fallon, Jimmy 9; and Obama 210; and Trump 47, 242–243
FDR *see* Roosevelt, Franklin Delano (FDR)
Federal Communications Commission (FCC) 92, 113, 130, 181, 246
Feiffer, Jules 46, 79, 83, 140
Ferguson, Andrew 57
Fern, Fanny 31–32, 222, 271; columns 266; "Male Criticism on Ladies' Books" 70
Ferrell, Will: as Bush (George W.) 10, 188–190, 197, 199–205; "Short Shorts for the USA" skit 192; *You're Welcome America* 199, 270
Fetchit, Stepin 38
Fey, Tina 2, 10, 13–14; Fern's influence on 32, 222, 271; as Palin 123, 178–179, 212–218, 264; and *Saturday Night Live* 266; and Second City 171; *see also* Palin, Sarah
Fineman, Chloe 267
First Family, The (1962) *see* comedy albums; Meader, Vaughn
Flicker, Ted 45, 83, 85–86
Flip Wilson Show, The 56–57, 265; *see also* Wilson, Flip
Flowers, Gennifer 158, 164, 165
Fonda, Henry 53
Ford, Betty 176
Ford, Gerald 15–16; Belushi as 117; Browne as 32; Chase as 2, 4, 10, 12, 24, 32, 59, 122–132, 143, 149–153, 199–200, 216; and *Saturday Night Live* 118, 120–129, 140, 175, 190
Forte, Will 199

Foster, George 90
Fox & Friends 182
Fox, Jesse David 234, 252
Fox Network 63, 163, 165; sketch shows 166
Fox News 68, 159, 180–182, 187, 264; and Obama 226; and presidency, defense of 205; rise of 190; and Trump 182, 251
Foxx, Jamie 139
Foxx, Redd 56, 62
Franken, Al 118, 126–127, 133, 141, 160
Franklin, Benjamin 1, 23, 33, 34, 39, 42, 48; as "American voice" 60, 262; as Poor Richard ("Richard Saunders") 24–25
freedom of speech 31, 33, 41, 45, 94, 191, 252, 267
freedom of the press 252
Freeman, Al 86
Fresh Off the Boat 270
Freud, Sigmund 5
Friar's Club 40
Fridays 62, 142–146
Frost, David 50, 53, 104
Frye, David, as Nixon 113–115
Full Frontal With Samantha Bee 69, 210, 245, 251
Funny or Die 70

Gaines, William 63
Galifianakis, Zach 210
Gallagher, Thomas 251
Galliver, Brian 211
Garson, Barbara 105
Gasteyer, Ana 177
gay and lesbian themes and issues: "Ambiguously Gay Duo" 168; *The Big Gay Sketch Show* 268; comedians 18, 212; marriage 186, 195
GayCo 71, 269
Gay, John 25
Gelb, Arthur 84
George III 273
Gianas, Tom 170
Gillis, Shane 18–19, 267
Gilmore, John 5, 17
Gingrich, Newt 68, 159
Giuliani, Rudy 190–191, 237, 243
Glaser, Jon 166, 170
Glaser, Nikki 235
Glover, Donald 220

Goldwater, Barry 54, 82, 87, 90, 104
Gore, Al 68, 165, 199; Hammond as 2, 188–190, 216
Graham, Lindsey 68, 243
Grant, Bob 181
Grant, Ulysses S. 31, 96
Gray, Herman 6
Gray, Jonathan 4
Gray, J.W. 32
"Great American Joke, The" 23, 25; and African Americans 59, 61; and female satirists 32; and Johnson 104; and Obama 219; tensions inherent in 270; and Twain 34
Green, Seth 198
Greene, Hugh (Sir) 50
Greenland 81, 233
Gregory, Dick 29, 47–49, 59–61
Grier, David Alan 163
Griffin, Kathy 254
Griffiths, D.W. 197
Groundlings 267
Grynbaum, Michael M. 270
Gulliver's Travels 3, 17, 34; *see also* Swift, Jonathan

Haberman, Maggie 247
Hackman, Gene 53
Haddish, Tiffany 268
Hagarty, James 91
Hakola, Outi 252
Hall, Arsenio *see Arsenio Hall Show, The*
Hall, Brad 142
Hall, Daheli 220
Hammond, Darrell: as Bush 199; as Cheney 202; as Clinton (Bill) 162, 172–175, 177; as Gore 2, 188–190, 216; as Nixon 118
Hanks, Colin 221
Hanks, Tom 7
Hannity, Sean 181–182
Hansberry, Lorraine 86
Harding, Warren 42
Harris, Aisha 224
Harris, Barbara 82, 85
Harris, David 109
Harrison, George 108
Hartman, Phil 142; as Clinton (Bill) 12, 161, 172–174, 176; as Kennedy (Ted) 154; as Reagan 143–145, 148

Hayman, Joe 36
HBO: *A Black Lady Sketch Show* 255; *The Dana Carvey Show* 166, 168; *Mr. Show* 63, 168; *Real Time With Bill Maher* 67
Helbig, Jack 170
Henry, Buck 126
Herblock (Herbert Block) 30, 111
Hertzberg, Hedrick 133
Hill, Anita 154
Hilton, Elena 226
Hinckley, John 143
Hitler, Adolf 87, 235
Hodge, Francis 26
Hoffman, Abbie 110
Hoffman, Robert 58
Holland, Tony 87
Honeymooners, The 44
Hooks, Jan 176
Hooper, Johnson Jones 26
Hope, Bob 39–42, 47, 132
Hope, Boots 38
Horace 1, 3
Horner, William 122
Horton, Willie 150
Hughes, William 152
Human Giant 70
Humphrey, Hubert 84, 107, 113
Hussein, Saddam 153, 198

impersonation 1, 19, 29, 50; Aykroyd as Carter 129–130; Aykroyd as Nixon 118; Baldwin as Trump 243, 250; Caliendo as Bush 197; Carrey as Clinton 163; Carvey as Bush 153, 173; Chappelle as Bush 196; Chase as Ford 123; Chase as Reagan 143; Cook as Macmillan 50; Ferrell as Bush 199–200; Fey as Palin 215; Frye as Nixon 113–115; Kennedy's use of 92; Meader as Kennedy 88–97, 102, 114, 263, 265; Morris as Bush 149; of Nixon 113–114; presidential 88, 91, 124, 139; Rogers as Coolidge 89; and *Saturday Night Live* 135, 172; *see also comedians and politicians by name*
impressionists 113–114, 139, 173, 188
Ingraham, Laura 243
In Living Color 6, 60, 62–63, 70, 149, 163–166
Inside Amy Schumer 69–70, 269

Iran 8, 178, 201; hostage crisis 137, 141, 143
Iran-Contra affair 5, 138–139, 144–145, 154, 175
Iraq 4, 138, 194–201; and 9/11 198
Iraq War 200, 203–204
irony 3–4, 6; failure of 190–193, 241
Irony and Outrage (Young) 181
I Think You Should Leave 70, 255

Jackie Gleason Show, The 44
Jackson, Andrew 26, 30, 73, 94
Jane the Virgin 270
Jay-Z 209
Jefferson, Thomas 30
JFK *see* Kennedy, John F.
Jimmy Kimmel Live 210; *see also* Kimmel, Jimmy
Johansson, Scarlett 243
John Birch Society 54
Johnson, Dwayne ("The Rock") 219
Johnson, Lady Bird 104; as Lady MacBird 105
Johnson, Lyndon Baines (LBJ) 15, 33, 39, 54, 86, 101–119; Frye as 113; and Goldwater 130; and humor 140; *see also* comedy albums; Smothers Brothers
joke candidates for the presidency 107
jokes 3–6, 8; and Bush 199; and Carson 47; censorship of 108–109; and Clinton (Bill) 158–159, 165–166, 169, 175, 183; and Clinton (Hillary) 166–167; and conservatism 180; and Cook 50; and democracy 33; exposure to 16; and Ford 122, 124, 126, 128–129, 131; and Gregory 49; and Hope 41–42; and Johnson 102; and Kennedy 80–84, 90–91, 97; about Lewinsky 158, 169, 193; about marginalized groups 180; in minstrelsy 17, 28, 35–36; and Nixon 102, 110, 112–118; and Noah 68; and Obama 210; and partisanship 47; and Perot 161; and politics and power 19, 39–41, 47, 191; and Pryor 59–60; and/about race 49, 60, 197, 222; and Reagan 138–140, 144, 146, 148–149; and Rogers 40, 42, 94; and Roosevelt 89–90; and Sahl 48, 94; about sexual harassment 154; about Soviet Union 138; and Stewart 68; and Trump 231–239, 242, 245, 251, 253–255; and Wolf 247; *see also* "Great American Joke, The"

Jolovitz, Jenna 170
Jones, Geraldine (character) 56
Jones, Irving 196
Jones, Jeffrey P. 4, 123–124, 153
Jones, Leslie 253
Jones, Paula 158–159, 174
Jones, Velvet (character) 61
Jortner, Maura 25
Jung, E. Alex 221
Juvenal/Juvenalian 3, 4, 71, 264

Kantor, Michael 43, 55
Kaufman, Andy 57–58
Kaufman, Charlie 166
Kaufman, Gerald 51
Kavanaugh, Brett 243–244
Kazurinsky, Tim 141
Keeping Up With the Kardashians 14
Kennedy, Caroline 94–95
Kennedy, Jackie 84, 86, 90, 94–96
Kennedy, John F. 20, 79–98: affairs of 32, 177; assassination of 53, 97–98, 101–102, 105; and Camelot 15; and Clinton 158, 166; humor of 81, 262; image control by 30; impressions of 14; and Johnson 104–105; and Khrushchev 95; and Meader 97, 114, 124, 153; and Nixon 111; and Obama 210; and Reagan 139, 146; and Sahl 48; and satirists 36, 53, 71; and Second City 98; and television 232; *see also* Cuban Missile Crisis
Kennedy, John John 94, 96
"Kennedy-Khrushchev Press Conference" 83–84, 263
Kennedy, Robert 92, 107
Kennedy, Ted 58
Kenney, Doug 58
Kercher, Stephen 44–45, 53, 79, 103
Kerry, John 187, 193, 216
Kersands, Billy 28, 197
Key & Peele 19, 36, 60, 69–71; and Obama 195, 209, 218, 220–226
Key and Peele (comedy duo) 11, 32, 195, 220–221
Key, Keegan-Michael 63, 70, 210, 220, 223
Khrushchev, Nikita 82–84, 87, 91, 93, 95, 263
Kids in the Hall, The 62, 162
Kilduff, Malcolm M. 92
Killam, Taran 249

Kimmel, Jimmy 47, 210, 243, 245
King, Rodney 13, 163
Kissinger, Henry 118
KKK 54, 253
Klepper, Jordan 241
Klobuchar, Amy 244
Koblin, John 270
Koch, Stephen 3
Kopechne, Mary Jo 58
Korman, Harvey 55
Kornhaber, Spencer 7
Koterba, Ed 89
Kovacs, Ernie 44, 46, 167
Kroll Show, The 70
Kruse, Kevin 181

Lady Bird Johnson *see* Johnson, Lady Bird
Las Culturistas 267
Lask, Thomas 93
Last Week Tonight With John Oliver 69, 245, 251
Late Show with Joan Rivers, The 163
Late Show With Stephen Colbert, The 47, 210
Laugh-In 55–56, 101, 112–113
Laurel and Hardy 42
Lauterback, Preston 39
Lawrence, Vicki 55
Lazarus, Emma 236
lazzi 8–9
LBJ *see* Johnson, Lyndon Baines (LBJ)
Leblanc, Anthony 212
LeCompte, Elizabeth 193
Lehner, Jim 90–91
Lemmings 58, 116
Leno, Jay 47
Letterman, David 47, 166
Levin, Lawrence 6
Lewinsky, Monica 13, 82, 158–160, 174, 177, 193
Lewis, Jerry 167
Libera, Anne 16
"liberal bias" 19
liberalism 54, 87; 1960s 87; in comedy 81; corporate 45; failure of 147; Great Society 53
libertarianism 65–66
Limbaugh, Rush 181–182
Lincoln, Abraham 19, 26, 30–33, 94, 118, 198
Little, Rich 114, 139

Living Premise, The 86
Lopez, John 154, 174, 200, 216
Los Angeles riots 13, 160, 163
Lott, Eric 197
Louis C.K. 166, 267
Louis-Dreyfus, Julia 18
Lovitz, Jon 145, 149
Lowry, Brian 268

Mabley, Jackie ("Moms") 39
MacBird! 105
MacFarlane, Seth 234
Macmillan affair 86
Macmillan, Harold 50–51, 82, 86
MacMillan, Norma 91
Maher, Bill 67
Mailer, Norman 104
Maisel, Remy 69, 264
"Make America Great Again" 145–146, 231, 272
Markham, David ("Pigmeat") 38
Martel, Jay 224, 236
Martin, Dean 167
Martin, Dick 55, 112; *see also* Rowan and Martin
Martin, Millicent 50
Martin, Shabazz K. (character) 61
Martin, Steve 57–58
Marx Brothers 42
Marx, Groucho 84
Marxism 226
Marx, Nick 17
*M*A*S*H* 64
Maslon, Laurence 43, 55
May, Elaine 6, 52–53, 91
McCain, John 212, 214–215, 218
McCann, Chuck 90–91
McCarthy, Joseph 43, 87, 237
McCarthy, Melissa 243–244
McClennen, Sophia 69, 154
McConaughey, Matthew 217
McConnell, Mitch 209
McDaniel, Hattie 38
McDonald's 12, 172–173, 198
McEnany, Kayleigh 242
McFadden, Bob 91
McGovern, George 116
McGrath, Douglas 141
McKay, Adam 170–171, 202

McKinley, William 31, 42
McKinney, Chris 166
McKinnon, Kate 179–180, 243, 250
McMahon, Ed 254
McSweeney's 121, 239–241
Meader, Vaughn: Chase compared to 127; and *The First Family* 12, 102, 118, 264; as Kennedy 88–97, 102, 114, 263, 265; and Morris 149
Meadows, Audrey 104
memes 107, 210, 226, 237, 264
Meredith Corp. v. FCC 181
#MeToo movement 267
Mexico 152, 231–232, 248
Meyers, Seth 162, 254–255
Michaels, Lorne 1, 19, 125; and Armisen 217, 220; and Aykroyd 130; on Bush 189; and Carvey 149; on Chase 123; on Ford 125, 127; and Giuliani 191; and Obama 218; and Perot 160; and *Saturday Night Live* 61, 132, 141–143
Miller, Ira 109
Miller, James Andrew 135
Miller, Jonathan 50
Miller, Stephen 8
minstrelsy 5, 11, 18; *The Black and White Minstrel Show* 51; characters 61; minstrel show 27–30, 35–36, 57, 197; and racism 273; songs 196; stereotypes 37–38, 221–222
misogyny 2; and Clinton (Hillary) 32, 175–177, 241; in comedy 266; and Schumer 70
Model Majority 71
Mondale, Walter 133, 144
Monty Python 9, 167, 169
Moore, Dudley 50
Moore, Michael 193
Moreland, Mantan 38
Moreschi, Opus 210
Morgan, Edmund 24
Morgan, Heather 166–167
Morgan, Henry 53
Morgan, Winnifred 25
Morris, Brad 212
Morris, Garrett 61
Morris, Jim 139, 149
Morris, Jonathan 215
Moses (prophet) 108–109
Mr. Dooley 24, 35–37

Mr. Show 63, 171
MTV 18, 164, 268
Mueller Report 226, 237, 240, 242
Mueller, Robert 226, 243
Murphy, Dean 91
Murphy, Eddie 61, 142
Myerson, Alan 103, 105, 109

Nachman, Gerald 49
Najera, Rick 268
Nast, Thomas 30–31, 73
national debt 160–162
national discourse and destiny 20
national identity 1–2; 1960s and 1970s 52; and African Americans 63; and comedy 58; early American 23, 25–26; and folksiness 212; and minstrelsy 30; and Palin 212; and race 272–273; and satire 270–271; and social justice 271; and women 32; *see also* race
nationalism *see* white nationalism
National Lampoon 46, 50, 57–58, 115, 117, 127, 142
National Lampoon Encyclopedia of Humor 58
National Lampoon Radio Hour, The 58, 116
National Oceanic and Atmospheric Administration (NOAA) 239
national security 88, 213, 238
National Weather Service 239
Native American comedians 71
Nero, Dom 255
Nessen, Ron 126–129, 133
Nesteroff, Kliph 81
Netflix 254–255
Newhart, Bob 36, 46, 91
Newman, Laraine 128
Nichols and May 52, 91
Nichols, Mike 52–53, 91
Nicholson, Jack 113
Nixon, Larry 89
Nixon, Richard 4, 15–16, 31, 82, 85; and censorship 54; David as 147; "Dick" 118; "enemies list" 33; and *The First Family* 181; Ford pardoning of 122–123, 132; and Frost 50; and humor 140; impersonations of 139; and Kennedy 89, 130; and *Laugh-In* 55, 112–113; and LBJ 102–119; and Paar 46, 89; in political cartoons 30; and Reagan 146; resignation of 135; scandal 149, 209; and *The Smothers Brothers Comedy Hour* 54; "Sock it to me" 55, 112–113; *see also* Frye, David, as Nixon; Watergate
Noah, Trevor 68
North American Free Trade Agreement (NAFTA) 149, 160
Northerners 27, 30
North, Oliver 138
North Star, The 27
nostalgia 137, 145–146, 221
Not Ready for Prime-Time Players 123
n-word 221; *see also* Key and Peele (comedy duo)

Obama, Barack 208–226; 2008 election 212–216; *Chappelle's Show* 195–196; and *The Daily Show* 68; and election of 2, 67, 69; and *Key & Peele* 19, 32, 36, 70, 220–226; and "Luther the Anger Translator" 70, 195, 210, 220, 223–226; memes 226, 210, 264; "post-racial" mythology of 20; racist attacks against 29; "The Rock Obama" 219; satires of 15; and *Saturday Night Live* 17, 125, 127, 178, 216–220; and Trump 8
Obamacare 208–209, 231, 245, 250
Obama, Michelle 68, 211; racist attacks against 29, 39, 226; and *Saturday Night Live* 216, 218; White House garden 8
Obeidallah, Dean 234
O'Brien, Conan 47
Ocasio-Cortez, Alexandria 32, 255
Odenkirk, Bob 166, 168
O'Donnell, Kenneth P. 92
O'Donnell, Rosie 262
Oliphant, Patrick 30
Oliver, John 10, 69, 180, 192, 237, 243–247
Omar, Ilhan 255
Omarosa 248
Onion, The 3, 8, 46, 50, 66; and 9/11 191–192; *AV Club* 66; and Bush 193–194; and Obama 211; and Trump 233, 238–240
Orben, Robert 125
O'Reilly, Bill 68, 181
Orwell, George 3

Paar, Jack 46, 89
Paley, William 106
Palin, Michael 50
Palin, Sarah 16; absurdity and 116; Couric's interview with 14, 213–215; Fey as 2, 10, 13, 123, 178–179, 212–216, 218, 264
Parker, Nicole 220
Parker, Trey 66
Parnell, Chris 199
parody: of *Altered States* 145; blank 7–8; *Carol Burnett Show*, use of 55; of Carter 132; definition of 6–8; and *MADtv* 220; *National Lampoon*, use of 57–58, 115; of *Rocky Horror Picture Show* 146; of *Schoolhouse Rock!* 219; *Smothers Brothers Comedy Hour*, use of 54; Trump as 92, 232–241
Parton, Sara Willis 31; *see also* Fern, Fanny
Patinkin, Sheldon 11, 53, 109–110, 117
Paul, Rand 68
Paulsen, Pat 107
Peele, Jordan 63, 70, 220, 223
Peisner, David 62
Pence, Mike 8, 67, 257, 244, 254
Perot, Ross 160–162
Perrin, Dennis 143
Perry, Tyler 7
personality-policy spectrum 14–15
Pharoah, Jay 216, 218–219, 223
Pike, John 18
Piñata Full of Bees 170–171; *see also* Second City, The
Piscopo, Joe 118, 143
Playboy Club 49
Playboy magazine, Carter's interview in 131–132
Poehler, Amy 171, 178
political cartoons 30–31, 45, 54, 94, 111; and Bush 193; *Doonesbury* 153; and Watergate 115
Politically Incorrect With Bill Maher 67
Poor Richard's Almanack (Franklin) 24; *see also* Franklin, Benjamin
Pope, Elaine 143
Portlandia 70
Posch, Brooke 269
"post-racial" 20, 69, 208–209
Powell, Colin 201
Premise, the 81–87, 103

President Show, The 254
Pressley, Ayanna 255
Private Eye (newspaper) 50
Pryor, Richard 49, 58
Putin, Vladimir 213, 232

Quaid, Randy 143

race: and American identity 63, 194–197; comedic critiques of 39, 48, 60–61, 63–65, 70; and culture 163, 195; and normalcy 222; politics of 69; white 28, 30
race, class, and gender 39, 52
race problem *see* Saturday Night Live (SNL)
racism 2; absurdity of 103; in comedy 267; learned nature of 194; and Obama 57, 208–209, 226; satirical takes on 51, 64, 221, 263; and the South 221; systemic 23, 196; of Trump 238, 248; *see also* "birtherism"
radio 42–44, 57, 88; AM 180; and Booker 90; call-in 133; early 36; and Hope 41; and Kennedy 90–92; *The National Lampoon Radio Hour* 58, 116; and Reagan 137; and Rogers 40, 89, 94; and Roosevelt 40; talk 159, 181–182
Radner, Gilda 129, 176
Ramis, Harold 110
Reagan, Michael 146
Reagan, Nancy 146, 148, 176
Reagan, Ron (son of Ronald) 146
Reagan, Ronald 15, 19, 137–149, 159, 170; and conservative talk radio 181; and *The Flip Wilson Show* 56; minstrel stereotypes, invocation of 29; and Obama 205, 210, 212; and *Saturday Night Live* 61; speeches of 232; "Star Wars" missile defense plan 67
reality and absurdity 232, 236; parameters of 11–14
reality TV 14, 140, 183, 231–232, 236, 248, 251
Real Time With Bill Maher 67
Red Scare 87
Red Skelton Show, The 44
Reid, Elliot 53
Reston, James 89
Rice, Condoleezza 202
Richard Pryor Show, The 167

Richards, Michael 143
Rihanna 220
Rivers, Joan 32, 163
Robinson, Peter M. 24, 40, 92, 102, 139
Robinson, Tim 255
Rock, Chris 169, 211, 253
Rockefeller, Nelson 54
Rocket, Charles 143
"Rock Obama, The" *see* Obama, Barack
Rocky Horror Picture Show 146–147
Rogers, Katie 238
Rogers, Will 32, 39–42, 43; as Coolidge 89, 94; and Roosevelt (Franklin) 26, 32, 52, 91, 127; and Sahl 47
Romney, Mitt 219
Ronnie & Nancy Show 148
Roosevelt, Franklin Delano (FDR) 19, 26, 43, 52, 102, 127; "Fireside Chats" 34, 94, 232; and Hope 42; and Reagan 137, 139; and Rogers 32, 40–41, 89, 91
Roosevelt, Theodore (TR) 35–36, 39–40, 42, 94, 160
Rosato, Tony 118
Rosenblatt, Roger 191–192
Rosenwald, Brian 182
Ross, Wilbur 243
Rowan & Martin's Laugh-In see Laugh-In
Rowan and Martin 112
Rowan, Dan 55, 112
Rubin, Louis, Jr. 23
Rudolph, Maya 202
Ruffin, Amber 211
Ryder, Winona 9

Sahl, Mort 32, 48
Sahlins, Bernie 141
Sanders, Bernie 179, 253
Sanders, Sarah Huckabee 247–248
Sandinistas 138
Sands, Diana 86
Sanford and Son 64
Sasso, Will 166, 197
satire 11–13; anger-based 110, 148, 224, 235, 245–246; changing face of 265–270; conservative 180–181; definition of 3–6; Juvenalian 4; liberal 181; as normalizer 14, 16; personality-based 13, 172; political 103, 119, 180; power of 48; as reality 66; safe 154–155; sitcom 64–66;

social 54, 83, 103, 163; and the state 119, 270–274
satiric advocacy 5, 10, 14, 69, 246, 255, 264–265, 273
satiric authenticity 5, 14, 69, 110, 241–248, 255, 264–265, 273
satiric news 66–69
Saturday Night Live (SNL) 4, 8, 10–12, 14; audiences 58–59; and Carter 129–130, 133–135; "CBS Evening News: Katie Couric Interviews Sarah Palin" sketch 13; faux presidential debates 130–132; and Ford 118, 122–129, 140, 175, 190; race problem 216–220; sketch TV, challenges to dominance of 62–64; and Trump 107; "Weekend Update" 11, 124, 127–129, 131–133, 141; and whiteness, privileging of 17–19
Saunders, Richard *see* Franklin, Benjamin
scandals: Bush's lack of 149; and Clinton 158, 173–175; corruption 31; Lewinsky 13, 158–159, 177; Obama's lack of 209, 226; sex 15, 80, 94; and Trump 226, 232, 240–242, 248, 252; *see also* Watergate
Schlatter, George 55, 112
Schlesinger, Arthur, Jr. 79, 92
Schumer, Amy 11, 32, 69–71
Scruton, Roger 27
Second City, The 9–11, 45–46, 52–53, 211; in the 1980s 170; 1990s rebirth of 163, 170; *America: All Better!* 212; "Between Barack and a Hard Place" 211; and The Committee 103; and "consensus culture" 79; and the f-word 98; and Johnson 103–106, 109; and Kennedy 115; *The Next Generation* 110; *Piñata Full of Bees* 170–171; *A Plague on Both Your Houses* 109; and the Premise 81–87; and Reagan 140; and *Saturday Night Live* 141–142; *SCTV* 62; and Watergate 117
Second Industrial Revolution 35
Seeger, Pete 106
Seinfeld 13
Seinfeld, Jerry 45, 67
Sellers, Peter 130
Sessions, Jeff 243
Sharpie-gate 14, 239–240
Shearer, Harry 143
Shephard, David 44

Sheridan, Phil (General) 31
Sherman's Showcase 270
Short, Martin 142
Shriver, Lionel 211
Shuster, Rosie 127
Simpson, O.J. 13
Simpsons, The 3, 64–66, 193
sitcom satire *see* satire
Skelton, Red 44
sketch comedy 2–5; and Americanness 71; apolitical 56; black 62–64, 208; British 148; and Bush 187, 198, 201, 203, 205; and Clinton (Bill) 158–166, 172, 174, 183; and Clinton (Hillary) 176; definition of 8–11; and diversity 62–64, 70–71; early American 52–61; Ford 123–125; and Gore 189; male perspective of 177; and national malaise 135; new wave 170; and Nixon 122; and Obama 208–209, 217–225; offbeat 172; and Palin 212, 215–216; and parody 7; performance 10; political 23, 103, 129, 133, 154; about presidents and the presidency 4, 20, 124, 135, 140, 153, 177–183; and radio 42; revue 9; roots of 10; and satire 7, 13, 54–55, 240; satiric 196; show 11; and social activism 106; and star system 133; subversive 83; timing, importance of 140; traditional 169; and Trump 233–236, 243–245, 248, 250, 252–255; *see also* Second City, The
sketch comedy and television 14, 17, 43–44, 46–71; in 1960s and 1970s 57, 98; flops 167; Fox's entry into 163; growth of 158; late-night 46–47; mixed format 67; non-network 64, 168; and *SCTV* 141; tensions between 142; *see also* Saturday Night Live (SNL)
slavery 23; and Huck Finn 34; and stereotypes 27, 29
Smigel, Robert 166, 168
Smith, Bessie 38
Smith, Seba 24, 26
Smothers Brothers 33, 55, 57
Smothers Brothers Comedy Hour, The 31, 51–56, 106–110, 127, 263
Smothers, Dick 54, 109
Smothers, Tom (Tommy) 54, 107, 109, 112
"Sock it to me" *see* Nixon, Richard
Souls of Black Folk, The (DuBois) 10

South Park 64–66, 117, 192–193, 254
South/Southerners 27, 30–31, 36, 39, 49; Clinton 159, 174; Deep 111; drawl 130, 158, 173; Old 51; Senators from 54; "way of life" 221
Spicer, Sean 6, 241–244
Spolin, Viola 44
Stage Yankee 25–28, 32, 34, 39; Bush as 189, 201; Clinton as 165
Stahl, Lesley 144
Stamatopoulos, Dino 166
State, The 18, 268
Steinberg, David 108
Steinmetz, Johanna 128
Stern, Howard 12
Stevenson, Adlai 85, 103
Stewart, Jon 50, 67–69, 243; on 9/11 193; and Bush 204–205, 242; and CNN 182; and liberals 180; and satire, defense of 191
Stewart, Patrick 144
Stewart, Potter 3
Stockdale, James (Admiral) 161
Stone, Matt 65–66
Stone, Oliver 193
Stott, Andrew 3
Stuckey, Mary 1
Sudeikis, Jason 199, 219
Suez Crisis *see* 1956–1957 Suez Crisis
Sullivan, Andrew 43
Sullivan, Ed 43, 46, 52–53
Sullivan, Nicole 166
Swift, Jonathan 1, 12, 17, 23–24
Sykes, Wanda 235, 243
Sypher, Wylie 16

talk radio *see* radio
Tallboyz 71
Taormina, Latifah 103
Tartikoff, Brandon 142
Taylor, Clarice 39
television *see* reality TV; sketch comedy and television
Temple, Shirley 55
Test, George A. 4
That Was the Week That Was (TW3) 50–56, 98, 104
Theatre Owners Booking Association (TOBA) 37–39
The Committee *see* Committee, The

Thede, Robin 269
Thomas, Clarence 12, 154
Thomas, Norman 104
Thompson, Ethan 4
Thompson, Kenan 7
Three Stooges, The 42
Thurber, James 11
Tlaib, Rashida 255
Tonight Show, The 2, 47, 112, 115, 140, 243; *see also* Carson, Johnny
Tonight Show With Jimmy Fallon, The 210, 242
Tonight Starring Jack Paar 89
Tonight Starring Steve Allen 46
Tracey Ullman Show, The 65
Trebek, Alex 7
Tripp, Linda 158–159, 174
Trudeau, Gary 153
Trump, Donald J. 1–2, 4, 6–12, 14–17, 20, 231–255; and absurdity 81, 116; and America as reality TV 140; Americanness, definition of 273; anti-intellectualism of 26; and Atamanuik 88; and Clinton (Bill) 32, 80; comedians, fear of 33; and *The Daily Show* 68–69; and Fallon 47; and Greenland, attempt to buy 81; image, control of 30; and immigrants 23; and parody 92; and satire 42, 71, 85, 110; and *Saturday Night Live* 31, 59, 107, 125–126; and *South Park* 66, 117; and Twain 34–35; *see also* Baldwin, Alec, as Trump
Trump Foundation 240
Trump, Ivanka 240, 243, 245
Trump, Melania 254
Trump voters 241, 253, 272
Tucker, Ken 118
Turturro, John 118
TW3 *see That Was the Week That Was* (TW3)
Twain, Mark 1, 34–35, 39, 42, 48
Tweed, William "Boss" 31
Tyler, Royall 25

Upright Citizens Brigade 62
Upright Citizens Brigade (improv theater) 267

Van Dyke, Dick 55
vaudeville 35–37; and African-Americans 61; and Hope 41; and *Laugh-In* 55; and radio 42, 44; white 38; and Wilson 40

Vietnam 84, 152; Vietnamization 111
Vietnam War 101–102, 111, 119, 126, 165; and *The Carol Burnett Show* 56; failures of 137, 148; Kerry's service during 186
Vietnam War, comedy sketches about 11, 15, 16, 49; by The Committee 103, 106; satire 118; by Second City 82, 84, 105, 109; by *The Smothers Brothers Comedy Hour* 54
Voltaire 1, 23

Waggoner, Lyle 55
Waisanen, Don 244
Walker, George 37–39
Wallace, George 107, 111
Wallace, Nicole 238
Walters, Barbara 176
Walth, Natasha 215
Wan, William 114
Ward, Artemis (character) 24, 32
Ward, Stuart 50
Warren, Elizabeth 32, 243
Washington, Booker T. 36
Washington, D.C. 41, 84–85, 165, 181; football team mascot 269
Washington, George 1, 25, 30, 125, 198
Washington, Kerry 216
Washington Post (newspaper) 12, 60, 241
Wasson, Sam 44
Watergate 12, 15, 56, 102, 135, 137, 154, 237; cartoons 111; and comedy, impact on 115–119; and Ford 124–126; and Reagan 146, 148; and the state, distrust in 127, 247, 263; tapes 112; *see also* Nixon, Richard
Wayans, Damon 63
Wayans, Marlon 63
Wayne, John 150
"Weekend Update" *see Saturday Night Live* (SNL)
Weird Al 7
Welles, Orson 92
What's Going on Here? 53
white America 11
White House Correspondents Dinner 246
white nationalism 232, 252
whiteness: of America 209, 231, 272; duality of 222; normalcy of 18, 222; of *Saturday Night Live* 17, 217, 265

White, Walter (character) 219
White, William Smith 81
Williams, Albert 212
Williams and Walker *see* Walker, George; Williams, Bert
Williams, Bert 11, 29, 38
Williams, Mary Elizabeth 18
Williams, Robin 143
Williams, Zoe 193
Wilson, Bobby 269
Wilson, Flip 56–57, 62, 208, 265–266
Wilson, Richard 41
Wilson, Woodrow 40, 43
Winfrey, Oprah 220
Winters, Jonathan 91
Wolf, Michelle 246
Woods, Leigh 37
Woodward, Bob 118

Yang, Bowen 266, 268
Yang, Veronica 265
Yankee 46, 186, 190; *see also* Stage Yankee
Young, Dannagal G. 181, 245
Young, Harvey 16
Your Show of Shows 44, 166

Zelizer, Julian 181